POPULAR CATHOLICISM
in Nineteenth-Century Germany

POPULAR CATHOLICISM

in Nineteenth-Century Germany

Jonathan Sperber

PRINCETON UNIVERSITY PRESS
PRINCETON, NEW JERSEY

Published by Princeton University Press, 41 William Street,
Princeton, New Jersey 08540
In the United Kingdom: Princeton University Press, Guildford, Surrey

Library of Congress Cataloging in Publication Data will be
found on the last printed page of this book

ISBN 0-691-05432-0

Publication of this book has been aided by the Paul Mellon Publication Fund
of Princeton University Press

This book has been composed in Linotron Sabon

Clothbound editions of Princeton University Press books
are printed on acid-free paper, and binding materials are
chosen for strength and durability
Printed in the United States of America by Princeton University Press
Princeton, New Jersey

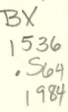

CONTENTS

LIST OF TABLES

ACKNOWLEDGMENTS

Many people have contributed to the creation of this book. I would like to express my thanks to all of them and point out to the reader that while their share in any virtues this study may possess is great, the faults it contains are solely my responsibility.

The text is a revised version of a doctoral dissertation accepted in 1980 by the University of Chicago. It was my good fortune to have Leonard Krieger, John Boyer, and Emil Karafiol as members of my thesis committee, three individuals who can only be described as scholars and gentlemen, stalwart exemplars of a rapidly vanishing academic ideal.

Research in Germany was made possible by funds provided by the *Deutscher Akademischer Austauschdienst*, whose generosity created an oasis in the economic desert of graduate student life. While in Germany, I was recipient of the hospitality of the *Institut für Wirtschafts- und Sozialgeschichte* of the University of Münster. The Director, Professor Richard Tilly, his *Assistenten*, Rolf Dumke, Rainer Fremdling, and Toni Pierenkemper, and all the students and staff of the institute, were willing to provide material facilities, advice, and assurance to a bewildered American in a foreign country. I also received advice and assistance from Professors Hans-Ulrich Wehler and Jürgen Kocka (Bielefeld), Hans-Jürgen Teuteberg (Münster), and Elisabeth Fehrenbach (then Düsseldorf). Having worked as an archivist, I have come to learn the difficulties of the profession, and would like to thank, somewhat belatedly, the staffs of the state archives in Detmold, Düsseldorf, Koblenz, and Münster, the (Arch)diocesan archives in Cologne, Münster, and Paderborn, and the municipal archives of Düsseldorf and Münster, for their patient assistance and willingness to fulfill even my more outrageous requests.

James Sheehan and Robert Wiebe read an earlier version of the manuscript and provided cogent and acute criticisms. The difficult transition from typescript to published work was eased by the assistance of R. Miriam Brokaw of Princeton University Press. I have learned much about social history and German history from my association with David Abraham, Henry Friedlander, Richard Greene, Gerd Hohorst, James Jackson Jr., Walter Kamphoefner, Heidi Kückelhaus, Peter Novick, William H. Sewell Jr., and especially Steve Hochstadt and Elizabeth Tobin, the warmth of whose friendship is matched only by the depth of their scholarship. Joan Ernst enabled me to continue my work at a time I thought I could not.

The first and most important influence on my life is that of my parents, Louis and Ruth Sperber, and with gratitude I dedicate this book to them.

A NOTE ON TRANSLATION

When translating German-language phrases into English, I have had in mind as a reader an American who is not necessarily knowledgeable in German, but has a general knowledge of European history. In general, I have avoided literal translation in favor of idiomatic English, except for offices and office-holders which I have tried to translate consistently, even at the risk of occasionally sounding stilted.

I have translated *Pfarrer* as "parish priest" for a Catholic clergyman and as "pastor" for a Protestant one. *Kaplan* has been translated "chaplain" and *Vikar* as "vicar," both referring to younger Catholic priests who still held transferrable positions and had not yet been appointed to a permanent post in charge of a parish. For *Dekan* I have used "dean" and for *Dekanat* "deanery." The reader is warned against the medieval impression created, as the deans were not archaic remnants of a vanished past, but agents of a structure of ecclesiastical administration required by the very large dioceses existing at the time.

With regard to state officials, I have translated *Oberpräsident* as "provincial governor," *Regierungspräsident* as "district governor," and *Regierungsbezirk* as "district." The frequently seen, literal translations "superior president" or "district president" should be avoided for they create a misconception. While in American usage, "president" refers to an elected chief executive, in nineteenth-century Germany, a "Präsident" was the presiding officer of an administrative or judicial *collegium*. I have translated *Regierungscollegium* as "district officials." *Regierung Aachen* thus appears as "Aachen district officials" or "Aachen district office."

I have translated both *Bürgermeister* and *Oberbürgermeister* as "mayor." The English expression "lord mayor" sounds rather silly in American usage, and creates a false exoticism about two groups of professional bureaucrats who performed similar functions in municipalities of different sizes and differing legal status. There is an exception to this translation. Throughout most of the nineteenth century in the Prussian Rhineland, the *Bürgermeister* in rural areas was an appointed official, the lowest level of full-time, professional bureaucrat. For these instances, I have used the term "area magistrate," as I also have for the Westphalian counterpart to the rural *Bürgermeister*, the *Amtmann*. I have left *Landrat* in the original German. Since the Prussian *Landrat* was sui generis, a translation simply does not serve. I have left the area administered by a *Landrat*, the *Kreis*, in the original German as well.

Stadtrat and *Gemeinderat* have been translated as "city council" or "town council" and "village council," depending on the area to which they refer. *Gemeindevorsteher* or *Ortsvorsteher* have been translated as "village foreman." The term *Landtag* has sometimes been left in the original, sometimes translated as "parliament." The translation "diet" for *Landtag* seems inappropriate, for a diet rather implies an assembly of feudal estates which the Prussian *Landtag*, for all its peculiar features, most emphatically was not. *Reichstag* has usually been left in the original German. The representatives of the various elected bodies, the *Abgeordneten*, have been referred to as "deputies"; their parliamentary organization, the *Fraktion*, has been translated "caucus."

A NOTE ON ARCHIVAL CITATION

Archival citation has been done in three different forms.

(1) The preferred form, with the name of the archives, the repertory, the number of the volume cited, and the folio number (*Blatt*): for instance, Staatsarchiv Münster Oberpräsidium Nr. 1601 I Blätter 33-54, or, in abbreviated form, STAM OP Nr. 1601 I Bl. 33-54.

(2) Many archival volumes are unpaginated, however. In this case, I have cited the document directly, and then the archival volume: Regierung Aachen to Oberpräsidium Koblenz December 17, 1825, Hauptstaatsarchiv Düsseldorf Regierung Aachen Nr. 4880, or, abbreviated, RA to OPK Dec. 17, 1825, HSTAD RA Nr. 4880.

(3) In some cases, even this is impossible, especially when citing from statistical tables and the like. I have in this case simply indicated the document and the archival volume where it can be found: for instance, illegitimacy rates calculated from the records of vital statistics in Staatsarchiv Münster Regierung Münster Nr. 93 I-III (STAM RM Nr. 93 I-III).

A LIST OF ABBREVIATIONS USED
IN THE FOOTNOTES

AGVP	Archiv des Generalvikariats Paderborn
BAM	Bistumsarchiv Münster
BM	Bürgermeister
GV	Generalvikariat
HAEK	Historisches Archiv des Erzbistums Köln
HSTAD	Hauptstaatsarchiv Düsseldorf
Kr.	Kreis
LA	Landratsamt or Landrat
LAK	Landesarchiv Koblenz
Lkr.	Landkreis
OB	Oberbürgermeister
OP	Oberpräsident
OPK	Oberpräsident (or Oberpräsidium) der Rheinprovinz in Koblenz
OPKN	Oberpräsident (or Oberpräsidium) der Provinz Jülich-Kleve-Berg in Köln
OPM	Oberpräsident (or Oberpräsidium) der Provinz Westfalen in Münster
Pf.	Pfarrer
PP	Polizeipräsidium
Pr.	Präsidialregistratur
RA	Regierung Aachen
RAR	Regierung Arnsberg
RD	Regierung Düsseldorf
RK	Regierung Köln
RM	Regierung Münster
RMI	Regierung Minden
RP	Regierungspräsident or Regierungspräsidium
STAD	Staatsarchiv Detmold
STAM	Staatsarchiv Münster
STDD	Stadtarchiv Düsseldorf
STDM	Stadtarchiv Münster

POPULAR CATHOLICISM
in Nineteenth-Century Germany

INTRODUCTION

THE PROBLEM

The nineteenth century was a period of rapid and intense social change on the European continent. A capitalist market economy, whose leading sectors were urban and industrial, replaced in a complex and non-linear way an economic system centered around small-scale peasant and craft production. Parallel to and interacting with this economic transformation, European states changed, their bureaucracies swelling in size and undertaking to control whole new areas of civil society while abandoning others, previously closely watched over, to the ostensibly self-regulating market. New elites arising from these social transformations confronted existing ruling groups, demanding a share of political power. The means of exercising such power and, in fact, its basic nature changed as revolutions, parliamentarianism, universal manhood suffrage created a mass participation in the affairs of state. Political implications of popular attitudes were no longer confined to the narrow circle of the village community or the artisan guild, and the mobilization of popular support became a central fact of political life.

These changes were not simply the result of the automatic workings of impersonal socioeconomic or political forces but a consequence of the interaction of such forces with the conscious human response to them. People, as individuals, or more importantly, in groups, used their received cultural heritage, the means they knew of expression and association, in order to oppose or to adapt to changes in their social environment occurring beyond their conscious control. Their resulting actions transformed, often without conscious intent, both social and political structures and the cultural framework used to interpret them. In this process of social change the elements of cultural response to socioeconomic or political forces have been less well studied than the forces themselves. If the outlines of the history of economic growth or the development of the nation-state in nineteenth-century Europe are clear enough, the history of forms of voluntary association, or of popular religious practices, are still terra incognita, except for a small (admittedly rapidly growing) group of pioneering studies. Even more difficult, both methodologically and empirically, is to integrate convincingly the interaction of these two elements to produce a study of the total process of social change.[1]

[1] Two examples of such studies, both of which have shaped the way I think about

In this book I will make such an attempt, taking as object of my study the Roman Catholic population of the area in northwestern Germany called Rhineland-Westphalia. I will discuss popular religion, its beliefs and practices, the forms of organization associated with them, in the context of the social tensions created by the crisis of the agrarian-artisan society of the late eighteenth and early nineteenth centuries and the first wave of industrialization and urbanization in Central Europe after the middle of the nineteenth century. This discussion will be followed by a consideration of the implication of these changes for political life, politics being used both in its narrower sense of elections and parliamentarianism and in its broader meaning of the exercise of power in society.

Confessional difference has been a constant presence in Central Europe since the Reformation. Both in its socioeconomic structure and its political behavior, the Catholic population of the region has been distinct from its Protestant counterpart. Long noticed by countless observers, of whom Max Weber was the most famous but scarcely the first, these differences remain perceptible today, strongly influencing political life in the Federal Republic of Germany. Although political Catholicism in Germany has received its share of attention, most work has focused on the actions of clerical parliamentarians, rather less on mass Catholic politics and its relation to both social change and changing forms of popular religion.[2] This work may therefore contribute a somewhat different approach to the study of a perennial problem of

these questions, are Gutman, "Work, Culture, and Society," and Agulhon, *La République au Village.*

[2] The extensive sociological literature on confessional differences in Central Europe is conveniently summed up by Burger, *Religionszugehörigkeit und soziales Verhalten.* The literature on Catholicism and politics in Germany is also extensive. The older works, oriented primarily toward parliamentary politics, include Bergsträsser, *Vorgeschichte der Zentrumspartei,* Schnabel, *Zusammenschluss,* and the still unsurpassed work of Karl Bachem, *Zentrumspartei.* Continuing this orientation are the more recent studies of Morsey, *Zentrumspartei;* Hömig, *Das preußische Zentrum;* and Ross, *Beleaguered Tower.* One of the best works in this tradition is Anderson, *Windthorst.* Since the 1960s, along with the general growth of interest in social history in Germany, there have been attempts to integrate social and economic interests into the history of political Catholicism, especially, Gall, "Problematik"; Blackbourn, *Class, Religion, and Local Politics;* and Möckl, *Die Prinzregentenzeit.* One of the few historians who has attempted to link religious life and politics is Christoph Weber, especially in his book *Aufklärung und Orthodoxie.* Political Catholicism in the Rhineland has been dealt with in the work of the students of Max Braubach, much of which has remained in unpublished form and is summarized by Müller, "Wahlsoziologie." On political Catholicism in twentieth-century Germany, the work of Plum, *Gesellschaftsstruktur und politisches Bewußtsein* is very suggestive, and I have learned much from it. On the continuing importance of confessional loyalties in the politics of the Federal Republic, see Blankenburg, *Kirchliche Bindung und Wahlverhalten,* and Pappi, "Parteisystem und Sozialstruktur." The methodological suggestions of K. Rohe, "Wahlanalysen," are helpful.

German historiography as well as dealing with an area which, in comparison to southern France or even Bavaria, is still social-historically underdeveloped.

THE SETTING

The Place

I decided to write a regional study, deliberately choosing an area homogeneous enough to permit common tendencies to be observed, small enough to enable one researcher to handle the material, yet broad enough to consider contrasts and similarities in the course of events in different places. Like all levels of analysis, this one has its defects: centralized policy-making appears in it as an exogenous element, affecting local events, while the effects of local or provincial happenings on centralized policy-making remain unconsidered. Nonetheless there are compensations for this. While the origins of the policies of the Papal Curia, the senior bureaucrats or parliamentarians in Berlin, can be approached only through secondary works, it is possible to see how their policies were actually carried out in the provinces: how German Catholics interpreted Pius IX's ultramontanism, how provincial authorities obeyed or sabotaged the commands of their Berlin superiors, how the parliamentarians got to parliament in the first place. The world looked very different in Cologne or Paderborn (to say nothing of Jülich or Attendorn) than it did in Rome and Berlin. Situations in the capital and the provinces were often quite different, at times exact opposites.

An alternative to a regional focus would have been an intensive local study, focusing on a single city or rural district. In this way, intimate connections between developments in different areas of social life could have been traced in detail and not, as is the case in a work covering a larger area, discussed somewhat schematically or episodically. A local study, though, lacks the element of comparison. The analysis of a single locality does not suffice to determine which elements of a perceived development were purely local and which were exemplars of a more general trend. Since this book deals with a theme which has been comparatively little studied and secondary sources for the purpose of comparison are, on the whole, lacking, it seemed advisable to sacrifice detail in favor of typicality.[3]

---

[3] A more pragmatic consideration may also be mentioned. Due to wartime losses, but even more to the peculiar records-retention practices of nineteenth-century archivists, the holdings of the relevant archives are very uneven. The records concerning one area may contain a good set of census materials, a second area elaborate election returns, a third a detailed description of popular religious practices, while virtually no area has

The area under study corresponds approximately to the contemporary West German *Land* of North Rhine-Westphalia. In 1815, the Congress of Vienna had awarded the region to the Prussian state, where it was administratively divided (after a brief period of greater complexity) between the two westernmost provinces: Westphalia, made up of the Arnsberg, Minden, and Münster districts, and the three northern districts of the Rhine Province—Aachen, Cologne, and Düsseldorf. The two southern districts of the Rhine Province, Trier and Koblenz, will not be dealt with directly in this book, although events there often did have an effect on the area studied, and I will not hesitate to mention them when necessary. In terms of the administration of the Catholic church, the area was part of the Ecclesiastical Province of the Lower Rhine, whose metropolitan was the Archbishop of Cologne and suffragans the Bishops of Paderborn and Münster. The archdiocese of Cologne extended over the entire Rhenish portion of the region, except for the northern half of the Düsseldorf District. This area was part of the Diocese of Münster, which also encompassed the entire Münster District. Catholics living in the Arnsberg and Minden Districts belonged to the Diocese of Paderborn.

As of 1871, sixty-five percent of the region's 4.2 million inhabitants were Catholics, most of the rest Protestants, and under one percent were Jews. The confessional distribution varied from area to area. While over ninety-five percent of the population in the rural parts of the Münster and Aachen Districts was Catholic—in many villages, neither Protestants nor Jews were to be found—there were equally Protestant rural areas in northeastern Westphalia and on the right bank of the Rhine. In general, the cities were confessionally more mixed than in the countryside, but the actual proportions varied sharply. Some—Barmen-Elberfeld, Solingen, or Bielefeld, to name a few of the larger examples—were over eighty percent Protestant. Others—Aachen, Cologne, Düsseldorf, or Münster, for instance—were upward of three-fourths Catholic. Examples of all proportions in between these two extremes can be found; the cities of the Ruhr basin were the closest to having equal proportions of both Christian confessions. Smaller towns usually followed the confessional pattern of the surrounding countryside, although there were a few examples of predominantly Protestant towns surrounded by predominantly Catholic rural areas.[4]

---

all of these records together. A regional study allows the possibility of using the good sources from one place to throw light on the less detailed records of another and thus to build up an overall picture which might not be obtainable in restricting oneself to a particular locality.

[4] *Die Gemeinden und Gutsbezirken*, Vol. VII (Westphalia) and Vol. VIII (Rhineland). Changes in confessional composition within the region are discussed below, pp. 44-47.

Socially and economically, the region varied as much as it did confessionally. There were areas of impoverished subsistence agriculture running from the Eifel districts to the west on the Belgian border through the *Bergisches Land* on the right bank of the Rhine and into the *Hochsauerland* in Westphalia. The land on the north German plain, the lower Rhine area and the Westphalian *Münsterland*, was more fertile, the agricultural holdings larger, and the peasants better off. There were many industrial regions, ranging from the heavy industry of the Ruhr basin to the textile districts of the left bank of the Rhine (in which both factory and artisanal production could be found throughout most of the nineteenth century) to the small metallurgical industry in rural areas in the hills. The cities varied from manufacturing towns, to large commercial centers—Cologne and Düsseldorf being the most prominent—to sleepy provincial administrative and market towns like Arnsberg or Paderborn.

For all this variety, the region possessed a certain socioeconomic unity. It was (and is) one of the economically most advanced areas in Germany. In the eighteenth and early nineteenth centuries, the organizationally and technologically most sophisticated forms of craft production—nowadays referred to by economic historians as "proto-industry"—had flourished. Several centers of early industrialization existed in Rhineland-Westphalia before 1850, and the area was one of the main centers of the post-1850 industrial boom and rapid urbanization, events which deeply affected even those parts of the region which remained predominantly non-industrial. The area, in short, was not a social or economic backwater but experienced some of the major socioeconomic transformations of the nineteenth century at an early date and in full force.[5]

Politically, the region was in the center of events as well. It was, of all parts of Germany, the most affected by the French Revolution: the left bank of the Rhine spent two decades as part of the French Republic and Napoleonic Empire; the territories east of the river had been for a lesser but still considerable period under the rule of the Napoleonic satellite states. Prussian rule in the region after 1815 created an anomalous situation. Like northern Germany in general, Prussia was a heavily Protestant country, and the existence of a Catholic majority in its two western provinces meant that the general lines of political development in nineteenth-century Prussia—the dominant state in Germany—took on a special form in the Rhineland and Westphalia. Just as the Rhenish-Westphalian Catholics by their religion were different from their Protestant counterparts in Prussia and northern Germany,

[5] On the economy of the region, see below, pp. 11-13, 39-44 and the sources cited there.

their living in the north—in a predominantly Protestant, socioeconomically advanced, and politically turbulent environment—made for
a different kind of Catholicism from that which existed in southern
Germany.[6]

The Time

The study concentrates on the years between 1830 and 1880. At the
beginning of the period, agriculture was the leading economic sector,
urban populations were small, and industrialization in its scarcely
apparent beginnings, far outweighed in importance by small-scale and
proto-industrial craft production. Neither constitution nor parliament
existed in Prussia; the handful of individuals interested in politics were
forced to resort to the powerless provincial diets, while an influential
and authoritarian bureaucracy kept nascent political tendencies firmly
in hand. The Catholic church was still recovering from the chaotic
conditions created by the French Revolution. Internal disputes between
Enlightened and orthodox elements, bureaucratic interference, and
lay-clerical conflict weakened its position. Fifty years later the region
was heavily urbanized and industrialized, with an even greater degree
of urbanization and industrialization about to begin. Organized mass
politics had taken on a definite form which set a pattern for the rest
of the history of the German Empire and in some ways until 1933.
Emerging from a period of intense state persecution, the Catholic
church in the area was firmly united under ultramontanist auspices
and enjoyed an unprecedented degree of popular support.

In between lay a period of economic crisis followed by a powerful
industrial boom, both events socially unsettling, albeit in very different
ways. The Revolution of 1848-1849 had crystallized *Vormärz* tendencies into lasting political groups whose interaction over the following
fifteen years had been conditioned by the peculiar nature of Prussian
parliamentary politics. Political life had been decisively transformed
by the upheavals following on the creation of German national unity
in 1866-1871, the introduction of universal, equal, and direct manhood suffrage, and the church-state confrontation of the 1870s. Perhaps less well known than these events but no less significant, a remarkable religious revival had transformed the nature of Roman Catholic
popular religious life and created a powerful unity of action within
the ranks of the clergy and between clergy and laity.

[6] There is a certain tendency among historians—especially English-speaking ones—
when considering German Catholics immediately to think of Bavaria. A concentration
on the Catholics of northern Germany may help to redress the historiographical balance.

In what follows, I will attempt to trace out the complex course of events, detailing the interaction between socioeconomic, political, and cultural change. The book will begin with an analysis of the changes in popular religious life occurring in the period between 1830 and 1870 and then move on to consider the political implications of these changes as they worked themselves out in the period between the Revolution of 1848-1849 and the *Kulturkampf* of the 1870s.

CHAPTER 1
POPULAR RELIGIOUS LIFE
DURING THE *VORMÄRZ*

THE BACKGROUND

The 1820s were a difficult decade for the Catholic church in Prussia's western provinces. French revolutionary and Napoleonic occupiers and administrators had abolished the ecclesiastical principalities of the Holy Roman Empire, and the disappearance of the temporal power of the Elector of Cologne, the Prince-Bishops of Münster, Paderborn, and Corvey had created a confused situation in the spiritual side of their administration as well. Whole dioceses remained in a chaotic condition for decades: vacant parishes went unfilled, popular religious life continued without clerical supervision. Monasteries were secularized, their property confiscated, the number of religious orders was greatly reduced, and their members barred from pastoral care. The universities of the old regime were closed, and the education of future clergy creaked along in badly understaffed seminaries.[1] While the reestablishment of an ordered administrative structure in 1822, following negotiations between Prussia and the Vatican, made it possible for the clergy to deal with these problems, the arrangements themselves became a source of new difficulties. The four dioceses of the newly created Church Province of the Lower Rhine—Trier, Cologne, Münster, and Paderborn, with the Archbishop of Cologne as Metropolitan—all covered enormous areas with equally large populations. Each diocese encompassed disparate territories with different social structures and varying historical traditions.[2]

The new political environment was, at best, a mixed blessing. Though the heavy hand of the Napoleonic regime was gone, the Prussian *Vormärz*, a period of authoritarian, bureaucratic rule, unchecked by a legislature or written constitution, was not necessarily a major improvement. The bureaucracy could and frequently did interfere in the internal life of the Catholic church, as it did in all spheres of society, the state authorities claiming the right to appoint many parish priests

---

[1] There is a good description of post-revolutionary conditions in Lipgens, *Spiegel*, 1: 337-61. The last word has not yet been said about the secularization, but two useful studies are Müller, *Säkularisation*, and Klein, "Säkularisation."

[2] Reuter, *Bistum Aachen*, pp. 159 ff.

and to approve the election of bishops by the cathedral chapters. The Jesuits and other religious orders were forbidden on Prussian territory, correspondence of the bishops with the Pope had to be sent through Berlin. Officials of church and state quarreled constantly over questions of public education and the civil validity of religious holidays.[3] The majority of the Prussian population, the ruling house, and the bulk of the leading officials were of the Protestant confession. If the hostility of the Lutheran state toward the Catholic church has perhaps been somewhat exaggerated in many historical accounts, there can be no doubt that in the pre-1850 period Prussian Catholics were harassed by a variety of discriminatory practices ranging from rules requiring Catholic conscripts to attend Protestant services to spectacular actions, such as the arrest of the Archbishop of Cologne in 1837.[4]

The social and economic environment of the first half of the century was one in which traditional structures were undermined without any order emerging to take their place. Population growth, beginning around 1750 and continuing steadily for a century in spite of temporary setbacks, had subverted the basis of the old-regime agrarian-artisan economy. The "excess" population no longer fit into the appropriate social niches—an artisanate divided into masters, journeymen and apprentices by an ordered guild system, a rural order of self-supporting peasant families and obedient unmarried servants, waiting to inherit a farm. Napoleonic-era reforms encouraged these developments by abolishing restrictions on marriage, the guild system, and other previously existing forms of socioeconomic restraint. The Prussian authorities, partisans of economic liberalism, preserved the reforms when the area came under their rule after 1815.

The progress of industrialization in Germany before 1850 was a sporadic one, however. Hampered by difficulties in finding markets and mobilizing capital, the few centers of early industrialization—in Rhineland-Westphalia, the Aachen region, the Wuppertal, and the County of Mark—could not absorb the growing population. The result was the creation of a large lower class, no longer part of an agrarian-artisan society but not yet integrated into an industrial world. Already existing lower strata—propertyless day laborers in towns and in the countryside, cottagers and peasants subsisting on parcels too small to support a family—greatly increased. Their ranks were swollen by traditionally better off social groups—master craftsmen and small merchants, for instance—facing economic impoverishment. The whole

---

[3] Huber, *Verfassungsgeschichte*, 1: 442-49; Schnütgen, "Die Feiertage"; material on controversies in elementary education in STAM OP Nr. 2163 I.

[4] Lipgens, *Spiegel*, 1: 394-535.

structure was shaken by crises resulting from crop failures in 1816-1817, the early 1830s, and again in 1846-1847.[5]

While conditions in Rhineland-Westphalia never quite reached the extremes they did in such genuinely impoverished regions as Silesia or southwestern Germany, the combination of population growth and Napoleonic-era reforms had produced a unique socioeconomic situation. Available statistics are clearest on the development of the artisanate. The abolition of the guild system meant that journeymen were free to go into business themselves so that, unlike the situation in the rest of Prussia, where certain guild restraints remained in force, in the first half of the nineteenth century the proportion of masters among all the artisans in Rhineland-Westphalia steadily increased. See Table 1.1. The growing proportion of masters in a retail market characterized by at best static purchasing power led to an increasingly difficult competition. At the same time, the ease with which economic independence could be obtained created a tight labor market and encouraged the journeymen to take an aggressive attitude toward their employers: less in the form of strikes and trade-union organization than in frequent job changes, drinking and carousing during working hours and a general defiance of their employers' authority. Throughout

TABLE 1.1

Journeymen and Apprentices per Master Craftsman
in Three Western Districts and All of Prussia, 1819-1849

	Journeymen and Apprentices per Master			
Year	Münster District	Aachen District	Düsseldorf District	Prussia
1819	0.56	?	?	0.51
1822	?	0.70	0.75	0.55
1828	?	0.61	?	0.57
1831	0.50	?	?	0.56
1849	0.57	0.56	0.60	0.76

SOURCES: STAM RM Nr. 120 I and 120 III; HSTAD RA Nr. 365-66; HSTAD RD Nr. 2159; *Tabellen und amtliche Nachrichten* ... 1849, 5: 530-66, 706-37, 618-77; Schmoller, *Kleingewerbe*, pp. 331-35.

[5] On the German and Rhenish-Westphalian economy of this time, see Köllmann, *Bevölkerung*, pp. 61-98, 208-228; Gladen, *Kreis Tecklenburg*; Kaufhold, "Handwerk und Industrie"; Reekers, "Die gewerbliche Wirtschaft Westfalens"; Tilly, "Entwicklung des Kapitalmarktes"; and Eyll, "Wirtschaftsgeschichte Kölns."

the *Vormärz*, the masters tried, without much success, one scheme after another to get their journeymen under control.[6]

Naturally, conflicts between master and journeymen had been an important feature of the traditional crafts economy. In early nineteenth century Rhineland-Westphalia, the guilds, the legal structure which previously regulated master-journeymen relations, had been abolished but the crafts economy continued to exist, basically unaffected by the first tentative steps toward industrialization. The resulting insubordination of journeymen against their masters was only one manifestation of increasing social disorder. Crime rates showed alarming increases; the sharp rise in illegitimate births dismayed contemporaries. It seemed as if private morality and public order were about to disappear.[7] Given such an unruly social atmosphere it would be surprising to find Roman Catholic religious life unaffected.

BETWEEN PIETY AND SECULARISM

The nostalgic picture of traditional piety and strict morality as yet uncorrupted by secularizing influences bears little relationship to the actual religious life of Catholic Rhinelanders and Westphalians in the early nineteenth century. Godlessness was hardly rampant, yet self-consciously secularizing currents were at work, and, even where they cannot be ascertained, developments within popular religious life itself were leading to lay-clerical conflict. The situation was in flux, as previously existing forms of clerical authority were dissolving without anything definite emerging to take their place. Conditions varied by region and by social class.

Most contemporary observers, and following them modern scholars, would not have held up the Catholic bourgeoisie of the region as a model of piety. Rather, as a group they would seem to have been heavily influenced by the secularizing currents of the French Revolution.[8] Masonic lodges, founded in the revolutionary era, made headway in spite of strong clerical hostility and were to be found in all the

---

[6] There are many examples of this in LAK 403 Nr. 7280 ff. See also LAK 403 Nr. 7285 Bl. 469-72 and LAK 403 Nr. 7300 Bl. 125-46.

[7] Blasius, *Kriminalität*, passim; Phayer, *Sexual Liberation*, pp. 32-50. Two contemporary perceptions of declining popular morality and increasing criminality are Pf. Lüking (Nieheim) to Bishop of Paderborn, Mar. 12, 1825, AGVP XVII, 1 and STAD M1 IP Nr. 960 Bl. 10.

[8] Lipgens, *Spiegel*, 1: 348-49; Keinemann, *Kölner Ereignis*, 1: 26-28, 359-69; Pf. Rieland (Warburg) to GV Paderborn, Jun. 30, 1828, AGVP XIV, 1. The Catholic nobility, on the other hand, was distinguished by its strict piety. Cf. Keinemann, *Kölner Ereignis*, 1: 351 ff.; Reif, *Westfälischer Adel*, pp. 435-49 and passim.

major cities of the Rhineland.[9] In 1852, the parish priest in Jülich complained that the religious indifference of the bourgeois Masons had contaminated the lower classes. The lodges provided just one arena for close social and business contacts with the generally well-to-do Protestant minority, contacts which did nothing to import a sense of militant Catholicism.[10] It would be an exaggeration to say that there were no pious Catholic bourgeois. Even around 1830, perhaps a low point in religious observance, there existed centers of middle-class Catholic piety, both in the old bishop's towns Münster and Paderborn as well as in heavily industrialized Aachen, where factory owners and merchants were prominent lay adherents of the "strict" tendencies in Rhenish Catholicism.[11]

Accounts of bourgeois laxity, however, usually close with a mention of the simple piety of the lower classes.[12] It is certainly true that the common people lacked the intellectual articulation of their social superiors. Workers, craftsmen, and peasants did not join Masonic Lodges, read liberal and left-wing newspapers, or write memoirs recalling the secular atmosphere of their youth. Popular opinion, insofar as it expressed itself, still employed the religious terminology of the old regime. Popular behavior, though, showed that these traditional notions were being interpreted in new ways—ones by no means pleasing to the clergy.

Priests complained of imperfect church attendance on Sundays and holidays. Even the minimal religious observance of the Catholic confession, the yearly communion at Easter, was not universally practiced in rural areas and small towns, to say nothing of in the larger cities.[13]

---

[9] LAK 403 Nr. 14599 Bl. 109-211. Catholics who belonged were denied the sacraments. LAK 403 Nr. 7037 Bl. 1-10, 23-26. For conditions in Westphalia, cf. Reif, *Westfälischer Adel*, pp. 405-408.

[10] On Jülich, between 1850 and 1870 a democratic and liberal stronghold in the strongly clerical Aachen District, see Gatz, *Volksmission*, p. 103. In 1851, the parish priest in Burtscheid noted that the Catholic bourgeoisie was "closely connected with the Protestants and therefore [religiously] lax." Ibid., p. 97.

[11] Keinemann, *Kölner Ereignis*, 1: 37-39, 365-68.

[12] See, for instance, Franz Schnabel, *Deutsche Geschichte*, 4: 44-47. A different opinion can be found in Phayer, *Religion*, passim.

[13] Instances of prolonged non-communication in the Westphalian countryside and small towns are documented in Pf. Hug (Herzenbroich) to Bishop of Paderborn, May 10, 1853, AGVP XVI, 12; Pf. Valenthen (Winterberg) to Bishop of Paderborn, Dec. 4, 1858, AGVP XVI, 14; Pf. Pees (Warburg) to Bishop of Paderborn, Dec. 7, 1859, AGVP XVI, 15. In mid-century Dortmund, a market town of some ten thousand inhabitants, just at the beginning of its industrialization (but admittedly three-quarters Protestant), about one-third of all Catholics never appeared for communion. Pf. Wiemann (Dortmund) to Bishop of Paderborn, Jun. 10, 1853, AGVP XVI, 12. Regrettably, only information on these scattered examples could be found, and evidence of large-scale surveys of the proportion of all Catholics attending weekly mass or receiving Easter

During Sunday services, the taverns were full of "boozers and brandy spirits"; instead of going into church, people stood around smoking and talking, while others preferred to go fishing or swimming. Artisans found Sundays a good day to catch up on a backlog of work or to prepare for a blue Monday. The Dean of Werl noted with disgust in 1845 that the churches were so empty on All Saints Day "it is almost superfluous to celebrate mass and give a sermon."[14] While attending services, church-goers showed a less than exemplary behavior. During the sermon, the congregation formed "tobacco collegia and conversation circles." Young people in overcrowded rural churches climbed into the rafters and onto the organ, talked during services, mocked the priest, and carried on in an unbecoming fashion. One young man went as far as to assault the clergyman who tried to call him to order.[15]

It was above all the tavern which was seen as the great enemy of religious life. The celebrations in honor of the patron saints were "more likely to lead people into the inns than the church." In Werden a.d. Ruhr, the factory workers would show up in the taverns bright and early Sunday morning and "carry on, scream, sing, drink and show not the slightest signs of morality and piety. . . ." In 1840, the Catholic church wardens in Essen complained that people would visit the taverns on Sundays, wander drunkenly through the streets disturbing divine services, and even stagger into church while the services were still being held.[16] Many came to morning services but spent the after-

---

communion could not. I would like to thank the now retired chief archivist of the *Archivstelle in der Erzdiözese Paderborn*, Dr. Cohausz, for taking the time to discuss some of the problems of source material with me.

[14] Dean Nubel (Werl) to *Kapitular Vikar* Paderborn, May 19, 1845 AGVP XIV, 2; Reports of Deans of Rietberg and Paderborn to Bishop of Paderborn, 1837, AGVP XIV, 1; HSTAD RD Nr. 129 Bl. 15-16, 28-33; Dean Sylan to RD undated (1837) HSTAD RD Nr. 3681; OB Düsseldorf to RD Sep. 28, 1860 HSTAD RD Nr. 13387; LAK 403 Nr. 6684 Bl. 678.

[15] GV Schade (Corvey) to RMI Apr. 27, 1817 and the GV of Paderborn to RMI (undated) STAD M1 IP Nr. 950; Pf. Fanlage (Darfeld) to BM Gröninger (Darfeld) Nov. 27, 1842 STAM LA Kr. Coesfeld Nr. 44; Dean Claeßen (Aachen) to the Aachen Police Commissioner Jan. 13, 1829 HSTAD PP Aachen Nr. 332; report of the Pf. in Wertheim to GV Paderborn, 1837 AGVP XIV, 1. The investigation of the assault revealed that the perpetrator was neither drunk nor crazy but a smith who did "masterful work"; the congregation sympathized with him, and similar incidents had occurred elsewhere. Dean Kemper to GV Paderborn Mar. 12, 1825 and GV Paderborn to Dean Kemper Apr. 7, 1825 AGVP XIV, 1.

[16] Dean of Büren to Bishop of Paderborn, 1837, AGVP XIV, 1; Dean of Mettmann to RD Oct. 26, 1837; Dean Heisman (Düsseldorf) to RD Jun. 6, 1837; BM Essen to RD Feb. 2, 1841 all in HSTAD RD Nr. 3861 and BM of Werden and Kettwig to LA Kr. Duisburg Jun. 20, 1835 HSTAD RD Nr. 3682. According to the last report, the peasants, unlike the workers, paid a quick visit to church on Sundays and then proceeded to "gather in the taverns and swill it down until they're totally drunk. . . ."

noons in the taverns.[17] Even more frequent was the practice of attending mass and dashing out of the church at the beginning of the sermon "and rinsing away the mass with beer." In the "pious town of Zons" the Dean became so annoyed with this practice that he had his chaplain give the sermon while he stood at the church door and turned back any of his thirsty parishioners who tried to get out.[18]

Drunkenness and absence from church on Sunday or holiday afternoons were closely linked in the clergy's eye with another major moral failing of the lower classes: their growing interest in dancing and worldly celebrations. "The interest in such pleasures in this area has gotten altogether out of hand. They usually degenerate into wild affairs filled with crude and immoral actions . . . not infrequently quarrels and brawls. . . . Now this peasant village holds a dance, now that one; now this miners' guild hires a band, now that one; and things have reached such a state that almost no Sunday goes by without dance music in one place or another."[19] The dances began in the morning, immediately after services, and continued through the afternoon until late at night. There was general agreement that the frequency of these worldly festivities had greatly increased in recent years, with dire consequences for sobriety, chastity, and the general level of morality.[20]

Catholic clergy as well as Prussian officials had no doubts about the origins of this moral decline. The French had abolished all ordinances of the old regime closing the taverns during the hours of worship as a way of showing their "contempt for divine service." It was the revolutionary heritage, the "French spirit of freedom," which was responsible for the "traces of disobedience to be felt here and there

[17] Reports of the clergy, 1837, AGVP XIV, 1. Visitation reports on the parishes of Marl and Ahsen, 1827, BAM GV Recklinghausen Nr. 49.

[18] LA Kr. Neuß to RD Oct. 1, 1827, HSTAD RD Nr. 3680; Dean of Warburg to Bishop of Paderborn, 1837, AGVP XIV, 1. Other examples of this practice: Pf. Bachmann (Buldern) to LA Kr. Coesfeld Mar. 20, 1843 STAM LA Kr. Coesfeld, Nr. 44; HSTAD RD Nr. 129 Bl. 15-16, 146-49. Although the sermon does not have the same major position in Catholic services as in Protestant ones, popular behavior of the time suggests a lessened authority of the Catholic clergy and a discontent with the existing forms of religious life. To anticipate a bit, if the church was to be the focus for political life and the priest a key figure in a political party, it would be necessary to have a congregation used to sitting and listening to the sermon.

[19] Dean Britzen (Stoppenberg) to RD May 20, 1837 HSTAD RD Nr. 3681.

[20] Reports of the Deans to the Bishop of Paderborn, 1837, AGVP XIV, 1; LA Kr. Wiedenbrück to RMI May 17, 1825 STAD M1 IP Nr. 950; Dean Kropf (Giershagen) to RAR May 20, 1836 STAM RAR II B Nr. 1037; STAD M1 IP Nr. 951 Bl. 50 ff.; reports of the Deans to the RD, 1837 HSTAD RD Nr. 3681; Pf., chaplain, and church wardens in Erkelenz to RA July 20, 1818; LA Kr. Geilenkirchen to RA Feb. 6, 1820 HSTAD RA Nr. 4782 and HSTAD OPKN Nr. 907 Bl. 153-54.

...," for the lack of "respect and religious devotion."[21] Everywhere the Catholic clergy drew the consequences and called for a battle against these baneful influences. The priests demanded that inns and taverns be closed during morning and afternoon services and that dancing as well as fairs and other worldly festivities be limited, restricted, or abolished.[22]

Should we dismiss these observations as just the perennial ruminations of the clergy, a group professionally inclined to view public morality with alarm, or as the product of a paternalist bureaucracy, intent on finding excuses to interfere in the private lives of its "administrees"? These are weighty objections, but not altogether convincing ones. Priests and bureaucrats did not always complain of deteriorating public morality. After 1850, the administrative correspondence of the ecclesiastical and governmental officials contained no condemnation of popular morality but praise for its improvement. The sharp drop in illegitimacy rates after 1850 shows that popular behavior really did change when compared with the first half of the century.

More importantly, there is a certain internal logic uniting these disparate complaints, stemming from the place of Sundays and religious holidays in nineteenth-century society. They were the only times when the lower classes could meet and associate—the one occasion when the Westphalian peasantry left its scattered farms and came to the market villages, the day urban laborers, factory workers, and craftsmen devoted to some other end than trying to stay alive. Neglecting services, vanishing from church before the sermon, putting the chief emphasis of the day on dancing and drinking implied a population sliding away from clerical supervision and influence.[23] Besides being the site of prodigious drinking bouts or immoral dances, the tavern was the meeting place for secular, lower-class organizations. After 1848, the inns would be frequented by liberal and democratic

[21] HSTAD OPKN Nr. 905 Bl. 353; LA Kr. Neuß to RD Nov. 29, 1817 HSTAD RD Nr. 3680; HSTAD RD Nr. 129 Bl. 15-16; proclamation of the Minden District Office in regard to the sacred character of Sundays and holidays, 1817 STAD M1 IP Nr. 951; Keinemann, Kölner Ereignis, 1: 29.

[22] These demands appear in every single one of the sources cited in the previous six footnotes. Paulus Melchers, Archbishop of Cologne in the Kulturkampf era, began his clerical career as a chaplain in the Münsterland in the 1840s, preaching against dancing and visiting the inns. Gatz, "Melchers," p. 151.

[23] Cf. the complaints of the clergy that young people, once out of school, had no organizational contact with the church and were slipping away from its moral influence. Reports of the Deans of Büren and Rietberg and the Pf. in Haaren to Bishop of Paderborn, 1837, AGVP XIV, 1 and Pf. Henning (Wiedenbrück) to Bishop of Paderborn, Sep. 18, 1827, AGVP XVII, 1.

partisans when they sought popular support.[24] Making presence in the taverns the highpoint of a religious holiday was just one aspect of a more general tendency toward the secularization and laicization of formerly clerically supervised practices and the creation of new, increasingly secular and laic practices and associations, which can be observed in many areas of religious life in the early nineteenth century. These developments were particularly apparent in two major areas of Catholic religious expression: pilgrimages and processions and religious associations.

Pilgrimages and Processions

Traditionally, processions and pilgrimages were an occasion for worldly amusement as well as religious inspiration. The village procession at Corpus Christi or in honor of the patron saint of the local church was followed by drinking bouts and dancing, the pilgrimages to distant shrines were as much worldly adventures as pious journeys, the shrines themselves as much circus sideshows as sources of devotion. This affinity between sacred and secular, the lack of a clear distinction between pious edification and profane amusement, was one of the most typical characteristics of Catholic religious life under the old regime.

Consider this description, written by a priest, of the scene at the miraculous image of the Virgin in Kevelaer on the Dutch border, an important goal for pious pilgrims in the early nineteenth century as well as today. The account portrays something which was as much a fair or popular festival as a religious celebration: "In addition to all these problems, there is the annoying mish-mash, at least in Kevelaer. In one place, people are chattering away, in another they are praying— in Dutch, or, a few steps away, in German. In one spot people are singing, in another they are wailing. While all this is going on, things are being sold or traded, people are drinking and eating, etc."[25] The unitary character of such experiences is apparent in the insistence of young people hiring on as farm servants that their masters allow them to go dancing on Saturday night or Sunday afternoon and allow them to go on a pilgrimage to Kevelaer—obviously, not for such different

[24] Even before the revolution, on the afternoon of Easter Sunday 1835, the journeyman saddler Friedrich Klyvert was singing revolutionary songs and distributing subversive literature brought from Paris to the other saddlers at the tavern where they gathered in Münster. STAM RM Nr. 265.

[25] HSTAD OPKN Nr. 905 Bl. 349-50.

reasons.[26] The connection between sacred and secular was found in another context. As in the middle ages, masses of pilgrims in the early nineteenth century were imploring divine assistance in curing physical illnesses: epilepsy, rabies, kidney trouble, or polio could all be dealt with in one sacred shrine or another.[27]

Going on a pilgrimage was not a universal activity but was largely confined to certain sectors of the Catholic population. Between 1816 and 1824, the government required all pilgrimages lasting more than one day to be accompanied by a priest, who had to turn in a list of pilgrims.[28] Several of these lists have survived and provide a basis for determining the social composition of the body of pilgrims. See Table 1.2. The pilgrims were overwhelmingly female, and a closer look shows they were mostly unmarried young women.[29] Virtually no male pilgrims were from the upper classes, another aspect of the alienation of the Catholic bourgeoisie from traditional forms of religious celebration.[30]

Since there is no good census, it is impossible to determine which social groups were proportionately overrepresented among the pilgrims. I would guess that, besides the bourgeoisie, the very lowest class—laborers and factory workers—was somewhat underrepresented and possibly the peasantry as well. The artisanate, on the other hand, seems to have formed a vanguard of clerically sanctioned pious practice. While the lists do not distinguish between master and journeyman, most of the artisans on them were married (thirty-one of the thirty-nine from the city of Neuß, for example) and so were probably established masters, not single journeymen still in their *Wanderjahre*. Outworking weavers from Odenkirchen were also enthusiastic pilgrims whose pious efforts met with clerical approval. Close bureaucratic supervision did not extend to processions, and lists of partici-

[26] HSTAD OPKN Nr. 907 Bl. 110; LA Kr. Neuß to RD Oct. 1, 1821, HSTAD RD Nr. 3783; Dean of Krefeld to RD May 3, 1837, HSTAD RD Nr. 3681; HSTAD RD Nr. 121 Bl. 17-18.

[27] See the reports of the *Landräte* of the Aachen District in 1825, HSTAD RA Nr. 4880.

[28] HSTAD OPKN Nr. 760 Bl. 2.

[29] One priest gave the ages of the pilgrims he led. Fifty-four percent of the women were between fifteen and thirty. Pf. Meers (Veen) to LA Kr. Geldern, Sep. 24, 1824, HSTAD LA Kr. Geldern Nr. 8.

[30] The lists rarely give the profession of the female pilgrims or that of their spouses or fathers. The only exception is the list of pilgrims from Neuß in 1816. Eighteen percent of the sixty-five married women on the pilgrimage were married to merchants, officials, or retailers, while only four percent of the fifty-three married male pilgrims belonged to such bourgeois professional groups. Not too surprisingly, bourgeois women seem to have been more firmly attached to traditional forms of piety than their husbands.

TABLE 1.2
Social Composition of Several Groups of Pilgrims, 1816-1824

	Düsseldorf 1816		Landkreis Düsseldorf 1816		Kr. Neuß 1816		Kr. Bonn 1820		Kr. Solingen 1824		Odenkirchen Kr. Gladbach 1819	
	%	N	%	N	%	N	%	N	%	N	%	N
Marital Status												
Men												
Single	(41)	37	(35)	18	(47)	178	(37)	47	(27)	.55	(62)	29
Married or Widowed	(59)	53	(65)	34	(53)	201	(63)	80	(73)	150	(38)	18
All	(100)	90	(100)	52	(100)	379	(100)	127	(100)	205	(100)	47
Women												
Single	(33)	102	(41)	60	(64)	453	(56)	192	(61)	116	(84)	92
Married or Widowed	(67)	207	(59)	85	(36)	254	(44)	149	(39)	74	(16)	18
All	(100)	309	(100)	145	(100)	707	(100)	341	(100)	190	(100)	110
Occupations												
Men Only												
Merchant, Rentier, Professional	(3)	3	—	—	(2)	6	(2)	2	(3)	7	—	—
Salaried Employee	(4)	2	—	—	—	—	—	—	—	—	—	—
Government Official	—	—	(2)	1	(1)	2	—	—	—	—	—	—
Innkeeper, Retailer	(9)	8	(4)	2	(1)	5	(2)	3	—	1	(6)	3
Artisan	(36)	32	(25)	13	(25)	94	(24)	30	(20)	40	(13)	6
Industrial artisan	—	—	(4)	2	(4)	15	(6)	8	(15)	30	(47)	22
Farmer	(4)	4	(31)	16	(26)	100	(35)	44	(24)	49	(13)	6
Laborer, Factory Worker	(18)	16	(4)	2	(9)	36	(6)	8	(24)	50	(11)	5
Servant	(2)	2	—	—	(4)	17	(4)	5	(3)	6	(4)	2
Other, Unknown	(2)	2	(28)	15	(2)	6	(4)	5	(3)	6	—	—
None (mostly minors)	(23)	21	(2)	1	(26)	98	(17)	22	(8)	16	(6)	3
All	(101)	90	(100)	52	(99)	379	(100)	127	(100)	205	(100)	47

SOURCE: HSTAD OPKN Nr. 760 Bl. 45-200; HSTAD OPKN Nr. 761 Bl. 39-48; HSTAD LA Kr. Solingen Nr. 147; LA Kr. Gladbach to Royal Consistory, Cologne, Jan. 18, 1819 HSTAD RD Nr. 3783.

pants were never made. Not requiring an extended absence from home and job, processions attracted a considerably greater attendance than pilgrimages, but scattered evidence suggests that the Catholic bourgeoisie was showing a declining interest in processions as well.[31]

By the 1820s, both pilgrimages and processions had come to have an increasingly bad reputation among the higher officials in church and state. The superstitious goals of many pilgrims were offensive to an enlightened upper class, while the loss of time in all the parading around appeared intolerable to a generation haunted by the specter of "pauperism" and concerned to accelerate the pace of economic growth. A continuous line of decrees restricting or abolishing these practices runs from the enlightened rulers of the closing years of the old regime through the revolutionary and Napoleonic period and into the first thirty years of Prussian rule. The last two Electors of Cologne had forbidden pilgrimages lasting longer than one day and abolished many religious holidays with attendant processions, the revolutionary and Napoleonic governments reaffirmed and expanded these restrictions. In 1814, the Prussian military governor allowed overnight pilgrimages to begin again, but after twelve years of elaborate and usually unsuccessful attempts to regulate and control them, Archbishop Spiegel of Cologne in conjunction with the Prussian government prohibited them once more.[32]

The Prussian bureaucrats, seeing themselves as the architects of economic growth and a more rational social structure, opposed pilgrimages as an archaic practice, harmful to economic development. Officials of the Aachen District Government drew up a list of all the pilgrimages in their district and concluded they were costing the economy exactly 38,451 *Thaler* and 22 *Silbergroschen* every year.[33] While carrying out their campaign against pilgrimages, the bureaucrats were careful not to appear as hostile, intruding East-Elbian Lutherans. They stressed the precedents set by the Catholic rulers of the old regime, carefully cooperated with the episcopal authorities, and never tired of pointing out that Catholic bureaucrats and "educated Catholics" in general approved of the measures of restriction and prohibition they

[31] Cf. HSTAD RD Nr. 119 Bl. 129-30; Keinemann, *Kölner Ereignis* 1: 365.

[32] There is a superficial and inaccurate discussion of these events in Lipgens, *Spiegel* I: 355. The details of the prohibition, its prehistory and execution, are in HSTAD OPKN Nr. 760 and 904, HSTAD RD Nr. 3783-3784, HSTAD RA Nr. 4880 and LAK 403 Nr. 16003-5. Also, see Schieder, "Trierer Wallfahrt."

[33] RA to OPK Dec. 17, 1825 HSTAD RA Nr. 4880; similar sentiments were expressed by the provincial governor of Westphalia, von Vincke in a letter to the Minister of Religious and Educational Affairs, Nov. 11, 1834 (draft) STAM OP Nr. 2686 I. In general, on the rationalist thinking of the Prussian bureaucracy in the *Vormärz*, Koselleck, *Preußen*.

wished to take. If Protestantism appeared in their considerations at all, it was only in the implicit assumption, held long before Max Weber, that the practices of the Protestant religion were favorable to economic growth and that Catholics might do well to emulate some of them.[34]

The attitude of the clergy was less unified and more complex. Scholarly opinion has seen it divided into two camps: "traditionalist," "orthodox," or "ultramontane," on the one hand, eager to uphold popular traditions and hostile to the government for attempting to suppress them, and an "enlightened" or "Hermesian" group, on the other, anxious to combat superstition and ignorance, disdainful of the stupid masses, and willing to cooperate with the Prussian state. In its most sophisticated form, this theory perceives the two groups in a social and political context. The "ultramontanists" are said to have had their support among the pious common people, their alliance forming the basis for Christian Democracy, while the enlightened clergy are seen as finding their supporters among the Protestant bureaucrats and, to a lesser extent, the Catholic bourgeoisie, thus becoming precursors of national liberalism and proponents of a *Staatskirchentum*, a church controlled by the state.[35]

This dichotomy is oversimplified because it focuses solely on the clergy's opinions while ignoring differences in popular piety. If priests had different attitudes about processions and pilgrimages, lay people did as well. Inhabitants of some areas and members of some social groups were willing to accept clerical leadership of these religious events; other laymen were not. The relative emphasis the population gave to the sacred and secular side of pilgrimages and processions, the relation between popular sexual conduct or attitudes toward work and these religious occasions varied as much from place to place as did the opinions of the clergy. The decisive element in the situation was the interaction between clerical and popular attitudes.

An exchange of opinions in the Münster District shows the complexities which could arise. In 1827, the government asked the bishops to determine if there were processions held outside the usual holidays, if these processions led to drinking and disorder, and if they kept people from their work. The bureaucrats wished to see such econom-

[34] See the sources cited in note thirty-two and STAM RM Nr. 17423 and 17614.

[35] This dichotomy goes back to the writings of Heinrich Schörs in the early twentieth century, although he had rather different sympathies from today's authors. The most sophisticated proponent of this theory is Christoph Weber, whose two excellent studies, *Kirchliche Politik* and *Aufklärung und Orthodoxie*, contain exhaustive bibliographies and useful critiques of the existing literature. A popularized version of some of these ideas can be found in Bucheim, *Ultramontanismus und Demokratie*, a vigorous criticism of them in Schieder, "Trierer Wallfahrt."

ically harmful celebrations moved to Sunday, when no one worked in any event.[36]

Dean Lüthekamp in Ahlen, like most of the clergy, was extremely suspicious of the state's motives:

> The reasons given for transferring the day when such processions take place could in fact be applied to any aspect of the Catholic religion. Indeed, should not everything be abolished, lumped together, or restricted which can be misused or can lead to the neglect of worldly business? Suggestions similar to those appearing in the essay [the memorandum initiating the inquiry, written by an official of the Ministry of Religious and Educational Affairs in Berlin] have recently been published in a journal, the *Economist* [probably the *Économiste*, organ of the French liberals during the Restoration] whose staff are well known to be subversives and revolutionaries. They promise the people as well as the statesman great profits from a lessening of the expenses for religious celebrations. . . .

> If neglecting work and visiting taverns are regarded as a reason to restrict divine services, then our holidays must be reduced, as in France, and, finally, following the former French practice, Sunday abolished and only one day in ten left free from work. . . .

> We should thank God that even on weekdays there are those among us Catholics who find their way to church, while on the other side all one sees, even on Sundays, are empty churches and crowded taverns.

These statements seem to be a classic formulation of the ultramontanist mentality: a priest defends popular holidays and the pious common people against the attack of an economically calculating bureaucracy, without missing the opportunity to take a sideswipe at the Protestants. However, the Dean's letter to the Bishop did not end there; the subsequent paragraph shows the previous ones in a different light:

> It is well known that these processions are held in almost every village on a different day. This custom, not based on any regulation of the church, probably arose in past times in order to heighten the celebration by allowing the participation of the neighboring clergy and their congregations. Nowadays, this participation has only led to mischief, for almost the whole summer

[36] Bishop of Münster to OPM Jun. 13, 1828 and Bishop of Paderborn to OPM Jul. 7, 1828, STAM OP Nr. 2686 I. The reports of the clergy of the Diocese of Münster are in BAM GV IV Nr. A94 and all quotations, not otherwise indicated, are from there.

through the young people do not go to church but run to the
dances which are held along with all the processions, now here,
now there. Not only does this state of affairs create a threat to
morality, it is also highly degrading to the divine celebrations,
because they appear in the eyes of the people as an excuse to
engage in worldly pleasures.

He therefore wished to see all these processions held on a single day
and the secular authorities empowered to prevent the inn-keepers from
holding dances at that time.

Dean Lüthekamp's report shows that a thoroughly ultramontanist
attitude toward the Protestant state could go along with a lively suspicion of popular religious practices—if the previously existing balance
between sacred and secular, between clerical supervision and lay initiative, had been changed in favor of the latter elements. The *Münsterland*, however, was (and is) famous for its piety; the report of Dean
Lüthekamp was an exception among the clerical comments.[37] In more
observant areas the processions appeared in a different light. Father
Reckers in Grevern noted: ". . . if young people want to accompany
these processions they must ask for special permission from their parents or employers . . . it is only given if they promise to make up the
missed work with a greater effort another day. . . ." The Dean of
Warendorf made a similar observation: ". . . services on those days
just last a short time and are attended mostly by those who can afford
to be away from their work, while those who are needed at home stay
there on the job. Finally, after services, everyone goes home and takes
up his work once more. . . ."

Similar observations were found in most of the reports; they defined
the sort of popular behavior the clergy saw as evidence of genuine
piety. The authority of the peasant paterfamilias was intact—unmarried children or farm servants had to ask his permission to leave their
work. Religious ceremonies did not appear as an excuse to have a
good time and escape the tiresome constraints of labor on the farm
or in the workshop. To the extent that popular amusements were an
addition to religious ceremonies, they showed no tendency to get out
of hand. The clergy noted neither a great increase in purely secular
festivities nor a growing secularization of religious holidays as in the

---

[37] The Deanery of Ahlen encompassed the *Kreis* Beckum, an area which stands out
from the rest of the Münster District. It had the highest illegitimacy rate (even higher
than in the city of Münster), was a center of peasant insurgency in 1848, a democratic
stronghold in 1849, and left-wing influences persisted in it until 1870. In general,
complaints about the secular enjoyment of processions follow the future political alignments in the area.

Deanery of Ahlen. If the clergy in the observant regions complained about secular festivities at all, these complaints were limited to a few traditional occasions, above all the *Fastnacht* in the week preceding the beginning of the Lenten season.[38]

The contrast between the two sets of popular attitudes toward religious festivities has an interesting sociological correlation. Although not an absolute rule, it seems that in those areas with a purely agricultural economy the worldly amusements were, in the eyes of the clergy, beginning to gain the upper hand over the religious celebrations to which they had once been subordinate, while in the regions of widespread rural linen-weaving the religious ceremonies retained a dominant position. This is an observation consistent with the previous figures presented on the social composition of pilgrimages which showed an unusually large contingent of weavers in clerically approved pilgrimages.[39]

Outworking rural weaving, whether conducted on a full-time basis, as in the Kempen-Krefeld silk-weaving region in the Rhineland, or on a part-time basis, as in Westphalia, was a socially stabilizing force. It enabled young people to set up their own household and get married without having to wait, as in the purely agricultural areas, for a farm owner or customary tenant to become senile or die. Illegitimacy rates were therefore lower in the weaving districts, and popular religious practices and the sociability associated with them appeared more benign to the clergy than in the purely agricultural areas, where economic difficulties in setting up a household led to elevated illegitimacy rates.[40]

The changing character of religious life in the Rhineland can be followed in greater detail. In 1821, the Governor of the Province of Jülich-Kleve-Berg (following the administrative reorganization of 1824 this area became the Düsseldorf and Cologne Districts of the Rhine Province) had a circular sent to every parish priest in his jurisdiction, asking if religious pilgrimages lasting more than one day were "salutary" [*heilsam*] or if they should be abolished. The government made no secret of its hostility to these pilgrimages. In view of its attitude and the political changes of the previous thirty years, with their ac-

[38] For similar accounts, see HSTAD RD Nr. 129 Bl. 449 and LA Kr. Geldern to RD Aug. 9, 1830 HSTAD RD Nr. 29137.

[39] Statistics on weavers from the 1827 census of looms and spindles in STAM RM Nr. 107 Bl. 53-58. The *Kreis* Beckum had, relatively and absolutely, the fewest weavers in the District.

[40] Illegitimate births made up only one to two percent of all births in the *Kreise* of rural weaving in the Münster District during the 1820s, while in the predominantly agricultural areas between five and nine percent of all births were illegitimate. Figures are from the records of vital statistics in STAM RM Nr. 93.

companying limitations on the public exercise of religious functions, one might expect a thoroughly intimidated and stereotyped set of responses. Just the opposite: most priests showed little hesitation in frankly expressing themselves, frequently in great detail, with a wealth of argumentation based on personal experience. Less than twenty percent of the replies took no position, or called for the suppression of overnight pilgrimages in such a way as to suggest the respondent was making an effort to curry favor with the government.[41]

All conceivable shades of opinion were represented, from very favorable appreciations of pilgrimages as manifestations of genuine piety conducted in an impeccably moral atmosphere, to expressions of open hostility, seeing in the events nothing more than an opportunity to avoid going to church, a hotbed of superstitious practices, a disaster for impoverished households, and an occasion for young people to enjoy illicit rendezvous. When analyzed systematically, the replies show distinct regional differences which provide a rough indication of where popular and clerical notions of religion were diverging, where secularizing (or, as the priests would have it, "immoral") tendencies were making an appearance and where clergy and laity retained a common viewpoint. I have separated the responses by Kreis (in their 1871 boundaries) and grouped them according to whether the respondent desired a prohibition of overnight pilgrimages, opposed such a prohibition, or gave no opinion. See Table 1.3.

Two clearly delineated areas of clerically sanctioned devotion appear: in the north, near the Dutch border—Kreise Kleve, Geldern, and Moers—and in the hills of the Eifel region and surrounding areas in the south—Kreise Bergheim, Bonn, Cologne (country), and Euskirchen. Both areas were heavily rural and predominantly agricultural, although the peasants of the northern region were distinctly better off than those to the south. In the big cities—Cologne, its suburb Mülheim a. Rhein, Düsseldorf, and Krefeld—the clergy had a poor opinion of popular religious practices, as was the case in the centers of factory industry in Duisburg and Essen and the areas of rural mining, metallurgy, and leather-working in the Siegkreis and Kreis Mülheim a. Rhein. The Rhine Valley between Düsseldorf and the pious border regions—Kreise Gladbach, Grevenbroich, Neuß, and Rees—held a middling position.[42]

---

[41] Circular and replies of the clergy are in HSTAD OPKN Nr. 904, 905, 905b, 906, 907, and 911b.

[42] The economic characteristics of the Kreise are taken from the material in Hahn and Zorn (ed.), Historische Wirtschaftskarte. As was the case in Westphalia, the post-1848 political line-up of the Kreise in the Rhineland followed closely the 1820s remarks on piety. See below, pp. 143-44.

TABLE 1.3
Opinions of the Clergy Concerning Overnight Pilgrimages

Kreis	Overnight Pilgrimages Should Not Be prohibited		Should		No Opinion		Total Asked	
	N	%	N	%	N	%	N	%
Cologne District								
Bergheim	26	(70)	7	(19)	4	(11)	37	(100)
Bonn	16	(59)	10	(37)	1	(4)	27	(100)
Cologne (city)			[a]					
Cologne (country)	19	(61)	8	(26)	4	(13)	31	(100)
Euskirchen	15	(65)	7	(30)	1	(4)	23	(99)
Mülheim a. Rhein	9	(45)	7	(35)	4	(20)	20	(100)
Siegkreis	10	(56)	6	(33)	2	(11)	18	(100)
Rheinbach	8	(31)	12	(46)	6	(23)	26	(100)
Waldbroel and Gummersbach	1	(13)	5	(63)	2	(25)	8	(101)
Wipperfürth			Replies missing					
Total Cologne District[b]	104	(55)	62	(33)	24	(13)	190	(101)
Düsseldorf District								
Düsseldorf	10	(40)	11	(44)	4	(16)	25	(100)
Duisburg	4	(36)	6	(55)	1	(9)	11	(100)
Essen	—	—	6	(75)	2	(25)	8	(100)
Geldern	22	(96)	—	—	1	(4)	23	(100)
Gladbach	8	(73)	2	(18)	1	(9)	11	(100)
Grevenbroich	10	(56)	8	(44)	—	—	18	(100)
Kempen	10	(59)	4	(24)	3	(18)	17	(101)
Kleve	23	(77)	3	(10)	4	(13)	30	(100)
Krefeld	2	(20)	6	(60)	2	(20)	10	(100)
Lennep-Mettman-Elberfeld	3	(25)	6	(50)	3	(25)	12	(100)
Moers	10	(67)	1	(7)	4	(27)	15	(101)
Neuß	11	(52)	6	(29)	4	(19)	21	(100)
Rees	9	(64)	4	(29)	1	(7)	14	(100)
Solingen	2	(17)	5	(42)	5	(42)	12	(101)
Total Düsseldorf District	124	(55)	68	(30)	35	(15)	227	(100)

[a] The parish priest of St. Cunibert replied that he was in favor of a prohibition; the remaining clergy of the city signed a joint letter recognizing the frequent abuses and immoralities occasioned by pilgrimages but recommending they be allowed with clerical supervision.

[b] Less Cologne city and *Kreis* Wipperfürth.

SOURCE: Circular and replies of the clergy in HSTAD OPKN Nr. 904, 905, 905b, 906, 907, and 911b.

In the Rhineland, the rural areas where popular and clerical conceptions of religion clashed most sharply were regions of rural industry, while in the Westphalian Münster District the areas of rural industry were where popular and clerical notions were most harmonious. The difference lies in the differing social context of different forms of rural industry. Unlike the outworking rural weavers, the rural metallurgical and leather-working industries implied the presence of a resident bourgeoisie—mine and mill owners, foremen, engineers, clerks— often Protestants, usually outsiders, who brought unsettling notions to the countryside.[43]

Finally, in the Catholic diaspora—*Kreise* Gummerbach, Waldbroel, Lennep, Mettman, and Elberfeld, most of *Kreis* Solingen and parts of *Kreise* Essen and Duisburg—the clergy either avoided the issue or agreed to support a prohibition in a way suggesting an attempt to conciliate the authorities. Living in areas where the public exercise of the Catholic religion was a rarity and had been long forbidden, ministering to widely scattered and usually very poor parishioners, they were not willing to make an independent judgment.

It is only when one places these regional differences in conjunction with the theological opinions of the clergy that their positions can be properly evaluated. If a priest found his parishioners using pilgrimages as an occasion for "immoral" behavior, he had to take some stand— whether he couched his argument in the language of a traditionalist lamenting the present-day decline in morality, or launched an enlightened attack on popular superstitious and immoral practices. The two options open were either to call for an outright prohibition, or to hope that clerical supervision could effectively combat negative tendencies. It may be that the first option was preferred by the enlightened clergy, who saw pilgrimages in wholly negative terms, not as an originally good thing, corrupted by abuses. Yet the choice of that option was tempered by many considerations: the negative experiences of past prohibitions, the fear that the "common man" would see prohibition as "religious oppression," or the conviction, eloquently expressed by Father Lemmers in Mülheim a.d. Ruhr: "The right to go on a pilgrimage is an expression of the freedom of religion. Every man has the right to worship his Creator in his own fashion, not just in temples built by human hands but in the great temple of nature."[44]

---

[43] On the social context of the rural metallurgical industry, see Bruckner, *Wirtschaftsgeschichte*, pp. 332-51.

[44] HSTAD OPKN Nr. 907 Bl. 14-15. He further explained that he would never let his own parishioners, impoverished day-laborers and factory workers, go on a pilgrimage, as it would expose them to immoral temptations and bring them into greater poverty.

In the more pious regions, on the other hand, the clash of opinions came more clearly to the fore. Unable to cite any concrete examples of immoral practices, the isolated enlightened opponents of pilgrimages and similar manifestations of popular piety could only fall back on philosophical hostility to "superstitious" practices and vague, secondhand gossip about immorality. The orthodox clergy in these areas, however, brought an extremely suspicious and hostile attitude toward any proposal to restrict or abolish the public exercise of religious functions. From a theological viewpoint they favored them, and from their personal experience they could see nothing morally objectionable in them. The stated motives of the proposals thus appeared suspect; a search for ulterior motives was only a logical consequence.

A culprit was found quickly enough: Freemasons, secret societies, liberals, "German clubbists"—in short, revolutionary conspirators were behind the proposals, seeking to shake the altar which held up the throne.[45] Long before any actual revolutionaries had made an appearance in the northern Rhineland or Westphalia, a large part of the Catholic clergy saw their hand at work.[46] They damned proposals, actually stemming from an enlightened bureaucracy, as the work of subversives and set themselves up as the true friends of monarchical order, thus creating a position which would strongly mark political Catholicism throughout the nineteenth century.

In spite of the opposition of the majority of the clergy, the Archbishop of Cologne in conjunction with the government prohibited overnight pilgrimages in 1826. His successor, the ultramontane Clemens August von Droste-Vischering, refused to renew the prohibition in 1837.[47] But some seventy years of hostility had taken their toll. Even during the great upsurge in religious sentiment following the arrest of Clemens August in the course of the so-called *Kölner Wirren*, the number of pilgrims was nowhere near that of twenty years pre-

[45] A few examples: HSTAD OPKN Nr. 905 Bl. 274; Nr. 905b Bl. 14; Nr. 906 Bl. 32. Passages from the letter of the Dean of Marl to the Bishop of Münster which made this point very forcefully (cf. the comments of the Dean of Ahlen, above pp. 23-24) were reproduced verbatim by the Bishop in his letter to the Westphalian provincial governor, Jun. 13, 1828 STAM OP Nr. 2686 I. Vaguely similar ideas had been expressed by a circle of Catholic officials and notables in Cologne and ventilated by the prominent Catholic publicist Joseph Görres in 1816-1819, so there may have existed a broader intellectual climate for these priests' ideas (cf. Faber, *Die Rheinlande*, pp. 350-67).

[46] On the lack of a left-wing political climate in Rhineland-Westphalia c. 1830, Keinemann, "Julirevolution," and Dowe, *Arbeiterbewegung*, pp. 43-49.

[47] LAK 403 Nr. 16003 Bl. 357-62. The government refused to renew the prohibition on its own as "under the present circumstances [the situation created after the arrest of Clemens August in 1837] it would only make matters worse." Ibid., Nr. 16004 Bl. 161-62.

viously. In the hunger years 1845-1847, pilgrims were few and far between, in sharp contrast to the old regime, when pestilence or crop failure set thousands in motion, imploring saints, the Virgin, or God for help against the hostility of nature.[48] By 1850, the traditional pilgrimage was dead; its triumphant resurrection in the following twenty years would see it in a new and different form.

Religious Associations

The traditional form of lay association in the Catholic Church was the religious brotherhood. Usually named after a saint, its members shared a common yearly mass or joint communion. They marched as a group in religious processions and at the funeral of one of their members. This by no means exhausted their raison d'être: brotherhoods performed charitable works, sponsored pilgrimages, constituted guilds or village self-government. They showed the traditional mixture of the sacred and secular, functioning as mutual benefit societies and sponsoring worldly festivities.[49]

As with other religious institutions of the old regime, the brotherhoods were in a chaotic condition by the 1820s. The revolutionary and Napoleonic legislation had theoretically abolished them and turned their property over to the parish church, but the laws were executed imperfectly at best, and many brotherhoods were refounded after 1815.[50] Three distinct types of religious brotherhood existed in Rhineland-Westphalia around 1830: the purely devotional, the mutual benefit society, and the sociable-festive association.

The first type, often under the name "Brotherhood of Christian Teaching," or "Brotherhood of Jesus, Mary, Joseph," had been introduced by the Jesuits during the Counter-Reformation. Brotherhoods of this type usually encompassed the entire parish, membership being bestowed after confirmation. Their chief function was to hold regular memorial services for deceased members. The services were typically held on Sunday afternoons, and so the fate of the brotherhoods varied with the tendencies of church attendance. In a pious

[48] On traditional practices, see Phayer, *Religion*, p. 38; Klersch, *Volkstum und Volksleben*, 3: 176-80. For the situation after 1837, see the reports of the *Landräte* in 1839, HSTAD RD Nr. 3784; LA Kr. Kempen to RD, Jan. 12, 1847 and Jan. 9, 1848, HSTAD RD Nr. 3785; LAK 403 Nr. 16004 Bl. 353-56. The sources on this question are considerably better for the Rhineland than for Westphalia, but events seem to have been similar there. Cf. Keinemann, *Kölner Ereignis*, 1: 362.

[49] The classic study of old-regime religious brotherhoods is Agulhon, *Penitents et franc-maçons*. Such groups have been less well investigated in Rhineland-Westphalia, but cf. A. Mönks, "Schützenwesen," or Klersch, *Volkstum und Volksleben*, 3: 163-73.

[50] Cf. HSTAD RD Nr. 240 Bl. 32.

region, they might exist peacefully, without change, throughout the entire nineteenth century. If the parishioners preferred to spend their Sunday afternoons in the taverns, as was often the case during the *Vormärz*, then the brotherhood simply withered away. An ambitious priest might attempt to revive it, but if church attendance did not improve, the brotherhood disappeared once more.[51]

The second type had existed in close conjunction with the old guild system. With the abolition of the guilds, both in the revolutionary-Napoleonic and Prussian legislation, these brotherhoods rapidly fell into decay. In Aachen, as a one-time Imperial Free City a stronghold of the guild system, Provost Claeßen noted in 1834: "The brotherhoods in St. Foilan's parish church, for instance, are of little importance today; in other churches, several seem on the verge of dissolution. Just last year the heir of the last master of the famous St. Anne's brotherhood, which had existed for over 400 years, brought me what little was left of the treasury. A typical example."[52] The need which these brotherhoods met—financial support for a member when he was too ill to work, money for a proper burial upon his decease—had not disappeared in the *Vormärz*, but had, if anything, increased. Another type of institution came into existence to meet these needs: the mutual benefit society.

The first of them date back to the closing years of the eighteenth century. In their most typical form, the members paid biweekly dues into a central treasury. At an annual meeting the entire membership elected a board of directors which gave quarterly reports (not without controversy: one set of statutes noted, ". . . it is forbidden to swear at the directors as they give their reports . . .") and oversaw the distribution of illness and death benefits. The societies were a largely secular form of association; the treasury was usually entrusted to an innkeeper, often the dominant figure in the group, and meetings took place in a tavern, generally to the accompaniment of a small drinking bout. Members were mostly skilled workers and artisans, with a sprinkling of day laborers, factory workers, master craftsmen, small businessmen, and market gardeners—in short, the typical early industrial proletariat. These mutual benefit societies were the mass organization of the proletariat, long before the existence of working-class political

---

[51] HAEK Cab.-Reg. XXII, 2 contains many examples. Similarly, cf. HSTAD RA Nr. 4856 Bl. 179-80 and Keinemann, *Kölner Ereignis*, 1: 365 n. 34.

[52] Provost Claeßen to Archbishop of Cologne, Jan. 4, 1834, HAEK Gen. XXIII, 2 I. A few of these brotherhoods seem to have eked out a meager existence in the industrial region surrounding Aachen, but not in the city itself. Cf. LAK 403 Nr. 16447 Bl. 100-106, 108-111 and Nr. 7281 Bl. 481-83; Pf. Schiffers (Dham, Kr. Düren) to GV Cologne, Aug. 10, 1837, HAEK Gen. XXIII, 2 I.

parties or cultural organizations. A survey of 1876, when they were clearly past their peak, counted 138,793 members in the Düsseldorf District, about ten percent of the entire population.[53]

The groups were not all entirely without ties to the old brotherhoods. In some, a mass for the soul of a deceased member was included among the death benefits, while in others the statutes called on all the members to attend a mass for their deceased associates on the morning of the annual meeting. Unlike a religious brotherhood, however, the members of the mutual benefit society were not incorporated into other aspects of religious life: they had no consecrated flag, took no collective part in processions, had no formal relation to the church.[54] If religious influences were on the wane, ideological influences of a quite different nature began to make themselves felt. Two societies, "Hope" [Zur Hoffnung] in Kleve and "Steadfast Harmony" [Beständige Einigkeit] in Düsseldorf, bore the same names as the local masonic lodges. In some of the larger towns, the journeymen of a particular trade formed their own mutual benefit societies. These groups were headquartered at an inn, where newly arrived journeymen could find lodging and help in looking for work. Catholic artisans from Bonn or Cologne would come into contact with their Protestant counterparts from northern Germany, thus diluting the intensity of their religious identification.[55]

The distinction between the second and third group of brotherhoods is not always sharp. The useful aspects of a mutual benefit society, whether secular or religious, by no means excluded the pleasures of meeting for its own sake. Many ceremonies were common to both forms of brotherhoods; should the treasury of a mutual benefit brotherhood give out, the brotherhood could easily continue to exist for

[53] What follows is based on the extensive collection of statutes and administrative correspondence in LAK 403 Nr. 7274-7298. Although an 1833 order of the royal cabinet required all mutual benefit groups to obtain approval of their statutes from the provincial governor, only the bureaucrats of the Düsseldorf District Office carried out this order, while their counterparts in Cologne and Aachen seem to have been unwilling or unable to do so. (Cf. LAK 403 Nr. 7288 Bl. 293-99 Nr. 7297 Bl. 339-49 and Nr. 7292 Bl. 592 ff.) The 1876 survey results can be found in HSTAD RD Nr. 25095. Assertions about the social composition of the membership are based on lists of members of mutual benefit societies in Düsseldorf, Steele, and Opladen in HSTAD RD Nr. 25098, Nr. 25096, Nr. 25119 and Nr. 25101.

[54] Of the forty-seven mutual benefit societies either founded or submitting newly written statutes for official approval between 1833 and 1848 in the predominantly Catholic industrial areas of the Düsseldorf District (Kreise Düsseldorf, Kempen, Essen, and the predominantly Catholic areas of Kreis Gladbach and Landkreis Essen) twenty-seven were secular organizations, fourteen included a mass for a deceased member as part of their death benefits, and only six were religious brotherhoods.

[55] Cf. LAK 403 Nr. 7277 Bl. 269-84, Nr. 7285 Bl. 573 ff. and Nr. 7287 Bl. 3-6.

social purposes alone. The situation around 1830 allows the two kinds of groups to be distinguished. When a member of either type of brotherhood died, his brothers would march with the bier to the cemetery. If the brotherhood was a mutual benefit society, the family of the deceased would receive a payment at the time of his death, while this was not the case with the sociable brotherhoods. In fact, it was frequently the custom for the family of the deceased to pay the brothers for their march and for the ensuing drunken wake in the local tavern.[56]

Another distinguishing characteristic of the sociable brotherhoods was their sponsorship of public festivities. The most common were the festivals of the brotherhoods of sharpshooters, the *Schützen*, for iconographic reasons usually named after St. Sebastian. The yearly *Schützenfest* was (and still is today, especially in small towns and rural areas) the high point of popular amusement. It provides a perfect example of the unity of popular religion, secular amusement, and an agricultural environment which typified "traditional" society in Western Europe. The festival was held on a religious holiday—Ascension, Pentecost, Assumption, the festival of the local patron saint—in the summer dead season of three-field agriculture between the end of the spring planting and beginning of the late summer harvest. In the morning, the *Schützen* marched in a festive procession to the church to hear mass, the whole village coming alongside to watch; in the afternoon, they held their shooting contest, followed by a dance. The *Schützen* also appeared in more strictly religious guise. They attended a special mass on the day of their patron saint and marched as a body in processions. At Corpus Christi, they "guarded" the Host in the procession (as they still do today, especially in the countryside) firing their rifles in the air, making a racket which could be heard for miles around.[57]

Tendencies toward the secularization of the *Schützen* began to make

---

[56] Some examples of this: STAM LA Kr. Warendorf Nr. 958; *Kreis*-Sekretär of Kr. Borken to RM, Jul. 28 and Aug. 8, 1832, STAM RM Nr. 1135; HSTAD RD Nr. 240 Bl. 30. Naturally, a secular mutual benefit society could also have a drinking bout after the burial of one of its members. Cf. HSTAD LA Kr. Duisburg-Mülheim Nr. 156 Bl. 8-19.

[57] Among the many descriptions of this in the archives, see HSTAD RA Nr. 184 Bl. 36-41; RA Nr. 4855 Bl. 44, 75 ff., 117, 222-29; RA Nr. 4856 Bl. 49-53; RD Nr. 240 Bl. 12; STDD II Nr. 1315; BM Kaiserswerth to LA Kr. Düsseldorf, May 17, 1824, HSTAD RD Nr. 3783; LAK 403 Nr. 8808 Bl. 63-86; STAD M1 IP Nr. 367 and 369; STAM OP Nr. 1047 I Bl. 41-59. These documents suggest another difference between the mutual benefit and sociable brotherhoods—namely, their social composition. The first seem to have existed largely in a proletarian milieu, where the benefits were especially necessary; the second among the petit-bourgeoisie and the peasantry, where they were less so, and the members had the time for extended festivities.

their appearance in the early nineteenth century. A group of young salaried employees and master craftsmen in Burtscheid, the industrial suburb of Aachen, became dissatisfied with the St. Sebastian's Sharpshooters Brotherhood, dominated by the Catholic notables, so they formed their own shooters' society in 1822, open to members of any confession. Their annual festival was not held on a religious holiday but on the anniversary of the battle of Belle Alliance.[58] In Solingen, the St. Sebastian's Brotherhood dissolved itself in 1832 and became a secular, interconfessional shooting club. The parish priest complained that according to Napoleonic legislation the parish and not the shooting club was the legal successor to the brotherhood. Agreeing with him, the Protestant mayor confiscated the members' insignia and silver shooting trophy.[59] One or another of these cases, the transformation of a religious brotherhood into a lay shooting club or the formation of a new, secular sharpshooters' society, can be documented as having occurred during the *Vormärz* in Aachen, Cologne, Düsseldorf, Essen, Mülheim a. Rhein, and Coesfeld (the second largest town in the *Münsterland* after Münster itself), where a Jew was elected as an officer of the *Schützen* in 1839. The revolution of 1848 acted as a stimulus to this process and the secular shooting clubs began to appear in smaller towns in the following years.[60]

A new ideology accompanied the changes in membership and activities of the sharpshooters' associations. In 1847, the St. Sebastian's *Schützen* in Düsseldorf, newly reorganized on a secular basis, issued an invitation to a "Great Rhenish-Westphalian Shooting Contest." The invitation's admittedly turgid rhetoric rang with a nationalist and vaguely democratic pathos explicitly put forth as superseding religion as a motivation for action:[61]

> Our forefathers were inspired by the same need to express their innermost desires as today openly and forcefully fills the heart of every German man. Under the pious auspices of a deeply felt religiosity they founded a Saint Sebastian's sharpshooters' association. The need to express a genuinely patriotic sentiment was felt in a union of men for whom the fatherland is more than just the plot of land on which they came into the world, for whom it

[58] HSTAD RA Nr. 4855 Bl. 80-117, Nr. 4856 Bl. 118-19, 141-42.

[59] A dossier on the affair: HSTAD RD Nr. 13229.

[60] For the *Vormärz*: STDD II Nr. 1315; HSTAD RA Nr. 4857 Bl. 23-24; HSTAD RK Nr. 8093 Bl. 46-47; LAK 403 Nr. 8808 Bl. 1-7, 87 ff., 345-49; Keinemann, *Kölner Ereignis*, 2: 281. After 1848, see LAK 403 Nr. 8809 and HSTAD RK Nr. 8093.

[61] Flier, dated Düsseldorf, June 1847 in STDD II Nr. 1315; the new, secular statutes of 1846 in ibid., Bl. 52 and 1848 membership lists (bourgeois with clearly Jewish and probably Protestant names) STDD II Nr. 1422.

is a great common possession of all those who perceive that only the unity of opinion can develop the strength absolutely necessary to protect the rights of the people and preserve and strengthen a genuine nationality.

Before 1848 these openly secular tendencies were probably confined to the more bourgeois of the shooters' brotherhoods. The rustic or petit-bourgeois *Schützen* or related brotherhoods, however, were not arenas of untroubled piety or harmonious relations with the clergy. Consider this disparaging description of the St. Matthew's Brotherhood in Rheydt (*Kreis* Gladbach) from the pen of the parish priest. After attending their mass on St. Matthew's Day, the brothers ". . . regularly go to a tavern and drink until late at night. . . . They only leave after swilling and fighting and after several have gotten so loaded they have to be carried home. Consequently, besides being called a 'brotherhood' they have come to be known as the 'boozers' company.' "[62] Just as was the case with pilgrimages and processions, the unity of sacred and secular in the religious brotherhoods appeared to be breaking down and the latter gaining the upper hand. The combination of these two aspects of religious life in the *Schützenfest* frequently appeared to the clergy as the perfect occasion for their parishioners to drink and engage in sexual misbehavior.[63]

The enlightened episcopate combatted the brotherhoods by abolishing the special masses said for them, cutting them off from all official connection with the church, and refusing to consecrate new ones. These measures were not terribly successful. If some brotherhoods disappeared, secular drinking clubs appeared in their place; existing brotherhoods, spurned by the clergy, devoted themselves less to religious affairs and more to drinking, shooting, and marching around.[64]

Conclusion

In 1853, the parish priest in Ratingen, a town near Düsseldorf, described his parishioners, dividing them into three groups: (1) An "up-

[62] Pf. Aussen (Rheydt) to Archbishop of Cologne Aug. 27, 1837 HAEK Gen. XXIII, 2 I.

[63] Report of the Dean of Marl and the Pf. of Wachtendonk to Bishop of Münster, BAM GV IV Nr. A94; reports of Deans of Höxter and Brakel to Bishop of Paderborn, 1837 AGVP XIV, 1; Clergy of the Deanery of Lichtenau to the Capitular Vicar of Paderborn, Dec. 28, 1841 AGVP XIV, 2; HSTAD RD Nr. 240 Bl. 30ff.; HSTAD RA Nr. 184 Bl. 11 ff.

[64] On measures of the episcopate, see: Lipgens, *Spiegel* 1 I: 355; Bishop of Paderborn to Pf. Lüking (Nieheim) Mar. 24, 1825 and to Dean Hammen (Wiedenbrück) May 25, 1827 AGVP XVII, 1. For the results of such actions, see: HSTAD RA Nr. 4856 Bl. 11-16, 27-30, 97-103; STAD M1 IP Nr. 358 Bl. 66-67; STAM RM Nr. 1175 Bl. 180-81.

per class with considerable wealth and a respect for culture and education." Their education, however, was "without scholarly foundation"
and based entirely on reading magazines. They were characterized by
"religious indifference and a certain smugness." (2) Most of the "better
Catholics" belonged to the middle class, which had, in general, a good
record with respect to the performance of its religious duties. (3) There
was, finally, the "class of day laborers, factory workers, and a mob
of proletarians." Many of them thought of "nothing but material
needs," were without "religious and moral education," and were inclined to alcoholism.[65] This description can serve as a good general
characterization of the ups and downs of Catholic religious life in the
Vormärz: a bourgeoisie influenced by enlightened ideas, a large group
of master craftsmen and peasants still loyal to the church, and a lower
class without any intellectual hostility to religion, but given to spending
a disproportionate amount of time in the taverns, and rather neglectful
of its religious obligations. It would be inappropriate to speak of the
situation as one of dechristianization. Easter communion was the general rule; regular Sunday church attendance the practice of a majority.[66]

Still, disturbing tendencies were beginning to appear. Regions of a
stable and clerically sanctioned piety existed next to areas where worldly
festivities were on the increase and once firmly religious institutions
were developing in a secular direction. These tendencies were not solely
the result of urbanization or industrialization. If the inhabitants of
Cologne or Düsseldorf were lax in their religious practice, those of
Aachen were models of devotion. Worldly peasants and pious weavers
were to be found in Westphalia and on the lower Rhine. The developments were as much a product of the crisis of the agrarian-artisan
social and economic order, coming from tendencies preexistent within
it, as they were products of the replacement of this order with a new,
urban-industrial one.

It was not always easy for the clergy to deal with the manifestations
of declining piety. By the 1840s it was becoming increasingly clear
that the methods used by the enlightened rulers of the old regime, the
revolutionary and Napoleonic governments, and the enlightened episcopate and Prussian bureaucracy were not terribly successful. If religious holidays were abolished, people would celebrate them anyhow—
in the tavern and not the church. If priests prohibited their parishioners
from going on a pilgrimage, they might well go without clerical su-

[65] Cited in Gatz, *Volksmission*, p. 113.
[66] Even in clearly dechristianizing areas in southern France, such practices were still
the rule. Agulhon, *République*, pp. 162-88.

pervision. Such measures of suppression and prohibition were made all the more ineffective by the refusal of a large number of the more orthodox clergy to carry them out.[67]

There were tentative efforts in an alternate direction—not toward prohibition or restriction but toward the restructuring of religious life. Enterprising priests tried to form new religious brotherhoods, which they would lead, and not a group of laymen. The brothers were to be required to avoid the taverns and to receive communion more frequently.[68] The majority of the clergy were not opposed to overnight pilgrimages, but wanted to see them continue under their supervision and control. These efforts were thwarted by a governmental bureaucracy with other concerns. In the end, the bureaucrats did not really care whether pilgrimages led to moral or immoral conduct, if the members of a religious brotherhood went to church or to the tavern following the funeral of a member. They simply wanted to see all these practices abolished as wasting economically precious time.[69]

The clergy and the bureaucracy were at cross-purposes over political as well as economic issues. The Prussian government was attempting to integrate the western provinces of the monarchy with areas having a very different history and equally divergent social and economic structures. Anything which emphasized these differences had to be avoided. Efforts to increase Catholic piety could only run in the opposite direction, underscoring differences between the Catholic majority and the Protestant minority in Rhineland-Westphalia and between the western and eastern provinces of the monarchy.

These tensions appeared in relatively trivial, local matters—when, for instance, the priest in Reusrath (*Kreis* Solingen) attempted to reemphasize the religious element in the sharpshooters' brotherhood and immediately alienated the local Protestants, who had previously par-

[67] Secular celebrations of abolished religious holidays: LAK 403 Nr. 6683 Bl. 45-48; reports of the clergy from the Rhenish part of the Diocese of Münster, 1827, BAM GV IV Nr. A94; Dekanatsverweser Rahte to RAR, Jun. 3, 1836, STAM RAR II B Nr. 1097. Clergy refusing to abolish traditional practices: Bishop of Paderborn to RMI, Aug. 12, 1827, STAD M1 IIA Nr. 459; LA Kr. Neuß to RD, Jul. 17, 1824; HSTAD RD Nr. 3680; LA Kr. Gladbach to RD, Aug. 23, 1830, HSTAD RD Nr. 29137; LAK 403 Nr. 6684 Bl. 213-16.

[68] Two examples of this: Pf. Sandfort (Ostenfeld) to LA Kr. Warendorf, Feb. 5, 1829, STAM LA Kr. Warendorf Nr. 958; Pf. Hessing (Wiedenbrück) to Bishop of Paderborn, Sep. 18, 1827, AGVP XVII, 1.

[69] The bureaucracy did not necessarily share the clergy's hostility to worldly amusements on Sundays, which were days off from work anyhow. The Düsseldorf District officials refused several times during the *Vormärz*, the last time in 1847, to order tighter restrictions on the opening times of inns or the holding of dances on Sundays and holidays. HSTAD RD Nr. 129 esp. Bl. 152-57, 286-87. Cf. also RAR to OPM, Nov. 9, 1836, STAM OP Nr. 2686 I.

ticipated, and increased the tensions between the two confessions in the area.[70] The most celebrated and dramatic example was the *Kölner Wirren* of the late 1830s. When the Archbishop of Cologne instructed his clergy to demand a promise of Catholic education for future children as a prerequisite to the solemnization of a religiously mixed marriage, he touched off a sharp conflict with the government, eventually ending in his arrest. The specter of an increasing alienation of the western provinces from the monarchy, led by a growing Catholic self-assertion, prompted the authorities to take this ultimately self-defeating step.[71]

The possibility of an unhindered reconstruction of religious life, provoking neither conflict with the government nor controversy within the ranks of the clergy, would occur only in the changed circumstances after mid-century. A new social and political environment would form the backdrop to a changing religious life.

[70] The District Office in Düsseldorf attempted in vain to mediate between the Protestants and Catholics. HSTAD LA Kr. Solingen Nr. 115.

[71] Cf. Keinemann, *Kölner Ereignis* passim, but esp. 1: 13-14 and 47-48, where he notes that the plans of the "strict party" in the church for a religious revival could lead only to conflict with the government.

CHAPTER 2

A RELIGIOUS REVIVAL:
1850-1870

A New Socioeconomic Environment

The two decades following 1850 were characterized by a large-scale economic boom, the first major wave of urbanization and industrialization in Central Europe. From the coal mines and steelmills of the Ruhr basin, to the growing commerce and finishing industries of the Rhine Valley cities, to the flourishing textile districts on the left bank of the Rhine, the northern Rhineland and Westphalia played a key role in this spurt of German economic growth. The majority of the area's population, however, lived in the countryside, and this was especially true of the Catholics, who were disproportionately rural. For the agricultural and preindustrial lower classes, the picture of the period is somewhat more mixed.[1]

It began disastrously, with a decade-long period of poor harvests between 1846 and 1857 which left the peasantry scrambling for a little income and the urban lower classes desperately trying to make ends meet. Circumstances improved in the 1860s, and real incomes probably rose above their *Vormärz* levels, but restriction and austerity continued to be a major presence in the lives of the lower classes.[2] This restriction was clearly reflected in demographic terms. The mid-century subsistence crisis sharply discouraged the formation of new households, and as a consequence the birth rate plummeted, reaching its nineteenth-century low point around 1860.[3] The proportion of the population living in celibacy also increased. See Table 2.1. Both the

---

[1] In 1871, 64.9 percent of the Catholic population of the northern Rhineland and Westphalia lived in rural areas, as compared with 54.8 percent of the Protestant population. Figures from *Die Gemeinden und Gutsbezirke*, Vols. VII and VIII.

[2] Historians, focusing on the industrial "takeoff," have tended to ignore the agrarian crisis of the 1850s, but cf. Walker, *Emigration*, pp. 157-61; Phayer, *Religion*, pp. 240-42; LAK 403 Nr. 2399, 2419, and 9509. In his 1857 Lenten pastoral letter, the Bishop of Münster described how, in his heavily rural and agricultural diocese, "the long-lasting rise in the price of essential necessities" had led to "unemployment, poverty and misery . . . illnesses of all kinds. . . ." *Kirchliches Amtsblatt der Diözese Münster* 1 Nr. 4, Feb. 19, 1857, pp. 1-2. On the modest improvements in standards of living during the 1860s, see the reports of the *Landräte* in STAM RM Nr. 260 and *Jahrbuch für die amtliche Statistik des Preußischen Staates* 2 (1867): 275-80, 315-31, and 345-48.

[3] Köllmann, *Bevölkerung*, pp. 59, 65, and 267 n. 33.

TABLE 2.1
Proportion of the Adult Population Married in
Three Western Districts, Two Eastern Districts, and
All of Prussia, 1837-1861

1. *Western Districts*
Percent of the Over-Sixteen Population Married

	Münster District		Aachen District		Minden District[a]		Minden District[b]	
Year	Men	Women	Men	Women	Men	Women	Men	Women
1837	50.8	48.2	53.2	50.2	64.5	62.7	55.6	56.7
1846	49.1	47.9	49.0	48.5	59.6	57.2	55.2	52.9
1855	48.4	48.0	47.6	48.8	?	?	?	?
1861	47.6	46.8	46.8*	47.9*	57.5	56.7	51.6	50.3

2. *Eastern Districts and All of Prussia*

	Gumbinnen District		Posen District		Prussia	
Year	Men	Women	Men	Women	Men	Women
1837	?	?	?	?	?	?
1846	55.3	53.0	57.2	55.8	54.7	53.6
1855	?	?	?	?	?	?
1864	63.5	57.5	61.3	54.5	57.4	54.4

*1864

[a] The heavily (over ninety percent) Protestant *Kreise* Bielefeld, Halle, Herford, Lübbecke, and Minden.

[b] The heavily (over ninety percent, with one exception) Catholic *Kreise* Büren, Höxter, Paderborn, Warburg, and Wiedenbrück.

The Aachen, Münster, and Posen Districts were over ninety percent Catholic; the Gumbinnen District over ninety percent Protestant.

SOURCES: STAM OP Nr. 672-75; HSTAD RA Nr. 310, 375; *Tabellen und Amtliche Nachrichten* . . . 1849, 1: 275-76; *Preußische Statistik* 10 (1867): 3-6, 64, 70.

predominantly Protestant and predominantly Catholic areas in the Rhineland and Westphalia showed this trend, in contrast to the population in the East Elbian Districts of Gumbinnen (heavily Protestant), Posen (heavily Catholic but ethnically Polish), or Prussia as a whole. A considerable number of inhabitants of Prussia's western provinces responded to the mid-century subsistence crisis by renouncing, whether temporarily or permanently, family life, a decision that would have important consequences for popular attitudes toward festivity and religion.

The condition of rural overpopulation, revealed in the mid-century subsistence crisis, was not solved simply by means of austerity on the part of the lower classes. Rural-urban migration occurred on a large scale after 1850 in Rhineland-Westphalia as people streamed out of the overpopulated rural districts and, seeking work, came to the growing urban-industrial areas. Although similar tendencies could be observed in the *Vormärz*, this migration increased enormously after 1850.[4] See Table 2.2.

The net population loss in rural areas due to the post-mid-century migration reached extraordinary proportions. Net emigration amounted to ninety-nine percent of the population increase between 1858 and 1871 in the Münster District. The region was totally unable to support any new inhabitants. *Kreis* Ahaus in the northwestern corner of the district was an area especially hard hit by the collapse of the rural linen weaving industry: its net population loss due to emigration was five times the natural increase in the population. Extrapolation from the above and other fragmentary figures suggests that upward of 150,000 individuals left the predominantly Catholic rural districts of the northern Rhineland and Westphalia in the two decades after mid-century.[5]

Not only was this emigration much more massive than in the *Vormärz*; it was headed in a very different direction. Unlike conditions in southwestern Germany, where overseas migration continued on a large scale both before and after 1850, or in East Elbia, where it began only after mid-century, in the northern Rhineland and Westphalia emigrants were increasingly likely to forsake the longer journey to North America after 1850 in favor of the shorter move to the booming industrial cities of the Rhine Valley and Ruhr basin.[6] Between 1850 and 1867, Aachen gained over 10,000 new inhabitants through immigration, from a total population of just 50,000 in 1849. The three Westphalia Ruhr basin *Kreise* of Dortmund, Bochum, and Hagen

[4] The migration figures are calculated differently for different areas: those from the Aachen and Münster Districts were calculated indirectly from census and vital statistics records; those from the Düsseldorf District directly from the records of the *Meldeämter*. Each source has its own biases and problems, which are discussed in Sperber, "Rhineland-Westphalia," pp. 120-27.

[5] Besides the sources cited in Table 2.2, see STAD M1 IL Nr. 199-200.

[6] In the Münster District, for instance, a little over five hundred inhabitants per year left Prussia during the 1850s and 1860s (Obermann, "De quelques problemes," pp. 120-32 and *Preußische Statistik* 10 [1867]: 95, 109, 133). During this time, however, the area was losing some 2,000 inhabitants yearly to migration, so three-fourths of them must have been headed for destinations inside Prussia—most probably the cities of the neighboring Ruhr basin—and not overseas. In general, on tendencies in population movements, see Hochstadt, "Migration and Industrialization," and the two essays of Karl Obermann, "Die Arbeiteremigration" and "Die deutsche Auswanderung."

TABLE 2.2
Population Change Due to Migration
in Three Districts, 1820-1871

1. Aachen District
Average yearly net population change due to migration

Region	1820-1836	1837-1849	1850-1867
Industrial areas[a]	+279	+858	+1045
Areas of rural industry[b]	−129	−175	−224
Predominantly agricultural[c]	−273	−55	−725

[a] *Stadtkreis* Aachen, *Landkreis* Aachen, *Kreis* Düren.
[b] *Kreise* Schleiden and Monschau.
[c] *Kreise* Erkelenz, Eupen, Geilenkirchen, Heinsberg, Jülich, and Malmedy (these areas also included some artisanal, outworking rural industry).

2. Münster District
Average yearly net population change due to migration

Region	1820-1830	1831-1839	1858-1871
Münster and suburbs[a]	+369	+212	+94
Areas of rural industry[b]	+313	−218	−1439
Predominantly agricultural[c]	−208	−184	−876

[a] *Stadtkreis* Münster and *Landkreis* Münster.
[b] *Kreise* Ahaus, Borken, Coesfeld, Steinfurt, and Tecklenburg (areas of rural linen-weaving).
[c] *Kreise* Beckum, Lüdinghausen, Recklinghausen, and Warendorf (toward the end of the 1860s, coal-mining began in *Kreis* Recklinghausen, but it, like the other *Kreise*, remained basically agricultural throughout the entire period).

3. Düsseldorf District
Average yearly net population change due to migration

Region	1824-1839	1840-1849	1850-1854
Urban or industrial areas[a]	+3079	+2319	+3808

TABLE 2.2 (*cont.*)

1. Düsseldorf District
Average yearly net population change due to migration

Region	1824-1839	1840-1849	1850-1854
Areas of rural or artisanal industry[b]	+1052	+97	+970
Predominantly agricultural[c]	−489	−442	−1022

[a] *Kreise* Düsseldorf, Elberfeld, Duisburg-Essen, Krefeld, and Gladbach.
[b] *Kreise* Kempen, Lennep, and Solingen.
[c] *Kreise* Geldern, Grevenbroich, Kleve, Neuß, and Rees-Moers.
NOTE: These divisions are only approximate as economic life was much more varied in the Düsseldorf District than in the Aachen or Münster Districts.
SOURCES: Aachen District: Calculated from census results in HSTAD RA Nr. 310, 342-44, 351 and vital statistics in HSTAD RA Nr. 322-26, 348-50.
Münster District: (1) For 1820-39, calculated from census results in STAM RM Nr. 96 III and STAM OP Nr. 672-73 and from vital statistics in STAM RM Nr. 93 I-III. The 1840 population was extrapolated from the 1837 and 1841 census results. Vital statistics from the years 1840-1858 are unavailable at the *Kreis* level.
Düsseldorf District: Calculated from the yearly reports of population movement in HSTAD RD Nr. 415-16. Post-1854 figures are only fragmentary but show a similar trend.

gained 83,345 inhabitants through migration between 1858 and 1871, with the bulk of this new population coming from the neighboring rural areas.[7]

The increasing migration meant that an ever-growing proportion of the inhabitants of large cities was new to them. In 1871, only 33.2 percent of the population of Essen had been born there, and while Essen was an extreme case—native-born made up on the average about half of the urban population of the area in 1871—the proportion of the adult population native to the cities would always be lower than the proportion of the total population. It seems likely that between two-thirds and three-fourths of the adult inhabitants of large cities and industrial areas of the northern Rhineland and Westphalia in 1871 had not been born in them and were newcomers to the urban-industrial way of life.[8]

[7] Calculated from Reekers, *Westfalens Bevölkerung*, pp. 302-352 and HSTAD RA Nr. 348-50, 344, 351. For the origins of these new inhabitants, see Degen, "Herkunft," Brepohl, *Aufbau*, pp. 72-73, and the discussion of the sources in Sperber, "Rhineland-Westphalia," pp. 129-31.
[8] Figures on the proportion of locally born are from the 1871 census results in *Die Gemeinden und Gutsbezirke*, Vols. VII and VIII.

A related factor in this population movement was an ever-increasing population turnover. With a growing migration, the instability of the population grew; people were more likely to move from the country-side to one city and then move on to another. In *Kreis* Düsseldorf, 4,405 individuals moved in or out of the *Kreis* in 1824, 7.9 percent of the *Kreis* population. In 1865, 16,939 people moved over the *Kreis* boundary, 17.0 percent of the population, the population mobility more than doubling in forty years.[9]

Twenty years of rural-urban migration had changed the confessional composition of the urban areas. Not, as the sociological cliché would have it, in the direction of a greater mixture of the confessions; rather, in many predominantly Protestant cities the Catholic proportion of the population increased sharply, while the reverse was not the case: the Protestant and other non-Catholic proportion of the population of predominantly Catholic cities grew, at most, rather feebly, and even declined in some instances. See Table 2.3.

The development between 1850 and 1870 differed from the previous twenty or thirty years, when an appreciable non-Catholic minority appeared in cities which had been almost exclusively Catholic under the old regime. Cologne, for instance, was 95.8 percent Catholic in 1816. By 1849, the Catholic proportion of the population had declined to 86.2 percent and remained almost stable there, as the city was still 84.1 percent Catholic in 1871. Düsseldorf was 89.2 percent Catholic in 1823, 81.2 percent in 1849, and 76.5 percent in 1871. Aachen was a heavily Catholic city throughout the century, but, while Protestants and Jews made up 2.6 percent of its population in 1820, their pro-portion more than doubled to 6.0 percent in 1849, yet only increased to 6.8 percent in 1871.[10]

This different development was a consequence of the different social structures of the Catholic and Protestant populations in the cities of the northern Rhineland and Westphalia. The Protestant minority in predominantly Catholic areas was disproportionately bourgeois, with well more than its share of large-scale merchants, industrialists, profes-sional men, and upper-level bureaucrats. (Except for the bureaucrats, the same could be said of the Jews, who were, however, a much smaller group than the Protestants.) For most of the nineteenth century, the factory owners and large entrepreneurs of the industrial cities of the lower Rhine and of the Ruhr basin were almost exclusively Protestant.

[9] Calculated from figures in HSTAD RD Nr. 416 and HSTAD LA Kr. Düsseldorf Nr. 119. I would like to thank Steve Hochstadt for making these figures available to me and explaining their significance.

[10] For the earlier figures, see HSTAD RA Nr. 342; HSTAD RD Nr. 416 Bl. 29-33; and van Eyll, "Wirtschaftsgeschichte," 2: 179. Later figures are from Table 2.3

TABLE 2.3
Changes in the Confessional Composition
of the Population of Selected
Rhenish and Westphalian Cities, 1849-1871

City	Year	Catholic	Protestant	Other	Total Population
Cities of the Ruhr Basin					
Dortmund	1849	27.1%	71.2%	1.8%	10,515
	1871	42.4	56.0	1.7	44,420
Duisburg	1849	36.7	62.3	1.0	8,934
	1871	49.1	49.6	1.3	30,533
Essen	1849	60.4	36.1	3.4	8,732
	1871	65.9	32.3	1.9	51,513
Cities of the Rhine Valley					
Cologne	1849	86.2	12.4	1.4	88,356
	1871	84.1	13.4	2.5	129,233
Düsseldorf	1849	81.2	17.0	1.8	23,860
	1871	76.5	22.1	1.5	69,365
Mülheim a. Rhein	1849	80.8	17.6	1.6	5,901
	1871	79.8	19.0	1.2	13,511
Cities of the Industrial Region on the Left Bank of the Rhine					
Aachen	1849	94.0	5.4	0.5	50,533
	1871	93.2	5.6	1.2	74,146
Krefeld	1849	70.1	26.1	3.8	36,111
	1871	72.3	24.2	3.5	57,105
Mönchengladbach	1849	72.9	25.1	1.9	3,736
	1871	79.1	19.5	1.4	26,354

SOURCES: *Tabellen und amtliche Nachrichten* ... *1849*, 1: 191 ff.; *Die Gemeinden und Gutsbezirke* ... *1871*, Vols. 7 and 8.

Only in Aachen was there a relatively well-established group of Catholic industrialists. In the predominantly Protestant cities of the same region, the Catholic minority was very largely confined to the lower strata of the population, working in the factories and mines or as day laborers, at best as independent small businessmen or master craftsmen.[11]

[11] See, for instance, Zunkel, *Der rheinisch-westfälische Unternehmer*, pp. 29-33; Adel-

Changes in the proportions of the respective confessional minorities represent two very different social processes. The growth of the Protestant population in heavily Catholic areas was a consequence of the arrival of Prussian officials and soldiers following the territorial realignments of the Congress of Vienna in 1815, and the movement of merchants and industrialists (and associated professional men such as notaries and lawyers) to areas of untapped markets and cheap labor, formerly closed to them by the discriminatory practices of old regime governments.[12] The growth of the Catholic minority in predominantly Protestant areas, on the other hand, was a result of rural overpopulation, and the subsequent rural-urban migration. Since the rural population was disproportionately Catholic, this internal migration tended to increase the proportion of Catholics in predominantly Protestant cities and maintain the large Catholic majorities in predominantly Catholic ones.[13] In either case, these rural emigrants contributed to the formation of a self-consciously Catholic working class in the in-

---

mann, "Führende Unternehmer," pp. 348-49; Croon, "Stadtvertretung in Krefeld und Bochum," pp. 389-96; and Croon, *Die gesellschaftlichen Auswirkungen*, passim. Among the many contemporary observations of the relationship between religion and class are Thun, *Die Industrie am Niederrhein*, 1: 197-98; the remarks of the *Landrat* of *Kreis* Duisburg cited in Hunly, "The Working Classes," p. 145 n. 47; *Germania* Dec. 29, 1871 (Elberfeld) and Oct. 15, 1873 (*Kreis* Gladbach); Pf. Wiemann (Dortmund) to Bishop of Paderborn, Jun. 10, 1853 AGVP XVI, 12; Franz Rennebaum et al. (Menden) to G. V. Paderborn, Jun. 16, 1860, and Vicar Petri (Lütgendortmund) to G. V. Paderborn, Mar. 20, 1866 AGVP XIV, 2; Pf. Aussen (Rheydt) to the Archbishop of Cologne, Sep. 27, 1837 HAEK Gen. XXIII, 2 I and HSTAD OPKN Nr. 907 Bl. 14-15.

These are all very impressionistic, of course, but quantifiable evidence is hard to come by. A cautious survey of sociological studies can be found in Burger, *Religionszugehörigkeit und soziales Verhalten*, which is, unfortunately, so careful and judicious that it comes to no definite conclusion. In the region under study, the only quantifiable material I have found are the 1864 school-tax receipts for *Kreis* Dortmund (STAM LA Kr. Dortmund Nr. 843). The figures are fragmentary (there are no figures separated by confession for the city of Dortmund itself), but they show consistently higher per-capita direct taxes paid by Protestants than Catholics. The discrepancy is greatest in the *Gewerbesteuer*, the tax on commercial and industrial enterprises, where the Protestants paid between three and four times as much per capita as Catholics did. For a detailed discussion of this source, see Sperber, "Rhineland-Westphalia," pp. 137-38.

[12] The movement began before 1815, in the era of revolutionary and Napoleonic government, and in some instances even before that, in the closing years of the old regime. Dreyfus, *Sociétés et mentalités*, pp. 303-308 and passim.

[13] In predominantly Protestant cities with a predominantly Protestant hinterland, such as Bielefeld, Solingen, or Barmen-Elberfeld, the Catholic proportion of the population did not increase to any great extent between 1850 and 1870 because the rural migrants came from the neighboring Protestant areas. As the rural population of the Rhineland and Westphalia was disproportionately Catholic, however, the overall effect of large-scale rural-urban migration was to increase the Catholic proportion of the urban population.

dustrial cities of the lower Rhine and the Ruhr basin, distinctly suspicious of and hostile to the predominantly Protestant entrepreneurial bourgeoisie of those areas.

REVOLUTION AND REACTION: PRUSSIAN STATE AND CATHOLIC CHURCH, 1848-1870

The activity and influence of the Catholic church in the Rhineland and Westphalia during the revolution of 1848-1849 reflected the ambiguous position of the church during the *Vormärz*. At first the clergy was able to assert its authority over the Catholic population and thus create the basis for a nascent political Catholicism, but in the face of an organized radical-democratic challenge in the latter half of 1848 and early 1849 the clergy's authority withered and was often openly defied. The struggle of the clergy and Catholic lay activists against a radical-democratic revolution nonetheless proved significant, for the church's counterrevolutionary activities helped to foster a rapprochement with the Prussian state, creating an uneasy alliance which lasted the better part of two decades.[14]

The news of the 1848 March uprising in Berlin produced widespread social disorders in the provinces and the Rhineland and Westphalia were no exceptions. Peasants acted to regain their forest rights or their share of the divided common lands; artisans attacked modern machinery competitive with traditional craft production; journeymen and proletarians (but also master craftsmen working under the putting-out system) demanded higher wages and an end to such exploitative practices as paying in truck. Residences of the wealthy—merchants, money-lenders, nobility—were attacked; mortgage records, promissory notes, charters of feudal privileges destroyed. The authority of

---

[14] There is a large body of literature on the revolution of 1848-1849 in the Rhineland and Westphalia, although certain aspects of the events have still not been well studied. The excellent, if a little old-fashioned, book of Wilhelm Schulte, *Volk und Staat*, covers events in Westphalia thoroughly, but there is nothing comparable for the Rhineland. Konrad Repgen, *Märzbewegung und Maiwahlen*, ends with June 1848 and consequently does not provide a complete picture. His essay "Klerus und Politik" is an interesting if very tentative work. The studies on special themes, Dowe, *Arbeiterbewegung* and Hömig, *Rheinische Katholiken und Liberale*, are useful, although somewhat limited. Finally, there are the regional studies prepared by the students of the late Max Braubach, one of the leading Catholic historians in Germany, the first of which was the book by Repgen mentioned above: Denk, "Die Wahlen in Köln"; Haas, "Die Wahlen in Regierungs-Bezirk Aachen"; Kaiser, *Die politischen Strömungen*; Röttges, *Die politischen Wahlen*; and Weinandy, "Die Wahlen des Regierungsbezirkes Köln." There exists no history of the democratic movement in the Rhineland or Westphalia; such a work would be of considerable interest.

the government was equally a casualty of events: unloved area magistrates, tax collectors, customs officials, or foresters were forced to
flee; the Prussian eagle was symbolically buried in a dung-heap.[15]

The restoration of order followed quickly on the heels of these
popular disturbances as the newly installed, liberal Berlin ministry did
not hesitate to employ troops against lower-class insurgencies. Free
expression of opinion being as important to liberalism as the protection
of property, the ministers did suppress the apparatus of the *Vormärz*
police state and allow adherents of all political tendencies to propagate
their ideas. The elections to the Frankfurt National Assembly and the
Prussian Constituent Assembly thus took place in a politically unfet-
tered atmosphere, but one from which all specters of social disorder
had been, at least temporarily, banned.

While firmly opposing such social disorder, the Catholic clergy and
lay activists happily accepted the new political situation. Freed from
the heavy hand of the authoritarian *Vormärz* government, they sought
to use the occasion to ensure a favorable position for the church in
the new Germany. The bishops sent out pastoral letters calling on the
faithful to elect good Catholics, and the clergy carried the message to
their parishioners. An observer described the scene in a Westphalian
village where, as was usually the case, the elections were held in the
parish church:

> Early in the morning the congregation gathered in the church.
> The priest . . . held the services and following them gave a short
> speech. He explained that today was the day of the elections and
> since it was permitted to hold them in the church he requested
> his parishioners to behave as was appropriate in a sacred place.
> He called on them to keep in mind the importance of the election.
> In these great events, God's voice was to be heard; therefore he
> asked God to enlighten them and guide them in this important

[15] Schulte, *Volk und Staat*, pp. 161-82 gives an excellent account of the events in
Westphalia. Much less satisfying is Repgen's dismissal of the popular disturbances in
the Rhineland as "unpolitical." (*Märzbewegung und Maiwahlen*, pp. 50-55.) The def-
inition of politics implied in this dismissal seems overly narrow—especially in a revolutionary situation—and the connection between the events and future "political" action
is never considered. Röttges carries this notion to extremes when he asserts the unpolitical and moralistic-conservative viewpoint of the rioting lower classes in the Kempen-Krefeld weaving district in the spring of 1848, yet notes that some six months later
the Democratic Club in Krefeld was made up mostly of workers and artisans. (Röttges,
Die politischen Wahlen, pp. 54-55, 83-84.) Similarly, the rural areas of the Münster
District, where disturbances were widespread in the spring of 1848, were also the
democratic strongholds of a year later, while the more peaceful regions in March 1848
remained politically in the clerical-conservative camp throughout the revolution. (Cf.
Schulte, *Volk und Staat*, pp. 169-72, 289-90, 310, 706-708.)

business. They would help decide on the entire future position of the Christian religion, of the holy church, of the entire nation, the government, and, finally, of the recreation of the German Empire. They should only elect thoughtful men who would conscientiously vote for the most worthy candidates. [The elections were indirect and these were the elections of the electors who would in turn select the deputies who would actually sit in the assemblies.]

Nothing seems to have been planned in advance. As the election began, everyone sat on the benches in the church; they held no discussions; they did not whisper to each other. Their names were read out, the ballots distributed. Each man wrote down a name on his ballot or had his neighbor write one for him. When the ballots were opened, read aloud, and counted, it turned out that the priest had been elected almost unanimously as an elector for the election of a deputy to the Berlin Assembly; the elector to the Frankfurt Assembly was the former feudal lord of the village.[16]

As the observer specifically noted, the parishioners were on their best behavior for this special occasion, unlike the often unruly *Vormärz* congregations. Under these conditions it is not surprising that the elections resulted in a great clerical victory. Catholic deputies were sent to the Frankfurt Assembly from all the predominantly Catholic regions of the northern Rhineland and Westphalia. The only exceptions were the cities of Cologne and Essen, where the (disproportionately Protestant) bourgeois liberals were victorious, and Düsseldorf, which was dominated by radical democrats.[17]

Düsseldorf was virtually the only place in the Rhineland and Westphalia where the radical left had been well organized in the spring of 1848. Many more naive and optimistic democrats had expected to win the elections without doing any more campaigning than putting a few notices in little-read newspapers. The actual outcome of the elections proved a great shock, and throughout the spring and summer of 1848 the leftists systematically organized and agitated, striving to gain the support of artisans and workers, reaching out from their urban centers to hold meetings in the countryside, attracting large crowds and signs of support from the peasantry. The efforts of the democrats coincided with an increasing radicalization of the inhabitants of Prussia's western provinces. From the summer of 1848 on-

[16] Cited in Schulte, *Volk und Staat*, p. 647; cf. Gatz, *Volksmission*, p. 64.
[17] Schulte, *Volk und Staat*, pp. 183-96; Repgen, *Märzbewegung und Maiwahlen*, pp. 225-304.

ward, the popular mood was steadily more militant as the difficulties and failures of the Frankfurt and Berlin assemblies became ever more evident. The increasingly open appearance of reaction in the fall of 1848—the Malmö armistice; the return from exile of the Prince of Prussia, symbol of the extreme right; the dispersal of the Prussian Constituent Assembly by royal troops; and the naming of the reactionary Brandenburg ministry—were met by radical countermeasures, spearheaded by a tax-refusal campaign. The authorities responded by arresting democratic leaders, thus inciting numerous minor incidents and major clashes between troops and populace in Münster and Düsseldorf.[18]

During this period of popular radicalization, political Catholicism was moving toward an accommodation with the Prussian government. Frightened by growing republican sentiments, the Catholic deputies in Berlin took their places on the right side of the assembly. The constitution imposed by the Brandenburg ministry without the assembly's consent (commonly known as the "decree-constitution"), on the other hand, contained important guarantees for the church, placing its internal affairs outside state control. The democrats knew they would have to confront the clergy if they were to gain popular support. A correspondent writing for Karl Marx's *Neue Rheinische Zeitung* stated, "In Westphalia, it is above all important to break the power of the clergy. . . . In order to do this, the rural inhabitants must be cleverly propagandized. . . ." The forces of order concurred with the democrats. Rhenish Provincial Governor Franz August Eichmann noted, "Where the democrats are victorious, the influence of the clergy disappears."[19]

In January 1849, new elections were held for the Prussian legislature, the last under equal (if indirect) suffrage for seventy years. The bishops reissued their pastoral letters of the previous March, or, in new ones, called on the faithful to oppose the leftists and support more conservative elements. The bishops' efforts found the support of the majority of the clergy and lay activists. Loosely organized in a network of "Pius Associations," they distributed leaflets, held rallies, and gave sermons denouncing the left and calling on the voters to support moderate or

[18] Dowe, *Arbeiterbewegung*, pp. 163 ff., 149-51; Pülke, "Kreis Recklinghausen," pp. 38-52; Schulte, *Volk und Staat*, pp. 163 ff.; Haas, "Die Wahlen im Regierungs-Bezirk Aachen," pp. 40-41; Röttges, *Die politischen Wahlen*, pp. 83-93; Weinandy, "Die Wahlen des Regierungsbezirkes Köln," pp. 54-62; Kaiser, *Die politischen Strömungen*, pp. 35-44. All of these works mention the radicalization of the peasantry, a portion of whom came to support the democrats. This development, which runs counter to the historiographical consensus of an increasingly conservative peasantry after the spring of 1848, deserves further investigation.

[19] Hömig, *Katholiken und Liberalen*, pp. 29-57, 83-96, 109; Pülke, "Kreis Recklinghausen," p. 60.

conservative candidates. A small minority of the clergy, mostly younger priests at the lowest levels of the ecclesiastical hierarchy, broke with the bulk of organized Catholics to support the democrats.[20]

The radicals scored a major electoral victory in the predominantly Catholic areas of the Rhineland and Westphalia, carrying every city except Aachen and most of the rural constituencies, except for those in the western *Münsterland*, parts of the Eifel district, the *Hochsauerland*, and the lower Rhine region near the Dutch border: all areas noted in the *Vormärz* as being unusually devout so the democratic campaign was unable to make headway against popular piety and clerical influence. Elsewhere, the democratic victory was characterized by open defiance of clerical authority. During the election-day sermon in favor of law and order preached by the Bishop of Münster, the members of the congregation whispered to one another in their seats throughout the speech, left the cathedral, and voted for candidates of the extreme left. If the *Münsteraner* repudiated the good behavior of the spring of 1848 and reverted to *Vormärz* practices as a way of showing their disapproval of clerically sponsored conservatism, the inhabitants of Siegburg (Cologne District) took more drastic steps, bombarding with stones a priest who had come down from Bonn to speak at an electoral meeting of the "constitutional" party, a liberal-conservative grouping favored by Archbishop Johannes Geissel of Cologne.[21]

[20] Schulte, *Volk und Staat*, pp. 65-66, 72; Haas, "Die Wahlen im Regierungs-Bezirk Aachen," pp. 46-50; Röttges, *Die politischen Wahlen*, pp. 105-108; Kaiser, *Die politischen Strömungen*, pp. 49-63; Pülke, "Kreis Recklinghausen," p. 52; Hömig, *Katholiken und Liberalen*, p. 106 esp. n. 41. The small minority of democratic priests were cut off from the main currents of political Catholicism as the only one to play a further role in political life, Chaplain van Berg of Jülich, sat in the Prussian Parliament during the 1860s as a left independent, conspicuously avoiding any association with the Catholic caucus (Hömig, *Katholiken und Liberalen*, p. 272).

[21] Schulte, *Volk und Staat*, pp. 287-90, 705-708; Weber, *Aufklärung*, p. 159 n. 32; Denk, "Die Wahlen in Köln," pp. 162-69; Haas, "Die Wahlen im Regierungs-Bezirk Aachen," pp. 46-51; Kaiser, *Die politischen Strömungen*, pp. 49-63; Röttges, *Die politischen Wahlen*, pp. 106-16; Weinandy, "Die Wahlen des Regierungsbezirks Köln," pp. 78 ff. The contention found in some of these works that elections were a victory for the Catholics or a Catholic-democratic alliance (most extreme in Hömig, *Katholiken und Liberalen*, p. 104 ff., but cf. Röttges, *Die politischen Wahlen*, pp. 105-108 and Weber, *Aufklärung*, pp. 156 ff.) is not borne out by their own evidence, which shows the opposition to the democrats of the episcopate, the majority of the clergy and Catholic associations. Röttges asserts that the clerical electors in the constituency Kleve-Geldern had democratic sympathies, but the ostensibly democratic candidate they supported accepted the decree-constitution of the Brandenburg ministry, the rejection of which had been the main plank in the democrats' electoral program. His own account shows the reason the Catholic electors supported this candidate (while rejecting a genuine democrat) and opposing the official conservative was their poor relations with the hostile, Protestant *Landrat* (cf. Röttges, *Die politischen Wahlen*, pp. 106-108, 180-87).

The democratic movement in Germany reached its high point in the spring of 1849, its actions culminating in a series of uprising across Germany. In the Rhineland and Westphalia, the centers of insurrection were the predominantly Protestant cities of Elberfeld and Iserlohn, but the largely Catholic regions were also involved. There was street fighting in Düsseldorf, and attempts were made to storm the arsenals in Neuß and Siegburg. The reserves were called out in Westphalia to suppress the Iserlohn uprising, but the reservists mutinied at their gathering points in Soest, Münster, Paderborn, and Warendorf and refused to participate in the campaign. Regular troops suppressed the insurgencies, and reaction was openly triumphant: democratic leaders were arrested or forced into exile; democratic political clubs and newspapers prohibited; the constitution revised in an anti-democratic fashion in 1850, although the concessions granted the Catholic church remained in the revised version. While the political authority of the clergy had been shown to be shaky and regionally limited in 1848-1849, a reflection of the insecure position of priests in *Vormärz* religious life, the opposition of the church to the radical-democratic phase of the revolution had greatly strengthened its institutional position and created an accommodation with the Prussian state.[22]

The new Prussian constitution guaranteed the independent self-government of the major religious groups. For the Catholic church this meant an end to certain kinds of crippling bureaucratic interference all too common in the *Vormärz*: the religious orders were allowed to settle freely in Prussian territory; the bishops' correspondence with Rome no longer had to be inspected by the authorities. The government's claim to a right to appoint priests to parishes in Westphalia and on the right bank of the Rhine was disposed of, through amiable negotiations in Westphalia and through the unilateral action of the Archbishop of Cologne for the disputed parishes in his diocese.[23]

The mixed marriage controversy, catalyst of the *Kölner Wirren*, the major clash between church and state in Prussia before 1848, if not disappearing from polemical view, became ever less a matter for governmental interference. In May 1866, Paulus Melchers, the new Archbishop of Cologne, took a step beyond that of his predecessor, Clemens August von Droste-Vischering, some thirty years previously. Not only did the new archbishop require all religiously mixed couples to have their marriage solemnized by a priest; he prohibited the Catholic spouse from taking part in a second ceremony performed by a Protestant

[22] Schulte, *Volk und Staat*, pp. 249 ff., 329 ff.; Röttges, *Die politischen Wahlen*, pp. 117-26; Weinandy, "Die Wahlen des Regierungsbezirks Köln," pp. 126-27; Dowe, *Arbeiterbewegung*, p. 228 n. 857.

[23] Heckel, "Die Besetzung," pp. 275-79, 290-96 and passim.

pastor. The order was enthusiastically enforced by the lower clergy, and as a consequence such second ceremonies, once quite common in religiously mixed areas, ceased to exist.[24]

Staatskirchentum did not completely disappear after 1850. The government retained the right to name certain canons of the cathedral chapters and the legal power to veto the chapters' choices when they elected a new bishop. Conflicting claims in these areas gave rise to long-standing disputes, and the death of a bishop was always the occasion for complicated intrigues as the government sought to bring a politically agreeable candidate to the vacant see. These controversies, though, were neither as drastic as their *Vormärz* counterparts nor as widespread. After mid-century, the state conceded that it had no business interfering in many aspects of ecclesiastical administration where it had meddled before 1850.[25]

The new relationship between state and church did not involve just a liberation of religious activity from state control. In the wake of the shattering events of 1848-1849 a positive cooperation developed as well, the church exercising aspects of its authority with a new or renewed legal mandate.[26] The classic arena for cooperation between church and state was the school system. In the "regulation" of 1854 the reactionary bureaucrats of the Ministry of Educational and Religious Affairs denounced the school teachers as responsible for the revolution of 1848, renounced all methods of enlightened pedagogy, and proclaimed as the chief goal of elementary education for Prussia's Protestants the inculcation of Lutheran orthodoxy. At the same time, the authorities were renouncing their pre-1848 claims to a dominant position in the public education of Prussia's Catholic population (to say nothing of the 1848 democrats' demand for the introduction of secular public education) and turning this position over to the church. By the 1850s the local and *Kreis* school inspectors for the Catholic state schools were priests, and the parish priest was by virtue of his position local school inspector and president of the local school board. The principals of the Catholic normal schools and all their staff were priests, representatives of the bishops took part in the qualifying examinations for potential schoolteachers, and all appointments to positions as teachers occurred with the consent of the respective bishop. Religious instruction, the single most important and time-consuming topic in the curriculum, was given by the parish priest or someone he

[24] HSTAD RD Pr. Nr. 1245 Bl. 66 ff.

[25] See Hohmann, "Domkapitel und Bischofswahlen . . . 1826-1856," and by the same author, "Domkapitel und Bischofowahlen . . . 1856 bis 1892," and Trippen, *Domkapitel und Erzbischofswahlen.*

[26] Cf. Weber, *Aufklärung*, p. 186.

designated. The Catholic branch of the Prussian public school system was thus largely administered and directed by officials of the church.[27]

The vexing question of the legal validity of religious holidays, which had embittered relations between church and state in the *Vormärz*, was settled after 1850 with a new set of regulations, which granted the parish priest in predominantly Catholic areas a say in the appropriate restrictions to be imposed upon public business during these holidays. Unlike their liberal *Vormärz* predecessors, reaction-era bureaucrats were willing to accede to clerical demands for the closing of taverns and the restriction of worldly festivities, for they shared the clergy's perception of popular immorality as an important precursor to the insurgencies of 1848-1849.[28]

The Prussian state and the Catholic church were two independent powers. Ultimately, the Berlin authorities would not give up their claims to final authority, nor the ecclesiastical hierarchy its to institutional autonomy. After 1866 and 1871, these contrasting claims would drive the two institutions into conflict; in the two decades before, though, a cooperation, centered around common goals, proved possible. Things went most smoothly in Westphalia, where Provincial Governor Theodor Duesberg was himself a Catholic, one of the first representatives of his confession to enjoy a distinguished career in the Prussian bureaucracy, eventually being ennobled for his efforts. A firm believer in the unity of throne and altar, Duesberg formed a close working relationship with Bishop Müller of Münster and took care to remain on good terms with the different individuals who occupied the see in Paderborn during his twenty-year tenure as Provincial Governor. The Rhenish Provincial Governor during the 1850s, on the other hand, Hans von Kleist-Retzow, was a stubborn East Elbian, a bigoted Pietist, who carried his fanatic hatred for popular festivities far beyond the point which the Archbishop of Cologne, the lower clergy of the archdiocese, or Kleist-Retzow's own subordinates, for that matter, regarded as reasonable. Yet even Kleist-Retzow's relationship with the

---

[27] On state educational policy among Prussian Protestants, see Meyer, *Schule der Untertanen*, pp. 35-39; developments in Catholic areas can be followed through documents in STAM OP Nr. 2163, I, esp. RAR to OPM, Jul. 12, 1853 and Nov. 29, 1854. It is difficult to ascertain how these arrangements worked in practice, for the bulk of the records of the *Provinzialschulkollegien* of both the Rhineland and Westphalia were destroyed in the Second World War. Some notion of the enormous emphasis put on religion and proper religious and moral conduct in teacher training can be gleaned from the draft for a set of entrance requirements to the Catholic normal schools in Westphalia, dating from 1869, in STAM Provinzialschulkollegium Nr. 1666.

[28] The history of Sunday and holiday ordinances can be traced through LAK 403 Nr. 6686-87, HSTAD RD Nr. 8970, and STAM OP Nr. 2686 II. A detailed discussion is in Sperber, "Rhineland-Westphalia," pp. 154-61.

Catholic church was one in which both parties worked toward ultimately similar goals, albeit with different means and priorities.[29]

Duesberg's and Kleist-Retzow's attitudes were shared by other high officials of the provincial and district administrations in the two decades after 1850 and can be seen as paradigmatic. Both forms of behavior were far more favorable to the Catholic church than the authoritarian, omnicompetent, bureaucratic interference of the *Vormärz*. As with the social and economic situation, the practices of the Prussian authorities after 1850 helped to create conditions in which the Catholic clergy would find it far easier to carry out their plans for a religious revival than had been the case in the first half of the century.

Forms of a Religious Revival

Precursors

Efforts directed toward shoring up popular piety, resolving lay-clerical conflict, refuting enlightened ideas, and dissolving the institutions embodying them were prevalent in German Catholicism even before the end of the old regime. If the revolutionary and Napoleonic periods marked a break (even here there were exceptions, such as the 1810 Trier pilgrimage), the efforts were resumed in scattered instances after 1815 and were visibly quickening and intensifying in the late 1830s and early 1840s. The Catholic response to the arrest of the Archbishop of Cologne in 1837—renewed participation in pilgrimages and processions, improved church attendance, openly expressed hostility toward the authorities—both reflected and encouraged these efforts. Even more so, the renowned pilgrimage to the Holy Shroud of Trier in 1844 showed the creation of new forms of religious life. Nonetheless, all these factors are best seen as precursors of a religious revival whose main thrust came after 1850. The great surge of Catholic opinion following the arrest of the archbishop in 1837 was never institutionalized and organized; tensions were gradually reduced; a mutually agreeable settlement was worked out between the Prussian government and the Vatican, and by the mid-1840s there were signs of a return to the dominant *Vormärz* pattern of a lax religious life. Attempts to create new forms of religious association or devotion by energetic

[29] Wegmann, *Verwaltungsbeamten*, pp. 42, 86-90; *Allgemeine Deutsche Biographie*, Nachtrag, Vol. 2, article "Kleist-Retzow." Duesberg's judicious handling of problems of mixed marriages and Catholic processions in predominantly Protestant areas is documented in STAM OP Nr. 1866-67 and Nr. 1047 I; Kleist-Retzow's intransigent attitude toward Sunday and holiday ordinances can be followed through HSTAD RD Nr. 129, 8964, 29141; HSTAD RK Nr. 2224 and LAK 403 Nr. 6687.

clerics, or, on occasion, even by pious laymen, remained uncoordi-
nated, scattered, controversial, and often ephemeral. The 1844 Trier
pilgrimage was by far the most important *Vormärz* precursor of the
religious revival, receiving nationwide publicity and producing a great
effect on the lives of hundreds of thousands in the region, but efforts
to adapt its lessons to other pilgrimages were unsuccessful before mid-
century. It was only after 1850 that the clergy took on in a systematic
and organized way the encouragement of a new religious sensibility
and created a whole series of popular religious practices and associations in which this sensibility could be institutionalized. Occurring
in a favorable socioeconomic and political environment, these efforts
brought the tentative initiatives of the previous fifty to eighty years
fully to fruition.[30]

The Missions

The post-Tridentine Catholic church had always engaged in missionary
activity to convert those regarded as heathens and to win back for the
faith adherents of the Reformation. In eighteenth-century Central Europe, however, the Jesuits began holding missions for the faithful, not
to convert, but to revive a religious intensity worn down by the cares
of everyday life. In design and execution a typical expression of baroque religiosity, the missions were virtually brought to a standstill
by the abolition of the Jesuits in 1773. Several old-regime governments
tried to keep them alive, using the secular clergy or members of other
orders as missionaries, but the wars of the French Revolution put a
definitive end to these efforts. After 1815 the missions were not revived
in the German Confederation. Their baroque excesses, complete with
the self-flagellation of the preachers, were abhorrent to the enlightened
episcopate of the 1820s and 1830s. Protestant governments were suspicious of the religious orders; the Jesuits, for instance, were forbidden
on Prussian territory. Although excluded from direct participation,
German Catholics living in the border regions were interested spec-
tators of the missions held in Restoration Alsace, or, after 1830, in
Belgium. The first tentative efforts at renewed missionary activity
stemmed from the secular clergy of Westphalia in 1846-1847, but the

---

[30] Early examples of these initiatives in the Prince-Bishopric Münster are discussed
by Reif, *Westfälischer Adel*, pp. 183, 209, 437 ff. The difficulties of local efforts at
religious revival during the *Vormärz* and the controversies they caused can be seen in
Weber, *Aufklärung* (also, cf. above, pp. 37-38). On the *Kölner Wirren*, see the massive
study of Keinemann, *Kölner Ereignis* the settlement of the conflict is documented by
Lill, *Die Beilegung*. Weber's analysis of the event in *Aufklärung*, pp. 79-82, is well
worth reading. On the Trier pilgrimages, there is Schieder's remarkable study, "Trierer
Wallfahrt"; for an attempt to plot variations in religious sentiment, see Sperber,
"Confessional Identity."

movement really began after 1850, when the guarantees of religious freedom in the new Prussian constitution facilitated the holding of missions and allowed the use of German-speaking regular clerics from France and Switzerland, experienced in missionary techniques. At their most frequent in the first half of the 1850s, the missions continued at a steady if somewhat reduced pace until the outbreak of the *Kulturkampf*. They were systematically organized, and in the course of twenty years every single parish in the Rhenish and Westphalian dioceses had received at least one mission, and many had had several.[31]

The missions were extraordinary occasions, gigantic festivals, popular holidays. People came from near and far to hear the Jesuits, Franciscans, or Redemptorists preach. All work came to a standstill, even at harvest time. In one village, the peasants went so far as to hire Jews to watch their farms so that the whole family and all the servants could attend. Factory work hours were shortened in industrial areas, and special evening sermons held for the workers. At four or five a.m. the churches were opened for confession. There were three or four two-hour sermons during the day, and in the evenings another opportunity for confession. Toward the end of a two-week period there was a mass communion followed by a procession bearing a commemorative cross which was planted in front of the church or in another public place, thus culminating the mission. The imposing stone structure with the dates of the first and all subsequent missions in front of St. Maximilian's in Düsseldorf is still standing today.[32]

The emotional atmosphere was highly charged. The preachers spoke in a dramatic and popular style, replete with threats of hell-fire and promises of heavenly rewards. Extraordinary scenes were commonplace: skeptics who had not been to church in decades returned to the fold; bitter personal and family quarrels were resolved; great quantities of stolen goods were restored. Religious intensity was at a fever pitch: people whined and sighed during the sermons, covered their eyes or cast themselves to the ground out of a sense of unworthiness at the exhibition of the Host. Crowds of hundreds and thousands lined up before the confessionals until the small hours of the morning, and a team of twenty priests would not suffice to hear them all.[33]

The missions were an extreme example of a new form of Catholic

[31] Gatz, *Volksmission*, pp. 15-70.

[32] Both the missionaries and the local clergy made extensive reports on the missions. Gatz's book contains an excellent evaluation of them for the Archdiocese of Cologne (ibid., pp. 71-201). Reports for the Diocese of Paderborn are in AGVP XVI, 12-17. Corresponding reports for the Diocese of Münster were destroyed, along with almost all the post-1830 material, during the Second World War.

[33] Gatz, *Volksmission*, pp. 123-29; reports on the missions in Kirchenbachem, Obermarsberg, Deseburg, Soest, Dortmund, Herzebroich and elsewhere in 1853, AGVP XVI, 12.

piety which would come into its own in the years following 1850. Unlike "traditional" religious life, with its coupling of religious occasion and worldly festivity, during the missions the religious event itself was the festival. The mission was an extraordinary holiday—everyone stopped work and came in their Sunday best—but without the dancing and drinking which had previously characterized the festivities. The day was organized so there was no time for profane pleasures—even if anyone had had the desire for them. "The churches are full, the taverns are empty," was how the Police Commissioner described Düsseldorf during the mission of 1851. Similar observations were made wherever the missions were held.[34]

The missionaries shared the enlightened clergy's hostility toward "immoral" popular celebrations, but they did not ignore the desire for festivity and simply try to suppress it: they offered an alternative. This outlook is epitomized by the missionary sermons. Unlike the didactic, enlightened, and boring sermons of the *Vormärz*, which drove the congregation from the churches and into the taverns, the missionary sermons were carefully designed for dramatic and emotional effect, without thereby losing any of their didactic character.[35]

The missionary calls to repentance were issued following the revolutionary upheavals of 1848-1849; the stormy hopes raised in those years had proved to be in vain. Poor harvests and skyrocketing food prices accompanied the reaction era of the 1850s. In this time of blasted worldly hopes, the missionaries called on their hearers to consider their sins and look toward heaven. Even when politics was not overtly discussed (which was by no means always the case), the missions were a powerful political force, diverting popular attention away from secular social and political action, encouraging a passive acceptance of existing conditions. The missions made a massive and long-lasting impression, as they were probably the single largest public gathering in Catholic regions during the first two-thirds of the century.[36]

The missionary sermons served to direct the tremendous impact of the occasion. They began with a description of the basic elements of Catholic doctrine: sin, penance, and absolution, the significance of the

[34] HSTAD RD Pr. Nr. 1232 Bl. 158-60; cf. Gatz, *Volksmission*, pp. 61, 104; report on the mission in Wormeln, 1853, AGVP XVI, 12.

[35] The regeneration of the sermon through the missions is emphasized by Gatz, *Volksmission*, p. 116.

[36] For reports on the unprecedented size of crowds during the missions, see Pf. Rinten (Brunskappel) to Bishop of Paderborn, Jul. 28, 1858, AGVP XVI, 14; Keinemann, *Beiträge zur westfälischen Landesgeschichte*, p. 104. The report of the Aachen Police Commissioner on the 1868 mission shows that enormous crowds were also the case at a later date in a large city. HSTAD RA Nr. 817 Bl. 134.

incarnation, crucifixion, and resurrection. Special emphasis was placed on the veneration of the Virgin, for every mission included a sermon specifically devoted to this topic and to the consecration of an image of the Virgin, just one of many forms of a growing Marian devotion after 1850. The missionaries went on to describe the concrete applications of these doctrines to a moral and Christian life. Moral issues to be emphasized were usually discussed beforehand with the local clergy. Special problems varied from parish to parish, but several themes were handled almost everywhere—above all, the missionaries combatted dancing, sexual license, frequent visits to the tavern, and worldly festivities on Sundays and holidays, in short, those areas of popular morality which the *Vormärz* clergy had seen as getting increasingly out of hand.[37]

The improvement of popular morality is doubtless a staple of the clerical profession, but the struggle against sin occurred in a specific sociopolitical context. From the pulpit and in the confessional, penitent parishioners were urged to make restitutions for stolen goods, especially for the theft of wood from the holdings of large, often noble, landowners, a sinful action frequently appearing in the accounts of the missions. The theft of wood was an expression of the conflict between an impoverished rural community, clinging to its traditional collective rights to the use of forest lands, and the owners of those lands seeking exclusive control over them. It was the most common crime in the *Vormärz*, and far more than in any overtly "political" way wood theft was how the inhabitants of the countryside experienced the revolution of 1848: news of the March events in Berlin was everywhere the signal for peasants to dash into the forests and reclaim their traditional rights and their wood. Only a few years later the missionaries began demanding restitutions. One small parish paid the Count von Westphalen alone one hundred *Thaler*, a year's wages for an agricultural laborer. On other occasions the nobles graciously agreed to forgive the peasants for their thefts. In either case, the appropriation of the wood was delegitimized, viewed not as a right but as a sinful act.[38]

[37] Cf. Gatz, *Volksmission*, pp. 98, 126. Draft outlines of missionary sermons can be found in ibid., pp. 117-21, and Pf. Birns (Etteln) to Bishop of Paderborn, Feb. 18, 1861, AGVP XVI, 15.

[38] The account of missionaries' rebuke of wood thieves is based on reports to the Bishop of Paderborn by Pf. Teipel (Obermarsberg) Dec. 27, 1853; Pf. Scheele (Tingensteichen) Nov. 17, 1856; Pf. Rinte (Brunskappel) Jul. 28, 1859; G. Leonard Gessler OFM Dec. 18, 1860; and Pf. Peipenbroich (Bigge) Jul. 24, 1861, AGVP XVI, 12-16. On wood theft in the *Vormärz* and 1848, see Blasius, *Criminalität*, passim; Schulte, *Volk und Staat*, pp. 169-72; and Röttges, *Die politischen Wahlen*, p. 58. Father Scheele in Tingensteichen noted that the mission had led "to the restitution of many stolen

In campaigning against this sin, the missionaries and the local clergy were supporting the claims of the forest owners against the traditional rights of the peasant community and were taking a stand against the revolution of 1848, which had seen the last great effort to retain the collective use of the forest. The missions mark a crucial intermediate stage in the relations between the peasantry and the Catholic nobility: in 1848, the nobles' castles were targets of rustic insurrection, but by the time of the *Kulturkampf* they would be centers of political Catholicism.[39]

When the missionaries discussed politics, they did so in a similar context of sin and morality, denouncing socialism and democracy as the work of the devil, exalting obedience to the monarch by divine right as an exemplification of Christian virtue, and attributing the events of 1848-1849 to widespread irreligiosity. Both area magistrates and parish clergy called for missions to counter democratic influences persisting after the revolution; the Düsseldorf Police Commissioner even had the sermons of the Jesuits printed and distributed following their 1851 mission to help to restore law and order in a city which had been a center of radical democracy during 1848-1849. The missionaries appeared as open counterrevolutionaries, putting the weight of the Catholic church behind the political structure of the era of reaction. This counterrevolutionary theme also appeared in later missions, following the social democratic agitation and 1869 Essen miners' strike, and again after the end of the *Kulturkampf* and the lapse of the anti-socialist law.[40]

The response to the missions was largely determined by their counterrevolutionary dynamic. The provincial and regional bureaucracy was at first hostile and suspicious, given the reputation of the Jesuits as enemies of Protestantism, a reputation grown to legendary proportions through a total lack of contact with the religious orders. To the great surprise of the authorities, the activity of the Jesuits contained no religious polemics. Quite the contrary, they carefully avoided anything which might increase confessional tensions. The great spectacle of the missions attracted both Protestants and Jews who found nothing offensive in them.[41]

---

goods . . . especially in regard to wood thefts, which many in 1848 and 1850 did not consider a sin."

[39] Cf. Reif, *Westfälischer Adel*, p. 456.

[40] Gatz, *Volksmission*, pp. 64, 92, 112-14, 122, 169, 205-208; HSTAD RD Pr. Nr. 1232 Bl. 158-60 and RD Pr. Nr. 1252 Bl. 35.

[41] Gatz, *Volksmission*, pp. 89-90, 97, 99, 104; Pf. Nubel (Soest) to Bishop of Paderborn, Mar. 1, 1853, AGVP XVI, 12; Pf. Koop (Arnsberg) to Bishop of Paderborn, Dec. 9, 1858, AGVP XVI, 14, to mention just a few examples.

The anti-democratic campaign of the missionaries produced a very favorable impression. Protestant officials admitted that the experience of the missions gave the lie to their former prejudices. Even the most suspicious could find no confirmation for their fears. The grudging approbation of the Governor of the Minden District, a man who made little effort to conceal his suspicion of and hostility toward Catholicism, is as eloquent a testimony as the more enthusiastic accolades of other officials: "Up until now nothing of a politically damaging nature has been observed about the Jesuits: on the contrary, it appears their sermons have had a laudable effect. They have brought forth an energetic expression of loyal behavior from the inhabitants of Paderborn in recent times. It appears believable, as people maintain, that the Jesuits' lectures frequently discuss the obedience due the laws and the authority of the state, especially when one considers that the democratic party, which has entirely different goals in mind, has never found any encouragement from the Jesuits."[42] The industrial bourgeoisie, whether of the Catholic or Protestant confession, shared the enthusiasm of the bureaucracy. Encouraged by the missionaries' attacks on socialism, they gave their workers time off at full pay so they could attend the sermons.[43]

While the provincial bureaucracy was openly favorable, or, at worst, reluctantly admiring of the missions, the central authorities in Berlin had a quite different attitude. In May 1852, Minister of the Interior Ferdinand von Westphalen and Minister of Educational and Religious Affairs Karl Otto von Raumer issued a decree prohibiting missions in predominantly Protestant areas. They accused the missionaries of stirring up religious tensions and attempting to make converts. In response to this action, the Catholic deputies in the Prussian Parliament formed their own caucus, the political forerunner of the Center Party. Sharply confronting the government, the deputies took a firm stand on their church's constitutional right to religious freedom and forced a retraction from the reactionary ministry.[44]

Such events illuminate the Janus face of political Catholicism. The church was making full use of the freedom it had won in the revolution of 1848, a freedom embodied in the 1850 constitution, in order to denounce the revolution. In Berlin the Catholic deputies were defying the reaction-era ministry and defending the constitution, while in the

[42] RPMI to OPM Aug. 13, 1853, STAM OP Nr. 2533. Cf. Regierungs-Vizepräsident Naumann (Münster) to OPM Aug. 24, 1853, STAM OP Nr. 2048; Gatz, *Volksmission*, pp. 99, 153-54, 158-63.

[43] Gatz, *Volksmission*, pp. 129-70; Pf. Wiemann (Dortmund) to Bishop of Paderborn, Jun. 10, 1853, AGVP XVI, 12.

[44] Gatz, *Volksmission*, pp. 150-57; Bachem, *Zentrumspartei*, 2: 96-111.

provinces the missionaries were working in conjunction with the local
and provincial authorities, attacking democrats and subversives, striving to uphold the social and political order. This duality of behavior—
opposition to an authoritarian central government and cooperation
with the authoritarian policies of the regional representatives of that
government—would be typical of political Catholicism in nineteenth-
century Prussia.

Overt opposition to the missions came from the democratic camp.
One evening during the Düsseldorf mission of 1851, placards were
put up on every street corner, reading: "Citizens!! As you know the
Jesuits are preaching here. Go and hear them. Then you can convince
yourselves how these wretched swindlers are using the pure democratic
teachings of Jesus to stultify the people and win them for the monarchy
by grace of God."[45]

Hostility to the missions did not always take such overt forms but
a pattern of covert opposition can be traced in which political and
non-political motives were mixed. In rural areas, the small-town
bourgeoisie were often a center of opposition, as in Meschede, a democratic and liberal stronghold in the heavily clerical mountainous region of Westphalia, the *Hochsauerland*, where several notables ostentatiously refused to let their daughters join the Sodality of Maidens
founded at the end of the mission in 1854. In other parts of the
Hochsauerland, opposition came from the wandering peddlers. Because of the poverty of the soil in this mountainous area, virtually all
the male inhabitants of some villages were forced to spend eight or
ten months of the year in all corners of Europe, selling their wares.
They brought back the notions they had picked up on their travels,
and in isolated mountain communities the missionaries found "all the
sins of a big city." Sometimes the peasantry itself was the source of
opposition. During the 1861 mission in Niederau (*Kreis* Düren) a town
in the Aachen industrial area, the factory workers diligently attended
the sermons, appeared in large numbers for communion, and sacrificed
their hard-earned pennies to help meet the mission's costs, but the
peasants were openly hostile, skipped the sermons, refused to dig into
their pockets, and in general showed no signs of religious or moral
improvement.[46]

As one might expect, the tavern was a gathering place for opponents
of the mission. The bourgeoisie of Meschede as well as the mountain

[45] HSTAD RD Pr. Nr. 1232 Bl. 158-60. The police commissioner attributed the
placards to "members of the subversive party of the Catholic confession."

[46] Pf. ? (Meschede) to Bishop of Paderborn, Jun. 17, 1854 (the last page of the latter
is missing); Director of Missions Hillebrand to Bishop of Paderborn, Jan. 1, 1857,
AGVP XVI, 13; Gatz, *Volksmission*, p. 141.

peddlers in the *Hochsauerland* found the inns an appropriate place to make fun of the missionaries and impugn their motives—to the point where the local clergy began to fear for the missions' success, unjustifiably as it turned out. On the occasion of the 1858 mission in Coeurl, a mining village not far from Dortmund, the parish priest reported: "We have here an innkeeper who was previously an enthusiastic Catholic and was universally well liked. Since the year 1848 he has slandered everything Catholic and last year went over to an attack on the entire Christian revelation, incisively making propaganda for atheism. There were several in the parish who were inclined to such beliefs, and still more who were brought to have doubts." But after the missionary Hillebrand preached against "children of the devil," the "following of this dangerous individual has been reduced to nil." Hillebrand, the energetic Director of Missions for the Diocese of Paderborn, summed up over a decade of experience in a letter to the Bishop in 1859: "Several noisemakers in the inns, people who give a bad name even to otherwise right-thinking parishes, are determined to slander and frustrate a holy cause, for they fear their own downfall—especially in regard to unjust actions, bad acquaintances, and serious improprieties."[47]

Whether populated by apolitical drunkards, convinced atheists, militant democrats, or simply those who wished to spend their free time away from the influence of the church, the taverns were a center of non- or anti-clerical sociability, one the missionaries combatted with extraordinary vigor. Opposition to this sociability lay at the center of the missionaries' efforts, whether they were denouncing dancers or democrats. For the duration of the mission and the immediate aftermath they might hope for a considerable success. The memory of the mission would remain, albeit in weakened form, for years. But a decisive victory required the creation of new patterns of sociability, new forms of behavior. These new forms are exemplified by changes which occurred after mid-century in processions and pilgrimages and religious associations.

Processions and Pilgrimages after 1850

Limitations placed on the public exercise of religious functions, bureaucratic hostility toward processions and pilgrimages, clerical doubts about them, and popular indifference or preference for the worldly

---

[47] Pf. Denso (Coeurl) to Bishop of Paderborn, Jul. 19, 1858; yearly report of Director of Missions Hillebrand to Bishop of Paderborn, Jan. 3, 1859, AGVP XVI, 14. The failings listed by Hillebrand are revealingly ambiguous in nature: they can be either political or moral—or both.

side of these occasions had all combined to reduce their scope and extent in the first half of the nineteenth century. The decades following mid-century were a time when these barriers were overcome, and pilgrimages and processions, in a changed form, became more widespread and well attended than ever before.

In 1875, the Berlin government asked the local authorities to draw up a list of all the pilgrimages and processions in the areas under their administration. The inquiry was a measure of the *Kulturkampf* and was intended to lead to the prohibition of all public manifestations of the Roman Catholic religion which were not "traditional" [althervorgebracht], the authorities defining as traditional any pilgrimage continuously in existence since 1850.[48] A curious result emerges from comparing this list with the lists of pilgrimages drawn up in the 1820s and 1830s. Many of the "traditional" pilgrimages turn out to have been mid-century creations; others took place at a date several months away from the times they had been celebrated in the past, as can be seen in the following table of pilgrimages to the miraculous image of the Virgin in Kevelaer from places in the Düsseldorf District in the years 1824, 1839, and 1875. See Table 2.4.

The number of pilgrims increased as greatly as the number of pilgrimages. Between 1816 and 1824 the authorities counted a yearly average of 36,000 pilgrims at Kevelaer. In 1861 there were approximately 100,000 pious visitors, and eleven years later, at the beginning of the *Kulturkampf*, Catholic sources claimed 400,000.[49] Kevelaer was not the only shrine registering an increase in pilgrims. Lists of all the pilgrimages from places in the Aachen District for the years 1825 and 1875 have survived. See Table 2.5. The increase in pilgrimages was not shared equally by all shrines. While some were experiencing an unprecedented increase in visitors, others were being abandoned. Analysis of the changes in the goals of pilgrims from the Aachen District shows the nature of these transformations. See Table 2.6.

The change in destinations was simultaneously a change in the nature of the pilgrimages. The traditional festivities, delight of folklorists, had begun to disappear: villagers near Monschau no longer marched off to Conzen in May of each year to the shrine of St. Pancratius, or to Eicherscheid to pray for a good harvest.[50] In place of these partic-

---

[48] Circular of the Ministers of Interior and of Religious and Educational Affairs, Aug. 26, 1874, STAM OP Nr. 2047 I.

[49] HSTAD OPKN Nr. 760 Bl. 289, 296; reports of the BM Kevelaer in HSTAD LA Kr. Geldern Nr. 8 and Kreis-Sekretär Kr. Geldern to RD Feb. 9, 1826, HSTAD RD Nr. 3783; BM Kevelaer to LA Kr. Geldern Apr. 24, 1862, HSTAD LA Kr. Geldern Nr. 8; *Düsseldorfer Volksblatt*, Sep. 17, 1872, HSTAD RD Nr. 1257 Bl. 35.

[50] The process was probably more pronounced than it appears in the table, as it was

TABLE 2.4
Pilgrimages to Kevelaer

Kreis	Number of Pilgrimages in 1875	Existed 1839	Existed 1824 Same Date as 1875	Existed 1824 Different Date from 1875
Düsseldorf city	3	none	1	1
Düsseldorf country	2	none	2	none
Duisburg	a			
Essen city	a			
Essen country	2	none	none	none
Geldern	18	b	7	9
Gladbach	13	5	5	1
Grevenbroich	8	2	8	none
Kempen	c			
Kleve	13	b	11	1
Krefeld	8	a	3	1
Moers	8	none	5	3
Neuß	10	9	10	none
Rees	11	none	3	none
Solingen	7	1	1	none

[a] Reports missing.

[b] The reports just gave pilgrimages which lasted more than one day, but Kevelaer could be reached on foot from *Kreise* Kleve and Geldern in one day.

[c] See pages 67-68.

SOURCE: 1824: *Kreis* Sekretär Engelhardt (*Kreis* Geldern) to RD, February 9, 1826 HSTAD RD Nr. 3753; 1839: Reports of the *Landräte* HSTAD RD Nr. 3784; 1875: Reports of the *Landräte* HSTAD RD Nr. 3954.

ularistic, locally oriented events, pilgrimages became increasingly centered around several large shrines of the Virgin, common centers drawing worshippers from distant and disparate areas. Even the dates of the pilgrimages were changed in honor of the Virgin. In *Kreis* Geldern (Düsseldorf District), where half of the processions to Kevelaer were switched from their traditional dates in the course of the century, they were moved from times in May or June to Marian festivals: Assumption in August, or the Nativity of the Virgin in September.[51]

precisely the local, small-scale pilgrimages which were overlooked by the authorities in 1825. RA to OPK Dec. 17, 1825, HSTAD RA Nr. 4880.

[51] Michael Phayer's contention that Marian devotion was virtually nonexistent in

TABLE 2.5
Pilgrimages in the Aachen District

Kreis	Pilgrimages of Which				
	Held 1875	Held 1825 Same Date	Held 1825 Different Date	Not Held 1825	Pilgrimages Held 1825 but Not 1875
Aachen city	1875 lists missing; 4 pilgrimages in 1825				
Aachen country	32	8	2	22	8
Düren	53	29	2	21	14
Erkelenz	31	1825 lists appear incomplete			
Eupen	4	2	—	2	—
Geilenkirchen	12	2	1	9	—
Heinsberg	30	10	2	18	1
Jülich	48[a]	8	3	37	3
Malmedy	10	5	—	5	6
Monschau	23	20	—	3	10
Schleiden	64	46	3	15	14

[a] The 1875 lists of pilgrimages are missing for two districts of *Kreis* Jülich. The comparison has therefore only been made between those districts for which lists exist for 1875 and 1825.
SOURCE: Reports of the *Landräte* from 1825 and 1875, HSTAD RA Nr. 4880.

Unlike the *Vormärz*, observers noted the discipline and order with which the pilgrimages were carried out. There seemed to be a growing male participation. Almost everywhere, the marches were under clerical leadership, somewhat of a novelty, as the *Landrat* of *Kreis* Schleiden (Aachen District) noted: "The processions to Michelsberg and Barweiler, although originating in the distant past, were never accompanied by a priest. This has only occurred in recent years, on the part of priests who attempt, in the manner of the Jesuits, to win over the faithful for their goals. . . ."[52]

---

nineteenth-century Germany (*Sexual Liberation*, pp. 38-39) needs revision. Cf. above, p. 73.

[52] LA Kr. Schleiden to RA Jul. 4, 1875, HSTAD RA Nr. 4881. Cf. accounts in *Sonntagsblatt für katholische Christen* 9 (1850): 516; *Kölnische Zeitung*, Nov. 9, 1861; *Germania*, Oct. 9-10, 1871; LA Kr. Krefeld to RD May 15, 1875; LA Kr. Moers to RD, Jul. 27, 1875 and LA Kr. Gladbach to RD, May 20, 1875, HSTAD RD Nr. 8954. On similar tendencies in nineteenth century France, see Marrus, "Wallfahrten im Frankreich." His emphasis on the importance of railroad building for the growth of large centers, while doubtless an important factor, is not the full story for the Rhineland: the 1875 accounts of pilgrimages mention that most were still made on foot, even over considerable distances, and the railroads were just coming into use.

TABLE 2.6
The Changing Nature of Pilgrimages
in the Aachen District, 1825-1875

Type of Shrine	Number of Pilgrimages to These Shrines in 1875 not Existing in 1825	Number of Pilgrimages to These Shrines in 1825 not Existing in 1875
Shrine of the Virgin[a]	73	14
Other important centers[b]	22	21
Local shrines	37	21
Total pilgrimages existing in one year but not the other	132	56

[a] Aldenhoven, Barweiler, Heimbach, Kevelaer, Mariahilfe (near Koblenz) and Ophoven.
[b] Cornelymünster, Düren, Moresnet, Nievenheim and Trier.
SOURCE: Reports of the Landräte from 1825 and 1875, HSTAD RA Nr. 4880.

In 1875, the *Landrat* of *Kreis* Kempen (Düsseldorf District) drew up a list of non-traditional pilgrimages for the area under his administration. His observations reveal the decline of traditional pilgrimages in the first half of the nineteenth century and their reemergence after 1850. The pilgrimage from Kempen to Xanten, he noted, had originated c. 1770 but had fallen out of use and was first revived in 1847. No pilgrims went to Kevelaer from Tönisberg between 1835 and 1852, as was also the case at Born, where the pilgrimage to Kevelaer on the festival of the Nativity of the Virgin was still practiced in 1820 but had subsequently disappeared and was revived around mid-century. The greatest burst of revivals occurred c. 1850, but they continued through the 1870s. In Amern St. Georg, the Kevelaer pilgrimage was revived after a twenty-one-year absence in 1863, and had been "out of practice" since about 1840 in St. Tönis, but was "revived in recent years, is held, however, on another day than previously." A similar story was told of processions. The procession on All Saints Day in Breyell was begun again in the 1860s after twenty years of desuetude. Processions of the newly confirmed children appeared in several places after 1850. In Born, the processions on St. Marks (Apr. 25) and at Rogation had disappeared by 1840, were revived in 1862, but were limited to a march around the church and became full-scale processions through the village only after 1871.[53]

[53] LA Kr. Kempen to RD, May 8, 1875, HSTAD RD Nr. 8954. Cf. Churchwardens in Reuland to RA and BM Reuland to LA Kr. Malmedy, Oct. 16, 1877; BM of Coer-

The anti-clerical *Landrat* was very much an exception in his research into the past history of the processions. Most of the officials simply noted down every procession or pilgrimage and certified them as genuinely traditional. In part, this may be explained by the political sympathies of many Catholic area magistrates charged with drawing up the lists. Others, hostile to the church, spent their time engaging in petty bureaucratic harassment. If the route of a procession had been changed, it was denounced as non-traditional, as happened when a parish had become too large in the 1860s and had been divided in two. If both new parishes carried on the old processions, there were then two processions which could be forbidden fifteen years later.[54]

Neither conscious concealment nor diversion of attention seem to be complete explanations, however. Even if an official had been familiar with the area he administered—and many were not—the decisive changes had occurred some ten to thirty years in the past and had been largely forgotten. There would have had to have been something in the processions or pilgrimages themselves which alerted the officials to their relative novelty and triggered an investigation. Watching a procession go by, its participants led by a priest in strictest order and discipline; singing and praying; carrying crosses, consecrated flags, and images of the Virgin or the saints—how could a Prussian official, already suspicious of the "backward" and "black" Catholic inhabitants of the western provinces, have seen anything other than a traditional relic of the past, unchanged since the middle ages?

The seemingly traditional and unchanging religious ceremonies were actually complex amalgams of popular tradition and nineteenth-century innovation. The process by which this came about, the repression of some traditional elements and the transformation of others, is difficult to see in the "snapshot" approach (comparison of one point in time with another) used in this section. In most cases, sources illuminating the process of change are lacking, but the evolution of the septennial pilgrimage to the relics of the Aachen cathedral, one of the major religious events for the Catholic population of the northern Rhineland, is well documented.

THE AACHEN PILGRIMAGE

The pilgrimage to the Aachen cathedral had existed since 1349. Pilgrims came for two weeks in July every seven years to venerate the

---

renzig to LA Kr. Erkelenz, Sep. 5, 1875; LA Kr. Schleiden to RA Oct. 8, 1875; testimony of the policeman Schroeder, the field-watchman Lenzen, and the farmer Welter from Hambach, all in HSTAD RA Nr. 4881.

[54] There are many examples of this in HSTAD RA Nr. 4881; cf. also LA Kr. Geldern to RD, Apr. 24, 1875, HSTAD RD Nr. 8954 and RAR to OPM, Oct. 25, 1877, STAM OP Nr. 2047 I.

relics stored there: the maternity dress of the Virgin, the swaddling clothes of the infant Jesus, the rags worn by Christ at the crucifixion, and the cloth in which the head of John the Baptist had been wrapped. The enlightened Emperor Joseph II abolished the pilgrimage in 1776, but it was resumed under Napoleon's patronage in 1804 and continued at regular seven-year intervals until the First World War.[55] By the early nineteenth century, however, the religious character of the pilgrimage seemed to be on the wane, as irate Catholic observers noted in 1846:

> While on the one side people are venerating the relics, on the other, the crowd, having nothing better to do, is chattering, laughing, eating, drinking, pushing, shoving, running to and fro. Pickpockets and other questionable characters ply their trade in the press; even the choir boys of the cathedral in their white robes do a little business selling rosaries. Wagons and carts dart on by, especially on weekdays, when the mass of pilgrims is not so great. In houses near the cathedral, where, for a fee, a pleasant seat is to be had, people are enjoying themselves, drinking and smoking or having a cup of coffee. When, after these not especially devout preparations, the moment comes for the relics to be shown, the crowd begins to pray once more, but the thoughtless curiosity seeker and the cold scorner can, at least in their bearing, show their disrespect. . . .

> On the neighboring streets, booths of all kinds are set up, and after venerating the holy relics in the morning, one can spend the afternoon seeing wild animals and wax figures . . . or going for a ride on a carousel—things which are in and of themselves innocent, but are as little appropriate in the neighborhood of the relics as the moneychangers were in the Temple. . . .

> The pilgrimage to the relics in Aachen, introduced in another era and appropriate in its way for a past time, has sunk in our day to the level of a secular popular festival where more attention is paid to earthly profits than to divine grace.[56]

It was the traditional setup of the pilgrimage which had occasioned its growing secularization. In the mornings, the relics were shown from the tower of the cathedral to a disorganized mass of pilgrims on the cathedral square below, while in the afternoons they were on display in the cathedral, but only to those fortunate enough to have purchased one of the four hundred entry cards.[57] Left to their own devices, the

[55] Schiffers, *Aachener Heiligtumsfahrt*, pp. 10-14 and passim.

[56] Constantia Society to Provost Grossmann of the Aachen Cathedral, undated (early 1846) (copy) HSTAD PP Aachen Nr. 86 I. Cf. HSTAD RA Nr. 10810 Bl. 3-5.

[57] Ibid.

pilgrims showed an increasing interest in the more secularly festive tendencies of the occasion, something not entirely surprising in view of the lax religious atmosphere of the *Vormärz*.

The first estimates of the total number of pilgrims for the entire two-week period of the pilgrimage date from the latter part of the century. Before that, the local officials tried to get a rough count by stationing policemen at every gate of the city on the Sundays of the pilgrimage period. The figures in Table 2.7 give their estimates for the Sunday when the crowd was at its maximum. Participation fluctuated considerably before 1850. The impact of the arrest of the Archbishop of Cologne in 1837 is manifest in the increased number of pilgrims in 1839, but in 1846 participation had fallen off once more. The pilgrimage to the Aachen relics shared two of the characteristics of Catholic religious life in the *Vormärz*: a fluctuating, but often low level of participation, and a tendency for the participants to stress the secular side of the combined sacred/secular festivals typical of traditional religious life. Like other aspects of religious life, the Aachen pilgrimage underwent a decisive change in character after mid-century.

The first example of a new type of pilgrimage, a model for developments after 1850, was the pilgrimage to the Holy Shroud of Trier in 1844. Unlike many manifestations of popular piety in the *Vormärz*, the Trier pilgrimage was strictly and bureaucratically organized from the top down. All the parishes in the Diocese of Trier were assigned a date when they were to appear in Trier to venerate the relic. The pilgrims, instead of straggling along the roadside as individuals or in small groups under questionable lay supervision, were led by priests in strictest order and discipline. The pilgrimage was planned by the bishop and senior clergy of the diocese in close conjunction with the

TABLE 2.7
Pilgrims in Aachen, 1825-1846

Year	Pilgrims on the Peak Sunday
1825	20,000-30,000
1832	c.45,000
1839	c.60,000
1846	c.28,500

SOURCE: HSTAD RA Nr. 10819 Bl. 3-5, 9; reports of the Aachen Police Commissioner and remarks of the Constantia Society in HSTAD Polizei-Präsidium Aachen Nr. 86 I.

Governor of the Trier District and the Rhenish Provincial Governor, who dropped the previous hostility of the bureaucracy and saw the pilgrimage as a counterrevolutionary enterprise, an opportunity to divert the minds of the impoverished inhabitants of the region from their worldly troubles to divine palliatives.[58]

While the extraordinary publicity surrounding the Trier pilgrimage made it an obvious model for the reform of its Aachen counterpart, the reform initiative came not from the clergy but from the lay Catholic political club, the Constantia, and was the first public action of the newly constituted group. Explicitly citing the precedent set in Trier, the Constantia's members denounced the traditional, increasingly secularized event and in early 1846 called for the reordering of the pilgrimage set for the following summer. They requested that the Archbishop of Cologne set fixed dates for each deanery in his diocese to come to Aachen, every parish to be led by its priest. The police were called upon to remove the vendors and wild animal shows from the streets. Finally, and most importantly, the Constantia wished to see the whole process of showing the relics changed. After a brief showing from the tower of the cathedral in the morning, the relics were to be shown inside the cathedral in the afternoon to the pilgrims, who would march in ordered processions, led by their priests, from prearranged points in the city to and through the cathedral. The whole experience of the pilgrimage was to be changed, the undisciplined, individualized, traditional pilgrimage, with its combination of sacred and secular, giving way to a highly organized, collective, and clerically led public manifestation. According to the Constantia, in a reformed pilgrimage "... the fire of Catholic enthusiasm ... will be carried throughout the entire land by processions with song and prayer. How much more passionate will be the devotion before the holy relics themselves! Strengthened by common prayer, instructed and encouraged by the speech of the accompanying priest, the faithful pilgrim will at last step into the venerable halls of our thousand-year-old cathedral. With every step his longing will increase, his heart beat faster, until at last, kneeling before the holy symbols of our salvation, he can pour out all his desires and needs to the Lord."[59]

This expression of romantic sensibility may seem a bit surprising, coming from the hard-headed group of merchants, industrialists, professionals, and local officials who made up the Constantia. As they were well aware, their political importance, their influence in an era

[58] On the Trier pilgrimage, see Schieder, "Trierer Wallfahrt."
[59] See the letter of the Constantia Society, cited above, n. 56; LAK 403 Nr. 13867 Bl. 183 ff.; Repgen, *Märzbewegung und Maiwahlen*, p. 111.

of nascent mass politics, was dependent on the existence of a lively religious sentiment among the Catholic lower classes. Popular morality was a means to a successful clerical politics for the Constantia, and an important goal of its clerical politics was the improvement of popular morality.

The officials of the Aachen District Office were more skeptical than their opposite numbers in Trier, and the Constantia's proposed reorganization of the pilgrimage was first completely carried out in 1853. In a festive ceremony on Saturday, July 9, involving the clergy of the city, the mayor, the city council, and representatives of the Prussian government, the relics were unsealed. For the following two weeks they were exhibited from 10:00 a.m. to noon, "with singing of psalms and other religious music." Every afternoon, from 1:00 p.m. to 7:00 p.m., processions from a different deanery of the diocese, each led by a priest, passed through the city from their starting points in St. Pauls and St. Michaels churches to the cathedral. A great celebration at the cathedral on July 24, with all the dignitaries once more present, marked the end of the pilgrimage.

The Prussian officials were very impressed with the orderliness of the pilgrimage, all the more so as the violent events of 1848-1849 were still fresh in their minds. The *Landrat* of the city of Aachen noted it was a "rare and most enjoyable occurrence . . . that there were no noticeable 'excesses' or disturbances of public order. . . ." Clergy and municipal officials concurred: the experience with the new system had been so favorable that it was to be introduced at the yearly pilgrimages to Burtscheid and Cornelymünster (both in *Landkreis* Aachen). The new form remained essentially unchanged in Aachen throughout the rest of the century. There was only one major innovation occurring in 1867, when the pilgrimage was closed by a great procession bearing the relics through the city, with the new Archbishop of Cologne, Paulus Melchers, at its head.[60]

More of the faithful experienced this new pilgrimage than had ever seen the old one, in part because railroad building made Aachen more accessible to pilgrims living at a distance, but there were also a greater number of participants arriving on foot than in the *Vormärz*. See Table 2.8.

In Aachen a traditional form of religious practice had come to an end in the second half of the nineteenth century. Yet the result was

---

[60] LAK 403 Nr. 13867 Bl. 190 ff.; HSTAD RA Nr. 10819 Bl. 105-110, 135 ff., 175 ff. In 1846, the relics were shown inside in the mornings and from the tower in the afternoon, but since the pilgrims generally did not reach Aachen until the afternoon, the carefully organized morning processions did not occur, and the old chaos was once again to be found, this time in the afternoon.

TABLE 2.8
Pilgrims in Aachen, 1853-1881

Year	Pilgrims on the Peak Sunday	Pilgrims Coming on Foot	Pilgrims Coming with the Railroad
1853	?	Over 62,000	?
1860	65,000	55,000	10,000
1867	71,000	61,000	10,000
1874	69,000	44,000	25,000
1881	110,000	60,000	50,000

SOURCE: HSTAD RA Nr. 10819 Bl. 105-10, 151-52, 207-13 and 246-50. Police Commissioner Hellweg to OB Conzen, July 15 and July 21, 1865 HSTAD Polizei-Präsidium Aachen Nr. 86 I.

not an increased secularization but a strengthened piety. It is precisely this replacement of traditional but laic and secularized forms of religious practice with new clerically controlled, politically relevant ones, which was a characteristic element of the Catholic milieu in the northern Rhineland and Westphalia in the two decades after 1850.

New Forms of Religious Associations

The changes in Catholic associational life after 1850 paralleled the simultaneously occurring changes in the nature of public manifestations of religion. In both cases, seemingly traditional institutions were imbued with new content and direction. After 1850 the single most important form of lay Catholic association remained the religious brotherhood. The 1874 governmental investigation of Catholic associations turned up whole areas where no organization but the brotherhoods existed. Even in the largely urban and industrial Düsseldorf District, 346 of the 609 Catholic associations counted were brotherhoods—and the returns on the brotherhoods from three Kreise still had not come in when the total was drawn up. Therefore the emphasis in the following sections will be placed on the brotherhoods and related organizations; the Catholic political clubs, peasant leagues, and Christian Social workers' associations, groups which came into existence primarily in the latter half of the 1860s, will be discussed in Chapter Four, which deals with political events at that time.[61]

[61] The main source for this section is the investigation of Catholic associations ordered by the Ministry of the Interior, following the attempt on Bismarck's life in 1874 by a

SODALITIES AND CONGREGATIONS

By far the most common and widespread of the new religious associations were the Marianic sodalities and congregations. In many
ways they were similar to the traditional brotherhoods. Members took
joint communion at the festivals of the Virgin, marched as a group in
processions, and were usually expected to turn out for the funeral of
a member. Piety and moral behavior, however, were strongly emphasized in sodalities: members were expected to recite a Marian devotion
or say their rosary daily, attend Sunday services regularly, meet once
a month on Sunday afternoons in the church for a devotional, and
shun taverns, dance floors, and other places providing occasions for
immorality. The most important difference between these groups and
the traditional brotherhoods was in their leadership. Brotherhoods
were organized and administered by laymen; the parish priest was in
some ways just an employee, the almoner who said mass for the
brothers' souls. At best, the priest was a guest of the members; at
worst, as frequently happened in the early nineteenth century, he and
they were bitterly at odds. A clergyman was always president [Präses]
of the sodalities and congregations, although backed by a lay executive
committee [Vorstand]. The Präses had the final say in the decision to
admit new members or expel old ones for failing to meet the requirements of the group. He presided over all the meetings and was the
central figure of the association.[62]

There was nothing inherently novel about the sodalities or congregations and no reason to see them as necessarily of more recent origin
than the brotherhoods. Some groups were demonstrably quite old: the
Marianic Sodality in Emmerich had existed since 1596; its counterpart
in Düsseldorf was in existence at the beginning of the eighteenth century. Others had been founded or refounded in the 1820s after the
end of the Napoleonic regimes.[63] But here as elsewhere, these scattered

---

former member of the Catholic journeymen's association (STAM OP Nr. 1601 II Bl.
25-26). Complete results of the investigation do not seem to have been preserved, and
the objectivity and insight of the bureaucrats responsible for carrying it out is frequently
open to question, but a judicious reading of the official replies provides an enormous
amount of information. Surviving reports are in HSTAD RD Nr. 288-89; HSTAD RA
Nr. 4817; LAK 403 Nr. 6695; STAD M1 IP Nr. 363; STAM RAR I Nr. 101; STAM
RM Nr. 1039 and STDM Polizeiregistratur Nr. 8. More generally, on the development
of Catholic associations, see Sperber, "Transformation of Catholic Associations."

[62] Statutes illustrating these points: LA Kr. Coesfeld to RM, Sep. 29, 1874, STAM
RM Nr. 1039; AGVP XVII, 4; LAK 403 Nr. 10447 Bl. 223-26; HSTAD RD Nr. 288
Bl. 165-76 and the 1874 report of the LA Kr. Hagen in STAM RAR I Nr. 101.

[63] Officers of the Marian Sodality of Bachelors to OB Fuchsius (Düsseldorf) undated
(July 1845), STDD II Nr. 1315; LAK 403 Nr. 10447 Bl. 121-22; unsigned and undated
memorandum (probably written c. 1820) on the Marianic Sodalities, STAM RM Nr.
17422.

examples create a false impression of antiquity. According to the 1907 *Schematism* of the Diocese of Münster, an area where then as today a great importance is placed on tradition and venerable age, ninety percent of the diocese's 490 sodalities had been founded after 1850, and of those formed before 1870, seventy-three percent had been formed in the two decades preceding that date. The sodalities were another aspect of the post-mid-century growth of Marian devotion. Like other forms of this devotion, they were strongly encouraged by the missionaries, who founded one or several sodalities after each mission.[64]

While the activities of the sodalities were centered around the clergy and the church, they were not limited to religious devotion. Like the traditional brotherhoods, the congregations and sodalities were sociable organizations; unlike them, however, their sociability was firmly fixed in a religious milieu. Father Zander in Gürzenich (*Kreis* Düren) described the activities of the Marianic Sodality of bachelors in his parish at the beginning of the 1870s: "[There exists] a Marian league which all the sixteen-year-olds join, for at that age they are finished with their religious instruction. . . . They have a common monthly communion with a special service for them on communion day. Along with that goes a speech recommending the reading of good books, the gathering of contributions for religious purposes, for the beautification of the church, etc. In this way, they maintain their contact with the parish priest."[65]

Sodalities could replace traditional brotherhoods, as happened in the Eifel town Euskirchen. The brotherhood of bachelors had held the *Schützenfest* until c. 1860, when the bachelors "lost" it and the innkeepers took it over. Deprived of its festive raison d'être, the brotherhood declined rapidly in importance, and in 1866 the parish priest proposed to revive it as a sodality. Besides the usual religious duties, he planned to have the members help restore the town's old *Klosterkirche* and lead the pilgrimage to Kevelaer—a pilgrimage initiated that year as a consequence of the newly opened railroad line. The sodality, he thought, would "do good service for religious and moral life, for the preservation of chastity and orderly family relations. . . ."[66]

---

[64] Calculated from *Schematismus Münster*, pp. 244-61. I have assumed that all sodalities whose founding date was not given in the schematism, or given as unknown, were founded before 1850, so, if anything, the proportion of pre-1850 foundings has been exaggerated. On the missionary founding of Marianic sodalities, Gatz, *Volksmission*, p. 126; AGVP XVI, 12-17 passim; AGVP XVII, 14 passim.

[65] Pf. Zander to Archbishop of Cologne, Dec. 4, 1871, HAEK Gen. XXIII 4 I; cf. the accounts of the Marianic Sodalities of Bachelors in STAM LA Kr. Ahaus Nr. 92 and LA Kr. Tecklenburg to RM, Oct. 6, 1874, STAM RM Nr. 1039.

[66] Pf. Dubelmann to G. V. Cologne, Sep. 6, 1866, HAEK Gen. XXIII 4 I. Father Dubelmann, well aware of the novelty of his proposal, noted that the new sodality

The clergy in the early part of the nineteenth century had complained about their lack of influence on youth once they were out of school; they rebuked the young people's excessive drinking and dancing, their declining sexual morality and growing wildness. Often as not, priests saw the brotherhoods of bachelors as a cause of the problem rather than a cure. These tendencies could be successfully combatted via the Marianic Sodalities: the church replaced the tavern as the center of youthful sociability, the self-organization of youth gave way to an association led by a priest. Marian devotion, with its glorification of chastity and renunciation, eased the transition to a more sober youthful life-style inherent in the new demographic situation of low marriage and illegitimacy rates. In religiously mixed urban areas, the sodalities served to keep alive a strong sense of confessional identity. Members of the Congregation of Maidens founded in Krefeld in 1869 were required to swear they would not enter into a mixed marriage; when similar groups were founded in the eastern part of the Ruhr basin in the 1890s, the girls swore to have no Protestant boy-friends. In all these respects, the Marianic Sodalities appear as forerunners of modern Catholic youth groups.[67]

The sodalities of married men, like the sodalities of the youth, were strongly oriented around the priest and the church. Their activities extended beyond prayer and contemplation, in socially or politically relevant directions. Sodalities in urban or industrial regions often took the form of mutual benefit societies (as did some sodalities of bachelors). In Hattingen, on the southeastern edge of the Ruhr basin, the members of the Marianic Sodality, founded after the 1854 mission, gathered every Monday evening in the schoolhouse to discuss the latest issue of the *Westfälisches Volksblatt*, one of the leading clerical newspapers in Westphalia.[68]

In the cities where the Jesuits settled after 1850, they organized Marianic Congregations. Being *Präses* of one of these was a full-time job. All day Sunday the Jesuit father had to be on hand for spiritual consultation; on weekdays, as part of the group's mutual benefit fund, he visited the sick members, "the healthy members as well," and was

---

would "in order to preserve tradition and not insult popular consciousness, appear as much as possible as a continuation of the existing old sodality. . . ." By the 1930s, when folklorists took up the investigation of popular customs, the *Schützenfest* had passed out of the hands of the bachelors almost everywhere, with the exception of the rural area around Cologne. Zender, "Das Kölnische 'Niederland,' " p. 258.

[67] HAEK Gen. XXIII 4 I and AGVP XVII, 4-5. As late as the 1930s, Catholic youth groups in the Aachen District were still known as Marianic Sodalities. Cf. the documents from the Nazi era in HSTAD RA Nr. 1052, and Plum, *Gesellschaftsstruktur und politisches Bewußtsein*, p. 104.

[68] HSTAD RD Nr. 288 Bl. 165-76 and the 1874 report of the LA Kr. Bochum, STAM RAR I Nr. 101.

expected always to be available for burials.[69] Unlike the rural sodalities, the Jesuits' congregations were more likely to be divided by class than by marital status: there were congregations for factory workers, for artisans, for "young merchants" (i.e., salaried employees), or for *Bürger*. Organizational life in each of these groups took a form corresponding to the social composition of their respective memberships. The congregation of young merchants in Cologne, for instance, maintained a meeting room with a library where the members would gather weekly to read newspapers, socialize, and hear lectures on religious and secular topics, their sodality thus taking on the characteristics of a bourgeois private club. Workers' congregations were outfitted with mutual benefit funds; they were to play an important role in the origins of the Christian Social movement around 1870.[70]

DESTINY OF THE TRADITIONAL BROTHERHOODS

Relations between the church and the lay brotherhoods at the local level varied considerably after 1850. In areas which had preserved a traditional devotion, even in the unruly first half of the century, the lay brotherhoods continued to practice their rituals as they always had, while maintaining good relations with the clergy.[71] Left to their own devices, the brotherhoods could also move in quite different, increasingly secular, directions, as happened with both the bourgeois *Schützen* discussed in the previous chapter and with more plebian groups like the St. Sebastians *Schützen* in Mülheim a. Rhein, who opened their hall to Social-Democratic agitators for a meeting in 1871.[72]

Traditional brotherhoods were often transformed by the interven-

[69] Dean Koth (Cologne) to Archbishop of Cologne, Aug. 22, 1872, HAEK Gen. XXIII 4 I. The letter was in reference to the Men's Congregation in the parish church St. Caecilia in Cologne, which had 1,600 members. Congregations in Aachen were of a similar size: see the report of the *Landrat* in 1874, HSTAD RA Nr. 4817.

[70] Dean of Aachen to Archbishop of Cologne, Aug. 19, and Nov. 8, 1872; "Jahresbericht der Marianischen Congregation für junge Kaufleute zu Köln 1872," all in HAEK Gen. XXIII 4 I. A congregation of "young merchants" also existed in Münster: STDM Polizieregistratur Nr. 8 Bl. 38, 40. In the *Vormärz*, it was precisely the "young merchants" who had a reputation for impiety (cf. Keinemann, *Kölner Ereignis*, 2: 19). The Congregations of Young Merchants, founded in Aachen in 1856 as a "spiritual army" against the "subversive ideas of the time" (Reuter, *Bistum Aachen*, p. 215) and in Cologne in 1858, provided a form of sociability which had only been available in secular guise during the *Vormärz*—as the Burtscheid *Schützen* (see above, p. 34) or the masonic lodges. The development of the working-class organizations is discussed below in Chapter Four.

[71] Cf. the 1874 accounts of the Gregorious Bruderschaft in Kleve, HSTAD RD Nr. 289 Bl. 130; the Johannis Bruderschaft in Riesenbeck and the Männerbruderschaft in Borken: LA Kr. Tecklenburg to RM, Oct. 6, 1874 and LA Kr. Borken to RM, Oct. 14, 1874, STAM RM Nr. 1039.

[72] Hombach, "Reichs- und Landtagswahlen," p. 245.

tion of the local priests, who worked to bring them under clerical control. The parish priest in Wiesdorf (*Kreis* Solingen) was one of the first to try such an intervention, joining in 1839 the *Schützen* brotherhood which had existed in the village since the sixteenth century. Adolf Janssen, the local innkeeper, described what happened next: "He formed an executive committee of the brothers [Brudervorstand] and appointed himself president of it. The committee wished to make new laws, which they called statutes, something which many brothers felt was not right. The committee justified its actions by its having a majority of the votes." The statutes carefully set down the religious aspects of the brotherhood's life: masses on St. Sebastians Day, during the *Schützenfest*, and after the burial of a member. A mutual benefit society was initiated in conjunction with the brotherhood, while the *Schützenfest* was to be limited to once every other year. The yearly business meetings were to be held in the village taverns on a rotating basis.

At the first meeting, held in Janssen's tavern, a dispute arose between the priest and the innkeeper over the disposition of the brotherhood's property, should it dissolve. The priest wanted to see it go to the parish; the innkeeper felt it should be distributed among the members. As the argument heated up, the priest announced, "From this day on, no more meetings will take place in this house of discord," and led the brothers out the door. The innkeeper had formerly been the dominant figure in the group: he had been a member since 1803, was twice "king" of the *Schützen*. His inn had been the locale of the brotherhood's meetings, and he had administered its property for many years. Outraged at this attack on his position, he complained to the *Landrat*, but in vain: the area magistrate, when queried by his superior, was firmly on the clergyman's side.

The comic aspects of this little episode notwithstanding, several important changes had been effected in the *Schützen* of Wiesdorf: (1) Leadership had passed from a layman, and an innkeeper at that, to a priest. (2) The moral and useful aspects of the institution, the masses, illness and death benefits, had been emphasized at the expense of the worldly festivities. (3) A written statute had replaced oral tradition in defining eligibility for benefits and obligations of membership. (4) Finally, the circle of members had expanded: any adult male of the community was eligible for membership, except for servants and non-resident day laborers. The membership had jumped from forty-nine to ninety following the writing of the new statutes—an expansion which probably gave the village priest a majority for his efforts to reconstitute the brotherhood. The *Schützen* were transformed from a sort of private club into a parish institution.[73]

The brotherhood was beginning to look suspiciously like a sodality. After 1840, and with increasing frequency after 1850, local clergy carried out similar operations on the *Schützen* or related brotherhoods in their parishes. The occasion might be given by a mission, in which case the brotherhood could be reorganized as a Marianic Sodality, or a parish priest might introduce a mutual benefit society as a way of effecting the reorganization. In Gymnich (*Kreis* Euskirchen), the priest and area magistrate combined to form a St. Cunibertus Society for the bachelors of the parish in June 1849, in order to combat revolutionary influences.[74]

The revised *Schützen* became a means of improving the moral atmosphere and not like their pre-1850 counterparts burying it. Following the mission in Oedingen (*Kreis* Meschede), the only dance held in the village was during the yearly *Schützenfest*. Festivities began following afternoon services and ended at sunset. The priest had only words of praise for the improved moral atmosphere in his parish: there had been no illegitimate births in the eight years since the adoption of this new system.[75]

The municipal archives in Düsseldorf contain the account of a religious brotherhood whose development in the nineteenth century exemplifies many of the trends discussed in this section. The St. Sebastians Brotherhood of sharpshooters in Hamm, a Düsseldorf suburb inhabited mostly by truck farmers, announced in 1828 that they were moving their yearly celebration from the festival of the patron saint to

[73] On the events in Wiesdorf, see HSTAD LA Kr. Solingen Nr. 117. It seems to have been typical for the traditional *Schützen* to have restricted their membership in one way or another. Cf. HSTAD RA Nr. 184 Bl. 36-41, 81-82, Nr. 4855 Bl. 72, Nr. 4856 Bl. 97-103 and the report on the brotherhood in Riesenbeck, cited above, n. 71.

[74] HSTAD RK Nr. 8093 Bl. 36. Examples of the transformation of the *Schützen* or similar brotherhoods (and this list makes no pretensions to completeness): HSTAD RA Nr. 4856 Bl. 178-79 (Birkesdorf, 1845); HSTAD RA Nr. 4857 Bl. 182-94 (Golzheim, 1864); LAK 403 Nr. 10447 Bl. 100-111 (Burtscheid and Wursteln, 1848); LAK 403 Nr. 7284 Bl. 575-82 (Gerresheim and Angermund, 1841); HSTAD RD Nr. 25100-01 (Ratingen, Rath, Hückeswagen, and Kaiserswerth, 1843, 1848, 1850, and 1856 respectively); HSTAD RD Nr. 25161 (Sturzelberg, 1870); HSTAD LA Kr. Solingen Nr. 116 (Schlebusch, 1856); HSTAD RD Nr. 288 Bl. 73-78 (Neviges, 1858); *Sonntagsblatt für katholische Christen* 11 (1852): 88 (Horstmar, 1848). Cf. HSTAD RA Nr. 4817, reports of the LA Kr. Düren on the brotherhood in Nothberg and the LA Kr. Erkelenz on the brotherhoods in Erkelenz, Immerwald, Holzweiler, and Keyenberg.

[75] Pf. and Churchwardens in Oedingen to GV Paderborn, Jun. 9, 1854, AGVP XVI, 12; similarly, Pf. Bockhaus (Cörbecke) to GV Paderborn, Dec. 23, 1857, AGVP XVI, 13 and HSTAD RK Nr. 8093 Bl. 31.

August 3, the birthday of the king of Prussia. Throughout the *Vormärz*, the *Schützenfest* remained in early August and was carried out without the slightest hint of a religious celebration. The statutes of 1837 make no mention of a mass on St. Sebastians day, and the yearly meeting of the brotherhood was not to be held then but within two weeks of the *Schützenfest*. The goal of the group, the statutes announced, was to "enliven the social life of the members and further their mutual intimacy and friendship." Religion was not totally forgotten, but had shrunk to a minor role: "to make the society also useful with respect to religion," the brothers were required to accompany the bier of one of their deceased fellows and attend the subsequent funeral services. The brothers' relation to the local clergy went beyond mere indifference. In 1845, members of the brotherhood's executive committee were the leaders in a drive to reduce the salary of the vicar in Hamm, a move which had drawn the considerable ire of the parish priest, who wondered how the inhabitants of Hamm could afford their extravagant and morally questionable *Schützenfest* yet could find no money for the clergy who tended to their souls.

Yet after mid-century the situation was completely reversed. In 1851, the *Schützenfest* reverted to the feast of the patron saint; a festive high mass was added to the program of events and remained there throughout the 1850s and 1860s. These changes were connected with the arrival of a new parish priest in Hamm. His name appeared on the brotherhood's 1853 membership list, and in that same year the last two members of the old executive committee who had caused the former priest so much trouble were voted out of office. Nor does the story end at that point. In June 1871, the *Schützen* from Hamm took part in the great parade held in Düsseldorf in honor of the Pope. During the *Kulturkampf*, prominent members led the Catholic reading club and were local activists of the Center Party. The recreation of the authority and prestige of the priest was a necessary intermediate step in the transformation of the secularized association of the *Vormärz* into the militantly religious-political organization of Imperial Germany.[76]

ADAPTATIONS TO AN URBAN AND INDUSTRIAL ENVIRONMENT

Before the rise of the Christian-Social movement in the late 1860s, there were essentially no sociopolitical organizations in German Ca-

[76] Letters of the *Schützenvorstand* in Hamm to OB Düsseldorf, Aug. 3, 1828, Aug. 10, 1834, Aug. 5, 1837, and Jul. 26, 1845, and the letter of Pf. Greisen (Hamm) to OB Düsseldorf, Jul. 21, 1845, STDD II Nr. 1315; STDD II Nr. 1421 Bl. 9, 11, 17, 19 ff.; HSTAD RD Nr. 288 Bl. 211; Chaplain Hömmacher to Dean Herten, Oct. 6, 1871 (copy) HAEK Gen XXIII 4 I.

tholicism. Notions of charity and moral improvement remained the dominant conceptions for the clergy and Catholic notables in their efforts to deal with the emergent social question.[77] The predominant form of association remained the religious brotherhood, whose socio-political workings were limited to the possible existence of a mutual benefit fund.

The sociopolitical importance of morality ought not to be slighted, however. Even without conscious sociopolitical intent, the moral imperative which led to the post-1850 formation of sodalities or congregations proved remarkably well adapted to city or factory life. Unlike the traditional brotherhoods, with their cycle of festivities tied to the agricultural calendar, the activities of the new religious organizations were designed to be carried out on Sundays and weekday evenings, the available free time of the urban laborer. Leadership of a priest, and not a lay committee, guaranteed an organizational continuity in the context of a lower-class urban population whose ever-growing geographic mobility was in strong contrast to the more sedentary ways of past rural society. The moral demands of the organizations, their emphasis on sobriety and frugality, were in and of themselves important elements of adaptation to the conditions of proletarian existence in the capitalist society of the early industrial era.[78] These characteristics can also be found in the two groups of Catholic associations founded after 1850 whose members came exclusively from the laboring classes: the associations of miners (Knappenvereine) and of journeymen artisans (Gesellenvereine, also known after their founder as Kolpingsvereine).

These Catholic organizing efforts occurred in the context of a weakening of their secular alternatives, the mutual benefit societies. In curious contrast to their flourishing in the *Vormärz*, these groups entered a period of stagnation and decline after 1850. Between 1833 and 1848, ten mutual-benefit societies had been formed in the city of Düsseldorf (one of which, admittedly, had existed since 1798 and had just had its statutes reconfirmed in 1833); between 1848 and 1870 just three new ones came into existence. Nine mutual benefit societies had been

[77] Gatz, "Aachener Karitaskreis," pp. 207-208.

[78] In other respects as well, the Catholic church in Rhineland-Westphalia appears to have acted as an element of adaptation to urban-industrial life and not in opposition to it. The clergy usually made no effort to preserve a long list of traditional saints days and festivities when they conflicted with the demands of industrial production. Workers were counseled instead to attend an early mass before work and give a portion of their extra earnings to charity. LAK 403 Nr. 6684 Bl. 51; Pf. Memer (Menden) to GV Paderborn Feb. 28, 1860; Dean Fleischmann (Huckarde) to GV Paderborn, Apr. 28, 1863, AGVP XIV, 2. (A different attitude could be found in Aachen early in the century: LAK 403 Nr. 6687 Bl. 213-16.)

formed during the *Vormärz* in *Kreis* Geldern, but only one in the years 1848 to 1870. Yet at least all ten of them still existed in 1876; in neighboring *Kreis* Grevenbroich, where seven mutual benefit societies had been formed before mid-century, none came into existence after 1848, and by 1876 all the previously existing ones had disappeared. There were thirteen mutual-benefit societies in *Kreis* Gladbach in 1836. Forty years later, in spite of a doubling of the population and the rapid expansion of the textile industry, with the consequent growth in the number of economically dependent workers, there were only sixteen such groups. The population in *Kreis* Kempen increased some sixty percent in the same interval, but the number of mutual-benefit societies increased only from twenty-one to twenty-four. This trend was by no means limited to predominantly Catholic areas, as the number of mutual benefit societies in the heavily Protestant *Wuppertal* actually fell in the interval, from 183 in 1836 to 150 in 1876.[79]

The reasons for this decline are obscure. Some groups ran into trouble with the authorities because of their political and trade union activities in 1848-1849 and were prohibited. Others could not compete with the compulsory insurance systems, introduced by several municipal governments after 1850.[80] The most likely cause of the groups' decline was rural-urban migration. Newly arrived urban inhabitants did not join the societies; the growing population mobility among the lower classes made it ever more difficult to develop a stable leadership.

The organizations were far from having died out by the 1870s. Whether for the rural silk weavers of the Kempen-Krefeld region or for the urban laborers of Cologne and Düsseldorf, the mutual-benefit societies still represented an independent form of association, one generally not under clerical tutelage.[81] But they were clearly in decline,

[79] Number of associations in 1836 and 1876: HSTAD RD Nr. 13660 and 25095; HSTAD LA Kr. Gladbach Nr. 331; LA Kr. Kempen Nr. 394. Number founded 1848-1870: LAK 403 Nr. 7278-98 and HSTAD RD Nr. 25097-25102, 25114-16, 25143, 25144-46. It is, of course, possible that the relative decline in the number of societies reflects a greater average membership. Since the figures on membership (as compared to the number of societies) in 1836 have not survived, it is impossible to prove or disprove this. Most societies put a statutory limit on the number of members; it therefore seems unlikely they could have grown to meet the rise in population.

[80] Köllmann, *Stadt Barmen*, p. 180; van Eyll, "Wirtschaftsgeschichte Kölns," 2: 245; Dowe, *Aktion*, pp. 246-49. The organization of a compulsory municipal insurance plan in Aachen in 1856 led to minor street disturbances since the factory workers did not trust the industrialists who were to administer the funds. LAK 403 Nr. 7006 Bl. 76 ff.

[81] Of the thirty-nine mutual benefit societies founded between 1849 and 1870 in the predominantly Catholic industrial areas of the Düsseldorf District six were religious brotherhoods, six included a mass for deceased members as part of their death benefits, and twenty-seven were secular organizations. The proportion of religious and secular organizations was thus about the same as in the *Vormärz* (cf. above, n. 54, of Chapter

and their decline only facilitated the task of organizing Catholic working-class associations.

Miners' associations   Beginning in 1855 and continuing for the next fifteen to twenty years, a series of Catholic miners' associations were founded in the Ruhr basin. Their statutory *Präses* was the local parish priest or one of his chaplains. Members of the group had a consecrated flag, marched together in processions or at burials, had a special mass on the day of their patron saint or on the festivals of the Virgin. High moral standards and regular fulfillment of religious duties were prerequisites for membership; laxity in this respect brought on expulsion. Everything was not strict piety, though. One evening a month the members met in the local schoolhouse or tavern under the supervision of the priest to converse, have a beer (card playing and drinking hard liquor were prohibited) and hear a morally inspiring or educational lecture given by the clergyman or schoolteacher. Such associations occasionally sponsored festivals where the members put on theatricals or gave choral recitals. The groups generally provided illness and death benefits for their members. By the late 1860s, the Catholic Knappenvereine in the Ruhr basin concluded an agreement by which membership, including the insurance benefits, was transferrable from one association to another.[82]

These associations were founded simultaneously with major changes in the Ruhr mining industry. Before 1850, the industry had been closely regulated by the state. Officials of the Mining Office fixed prices and wages, set production quotas, and arranged for the marketing of the output. The miners had a quasi-official position: they were guaranteed steady employment, a rarity in the *Vormärz*, and could be transferred from one pit to another at the request of the Mining Office. Distribution of the work force and preservation of labor discipline were tasks of the government, not within the legal competence of the miners' "employers," the private owners of the mines.

The miners were organized by the state into *Knappschaften*, and only a *Knappschaft* member could work in the mines. The *Knappschaften* were more than formal-legal associations: the members had

---

One), but the number of new organizations formed declined markedly, especially considering the enormous increase in the proletarian population. Sources: besides those cited in n. 54 of Chapter One, HSTAD RD Nr. 24115-25116, 25137-41, 25147-48, 25096, 25144-46.

[82] This section is based on the brilliant work of Klaus Tenfelde, *Bergarbeiterschaft*, pp. 361-96 and passim. I would like to thank Dr. Tenfelde for taking the time to discuss some of his findings with me, but he is in no way responsible for my interpretation of them.

a special uniform, a marching band, a chorus, etc. There were officially sponsored festivals during which the miners took an oath to the king of Prussia as represented by officials of the Mining Office. Ruhr coalminers were regarded and regarded themselves in the *Vormärz* as a kind of aristocracy of the working class, with a well-developed consciousness of their special corporate position.[83]

In the decade following 1850 the government gave up its control over the industry and allowed the forces of a capitalist market economy free play. Prices, wages, output, and sales were left to the market; except for the enforcement of safety regulations and the limitation of the employment of women and children, the relation between entrepreneur and miner was deregulated, reduced to a private employment contract. The *Knappschaften* were stripped of all ritual and festivity and limited to a businesslike compulsory insurance program.

The miners saw their privileged position abolished, their wages and even their jobs exposed to the incalculable fluctuations of the market economy. A flood of migrants from overpopulated rural areas in the Rhineland, Westphalia, and Hessen overwhelmed old mining families, whose exclusivity had previously been protected by paternalist state regulations. Ruhr coalminers bitterly resented these developments, and for the rest of the century the memory of the traditional rights of their profession remained a powerful motivation for their collective social and political action.[84]

The Catholic miners' associations served as a replacement for the sociability, festivity, and ordered social existence which had been purged from the *Knappschaften*. In a sense, the church was acting to uphold a traditional social institution, but here as elsewhere the "traditionalism" of the church was of a very limited nature. The Catholic miners' associations were not traditional organizations but mid-century creations, strikingly similar to the sodalities and congregations formed at that time and unlike their predecessors, the *Knappschaften*, which had been institutions of the Prussian state without any connection to the Catholic church. The function of these new Catholic miners' associations can best be described as both the preservation of traditional ideas and patterns of behavior and their transformation in order to meet the demands of an industrial-capitalist economic and social order.

In the predominantly Protestant areas of the eastern Ruhr basin, on the other hand, the pastors made no effort to organize the miners; the first Protestant miners' associations date from the late 1880s. Following the dissolution of the old *Knappschaften*, the miners formed their

[83] Ibid., pp. 63-131.
[84] Ibid., pp. 162-282, 394-436 and passim.

own associations, frequently centered around an innkeeper. In the 1870s and 1880s, many of these groups were taken over by the Social Democrats.[85] The same protest against abolition of a pre-capitalist social order could thus be exploited by very different political tendencies.

Journeymen's associations   These organizations were closely linked to the efforts of one man, Adolf Kolping. Born in 1813 to a poor family living in the town of Kerpen in the Eifel region, Kolping was apprenticed to a shoemaker. At the age of twenty-four he decided to become a priest, and with the support of generous patrons he was able to attend *Gymnasium* and go on to study theology at the University of Munich. Ordained in 1845, Kolping took up his first position as a chaplain in Elberfeld. The condition of the working classes in one of Germany's major industrial cities made a deep impression on him, and the following year he founded the first journeymen's association, the Kolpingsvereine, as they came to be known. In 1849, Kolping obtained a post as vicar of the Cologne cathedral. He lived in Cologne until his death in 1865 (in 1862 he became rector of the *Minoritenkirche*), providing central leadership for the growing network of journeymen's associations, speaking as an authority on social questions at gatherings of Catholic associations, editing a popular magazine, and taking an active role in local politics as a member of the Catholic political party. At the time of his death, there were some 60,000 members of the journeymen's associations, all over the German-speaking world.[86]

Kolping understood his associations as a form of social-charitable activity not previously practiced. The groups would go beyond preaching morality to the young artisans by offering them practical help in their careers. Instruction would be given in reading, writing, arithmetic, bookkeeping, and other useful skills, preparing the journeyman for a future career as master craftsmen and thus contributing to the maintenance of a healthy *Mittelstand*. The journeymen's associations were not to have any official ties to the Catholic church. Religious polemics and political discussions were statutorily excluded from the organizations; Protestant journeymen were to be free to join.[87]

In practice, however, the groups acted very much like sodalities.

[85] Ibid., pp. 382-83, 388 n. 192, 489, 596.

[86] There is no complete scholarly biography of Kolping. The best study is the interesting work of Schmolke, *Kolping als Publizist*, which contains an extensive bibliography of the largely hagiographical literature. On Kolping's often overlooked political activities, see Denk, "Wahlen in Köln," pp. 149-50.

[87] The ideal of the Gesellenverein: Schmolke, *Kolping als Publizist*, pp. 47-70.

They were led by a priest as *Präses* who had the final say in all affairs of the association. The members celebrated joint communions, usually on the festivals of the Virgin; they had a consecrated flag and marched as a group in processions. They were required to attend church regularly, recite a daily devotion, stay clear of the taverns, and, in general, maintain high moral standards or face expulsion.[88]

The clergy viewed the Gesellenvereine as essentially similar to the sodalities of bachelors. Journeymen's associations were founded for young men who did not want to join the sodalities, or as a supplement to them when a priest felt that a sociable gathering on Sunday afternoon after services would profane the sacred character of the religious association. Some priests were hostile to the journeymen's associations, seeing them not as supplements to their sodalities, but as rivals. In any event, the groups were firmly embedded in a Catholic religious context, so it is questionable if many Protestants would have wanted to join, and in practice they seem to have been kept at arm's length.[89]

Seen in this light, the journeymen's associations appear less as a unique form of religious-social activity, and more as a variant of the predominant tendency of Catholic associational life after 1850. The uniqueness of the Kolpingsvereine is not to be sought in their organizational structure, which, on the local level, looked very much like the sodalities, nor on their being reserved for a single social group, as the Jesuits had founded congregations of artisans or young merchants. It was the object of the organizations' efforts, the journeymen artisans, which gave the groups their unique character and brought them considerable public attention.

The structure of the artisanate in the northern Rhineland and Westphalia was changing in the post-1850 period. The overcrowding and ruinous competition among the masters, so characteristic of the *Vormärz*, was giving way to a situation of greater prosperity, as growing

---

[88] Ibid., pp. 67-69; STAM RAR I Nr. 101 Bl. 18 ff., 188 ff., 288 ff.; HSTAD RD Nr. 288 Bl. 68-71; "Programm zum Empfang des Herrn Kardinal Erzbischofs von Geissel," Jun. 17, 1857, "Festordnung für die Grundsteinlegung zur neuen Marienkirche in Aachem am 22 Mai 1859," both printed fliers in HSTAD PP Aachen Nr. 86 V. I; HSTAD RK Nr. 8093 Bl. 90-91; Domvikar Spork to Bishop of Paderborn Jan. 17, 1869 and Rector Hellingen (Gesecke) to GV Paderborn Aug. 8, 1869, AGVP XVIII, 1; HSTAD RA Nr. 4818, documents on the Gesellenverein in Monschau; *Sonntagsblatt für katholische Christen* 17 (1858): 189-91, 794.

[89] *Sonntagsblatt für katholische Christen* 9 (1850): 552. Pf. in Hagen to Bishop of Paderborn, Feb. 17, 1859 and Pf. in Meschede to Bishop of Paderborn, Feb. 22, 1865, AGVP XVIII, 1. On the standoffish attitude toward Protestants, see Pf. Roper (Menden) to Bishop of Paderborn, Mar. 24, 1866, and the minutes of the meeting of all the *Präsiden* of the Gesellenvereine in the Diocese of Paderborn in Dortmund, Aug. 10, 1869, both in AGVP XVIII, 1.

TABLE 2.9

Journeymen and Apprentices per Master
Craftsman in Three Western Districts
and Prussia as a Whole, 1849-1861

| | Journeymen and Apprentices per Master | | | |
Year	Münster District	Aachen District	Düsseldorf District	Prussia
1849	0.57	0.56	0.60	0.76
1858	0.55	0.61	?	0.93
1861	?	0.66	0.75	1.04

SOURCES: *Tabellen und amtliche Nachrichten . . . 1849*, 5: 530-66, 706-737, 618-77; *Statistische Nachrichten . . . Regierungs-Bezirk Münster*, p. 44; HSTAD RA Nr. 372 and Nr. 348; HSTAD RD Nr. 2159; Schmoller, *Kleingewerbe*, pp. 331-35.

incomes increased consumer purchasing power and emigration or entry into industry reduced the "excess" population which had previously sought to earn a living in the crafts. See Table 2.9. Although still lagging behind the figures for Prussia as a whole, the concentration of capital in the artisanal professions was clearly occurring in the western provinces.[90] The number of journeymen and apprentices relative to the masters was increasing; it was becoming more difficult to obtain economic independence.

Historians have often pointed to the guild system as an important organizing or causal agent in this process. Since the origins of the increase in the proportion of masters can be found in the abolition of the guilds, then their revival may be regarded as the reason for the reversal of this trend after 1850. The hostility of the artisanate toward laissez-faire and its demand for a revival of traditional corporate structures have long been a staple theme for historians writing about nine-

[90] The Münster District appears to be an exception; however, the 1861 figures (unfortunately only preserved for several *Kreise*) show a noticeable increase in the proportion of journeymen and apprentices. In *Kreis* Steinfurt, for instance, the number of journeymen and apprentices per master craftsman went from 0.48 in 1819 to 0.43 in 1831 and rose to 0.46 in 1849, 0.54 in 1858, and 0.57 in 1861. (1861 figures from STAM LA Kr. Steinfurt Nr. 1667.) In *Landkreis* Münster, the relevant figures are 0.46 in 1819, 0.38 in 1831, 0.56 in 1849, 0.31 in 1858, and 0.69 in 1861 (1861 figures from *Statistische Nachrichten . . . Kreis Münster*, pp. 27-28). It is by no means impossible that the 1858 figure for *Kreis* Münster is a misprint, or involves an arithmetical error by the authorities, which sufficed to distort the average for the whole district in that year.

teenth-century Germany.[91] Whatever the validity of this conception
for other parts of Central Europe, it is not at all applicable to the
Rhineland and Westphalia. The post-1850 "revival" of the guild system was directed by the reactionary Berlin bureaucracy, which drew
up model statutes for the new guilds and imposed them on an unwilling
or indifferent population. More often than not, the guilds remained
purely paper organizations. When a guild actually was set up, only a
tiny fraction of the eligible masters joined; the guild's regulations were
universally ignored almost from the moment of its inception. By 1860,
most of the guilds had ceased to exist; the remainder vegetated amid
general apathy until the introduction of complete occupational freedom in 1869 ended their official character.[92]

The guilds had failed to organize and direct the new environment
in which artisans found themselves after mid-century. Who would lead
the adaptation of the artisans to new conditions: the master to the
prospect of being an employer, the apprentices and journeymen to an
ever-extended period of economic dependence, requiring ever greater
efforts until they would be in a position to open their own shop? The
Catholic clergy recognized the decline of the artisanate in the first half
of the century, attributing it, as one priest in Münster did (and not at
all inaccurately), to "the abolition of the guilds, the legalization of
freedom of internal movement and freedom of occupation, and the
great number of carefree and thoughtless marriages contracted by
artisans. . . ."[93] The post-1850 religious revival was to play an important ordering role in the changing of those conditions, a role the
guilds did not fill. The Jesuits, in their Aachen mission, preached
against early marriages for journeymen, fatal to their chances for
economic independence. Above all in the Kolpingsvereine, the clergy
acted as mediators between masters and journeymen, encouraging the
latter to obey their employers, cultivate the virtues of sobriety, orderliness, and punctuality, work for self-improvement, and save for

---

[91] An attitude most prominently represented in America by Theodore Hamerow, in
Restoration, Revolution, Reaction, pp. 21-37, 102-106, 141-55, 228-37, 438-48, and
Social Foundations, 1: 77-83, 118-32.

[92] HSTAD RA Nr. 14114 Bl. 1-2, 19 ff., 94-95, 184-89, 192, 201-204; STDM Fach
27 Nr. 10; van Eyll, "Wirtschaftsgeshichte Kölns," 2: 184; *Statistische Nachrichten
. . . Kreis Coesfeld,* p. 55; Matzerath, "Städte Rheydt und Rheindahlen," p. 79, n. 146.
In 1883, when the Bismarckian social legislation called for the revival of the guilds, the
authorities counted no guilds existent in the Münster District, five in the Arnsberq
District, twenty-one in the Minden District, thirty-six in the Düsseldorf District, twenty-
three in the Cologne District; and four in the Aachen District. In the eastern provinces,
on the other hand, there were several hundred guilds still existent in each district.
HSTAD RA Nr. 14115 Bl. 164-66.

[93] *Sonntagsblatt für katholische Christen* 14 (1855): 148.

the day when they might hope to be independent. The *Vormärz* journeyman, insubordinate to his master, given to celebrating blue Mondays and demanding higher wages, was to be replaced by a hardworking, obedient employee. Not surprisingly, Kolping's efforts found the enthusiastic support of the master craftsmen.[94]

Kolping's efforts were only superficially related to the advocacy of the restoration of the guild system. Although nineteenth century Catholic social rhetoric was filled with nostalgia for a vanished, medieval, and corporate world, and contained frequent broadside blasts at modern, urban-industrial society, Kolping's associations were in no way medieval revivals.[95] The traditional artisan guilds were lay-run brotherhoods; in the Kolpingsvereine, like other Catholic associations formed after 1850, the clergy had a key role. The artisanate to which Kolping spoke was not an impoverished and declining group of traditionalist craftsmen, but a stratum of small businessmen beginning to adapt to a new socioeconomic environment, and the journeymen's associations played an important role in bringing this adaptation about.

Kolping described the journeymen artisans in the 1840s as an immoral and even subversive group. They did not go to church on Sunday, celebrated blue Monday, spent all their free time in the taverns, were "usually in possession of the worst books, are infected with the most dangerous doctrines, are presently [1849] at work on the subversion of all order as they have previously spread the crudest immorality about in all circles in which they moved." Kolping saw his associations as counterrevolutionary organizations; in his speeches, he thundered against socialism and democracy.[96] Although the organization's statutes explicitly underlined the exclusion of politics, attacking revolution and subversion, upholding the social and political order was naturally not regarded as "political."

Moral, socioeconomic, and political aims converged in Kolping's scheme of things. A pious, industrious, and obedient class of journeymen, forming the basis for a prosperous and satisfied *Mittelstand*

[94] Gatz, *Volksmission*, p. 98, n. 121. Kolping founded his local associations by first looking for a priest willing to act as *Präses*, then finding some master craftsmen who would sponsor the group (they formed a *Schutzvorstand*, a "guardian executive committee") and only then arranging for journeymen to join. Kracht, "Gründung der ersten Gesellenvereine," pp. 195-213.

[95] On Catholic social theory, see Grenner, *Wirtschafts liberalismus und katholisches Denken*. The pages of the *Sonntagsblatt für katholische Christen* in Münster were filled with praise for the guilds and the medieval world and showed a blatant hostility toward cities and modern industry.

[96] See Kolping's pamphlet, *Der Gesellenverein: Zur Beherzigung für Alle, die es mit dem wahren Volkswohl gut meinen* (Cologne and Neuß, 1849) in HAEK Gen. XXIII 2 I.

of master craftsmen, would render society immune to a recurrence of the revolutionary upheavals of 1848-1849. In the counterrevolutionary atmosphere of the 1850s, this conception found support outside Catholic circles. A petition from 1854 in support of the Cologne journeymen's association's request for incorporation papers was signed by a cross-section of leading citizens of the city, including such distinctly non-Catholic figures as representatives of the Schaafhausen and Oppenheim banking houses.[97]

Even Hans von Kleist-Retzow, the Provincial Governor of the Rhineland during the reaction era, whose pietistic attitudes led him into countless conflicts with Rhenish Catholics, found nothing but good words for Kolping. He defended the journeymen's associations against the attacks of the Cologne District Governor, Eduard von Moeller, and praised Kolping's efforts in his inimitable pious-bureaucratic style: "I . . . believe these associations, in order to reach the solemn goals to which they aspire, must be pleasing to God and do not fail to have His blessing. Therefore, they are deserving of the support of the royal government."[98] For the arch-conservative provincial governor, the organization of the journeymen was a perfectly legitimate way to restore an unruly social group to its appropriate position in a well-policed society. Protestant-conservative and Catholic sociopolitical aims coincided, and they both found support from a sometimes liberal upper bourgeoisie for whom the disturbing memories of social upheaval in 1848-1849 remained all too present.

TENDENCIES OF CATHOLIC ASSOCIATIONAL LIFE, 1850-1870

It is very difficult to provide even an approximate estimate of the proportion of Catholics who belonged to a religious association. Membership figures were not always scrupulously recorded and, even when they were, they have usually not been preserved. At most, some guidelines can be offered.

Most obviously, the extent of membership depended on the commitments accompanying it. An organization which collected dues and held regular meetings would attract a smaller circle of members than one whose sole organizational requirement was the performance of a daily devotion. Another important determinant was the social environment. Rural areas and small towns, even small industrial or mining towns, were more conducive than large cities to having a high proportion of members. A bachelor's or maiden's sodality would probably encompass every single eligible individual in a rural or small town

[97] LAK 403 Nr. 7360 Bl. 223-25.
[98] Ibid. Bl. 252; cf., also, Bl. 249-60 and 480-81.

parish; an urban congregation or Catholic miners' association might reach between five and ten percent of those eligible for membership at any given time, although higher proportions were by no means unknown. The Kolpingsvereine fell between these two extremes, reflecting the social ambiguity of an organization whose members were drawn both from proletarianized artisans living in big cities and journeymen in small towns who could still expect to become masters themselves one day.

In comparison to the *Vormärz*, a considerably greater proportion of the faithful were members of religious organizations. One reason is simply that there were more organizations. Sodalities were founded in great number after the missions; Catholic journeymen's and miners' associations encompassed previously unorganized (or at least not organized by the church) social groups. Although the indications are less sure, it would seem that, in addition, existing religious organizations increased their membership in the post-1850 era when compared with the situation before mid-century.

If we turn from the quantifiable to more qualitative aspects of associational life, the one dominant tendency which came to the fore after 1850 was the growing centrality of the clergy. The traditional lay-run brotherhood gave way to the association presided over by a priest, whether that association existed for purely religious reasons, or if it engaged in social-charitable or sociable activities.[99] Many traditional brotherhoods developed in a secular direction in the *Vormärz* or were replaced by more secular organizations. The clergy might deplore this trend, feud with the brotherhoods, and denounce the journeymen's frequent visits to the taverns, the moral failings of the *Schützenfeste*, and the excessive dancing of young people. But without providing an alternative form of sociability, all their efforts would be in vain. The religious associations of the post-1850 period provided for precisely that alternative; they became a means by which the clergy attempted to improve popular morality and revive religious feelings.

A NEW CLERICAL LEADERSHIP; A NEW MORAL ATMOSPHERE

The 1850s and 1860s appeared as a time of moral and religious improvement. In comparison with the lax and somewhat irreverent mood of the *Vormärz*, the following decades saw a growing morality and sobriety. As a result of the efforts of the clergy, the Bishop of Paderborn

[99] Erwin Gatz's call on scholars to investigate the "change from brotherhoods to Catholic associations run by laymen," in the nineteenth century ("Melchers," p. 145) presents the problem backward: the change was from lay brotherhoods to religious and other organizations led by the clergy.

noted in 1860 with regard to conditions in Soest and its environs:
". . . religious life and the feeling for the importance of the church
have noticeably improved since 1845." Perhaps not all priests could
claim the success of Father Hippe in Lütgender (*Kreis* Warburg), who
proudly reported in 1863 that there had been only one dance held in
his parish during the previous eleven years, but he was by no means
alone in observing a changing mood.[100]

Dancing and related festivities, with their associated sexual misbehavior, were in decline. Young people, organized in their sodalities,
appeared under greater control and on better behavior. The influence
of the taverns was on the wane; the churches were increasingly filled
on Sundays and holidays. As one priest noted in 1861, after discussing
the long history of immorality and dissension in his parish, whose
inhabitants had gone as far as to sue one of his predecessors: "It can
be said in praise of the current generation that divine services are
zealously attended, the Holy Sacrament eagerly and frequently received, and religious instruction and edification in printed and spoken
form almost greedily snapped up."[101]

The stricter moral atmosphere was well suited to the socioeconomic
environment of the period. Condemnation of drinking, dancing, and
fast living, the spread of Marian devotion, with its high estimation of
the virtues of chastity and renunciation, were an important means by
which that large proportion of the Catholic lower classes still employed
outside the dynamic industrial sector of the economy adopted to the
harsh economic realities of the decade of the 1850s. Similar religious
practices and institutions provided an orientation point for those tens
of thousands of individuals who left the countryside to join the ranks
of the industrial proletariat. For the Catholic upper classes, as well as
the Prussian authorities, the counterrevolutionary and socially pacifying effects of the religious revival were visible and most welcome.

The more pious mentality of the post-1850 period is reflected in the
movement of the illegitimacy rate. Behind the widespread *Vormärz*

---

[100] Bishop of Paderborn to OPM, Dec. 24, 1860, STAM OP Nr. 2686 II; Pf. Hippe
(Lütgender) to Bishop of Paderborn, Oct. 23, 1863, AGVP XVI, 16.

[101] Pf. Kalbold (Atteln) to Bishop of Paderborn, Mar. 23, 1861, AGVP XVI, 16. Other
examples of a perception of improved morality and piety: Wardens of the Soest Ca-
thedral to Bishop of Paderborn (copy in Bishop of Paderborn to OPM Dec. 24, 1860);
RM to Interior Minister, Jul. 15, 1858, both in STAM OP Nr. 2686 II. Reports of the
Landräte of the Minden District on the sacred character of Sundays and holidays, 1862,
STAD M1 IP Nr. 951; letters to the Bishop of Paderborn from Pf. and Churchwardens
(Oedingen), Jun. 9, 1854; Pf. Mutlar (Grevenstein), Dec. 10, 1855; Pf. Arndt (Worm-
bach), Dec. 15, 1856; P. Sachs (Dahl), Apr. 3, 1856, AGVP XVI, 12-16; HSTAD RA
Pr. Nr. 741 Bl. 14, 33; reports of the *Landräte* of the Cologne District on the sacred
character of Sundays and holidays, 1859, HSTAD RK Nr. 2224.

TABLE 2.10
Illegitimacy Rates in Selected Areas, 1820-1867

District	Kreis	Percent of All Births Illegitimate				
		1820-29	1830-39	1840-49	1850-59	1862-67
Rural Areas with High or Moderate Illegitimacy Rates						
Münster	Beckum	7.8	6.4	?	?	4.0
Arnsberg	Soest	10.6	8.5[a]	?	?	4.4
Aachen	Jülich	6.0	4.4	4.3	4.2	3.8[c]
Rural Areas with Low Illegitimacy Rates						
Münster	Ahaus	1.6	1.5	?	?	1.8
Düsseldorf	Geldern	2.9[b]	?	?	?	2.2
Aachen	Schleiden	2.2	2.5	2.5	2.1	2.1[c]
Three Big Cities						
Aachen		6.1	5.9	4.7	3.9	3.7[c]
Düsseldorf		7.4	7.9	6.4	5.8[d]	6.8[e]
Münster		8.2	5.8	?	?	4.1[f]

[a] 1830-38.   [b] 1822-28.   [c] 1860-67.   [d] 1850-54.   [e] 1865-66.   [f] 1862, 1865-67.
SOURCE: STAM RM Nr. 93 I-III; STAM LA Kr. Soest Nr. 3; STAM RAR B Nr. 119; HSTAD
RA Nr. 322-26, 358-60; HSTAD RD Nr. 416 Bl. 138; STDD II Nr. 1298; *Preußische Statistik*
10 (1867): 190-95, 241, 247, 251; 17 (1870): 8-58.

criticism of growing worldly festivities or the secularization of traditional religious festivals lay the perception that these new appearances
were accompanied by a loosening of sexual morality. Through the
missions, the sodalities, the new forms of pilgrimages, the clergy struggled hard against popular sexual practices. See Table 2.10. The existing
evidence is somewhat sparse, as records of vital statistics have not
been well preserved. Nevertheless, as Table 2.10 shows (and the figures
are for the Catholic population of the respective areas only),[102] there
was a marked decline in illegitimate births or a continuation of an
already low level of illegitimacy. Illegitimacy rates are not solely a
product of moral attitudes, of course, but are influenced by demographic, social, and economic factors. Without slighting these (and a

[102] There are two exceptions to this: the figures for *Kreis* Beckum, 1862-1867, and
Kreis Geldern, 1822-1828 and 1862-1867, are for the entire population. As both of
these *Kreise* were heavily Catholic, this should make little difference. For *Kreis* Soest,
which was about sixty percent Protestant, the available figures for 1862-1867 are for
both confessions together. Vital statistics, separated by confession, are available for the
year 1858 (STAM RAR B Nr. 119), and I have assumed that the ratio of Catholic to
Protestant births and illegitimate births was the same in 1862-1867 as in 1858.

full analysis would go beyond the scope of this work), I feel it is
nonetheless possible to assert that the clergy's long and laborious
campaign to improve popular morality was not totally without effect.[103]

The clergy had fought these battles before 1850 as well as after.
But in the *Vormärz* they could only rail against popular tradition,
which had taken on an increasingly secular character—worldly celebration of Sundays and holidays, unsupervised pilgrimages, "immoral" practices at the *Schützenfest*, the gathering of religious brotherhoods in the taverns—and call on the authorities to restrict or prohibit
them. In the second half of the century, it was possible to offer an
organized alternative: the mission, an exciting break in the routine of
religious life, the sodality or Gesellenverein as replacement for the lay-
run brotherhood and mutual benefit society or model for their reconstruction, the clerically led pilgrimage to a shrine of the Virgin in place
of the local procession in honor of the patron saint. Popular practices
were not suppressed, but neither did they continue unchanged. They
were transformed: the secularizing elements disappeared or were greatly
reduced; the more purely religious elements—"religious" as defined
by the clergy—came increasingly to the fore.

The growing centrality, prestige, and authority of the local priest
was apparent in all aspects of Catholic religious life. After 1850 he
was at the center of affairs: preaching to an attentive congregation,
presiding over the Gesellenverein or sodality, leading the annual pilgrimage to Kevelaer or to another shrine of the Virgin. Alternate forms
of sociability, whether openly secular, or religious but lay-dominated,
were in decline. The tavern, in particular, could not compete with the
church, the innkeeper with the priest.

The changing position of the clergy in religious life naturally raises
the question of changes within the clergy itself. Since both mono-
graphic studies and detailed documentation are lacking, this is a difficult question to answer, and only a few indications can be given
here. During the *Vormärz*, vocations had been declining, especially in
relation to the rapid population growth. There were some 1,600 sec-

---

[103] In Prussia, unlike southern Germany, there were never any legal barriers to getting
married (Köllmann, *Bevölkerung*, pp. 96-98), so the fall in illegitimacy rates is not a
reflection of a laxer legal practice. Nor is it a reflection of a greater proportion of women
getting married: indeed through the 1860s, the proportion of adult females in the
northern Rhineland and Westphalia who were married was actually *declining* (see Table
2.1).

A different analysis of the religious and moral implications of illegitimacy rates can
be found in Phayer, *Sexual Liberation*, but cf. the criticism in Sperber, "Rhineland-
Westphalia," pp. 99-102.

ular clergy in the Archdiocese of Cologne in 1825, about one priest for every 531 Catholics, but by 1846 there were just 1,393 priests, one for every 805 diocesans. In the Westphalian part of the Diocese of Münster, the number of priests active in pastoral care increased slightly, from 520 in 1826 to 569 in 1851, but this increase was outstripped by population growth, for there was one priest active in pastoral care for every 632 diocesans in the former year, but only one for every 666 in the latter. *Vormärz* attempts to expand the clerical role, besides all the other difficulties they encountered, ran up against the problem of an insufficient priestly cadre.

After mid-century vocations increased, and by 1872 there were 1,822 secular clergy in the Archdiocese of Cologne, admittedly slightly less per diocesan than in 1849 (1 to every 839 Catholics) but at least marking a break with the precipitous decline during the *Vormärz*. Especially in the rapidly growing urban areas, the regular clergy was able to fill the gaps left by the seculars, since the 1850 constitution allowed them to settle freely in Prussia. In Aachen alone, the number of regulars grew from 11 in 1850 (a figure constant throughout the *Vormärz*) to 93 by 1872. The situation was even more favorable in the heavily rural Westphalian part of the Diocese of Münster, an area of almost no population growth after 1850, due to a falling marriage rate and a large rural-urban migration. Even without the undoubted increase in the number of regulars (for which I have been unable to obtain any figures), the number of secular clergy active in pastoral care reached about 623 by 1872, one priest for every 629 Catholics, a better priest-laymen ratio than in 1826.[104]

The growing number of priests was both cause and consequence of the religious revival, as an increasingly pious atmosphere encouraged vocations and the mounting prestige and authority of the clergy made the priesthood appear as a more desirable profession. Material considerations only reinforced the trend. Benefices in the Rhineland and Westphalia were supported primarily by parish lands and in the post-1850 economic boom the value of both rural and urban real-estate increased considerably. With some exceptions in impoverished mountainous areas and among the younger clergy, clerical incomes grew

[104] Figures for the Archdiocese of Cologne are from Reuter, *Bistum Aachen*, pp. 156-58, 211; for the Diocese of Münster from OPM to Minister of Religious and Educational Affairs, Apr. 23, 1826, STAM RM Nr. 17223; *Tabellen und amtliche Nachrichten*, 1: 276; *Adreß-Buch der Geistlichkeit; Die Gemeinden und Gutsbezirke* (Vol. VII, Westphalia) and STAM OP Nr. 1923 Bl. 1206. (The last-named source gives the total number of priests from which I have deducted twenty to account for those active in diocesan administration and secondary-school teaching and thus not directly involved in pastoral care.)

correspondingly. Improved personal finances enabled priests to expand the scope of their charitable activities and to avoid unseemly quarrels with their parishioners over fees for saying masses or performing baptisms, marriages, and burials, disputes which had emerged in the *Vormärz* and done nothing to help strained lay-clerical relations. The improved incomes of the large majority of the clergy also enabled them to avoid asking the state authorities for special assistance to bolster their income, weakening the possibilities for *Staatskirchentum*.[105]

Besides greater numbers, another factor favoring clerical activism may have been generational change, as older priests, many of whom had been educated by enlightened teachers in the late eighteenth and early nineteenth century, gave way to a younger clergy instilled with more ultramontanist notions. Before 1848, it seems to have been precisely the younger priests who were most interested in introducing new, especially Marian, devotions and preaching dynamic sermons. More generally, the religious revival in Rhineland-Westphalia was part of the broader "ultramontanist" tendency in nineteenth-century Catholicism as neo-scholasticism and a religious practice rich in devotions to the Virgin, the cross, and the Sacred Heart triumphed over enlightened ideas and a dry, rationalist religion.[106]

The question of a religious revival cannot, however, be reduced to the triumph of ultramontanism over enlightenment. The new religious practices and institutions lacked those features of lay control and popular misbehavior which the *Vormärz* enlightened clergy had found objectionable. Firmly under clerical control, the new institutions and practices could be used to exhort and instruct, to improve popular morality rather than to harm it. Enlightened priests could be found taking an active part in the religious revival, from the arch-Hermesian Dean Gottfried Reinarz, who in 1849 proudly led Krefeld's first Corpus Christi procession in living memory, to Johann Georg Müller,

---

[105] Material on clerical incomes can be found in two surveys, one carried out in 1842 and the other thirty years later. The results are in BAM GV VII Nr. A38; STAM OP Nr. 2111 I Nr. 2112 II-III, Nr. 2134 III; RAR IIB Nr. 938; RM Nr. 17301-17302; LAK 403 Nr. 10351, 10354-55, 10357. Information on the economic conditions of the poorer priests can be obtained from their requests for grants from the government, STAM OP Nr. 2113 I-III, Nr. 2112 I. One example of *Vormärz* quarrels over fees for masses and burials is in LAK 403 Nr. 7282 Bl. 87 ff; cf. above, p. 92, n. 101.

[106] On younger priests before mid-century, cf. Weber, *Aufklärung*, pp. 88-89, HSTAD RA Nr. 184 Bl. 11. In Weber, *Aufklärung*, pp. 113-48, there is a discussion of the struggle between Hermesians and ultramontanists for key clerical positions, eventually ending in the victory of the latter by the 1860s.

It would be interesting to know if changes in clerical attitudes reflected changes in the social origins of the clergy, but I have not been able to find anything definitive on this point.

Bishop of Münster from 1846 to 1870. Müller's rationalist and Hermesian connections had led orthodox elements to oppose his appointment, and he always strove to maintain good relations with the Prussian authorities, but he was no less favorable to missions, sodalities, Marian devotions and other aspects of the new piety in his diocese than his "ultramontanist" and politically intransigent contemporary, Johannes Geissel, Archbishop of Cologne from 1844 to 1866.[107]

A similar caution applies to the literally ultramontanist side of the religious revival. Pius IX was certainly a strong adherent of the new practices and parallel developments to those described in this chapter occurred throughout the Catholic world during his papacy. The Papal presence was more pronounced after mid-century, as the 1850 Prussian constitution allowed the bishops direct access to the Pope, and the Jesuits, Franciscans, and other orders sent by Rome played a greater role among the clergy than in the *Vormärz*, both in terms of their greatly increased numbers and their leading position in the religious revival, holding missions, founding and directing sodalities and congregations. Nonetheless, these central Roman instances did not dominate local initiatives but complemented them. The first of the revived missions were carried out by secular clerics even before the Jesuits were allowed back in Prussia, and Father Hillebrand, Director of Missions in the Diocese of Paderborn, probably the single most important individual in Rhenish-Westphalian missionary activity, was not a regular but a former chaplain in Dortmund. All the efforts of the Jesuits would have been in vain had not the parish clergy eagerly seized upon and implemented their proposals. These Jesuits' initiatives were so successful precisely because the secular clergy saw them as the solution to difficult problems of pastoral care that they had been contending with for decades. Roman ideas were taken up when appropriate; Pius IX would become in time a powerful symbol of Catholic unity in Germany (a development foreshadowed in the Pius Associations of 1848), but ultramontanism was never an end in itself for the Rhenish-Westphalian clergy and prominent laity, as their behavior in the controversy over Papal Infallibility would make clear.

Parallel to the growing post-1850 clerical consensus, whose existence removed a major impediment to the religious revival, went a reconciliation with the Prussian authorities. The events of 1848-1849 played a decisive role as the popular upheavals of those years gave an enormous impetus to tendencies toward a religious revival already apparent in the 1840s. Decades of accumulated moral and religious

---

[107] HSTAD RD Nr. 119 Bl. 112-14; Weber, *Aufklärung*, pp. 118-29, 145; Gatz, "Melchers," p. 153; Pfülf, *Geissel*, passim.

disorder were perceived as having led to the revolution; the clergy saw a clear connection between religious laxity, moral failings, and democratic sympathies. Coming into being under counterrevolutionary auspices, the religious revival won the approval, or at least the toleration, of a bureaucracy engaged in trying to pacify the inhabitants of Prussia's western provinces after two years of upheaval.

The counterrevolutionary aspect of the religious revival did not take the form of supporting a specifically Catholic political party; rather, the emphasis on the renewal of piety as a counter to subversion tended to lead the faithful away from political action of any kind. Between 1850 and 1866, political Catholicism in the Rhineland and Westphalia achieved, at best, only partial successes. Its mass political potential remained latent, hidden behind a group of new religious institutions which were coming into existence. The new moral atmosphere had not yet become political reality.

CHAPTER 3

CLERICALISM, LIBERALISM, AND THE STATE: 1850-1866

The Characteristics of Political Life

The suppression of the revolutionary movement in 1849 did not return Prussian politics to their *Vormärz* condition of authoritarian-bureaucratic rule and only quasi-legal opposition. After 1850, political life was broader, more open, than in the *Vormärz*, with many more opportunities for public participation, creating a situation where individual or group interests could be more easily expressed. The press, if still not entirely free, was no longer censored in advance. Associations could be formed and public meetings held, although both processes were hampered by restrictive legislation. Suffrage encompassed most males over twenty-five, excluding only recipients of public poor relief in the year preceding the election and those who had changed their place of residence in the previous six months, but the individual's vote was weighted according to the amount of taxes he paid. Finally, the main focus of the electoral process, the House of Deputies of the Prussian Parliament, was a political body with constitutionally defined powers, and not a mere consultative organ, as had been the *Vormärz* provincial diets.

For all the changes when compared with the first half of the century, the post-1850 political system set definite limits on the extent of public participation and the sharpness of interest-group articulation. While close to universal (for males), suffrage was public, unequal, and indirect. The eligible voters of each precinct, who were grouped into three classes based on the total direct taxes paid, proclaimed orally before a local election commission their choice of electors. Several weeks later, the chosen electors from all the precincts of a parliamentary constituency, usually made up of several *Kreise*, gathered at a central location and elected, once again orally, the parliamentary deputy or deputies representing the circumscription.

The blatant inequality of the franchise, where the few wealthy individuals who paid one-third of the total direct taxes in the precinct selected as many electors as the bottom eighty percent who paid the same amount, did not encourage electoral participation. Nor did the openness of the ballot, with governmental officials, employers, and other powerful but interested parties observing every vote, act to raise the level of the turnout. Participation rates almost never went above twenty percent in the third class, where eighty percent of the voters were grouped; often as few as five percent of the eligible voters went to the polls.

The election campaign conformed to the limitations placed on the electorate. Mass public meetings were a rarity, occurring only in the big cities during the hotly contested elections of the 1860s. Political business was performed by small, usually self-appointed local committees which often ceased to exist after the election was over. It was only toward the end of the period that these local committees began to nominate slates of candidates to serve as electors. Before that, and throughout the entire period in many rural areas, the few voters who came to the polls simply voted for a locally influential person known for an interest in political affairs. More often than not, candidates for a seat in parliament were not nominated until after the selection of the electors. It was only then, and among the limited circle of several hundred electors, rather than the tens of thousands of eligible voters, that an intensive election campaign took place.

Political parties had only a shadowy existence. Between the local committees and informal groups of electors who went about the business of nominating and electing parliamentary deputies, and the caucuses formed by those deputies when they met in Berlin, there existed only the loosest of connections. Political groups and alliances at the local level in the provinces often looked very different from the way they appeared in the capital; at times, the two sets of connections could even be diametrical opposites.

Prussian politics in the 1850s and first half of the 1860s was a notables' politics. Electoral campaigns were dominated by small, informal gatherings and not by mass meetings. Nominations and elections were arranged by independent local committees and not by centrally organized political parties. The political process was dominated by the unstructured cooperation of locally influential men and not by the interaction of well-organized interest and pressure groups.

Although not formally structured, the political process nonetheless followed definite patterns. Two groups of notables, emerging from vaguely contoured *Vormärz* tendencies in 1848-1849, dominated political life in the Catholic areas of the Rhineland and Westphalia during the two decades following mid-century. They can be referred to as liberal-democrats and clerical-conservatives. Unlike the rest of Prussia, including the predominantly Protestant areas of the western provinces, there was no conservative party, no unambiguously loyalist and royalist grouping. Even among the regional bureaucracy, loyalist officials

were just one faction, competing with their liberal and clerical counterparts, as the *Vormärz* political and social unity of the bureaucracy
dissolved, and it began to reflect tendencies in the surrounding society.

The two elite groups in the provinces related to each other in a
different way than did the parliamentary deputies they sent to Berlin.
Both Catholic and liberal parliamentarians opposed the reaction-era
ministry, supported the moderately liberal "new era" government of
1858-1861, and then drifted apart in the following five years, the era
of the Prussian constitutional conflict, as the liberals moved into sharp
opposition to the ministry of Otto von Bismarck, while the bulk of
the clerical deputies supported it, albeit with reluctance. Events in the
provinces had their own dynamic, independent of the development of
parliamentary alliances and rivalries, although interacting with them.
Clerical and liberal partisans formed relatively cohesive blocs. The
attitude of each of these groups toward the Berlin ministry or parliamentarians might change, but the two groups were largely impermeable relative to each other: notable supporters of one group almost
never switched over to the other, regardless of political regroupings
in the capital. Changes in electoral results rarely occurred because
voters from one party switched to the other; rather, leaders of one
group succeeded in out-mobilizing the other, bringing more of their
usually passive supporters to the polls.[1]

The two blocs were determined by differing social milieus. Confessional differences were the most obvious: virtually the only Protestants
supporting the clerical party were bureaucrats acting (often enough
unwillingly) on the orders of their superiors. Less devout Catholics
were also likely to be supporters of the left. Occupational groups with
anti-clerical histories, such as the innkeepers, were often liberal partisans, and regions with a tradition of lay-clerical conflict were not
entirely hospitable to political Catholicism.

Liberal and clerical adherents were found in different socioeconomic
positions. Liberals enjoyed strong support from groups both in the
city and the countryside which were oriented towards a capitalist
market economy, while the clericals, although certainly not lacking
affluent supporters (one need only think of the Westphalian Catholic
nobility), in general drew their support from somewhat less well-off
and definitely less capitalist social strata. The confessional and soci-

---

[1] There were two occasions when these blocs dissolved and allegiances were created
across their boundaries, democrats and militant clericals coming together against moderate liberals and conservative Catholics. Both of those occasions, however, the elections
of January 1849, and, much more prominently, those of February 1867, occurred in
periods of mass political participation, beyond the framework of notables' politics. Even
in them, such bloc-spanning alliances occurred only in a minority of constituencies.

oeconomic orientations tended to converge, since capitalists were dis-proportionately Protestant and an articulate anti-clericalism made more headway among the Catholic bourgeoisie than other social groups.

Catholic politics cannot be equated with petit-bourgeois anti-cap-italism. Attempts by clerical politicians to push a guild-oriented, anti-occupational freedom, anti-usury political program during the 1860s were a dismal failure. Clerical politics remained clerical, that is, cen-tering around confessional issues and the defense of religion. Such a religiously based politics by no means excluded social questions since the ongoing religious revival had placed both religion and the clergy in the center of adaptation to a new socioeconomic environment. In the limited realm of notables' politics, with its restricted participation skewed toward the wealthier sectors of the population, the mass appeal of the religious revival went politically unused; its mobilization would have to wait on the events of 1866-1867.

The Era of Reaction: 1850-1858

After the suppression of the risings of the spring of 1849, the demo-cratic movement was outlawed. Its leaders quickly found themselves in jail, in exile, or, at best, free but silenced and politically isolated. The more moderate liberals, driven into opposition to the reactionary ministry, continued to enjoy a certain restricted liberty of expression in their strongholds in the big cities, but the government employed all the means of bureaucratic harassment and petty obstruction to ensure that their representatives did not obtain seats in the legislature. The elections were scenes of apathy and non-participation. Only 9.5 per-cent of the eligible voters in the Münster District appeared in 1852; in the Aachen District, 8.5 percent; in the Minden and Düsseldorf Districts, 12.0 percent. The democratic appeal for a boycott of the elections, widespread apathy and disillusionment with politics after the disappointments of 1848-1849, the problems of earning a living in economically difficult times—all contributed to such a mediocre turnout.[2]

In face of this massive apathy, the forces of order scored an easy triumph. Of the 1,675 electors chosen in the Minden District in 1852, the district governor noted, almost all were conservative; in the Cath-olic *Kreise*, "almost all the conservative electors, however, are of the predominantely clerical tendency. . . ." In the Münster District, some sixteen percent of the electors were priests, who dominated the elec-

[2] STAM OP Nr. 495 Bl. 79, 89; LAK 403 Nr. 8444 Bl. 251 ff.; Röttges, *Die politischen Wahlen*, p. 173.

toral process, the results being favorable to the "conservative party." Aachen District Governor Friedrich Kühlwetter, considering that the government would prefer to see a "strongly confessionally oriented [i.e., Catholic-clerical] deputy" in preference to the oppositional liberal Dr. Claeßen had the state officials acting as electors in the constituency Geilenkirchen-Heinsberg-Erkelenz vote for the clerical candidate, *Landesgerichtsrat* de Syo. Both Kühlwetter and the pietist provincial governor Hans von Kleist-Retzow were quite pleased with the election results in the Aachen District, even though all the deputies elected there were Catholic and clerically minded.[3]

This accord in parliamentary elections was part of a broader cooperation between Prussian state and Catholic church. While the authorities were approving the election of clerical deputies, they were busy negotiating a role for the church in the state educational system and in the drawing up of Sunday and holiday ordinances or admiring the counterrevolutionary content of the Jesuits' missionary sermons. The common impetus to these developments was the desire to improve popular morality, whose decline was seen as the cause of the radical insurgencies of 1848-1849. Even as the counterrevolutionary alliance between throne and altar seemed firmly sealed, it was being undone in the electoral realm. Paradoxically, it was not the failure of the alliance which led to this result, but its success, a consequence of the counterrevolutionary atmosphere of the early 1850s.

Although order seemingly reigned throughout the Prussian state, the central government was nervous and uneasy. The ministry saw subversives everywhere and bombarded the provincial authorities with reports of democratic and communist conspiracies, occasionally real but usually totally imaginary. Lists of dangerous men were circulated; most of the names on them had no connection with actual people. Police officials in the largest cities were required to submit weekly reports on any suspicious occurrences, analyzing in detail even the most trivial happenings. The beginning of the struggle between Prussia and Austria for hegemony in Central Europe only sharpened the tense atmosphere. Tensions were increased still further by the outbreak of the Crimean War and the possibility the German states might become involved in it.[4]

In this situation, the activities of the clerical notables and politicians

[3] STAM OP Nr. 495 Bl. 76-83; Haas, "Die Wahlen im Regierungs-Bezirk Aachen," pp. 75-84.

[4] See, for instance, STAM OP Nr. 2691 Bl. 35-45 and passim; HSTAD RA Pr. Nr. 702 Bl. 141-45, 171 ff.; LAK 403 Nr. 2182; STAM OP Nr. 1122. A similarly paranoid fear of revolutionary conspiracies existed in French official circles during most of the 1850s. Payne and Grosshens, "French Political Police."

appeared extremely suspicious to the Berlin government. The church
was certainly open in its hostility to the democratic revolution, but
the Catholic notion of counterrevolution did not stop at Prussia's
borders. It embraced the position of the Emperor—ruler of Catholic
Austria and *primus inter pares* among the German princes. In January
1851, a group of Pius Associations from Westphalia published an
address in the *Wiener Zeitung*, praising the Emperor for having saved
the "imperial estate from the abyss of the revolution" and having
restored to the church all its "traditional liberties" by signing a Con-
cordat. The Berlin authorities ordered an immediate investigation. As
organs of political Catholicism in 1848-1849, the Pius Associations
had taken a leading role in the struggle against democracy in Westphalia, but the praise of the Habsburg monarch just a few months
after Prussia's diplomatic humiliation at Olmütz raised entirely different perspectives. The local authorities all insisted on the benign
nature of the organizations, and the Interior Minister reluctantly agreed
with them, but two years later he was calling for a renewed investigation.[5]

Every incident fed the suspicions of distant and hostile authorities.
What were they to think when Father Hillebrand, director of missions
for the Diocese of Paderborn, in a sermon following the 1854 Corpus
Christi procession in Lichtenau, called on his listeners to pray ". . .
may the Lord God uphold the House of Austria, bulwark and protector
of the Catholic church for many years . . ."? How were the loyalties
of the Catholic nobility to be regarded upon learning that the sons of
the Count von Westphalen served in the Austrian army or the views
of the Catholic press, knowing that the brother of the publisher of the
Westfälisches Volksblatt was a lieutenant in the Austrian navy?[6]

These incidents point to a basic dilemma of Prussian politics in the
era of reaction. The suppression of the democratic movement in the
spring and summer of 1849 brought conservative and authoritarian
elements to the fore throughout Germany. In most of Prussia, "conservative" meant "absolutely obedient to the king and his ministers,"
but in the Catholic areas of the Rhineland and Westphalia the conservative elements were independent of the government and would
cooperate only as long as it was in their interest to do so. The extent
and nature of this cooperation depended on the attitude of the governmental authorities. Many, but by no means all, of the local and
provincial officials were ready to work with the church and political

[5] STAM OP Nr. 1914.
[6] Royal Police Lieutenant Kluge to RPMI, Jan. 17, 1855, and *Landrat* Grasso (Paderborn) to RPMI, Mar. 10, 1855, STAD M1 Pr. Nr. 461.

Catholicism, but Interior Minister Ferdinand von Westphalen, the bulk of his colleagues in the reactionary ministry, and the court camarilla in Berlin paraded an ostentatiously Protestant suspiciousness of the "ultramontanists."

The 1852 elections were already affected by these suspicions. Shortly before the balloting, the government decreed that missions could not be carried out in areas with predominantly Protestant populations. This, the so-called "Raumer decree," named after the Minister of Educational and Religious Affairs, also declared the Jesuit-run Collegium Germanicum in Rome off-limits to Prussian clergy. Everywhere the Catholic electors and deputies announced their intention of opposing the decree. The priests in *Kreis* Geldern (Düsseldorf District) made the rather exaggerated claim that the situation was as serious as at the time of the *Kölner Wirren*. In the religiously mixed electoral districts of the lower Rhine, the elections were fought on an openly confessional basis, the Catholic electors outvoting the Protestant ones and electing Catholic deputies.[7]

Most of the local officials saw nothing dangerous in these results. They were aware of the conservative opinions of the clergy and clerical notables and had a favorable view of the pacifying and counterrevolutionary effects of the missions. A minority disagreed and saw the election of conservative but Catholic deputies as a triumph of "opposition" to the government's policies.[8] The Catholic deputies, on arriving in Berlin, formed their own parliamentary caucus, opposed the Raumer decree and forced the government to retract it. The newly formed Catholic caucus in the Prussian parliament was a politically heterogeneous group, but its members firmly supported the constitution, which guaranteed the rights of the church, and opposed proposals surfacing within the ministry and the court camarilla to abolish it. Consequently, the clerical deputies frequently voted with the liberal opposition on issues not strictly related to religion.[9]

In contrast to the parliamentary action in Berlin, the confrontation between church and state in the provinces took the form of a clash between two different versions of counterrevolution. The authorities suppressed the *Deutsche Volkshalle* in Cologne, but hardly for its left-wing sentiments. Counterrevolution had dominated the newspaper's editorial policy; it even had supported the extreme reactionary demands for the abolition of the Prussian constitution which the Catholic

---

[7] LAK 403 Nr. 8444 Bl. 155, 225-28, 402-403; Röttges, *Die politischen Wahlen*, pp. 159-68.

[8] STAM RAR I Pr. Nr. 81 Bl. 269.

[9] On the early history of Catholic parliamentarianism in Prussia, Donner, *Die katholische Fraktion*, passim; and Bachem, *Zentrumspartei*, 2: 96-152.

parliamentarians had so firmly opposed. The *Volkshalle*, however, always insisted that genuine counterrevolution meant the restoration of the primacy of the Austrian Emperor in Central Europe. For that reason it was constantly in trouble with the authorities throughout its six-year history and was finally suppressed on order of the Interior Minister in 1855.[10]

State and church each tried to paint the other as a false counterrevolutionary, secretly in league with democratic elements. As early as 1850, the *Sonntagsblatt für katholische Christen* in Münster announced, "In the modern age, non-Christianity has appeared in double form: as modern democracy and as old bureaucracy, both hostile to Christianity. Genuine bureaucracy is therefore nothing other than the organized modern democracy. . . ."[11] The reactionary ministry mounted a campaign to smear the Catholic church by portraying it as being in alliance with the democrats. Interior Minister von Westphalen sent out a circular accusing the Rhenish clergy of working with the democrats. A flood of protest letters from outraged priests, pointing out their conservative sentiments, reached the Archbishop of Cologne and the Bishop of Münster; the embarrassed minister was forced to apologize.[12] On the eve of the 1855 elections, the government press agency placed an article in friendly newspapers, pointedly asking Catholics whether they had more to expect from the "Principles of 1789" than from the Hohenzollerns and orthodox Lutherans. Small wonder the Catholics in Paderborn complained in 1855, as a police report noted: "They [the Catholics] say the government lacks gratitude [in accusing Catholics of collaboration with the left] and maintain . . . that it was precisely the ultramontane party which saved the state in 1848 and 1849 and that the party press organs are inspired by conservative sentiments."[13]

[10] Bachem, *Joseph Bachem*, 1: 225 ff. and 294-98. The *Westfälisches Volksblatt* in Paderborn followed a similarly counterrevolutionary but clerical and pro-Austrian line. Only the intervention of Westphalian Provincial Governor Duesberg saved it from the same fate as the *Deutsche Volkshalle*. STAM OP Nr. 1085 Bl. 159-77, 183-216.

[11] *Sonntagsblatt für katholische Christen* 9 (1850): 22-24. A similar point was made in the article series on the conflict between church and state in Baden in the *Westfälisches Kirchenblatt*, the Sunday supplement to the *Westfälisches Volksblatt*, and almost led to the newspaper's suppression.

[12] Ibid., 13 (1854): 494, 528.

[13] *Preußische Correspondenz* Nr. 227, Sep. 30, 1855; copy in STAM OP Nr. 500; Royal Police Lieutenant Kluge (Paderborn) to RPMI, Jul. 23, 1855, STAD M1 Pr. Nr. 461. The grain of truth in these mutual accusations stemmed from 1848-1849 when a small minority of both bureaucrats and priests had supported radical movements. A major aspect of the bureaucrats' radicalism was their anti-clericalism, and a major aspect of the priests' radicalism was their anti-Prussianism, hostilities both groups shared with their conservative colleagues.

The government took steps to ensure good results in the 1855 elections. On instructions from the Interior Minister, the electoral districts were gerrymandered to leave oppositional electors outvoted, which meant in several instances that a Catholic *Kreis* was combined with two Protestant ones.[14] In spite of pressure on the mass of lower officials, on the one side, and pastoral letters and exhortatory sermons, on the other, the elections took place in an atmosphere of unparalleled apathy. Turnouts were at one of the lowest points in the century. Turnout rates were rarely over fifteen percent, and in most constituencies they were half that proportion. In some villages, no one at all showed up at the polls, and the elections were cancelled.[15]

The *Kölnische Zeitung,* organ of the moderate liberal opposition, called on liberals and clericals in the Rhineland and Westphalia to work together against the ministry. In Cologne and the immediate vicinity, the two groups cooperated without great difficulties, but elsewhere tensions persisted. Two deputies were to be chosen for the electoral district Düren-Jülich. The first deputy chosen by the electors was a priest, who was elected with liberal support, but on the second ballot the clerical electors turned around and voted for the official candidate over the man supported by the liberal opposition. By clever manipulation, the government had combined the Protestant, rural, and conservative *Kreis* Halle, the Protestant but urbanized and liberal *Kreis* Bielefeld, and the largely Catholic *Kreis* Wiedenbrück (all Minden District) into one electoral district. The Protestant liberals would not vote for a Catholic candidate, and the Catholics would not vote for a liberal candidate, so three Protestant conservatives were elected.[16]

In most predominantly Catholic Rhenish-Westphalian constituencies, deputies belonging to the Catholic caucus in the Prussian Parliament were elected, usually by quite large margins, receiving between seventy-five and ninety percent of the votes of the electors. "Official" or "governmental" candidates could make a reasonable showing only where there existed a sizeable Protestant minority, and one from which all left-wing elements had been purged, to vote for them. Such elections

[14] Weinandy, "Die Wahlen des Regierungsbezirks Köln," pp. 129-30; RPMI to OPM, May 31, 1855; OPM to Interior Minister, Jun. 8, 1855, and Interior Minister to OPM, Jul. 22, 1855, STAM OP Nr. 500.

[15] Weinandy, "Die Wahlen des Regierungsbezirks Köln," p. 133; Denk, "Die Wahlen in Köln," p. 113; Röttges, *Die politischen Wahlen,* p. 196; STAM LA Kr. Ahaus Nr. 347; STAD M1 IL Nr. 34.

[16] Denk, "Die Wahlen in Köln," pp. 111-15; Haas, "Die Wahlen im Regierungs-Bezirk Aachen," pp. 92-93; LAK 403 Nr. 8845 Bl. 14-15; "Verzeichnis der im Regierungsbezirk Minden gewählten Abgeordneten" (1855), STAM OP Nr. 500.

were less a struggle between government and opposition than a conflict between two religiously tinged forms of conservatism.[17]

Indeed, it is not at all clear that there was a sharp confrontation between governmental and clerical elements in the Catholic areas. State and church had worked together closely in opposing the revolution; in the 1852 elections; the "clerical" candidates had usually enjoyed "official" support. During the height of the dispute between the Catholic deputies and the reactionary ministry in the Prussian Parliament, provincial and local authorities continued to cooperate with church officials on a broad variety of issues outside of electoral politics. Even in 1855, several successfully elected clerical deputies were state officials: the area magistrate Brüning in the constituency Beckum-Lüdinghausen-Warendorf (Münster District) or the Landrat of Kreis Brilon, Casper Maximilian Freiherr von Droste, elected in Brilon-Meschede-Wittgenstein (Arnsberg District). In these areas at least, the identification of official and clerical conservatism continued in spite of the official policy of the central government.[18]

The election of the deputies was recorded on official protocols which gave the name, occupation, and vote of all the electors in a constituency. Such protocols have rarely been preserved but are available for the 1855 election of the deputies representing the constituency Warburg-Höxter-Büren-Paderborn, four heavily Catholic Kreise in the Minden District, the electors voted for three deputies.

The electors had been selected by a small minority of the voters: only 8.2 percent of the voters in Kreis Büren had gone to the polls, 10.5 percent in Kreis Höxter, 12.4 percent in Kreis Paderborn, and 21.0 percent in Kreis Warburg (the last a relatively high turnout by 1855 standards). Meeting together, the electors chose three clerical deputies to sit in the Prussian Parliament. On the first ballot, they elected Joseph Schmidt, a judge on the Kreisgericht in Paderborn, by 392 votes to 142 for the official candidate, the Landrat of Kreis Höxter, Friedrich Freiherr von Wolff-Metternich. The second deputy elected was Wilhelm Rohden, justice on the Court of Appeals in Posen (but a native Westphalian) by a vote of 375 to 52 for Wolff-Metternich and 37 for Mayor Fischer of Warburg. The third deputy elected was

[17] In the constituency Ahaus-Borken-Recklinghausen of the Münster District, which was over 90 percent Catholic, the clerical candidates received 92 percent, 90 percent, and 73 percent of the electors' votes respectively, but in neighboring Steinfurt-Tecklenburg, some 35 percent Protestant, the victorious clerical candidates managed only 64 percent and 60 percent of the electors' votes. "Verzeichnis der Wahlkandidaten zum Hause der Abgeordneten," STAM OP Nr. 500. Similar examples can be drawn from the lower Rhine. Cf. Röttges, Die politischen Wahlen, pp. 186-90.

[18] Election results are in STAM OP Nr. 500.

a judge on the Höxter *Kreisgericht*, Neukirch, by a vote of 338 to 119 for Metternich.[19]

I have divided the electors into four groups: those who voted the straight governmental ticket, those who split their ballots, and those who were selected but either did not appear for the balloting, or appeared and cast a blank ballot, or voted for another individual than the ones mentioned above, one with no chance of having been elected. See Table 3.1. In addition, I have considered the social grouping of the electors and the candidates they supported. See Table 3.2.

The social distribution of the electors in all four *Kreise* is similar and reflects their rural and non-industrial social and economic structures.[20] Between forty and sixty-five percent of the electors voting for the official candidates or splitting their ballots were state officials or village foremen, who were elected by the larger property-owning peasants, but whose election required governmental sanction. The governmental electorate was thus made up of village foremen, tax collectors, postmen, foresters, or area magistrates—those whose position depended on official good favor or who were natives of the Protestant eastern provinces working in an alien environment. In addition, the scattered Protestant population in the towns of the area supported the

TABLE 3.1
Votes of the Electors in
Büren-Paderborn-Höxter-Warburg, 1855

Vote	Büren N	Büren %	Paderborn N	Paderborn %	Kreis Höxter N	Kreis Höxter %	Warburg N	Warburg %	All N	All %
Clerical	95	(72)	93	(68)	99	(54)	45	(34)	332	(57)
Governmental	12	(9)	11	(8)	38	(21)	48	(36)	109	(19)
Split	10	(8)	26	(20)	29	(16)	23	(17)	88	(15)
Other	14	(11)	6	(4)	18	(10)	17	(13)	55	(9)
Total Electors	131	(100)	136	(100)	184	(101)	133	(100)	584	(100)

SOURCE: Election protocols in STAD M1 IL Nr. 59.

[19] The protocols are in STAD M1 IL Nr. 59; turnout figures and election results are found in STAD M1 IL Nr. 34 and "Verzeichnis der im Regierungsbezirk Minden gewählten Abgeordneten zum Hause der Abgeordneten," STAM OP Nr. 500, respectively.

[20] More electors from *Kreis* Büren are in the category "other, unknown," because a larger number of electors from that *Kreis* had no occupational designation written down next to their name on the election protocols.

TABLE 3.2
Social Composition of the Electors in Büren-Paderborn-Höxter-Warburg

Social Group	Clerical No.	%	Governmental No.	%	Split No.	%	Other No.	%	All No.	%
				Kreis Büren						
Noble, estate-owner	2	(2.1)	2	(16.7)	2	(20.0)	—		6	(4.6)
Large farmer[a]	4	(4.2)	—		—		1	(7.1)	5	(3.8)
Peasant[b]	8	(8.4)	—		1	(10.0)	3	(21.4)	12	(9.2)
Merchant	1	(1.1)	—		—		—		1	(0.8)
Artisan-retailer	6	(6.3)	—		1	(10.0)	1	(7.1)	8	(6.1)
Upper level official	2	(2.1)	—		—		—		2	(1.5)
Lower, middle official	11	(11.6)	6	(50.0)	—		1	(7.1)	18	(13.7)
Village foreman	11	(11.6)	—		3	(30.0)	5	(35.7)	19	(14.5)
Professional	2	(2.1)	1	(8.3)	—		—		3	(2.3)
Clergy	26	(27.4)	—		—		—		26	(19.8)
Other, unknown	22	(23.2)	3	(25.0)	3	(30.0)	3	(21.4)	31	(23.7)
Total electors	95	(100.1)	12	(100.0)	10	(100.0)	14	(99.8)	131	(100.0)
				Kreis Paderborn						
Noble, estate owner	1	(1.1)	1	(9.1)	1	(3.8)	—		3	(2.2)
Large farmer[a]	18	(19.4)	2	(18.2)	—		4	(66.7)	24	(17.6)
Peasant[b]	9	(9.7)	—		6	(23.1)	—		15	(11.0)
Merchant	8	(8.6)	—		2	(7.7)	—		10	(7.4)
Artisan-retailer	8	(8.6)	—		1	(3.8)	—		9	(6.6)
Upper level official	3	(3.2)	5	(45.4)	2	(7.7)	1	(16.7)	11	(8.1)
Lower, middle official	8	(8.6)	2	(18.2)	5	(19.2)	—		15	(11.0)
Village foreman	8	(8.6)	—		6	(23.1)	1	(16.7)	15	(11.0)
Professional	6	(6.5)	1	(9.1)	—		—		7	(5.1)

TABLE 3.2 (*cont.*)

Social Group	Clerical		Governmental		Split		Other		All	
	No.	%	No.	%	No.	%	No.	%	No.	%
Clergy	21	(22.3)	—		—		—		21	(15.4)
Other, unknown	3	(3.3)	—		3	(11.5)	—		6	(4.4)
Total electors	93	(99.9)	11	(100.0)	26	(99.9)	6	(100.0)	136	(99.8)

Kreis Höxter

Social Group	Clerical		Governmental		Split		Other		All	
Noble, estate owner	2	(2.0)	1	(2.6)	3	(10.3)	1	(5.6)	7	(3.8)
Large farmer[a]	4	(4.0)	2	(5.3)	5	(17.2)	—		11	(6.0)
Peasant[b]	18	(18.2)	1	(2.6)	7	(24.1)	5	(27.8)	31	(16.8)
Merchant	5	(5.1)	2	(5.3)	2	(6.9)	—		9	(4.9)
Artisan-retailer	6	(6.0)	8	(21.1)	2	(6.9)	2	(11.2)	18	(9.8)
Upper level official	—		4	(10.5)	—		—		4	(2.2)
Lower, middle official	16	(16.2)	13	(34.0)	3	(10.3)	—		32	(17.4)
Village foreman	11	(11.1)	1	(2.6)	4	(13.8)	5	(27.8)	21	(11.4)
Professional	3	(3.0)	3	(7.9)	1	(3.4)	—		7	(3.8)
Clergy	31	(31.3)	—		—		5	(27.8)	36	(19.0)
Other, unknown	3	(3.0)	3	(7.9)	2	(6.9)	—		8	(4.3)
Total electors	99	(99.9)	38	(99.8)	29	(99.8)	18	(100.2)	184	(99.4)

Kreis Warburg

Social Group	Clerical		Governmental		Split		Other		All	
Noble, estate owner	2	(4.4)	2	(4.2)	1	(4.3)	—		5	(3.8)
Large farmer[a]	2	(4.4)	3	(6.3)	2	(8.7)	—		7	(5.3)
Peasant[b]	4	(8.8)	9	(18.8)	8	(34.8)	8	(47.1)	29	(21.8)
Merchant	1	(2.2)	5	(10.4)	1	(4.3)	1	(5.9)	8	(6.0)
Artisan-retailer	2	(4.4)	2	(4.2)	1	(4.3)	—		5	(3.7)
Upper level official	—		3	(6.3)	—		—		3	(2.3)
Lower, middle official	8	(17.8)	11	(22.9)	7	(30.4)	1	(5.9)	27	(20.3)

TABLE 3.2 (cont.)

Social Group	Clerical No.	%	Governmental No.	%	Split No.	%	Other No.	%	All No.	%
Village fore-man	3	(6.7)	11	(22.9)	3	(13.0)	4	(23.5)	21	(15.8)
Professional	2	(4.4)	2	(4.2)	—		1	(5.9)	5	(3.8)
Clergy	20	(44.4)	—		—		1	(5.9)	21	(15.8)
Other, unknown	1	(2.2)	—		—		1	(5.9)	2	(1.5)
Total electors	45	(99.7)	48	(100.2)	23	(99.8)	17	(100.1)	133	(100.1)

[a] Oeconom, Colon.
[b] Ackerer, Ackersmann.
SOURCE: Election protocols in STAD M1 IL Nr. 59.

authorities. The best example of this is the town of Höxter, over half of whose inhabitants were Protestants with a reputation for embracing an aggressive and obnoxious Pietism.[21] Eleven of the fifteen electors from Höxter voted for the governmental candidate. Where, as in *Kreis* Büren, no such Protestant enclaves existed, the number of governmental electors was much smaller.

The mainstay of the clerical electors, as one might imagine, was the clergy. Every single priest who appeared to vote, voted the straight clerical ticket; the tiny minority with other opinions chose discreetly not to appear. A large majority of the Catholic members of other social groups voted clerical as well. In particular, in three of the four *Kreise*, over half of the lower- and middle-level officials (including the schoolteachers) supported all the clerical candidates. The local representatives of the state's authority were thus to be found in considerable numbers in the ranks of the Catholic opposition.

Certain regional differences can be noted. The electors from *Kreis* Büren voted overwhelmingly for the clerical party—a consequence of the lack of a Protestant minority, but probably also representative of a certain halfhearted effort on the part of the *Landrat*. Unlike the other three *Kreise*, the *Landrat* of *Kreis* Büren was not selected by the voters as an elector, and it would seem that he made no particular effort to coerce the officials in his *Kreis* into voting for the official candidate.

---

[21] On the Protestants of Höxter, see the letter from members of the Catholic community there to the Bishop of Paderborn, Nov. 27, 1858, AGVP XVI, 12.

The governmental elements achieved their best results in *Kreis* War-burg. In part, this is attributable to the opposite circumstances from *Kreis* Büren—energetic pressure on the part of the *Landrat*, existent Protestant enclaves (Protestants made up about nine percent of the *Kreis* population). Governmental electors, however, were chosen from entirely Catholic villages. Furthermore, a greater proportion of the population of *Kreis* Höxter was Protestant than was the case in *Kreis* Warburg, and Höxter's *Landrat*, the Freiherr von Wolff-Metternich, was second to none in his unswerving loyalty to the Prussian state. Yet the official candidate did noticeably better among the electors from *Kreis* Warburg than among those from *Kreis* Höxter. It would seem that the political influence of the clergy was weaker in *Kreis* Warburg than in the other *Kreise* of the electoral district. The pro-portion of clergy chosen as electors was smaller than elsewhere: in the other *Kreise*, almost all the parishes routinely selected their priest or one of his chaplains as an elector, whereas about one-third of the parishes in *Kreis* Warburg did not. In 1855, this meant that the *Landrat* could successfully pressure the Catholic lower officials, village fore-men, and farmers into voting for at least one of the official candidates, while in the 1860s this relatively weak clerical position would be reflected in a stronger support of left liberalism in *Kreis* Warburg than in the other three *Kreise*.

It is difficult to say much about the political attitude of the original voters. Corresponding protocols on the selection by the voters of the electors have not been preserved, and the existing sources do not throw much light on the matter. Turnouts were low; the great surge of religious sentiment expressed in the contemporary missions could not be translated into mass political participation. It frequently appears from the lists of electors that many villagers chose as electors the priest, the village foreman, and a third influential or affluent person—a schoolteacher, estate owner, or well-off farmer. Their election seems less the endorsement of a political viewpoint than the recognition of their dominant position in the local society.

The electors thus chosen frequently voted in diverging ways. In Thüle (*Kreis* Büren), the voters chose as electors the parish priest, the village foreman, and a Catholic nobleman, Wilderich Freiherr von Ketteler. The priest voted the straight clerical ticket, the foreman for the official candidate, and Freiherr von Ketteler voted for the first clerical candidate, Schmidt, voted against the second, Rohden, and for the *Landrat* von Wolff-Metternich, and abstained on the third. Rohden stood on the extreme left wing of the Catholic parliamentary depu-tation, and Ketteler's electoral behavior was shared by other conser-vative Catholic aristocrats serving as electors. What is particularly interesting about this case, however, is that Ketteler was no noble outsider but the brother of the celebrated Bishop of Mainz, Wilhelm Emmanuel von Ketteler, and in his own right an important figure in political Catholicism and the organized Catholic movement in Westphalia and in all of Germany.[22] His election, along with a priest, and their subsequent differing votes is one more piece of evidence to suggest that the alternative clerical-governmental was not at all well defined in the eyes of the voters in 1855. On the local level, church and state still stood together as symbols of counterrevolutionary authority.

A TRANSITIONAL PERIOD: 1858-1861

For all the passion and militant parliamentary struggle in Berlin, the confrontation between Prussian state and Catholic church in the mid-1850s proved ephemeral. Ties formed in the fight against the democratic revolution retained their strength and greatly reduced the extent of the clash at the local level. Existing suspicions, also dating from the revolutionary era, prevented in several instances an effective cooperation in the constituencies between the moderate liberal and the clerical opposition to the reactionary ministry, regardless of what happened in Berlin. Church-state relations improved in the closing years of the reaction era. The circular of the Interior Ministry on the upcoming 1858 elections described the government's plans solely in terms of a struggle against liberalism and democracy; unlike three years previously, the clerical party was not included in the ranks of the opposition.[23]

These electoral preparations were the last act of the reactionary ministry. In the summer of 1858, a Regency Council declared the ruling monarch, Friedrich Wilhelm IV, hopelessly insane; his brother, Prince Wilhelm, became Regent. Wilhelm dismissed the reactionary ministers and closed his ears to the court camarilla. He appointed a new ministry, composed of cautious sympathizers with the most conservative elements of the former liberal opposition. The new Minister President was Anton von Hohenzollern, from the Catholic branch of the royal family.[24]

The "New Era" ministry, as it was known, abandoned the former practice of massive and centrally directed interference with the electoral process. It took steps to dismantle the police-state apparatus that

[22] Hohmann, "Die Soester Konferenzen," pp. 294-95.
[23] Circulars of Interior Minister von Westphalen to all provincial governors, dated Jul. 24 and Aug. 21, 1858. Copies in STAM OP Nr. 500.
[24] On the politics of the "New Era," see Haupts, "Die liberale Regierung," which contains extensive bibliographical references.

its predecessors had erected, and in doing so ended the confrontation between governmental and oppositional elements, which had, however ambiguously, dominated the previous elections of the decade and would be seen once more after 1861. Since the formerly oppositional clericals and moderate liberals were both more or less in agreement with the views of the new ministry, the lines of cleavage and cooperation in the elections of 1858 and 1861 were locally based and not determined by directives issued in Berlin.

Political alignments varied from one constituency to the next. Liberals and clericals in Wiedenbrück-Halle-Bielefeld worked together, unlike three years previously, electing two liberals and one Catholic deputy. Similar instances of liberal-clerical cooperation could be found on the lower Rhine and in the *Bergisches Land*. The 1855 patterns persisted in the Münster District and in several lower Rhine constituencies where the elections remained a struggle of Protestant against Catholic. Liberal-clerical antagonisms were also revealed: the liberal electors in Cologne selected two deputies over the opposition of their clerical counterparts before agreeing to a compromise on the third deputy from the constituency. A meeting of electors to discuss potential candidates in Stolberg (*Landkreis* Aachen) ended in a fist fight between liberal and clerical partisans.[25]

A new feature of the elections was the return of the democrats to the political process, less in the cities than in the small towns and in the countryside. Justice of the Peace Kampmann in Geilenkirchen, a leader of the radical democracy in 1848-1849, had been active in the subsequent decade, defending tavern keepers whom the government had threatened with withdrawal of their licenses. In 1858, he mobilized them for a democratic election campaign in the constituency Geilenkirchen-Heinsberg-Erkelenz (Aachen District). Democratic veterans led a campaign in Kempen-Geldern (Düsseldorf District), while in *Kreis* Beckum (Münster District), a democratic stronghold in 1848-1849, the nervous authorities could find no traces of an organized campaign, but somehow twenty-three electors turned up to vote for Benedikt Waldeck, the "peasant king," leader of the Westphalian democracy during the revolution.[26]

Although the ministry had renounced any effort at guiding the elec-

[25] LA Kr. Bielefeld to OPM, Nov. 23, 1858; "Verzeichnis der zum Hause der Abgeordneten gewählten Abgeordneten" (1858), both in STAM OP Nr. 500; Röttges, *Die politischen Wahlen*, pp. 208-10, 212-14; Weinandy, "Die Wahlen des Regierungsbezirks Köln," pp. 155-57; Denk, "Die Wahlen in Köln," pp. 126-27; Haas, "Die Wahlen im Regierungs-Bezirk Aachen," p. 100.

[26] Haas, "Die Wahlen im Regierungs-Bezirk Aachen," pp. 105-106; Röttges, *Die politischen Wahlen*, p. 211; HSTAD RD Pr. Nr. 564 Bl. 172; Regierungs Vizepräsident

tions, the bureaucracy was far from neutral.[27] As central guidance fell away, differing political tendencies within the ranks of the authorities appeared. Some officials continued to favor a conservative-authoritarian course, even without the backing of the ministry; a few even showed their radical-democratic sympathies. Most, though, supported either the clerical or moderate liberal position. In Düsseldorf, the *Landrat* and the veteran Catholic parliamentarian August Reichensperger were elected together. A few miles down the Rhine, in the electoral district Neuß-Grevenbroich, the authorities offered a certain support to the liberal candidate who was victorious over the individual preferred by the clergy. In the Aachen District, the authorities supported the clerical candidate in the constituency Aachen-Eupen and the liberal one in Düren-Jülich; in both cases, Catholic deputies were elected.[28]

The Berlin authorities refrained in 1861 as they had in 1858 from systematic electoral intervention, but the events of the intervening three years had created an increasingly polarized situation. Across Europe the waning of the reaction era had given way to a new period of nationalist, liberal, and democratic initiative, embodied in such events as the northern Italian war of 1859, the campaign of Garibaldi in southern Italy, the founding of the Nationalverein, and the appointment of a parliamentary ministry in Baden. Prussian politics moved in a similar path, and a number of left-wing deputies in the Berlin Parliament united to form the German Progressive Party, crystallizing out of the amorphous grouping of left-of-center parliamentarians a left-liberal bloc, joining old democrats and more militantly inclined liberals. In the provinces, like-minded notables followed their lead, meeting to coordinate their efforts and founding provincial branches of the new party.[29]

(Münster) to OPM, Sep. 5, 1858, STAM OP Nr. 500. The democratic campaigns were not very successful, managing to obtain only between five and seven percent of the electors' vote.

[27] The new ministry itself encouraged this, noting that in choosing the electors, "expectations, wishes, and hopes have been expressed, whose fulfillment the existing organs of the government are expressly obligated to oppose in consideration of the goals set for them by the royal authority." The *Landräte* were called upon to work in opposition to these never expressly defined tendencies, an appeal which could easily be interpreted as a blank check to act against whatever any official felt were anti-governmental forces. (Circular of the Interior Minister to all *Landräte*, Nov. 17, 1858; copy in STAM LA Kr. Meschede Nr. 268.)

[28] HSTAD RD Pr. Nr. 564 Bl. 203; Röttges, *Die politischen Wahlen*, pp. 215-16; Haas, "Die Wahlen im Regierungs-Bezirk Aachen," pp. 100-102.

[29] The atmosphere of the period is evoked by Hamerow, *Social Foundations*, 2: 3-

Some liberals were motivated by Protestant anti-Popery, others by a militant anti-clericalism, but even where there was no hostile intent, every victory for the program of the bourgeois left was a blow to the Catholic church. The territorial changes in Italy were a direct threat to the temporal power of the Pope, while the defeat of the Austrian army in Lombardy raised the specter of the expulsion of the Habsburgs from German affairs. Just such a step was the basis of the National-verein's *kleindeutsch* program of German unification, which would have left Catholics a permanent minority in a unified Germany minus Austria. Almost the first act of the new liberal-parliamentary ministry in Baden was to become involved in a bitter conflict with the Catholic church, pointing toward an unpleasant future should the Progressives or their bureaucratic sympathizers ever come to power in Prussia or a unified but *kleindeutsch* Germany. The same events which gave liberals and progressives a greater sense of self-confidence and encouraged them to increase their activities were for the clerical party signs of growing uncertainty and danger.

The Catholic parliamentarians were divided over the proper response to this dangerous situation. One faction, led predominantly by members of the Westphalian and Silesian aristocracy, but including most of the leading lights of political Catholicism, looked to an alliance with the Protestant conservatives, stressing a common opposition to radicalism, down-playing their differing attitudes toward the Prussian constitution. This faction's leading press organ in the west was the *Westfälische Merkur* in Münster. Another group, composed chiefly of back-benchers in the Catholic parliamentary delegation, with a press spokesman in the Bachem family's *Kölnische Blätter*, wished to continue a cautious cooperation with the liberals, in doing so hoping to moderate the stance of the left and also to preserve the constitutional guarantees of the church's independent position.[30]

Regardless of the potential parliamentary orientation of the Catholic deputies, it was increasingly difficult for the clerical notables to cooperate with their liberal counterparts in the constituencies. Defining themselves as an interconfessional movement, the liberals insisted that religion was no basis for politics and denied the Catholic party any legitimate grounds for existence. The Progressives of *Kreis* Wiedenbrück (Minden District) stated in a flier "Let us . . . give the world

---

48; the founding of the Westphalian branch of the Progressives was reported by the Hamm correspondent of the *Kölnische Zeitung*, Nov. 5, 1861.

[30] Bachem, *Zentrumspartei*, 2: 153-63; Wendorf, *Die Fraktion des Zentrums*, passim. For a hostile contemporary view of these differences, see the commentary of the *Kölnische Zeitung*, Oct. 9, 1861.

... a beautiful example ... of the harmonious cooperation of the Progressives of all confessions in our *Kreis*, where each confession gladly takes into account the justified demands of the other. We will not drag religion into politics; it is the sacred possession of every individual."[31] The differences between liberals and clericals had not yet everywhere hardened into total hostility. It was still possible in Cologne and Aachen for Catholic, liberal, and progressive electors to agree on common deputies. Such instances of amiable coexistence were the exception in 1861; more common was an increasingly bitter opposition. Priests in a number of constituencies, speaking from the pulpit and in election meetings, denounced the liberals and progressives as Freemasons, atheistic enemies of Christianity, as red subversives, warmongers, intent on a violent exclusion of Austria from Germany. Clerical newspapers, even those intent on retaining good relations with liberal parliamentarians, echoed the charges. The left, for its part, did not shrink from polemics and roundly denounced the Catholic party, accusing it of seeking to maintain its politically irrelevant existence by allying itself with the East Elbian reactionaries.[32]

Events in the constituency Warburg-Höxter-Büren-Paderborn exemplify in miniature the changes in political alignments occurring between 1858 and 1861. The fall of the reactionary ministry in 1858 had meant the dismissal of the anti-Catholic Minden District Governor Friedrich Wilhelm Peters and his replacement by Heinrich von Bardeleben, a man of quite different views from his predecessor. He reported to the Westphalian Provincial Governor: "After I had convinced myself that the Bishop of Paderborn had the interests of the govern-

[31] Flyer, "Aufruf zu den Wahlen," in STAD M1 Pr. Nr. 259; a similar point was made in the account of the elections in Lippstadt in the *Kölnische Zeitung*, Nov. 21, 1861 and by the liberals in the *Hochsauerland, Olper Kreis-Blatt*, Nov. 30, 1861, copy in STAM OP Nr. 500. The following year, the Rhenish Provincial Electoral Committee of the Progressives generalized these sentiments in a widely distributed flyer: "The holy religion concerns the heart and not the wallet. We are not electing men to a synod but to a worldly *Landtag*. . . . Therefore we should not vote for a priest." Cited in Haas, "Die Wahlen im Regierungs-Bezirk Aachen," p. 137.

[32] For examples of liberal-clerical cooperation, see Denk, "Die Wahlen in Köln," pp. 142-43; Haas, "Die Wahlen im Regierungs-Bezirk Aachen," pp. 119-23. The radical Justice of the Peace Kampmann, "symbol of the red democracy," and his army of agitating innkeepers so terrified the moderate liberals, the clergy, and the officials of the constituency Erkelenz-Heinsberg-Geilenkirchen that they buried their differences and united to defeat him (ibid., pp. 130-31). Liberal-clerical hostility is documented in Röttges, *Die politischen Wahlen*, pp. 226-44; Weinandy, "Die Wahlen des Regierungsbezirks Köln," pp. 182-84; the press polemics in the *Olper Kreis-Blatt*, Nov. 30, 1861, STAM OP Nr. 500; and the reports of correspondents from various localities in the Rhineland and Westphalia, *Kölnische Zeitung*, Nov. 21, 1861.

ment as much at heart as those of his church, I met with him for a personal conference concerning the upcoming [1858] elections. We soon reached complete agreement on the candidates to be elected."[33]

The electors from the four *Kreise* gathered in Driburg to elect the deputies. On the first ballot, the incumbent clerical deputy, Schmidt, choice of bishop and district governor, received 375 of 507 votes, *Landrat* Grasso of *Kreis* Paderborn receiving 76 and Justice Wickmann of the Paderborn Court of Appeals 43. (The latter two can be seen as the liberal and democratic candidates, respectively.) On the second ballot, estate-owner Derenthal in Marienmünster was elected with 481 of 485 votes. Derenthal had been the choice of bishop and district governor; in the 1860s he would stand as a liberal candidate against the clericals. He must have appealed to the partisans of all the parties, and his election shows that at the beginning of the "New Era" well-defined, sharply differentiated political groups did not yet exist. The third ballot saw the victory of the last agreed-upon candidate, Justice Schlüter of the Paderborn Court of Appeals, who, however, received only 257 votes, while the *Landrat* Grasso obtained 223, and 16 were scattered. Everything, it seemed, had gone quite smoothly. The Prussian Parliament then received a petition from seventy-four electors from *Kreis* Paderborn, protesting the election of Schlüter. Before the balloting began, several electors went around informing others that Justice Wickmann and *Landrat* Grasso were both bad Catholics who had not been to church in decades. A vote for them would put religion in danger. Before the third ballot, the keeper of the electoral protocol left the room and was replaced by deputies who had not sworn the required oath to keep an honest record. Several witnesses reported having heard a forester for Freiherr von Haxthausen vote four times. Conditions were chaotic; other irregularities were suspected; protests went unheard. The *Landrat* of *Kreis* Höxter, Friedrich Freiherr von Wolff-Metternich, the official election commissioner, refused to certify the results of the election until almost all the electors had left the room, and a new ballot had become impossible. The District Governor responded to these accusations of electoral fraud by calling on its probable perpetrator, *Landrat* von Wolff-Metternich, to investigate. Metternich, not surprisingly, decided the results were honest. The Parliament quashed Schlüter's mandate, but he was chosen again at a special election in 1859.[34]

[33] RPMI to OPM, Oct. 5, 1858, STAM OP Nr. 500. On Peter's fall and his replacement by von Bardeleben, see Wegmann, *Verwaltungsbeamten*, pp. 137-38.
[34] STAD M1 IL Nr. 63.

The charges of fraud are less important than the changes between the 1858 elections and their predecessors in 1855. The earlier elections had set state against church (although a good part of the bureaucratic apparatus openly let their clerical sympathies show through); in 1858, the balloting was dominated by the prearranged agreement between district governor and bishop. *Landrat* von Wolff-Metternich, in 1855 aggressively hostile to the clerical candidates, applied his talents at intimidation and manipulation in their favor three years later. While there was no complete realignment in 1858, as all the electors could agree on one candidate, and local loyalties as well as ideological differences probably played a role in the contest between Schlüter and Grasso, the outline of a conflict between clerical and progressive elements with the state bureaucracy supporting the church, was clearly prefigured.

The open clash came three years later. A reapportionment of the electoral districts separated *Kreise* Paderborn and Büren from Warburg and Höxter, and joined them to *Kreis* Wiedenbrück, the new constituency to elect two deputies to the Prussian Parliament. Representatives of the "constitutional" and "democratic" parties in the constituency met in Lippstadt and agreed to work together and support the Berlin program of the Progressive Party. They nominated as their *Landtag* candidate Benedikt Waldeck, the leader of the Westphalian democracy in 1848-1849. The clergy denounced the left from the pulpit; the *Landrat* of *Kreis* Paderborn noted it was the liveliest election of the previous ten years. The clerical party was victorious, reelecting Schmidt with 191 electoral votes to Waldeck's 107 and 22 for other candidates, and then Hermann von Mallinckrodt with 158 to 103 for Waldeck

TABLE 3.3
Votes of the Electors in *Kreis* Paderborn, 1861

Vote	Signatories of Protest Letter 1858		Other Electors	
	No.	%	No.	%
Clerical	12	(41)	89	(80)
Progressive	15	(52)	22	(20)
Absent, abstained scattered	2	(7)	—	
Total	29	(100)	111	(100)

SOURCE: Petition signers, STAD M1 IL Nr. 63; electoral protocols of 1861, STAD M1 IL Nr. 67.

and 54 for others.[35] A much larger proportion of the former signatories of the fraud charges supported the Progressive candidate in 1861 than was the case with the other electors. See Table 3.3.

Tensions between clerical-conservatives and liberal-democrats, dating from the revolution, had been in abeyance during most of the 1850s, since the latter group took no part in politics, and church-state quarrels occupied what little political interest was present. The tentative return to a broader political life in 1858 might not have been accompanied by any open hostilities had *Landrat* von Metternich's clumsy attempts at electoral manipulation not brought these long-dormant tensions to the surface. By 1861, the informal antagonisms of three years previously had taken on organized shape. Proceedings in this southeastern Westphalian constituency embodied in spectacular form the typical course of events in the Catholic regions of Prussia's western provinces. Once the restrictive hand of the reaction era police state was removed and political forces allowed free play, a confrontation between clerical and progressive elements began to develop. The confrontation was already far advanced by 1861; following that year, events in Berlin would lead to an intensification of the conflict but would also introduce a new, distorting dimension to it.

THE CONFLICT ERA: 1862-1866

The 1861 elections to the Prussian Parliament were a major success for the Progressive Party and its allies. The new, more militant, left-wing parliamentary majority soon found itself in conflict with the ministry over plans for the reorganization of the army. No compromise could be reached, and the Parliament refused to ratify the yearly budget or pass an appropriations bill; the government went on collecting taxes without legislative approval. The conflict between royal authority and liberal legislature rendered the position of the "New Era" ministers impossible. One by one, they resigned or were replaced, a process culminating in the naming of Otto von Bismarck as Prussian Minister President in the fall of 1862. For the following four years, political life in Prussia was dominated by the struggle between the reactionary ministry and the liberal-progressive parliamentary majority.[36]

In the elections of 1862 and 1863 the government spared no efforts to defeat its parliamentary opponents and elect deputies favorable to its position. The provincial authorities in the Rhineland and West-

---

[35] Reports of the *Landräte* and the election results are in STAD M1 Pr. Nr. 259.

[36] Anderson, *Conflict in Prussia*, passim; Hess, *Das Parlament das Bismarck widerstrebte*, passim; Pflanze, *Bismarck*, pp. 156-230.

phalia had a more difficult time exerting official influence at the elections than their counterparts elsewhere in the monarchy. In the Catholic areas of the west, there were only two political groupings, "the party of the priests and the so-called liberals," as the Cologne District Governor cynically put it in 1858. Only the administrative bureaucracy could usually be counted on as reliably governmental.[37]

The Protestant minority, bulwark of the official candidacies in the mid-1850s, was, if anything, farther left than the Catholics, as the 1861 elections had shown. Progressives had swept the predominantly Protestant constituencies of the Minden District that year, in spite of an aggressive campaign by conservative elements, combining official support, Pietist religiosity, advocacy of the guild system, and anti-Semitic agitation. The electors from the Catholic *Kreise*, on the other hand, voted down the Progressive candidates and elected clerical deputies regarded as reliably conservative. Similar results were achieved in the Düsseldorf District, the constituencies on the right bank of the Rhine, either predominantly Protestant or with considerable Protestant minorities, voting for liberal and progressive deputies, while in most of the heavily Catholic constituencies on the left bank of the river, the liberal-progressive candidates went down to defeat.[38]

If the government wished to break the influence of the left in the Rhineland and Westphalia, it had no choice but to rely on the Catholics. On the eve of the 1862 elections, Interior Minister Gustav von Jagow sent a circular to all the provincial governors calling on them to ". . . work toward the greatest possible unification of all conservative elements . . . rally them under one flag as a great conservative party loyal to the constitution in order to fight their common enemy, the democrats, at the elections." The Minister of Educational and Religious Affairs then sent a copy of this circular to all the bishops in the Prussian monarchy, with the disarming comment that he had no desire to influence their political action, but merely wished to make clear the government's resolve to combat the left-wing tendencies revealed in the previous election.[39] The ministry thus gave its official approval to the informal alliance between local authorities and the clergy and Catholic notables which had existed in many areas since 1848. In doing so, the central government did not create a clash between liberal-progressive and clerical partisans; rather, it intervened

---

[37] Cited in Weinandy, "Die Wahlen des Regierungsbezirks Köln," p. 146; cf. the opinions of the *Landrat* of *Kreis* Gladbach in HSTAD RD Pr. Nr. 565 Bl. 32.

[38] See the reports of the *Landräte* on the 1861 elections in STAD M1 Pr. Nr. 259; HSTAD RD Pr. Nr. 565 esp. Bl. 257; Röttges, *Die politischen Wahlen*, pp. 229-49.

[39] Copies of the circulars (dated Mar. 23 and Mar. 26, 1862) are in STAM OP Nr. 500.

in favor of one side, in a situation where open antagonisms were already existent.

A large majority of the provincial bureaucracy and the subordinate lower officials proved eager to carry out the policy formulated in Berlin. For the Catholic *Landräte* and lower officials who had not been afraid to show their clerical sympathies in the mid-1850s, when ministry and hierarchy were in conflict, the new situation presented no difficulties since both temporal and spiritual authorities were in agreement. Loyalist officials, committed to following orders from Berlin, performed a soldierly about-face, as in the Eifel constituency Schleiden-Monschau-Malmedy (Aachen District), where the officials gave up their twelve-year alliance with the largely Protestant industrial interests in 1862 and suddenly supported the efforts of the clergy.[40]

The government had difficulties only where liberal sympathies persisted, chiefly in the upper ranks of the official hierarchy. Such sympathies were most apparent in Arnsberg, where the district officials were divided into hostile bureaucratic-liberal and clerical-conservative camps. District Governor Friedrich Wilhelm von Spankeren was openly sympathetic to the Progressives and opposed the clerical party at the 1861 and 1862 elections, justifying his actions as anti-ultramontanism. Led by the *Landrat* of *Kreis* Arnsberg, Felix Freiherr von Lilien, and the Provost Koop of the Arnsberg cathedral (who was also the official in charge of educational affairs for the Catholic population of the district), an opposing group of officials denounced Spankeren to his Berlin superiors, who dismissed him and transferred the liberal official Ziegert to Silesia. The following year, several Protestant clerks in the district office who voted against the Catholic-governmental candidates (defending themselves by claiming anti-ultramontanist motives) were severely rebuked and temporarily demoted.[41]

The firm alignment of the state apparatus did not suffice to reverse the trend begun in 1861, as the Progressives improved their position, capturing several seats previously held by the Catholic party and increasing their support even where they remained a minority. Voters showed themselves less inclined to respond to appeals from the pulpit

[40] Haas, "Die Wahlen im Regierungs-Bezirk Aachen," pp. 139-49. On the attitude of the bureaucracy in 1862-1863, see ibid., pp. 151-55; Röttges, *Die politischen Wahlen*, pp. 255-60, 267-71, 286-89, 293-94; HSTAD RD Pr. Nr. 565 Bl. 45; RPMI to OPM, Apr. 6, 1862; address of the *Landrat* of *Kreis* Arnsberg, printed as a supplement to Nr. 15 of the *Arnsberger Kreisblatt*, 1862, in STAM OP Nr. 500; RPMI to OPM, Nov. 2, 1863, STAM OP Nr. 501.

[41] On the affair, see STAM OP Nr. 2679 I and Nr. 2680 as well as Wegmann, *Verwaltungsbeamten*, p. 147. It was a common practice in the predominantly Catholic areas of the Prussian state for the authorities to name a priest to the district office post for the educational affairs of the Catholic inhabitants.

and in the Catholic press to defend endangered religion and turn back the rising tide of atheism and Freemasonry. Even the candidacy of Archbishop Geissel of Cologne proved fruitless. In the Rhenish constituency Grevenbroich-Neuß-Krefeld (country) (Düsseldorf District), he was defeated by the left-liberal Sartorius, 214 electoral votes to 178.[42]

The elections of the following year, at the very peak of the conflict, brought new victories for the Progressives and fresh defeats for the clerical party, but the mood on the Catholic side in 1863 was more resigned than combative. The Archbishop of Cologne was said to have ordered his clergy not to take part in electoral agitation. Many of the lower clergy would not have done so in any event, angered by the increasingly anti-Austrian tone of Bismarck's foreign policy.[43] The Bishop of Paderborn entered into negotiations with the new, conservative Arnsberg District Governor, von Holzbrinck, but appears to have changed his mind at the last minute. He issued no pastoral letter on the election, and, unlike previous years, the clergy of the diocese did not act in a unified fashion: some continued to uphold the alliance of throne and altar, while others withdrew into passivity. Only in the Diocese of Münster did a bishop lead a more or less united clergy in alliance with the ministry.[44]

Without the active backing of the clergy, the Catholic notables were ever more dependent on the support of the state apparatus. The once dominant Constantia, the Catholic political club in Aachen, managed barely twenty percent of the electoral votes, and that only because District Governor Friedrich Kühlwetter ordered all the officials to vote for its candidate. In the *Hochsauerland* constituency Arnsberg-Brilon-Lippstadt (Arnsberg District), the clerical-conservative symbiosis reached its peak. The official candidates were the scions of a bourgeois Catholic notable family, the Plaßmann brothers, one of whom was a state's attorney and the other an estate owner and area magistrate. Both had a long history of activity as clerical politicians; their clerical and con-

---

[42] Röttges, *Die politischen Wahlen*, pp. 267 ff.

[43] Haas, "Die Wahlen im Regierungs-Bezirk Aachen," pp. 151-55; similarly, in parts of Westphalia, STAM RAR I Pr. Nr. 90 Bl. 29.

[44] No records of the negotiations between bishop and district governor exist, but see STAM RAR I Pr. Nr. 90 Bl. 26-27, 29, 42-43, 55-75; STAM LA Kr. Meschede Nr. 505; the reports on the elections in the Minden and Münster Districts, STAM OP Nr. 501; and Röttges, *Die politischen Wahlen*, pp. 276-89. A similarly standoffish attitude can be observed among Catholic politicians. Burghard Freiherr von Schorlemer-Alst, founder of the Westphalian Peasant League, discreetly declined when asked to come to Berlin for a meeting of the Volksverein, the planned conservative mass political organization. See his letter to Provincial Governor Theodor von Duesberg, Sep. 13, 1863, STAM OP Nr. 501.

servative views remained firm over the years, leading them alternately into cooperation and conflict with the ministry as the latter changed its policies. In 1848-1849, as Catholic counterrevolutionaries, they were leaders of the forces of order in Westphalia, while their opposition to the Raumer decree and the church policies of the reactionary ministry led the authorities to denounce them as oppositional. The common struggle against the Progressives brought them onto the side of the government, but their pro-Austrian sympathies in 1866 would put them in opposition once more and earn the area magistrate Plaßmann official condemnation as the "leading ultramontane agitator in the Kreis."

In 1863 the Plaßmann brothers were at the height of their governmental respectability. Heavy pressure was applied to the officials, even the Protestant ones, to support their candidacy. At the meeting of the electors, Mayor Franz Wulff of Arnsberg and school principal Becker from Brilon, two long-time leaders of the Catholic party in the area, attacked the liberal candidate for his "lack of good Catholic sentiment"—a rather odd remark to make on behalf of a candidate backed by Bismarck's ministry. The electors were unconvinced, and the district returned two Progressives to the Prussian Parliament, a left-wing victory and clerical defeat previously unheard of, even in the revolutionary year 1849.[45]

Unlike the Protestant conservatives, Catholic politicians were not directly tied to the monarchy, and, beyond the largely fruitless alternatives of resignation or firm alliance with the reactionary ministry, they had the option of trying to reach agreement with the left, with the intent of electing Progressive deputies who would, however, be responsive to Catholic opposition to the introduction of secular public education, civil marriage, and a *kleindeutsch* program of German unification. Such an option was fraught with difficulties and impossible to carry out in practice, for it meant the clerical politicians would have to ask their supporters to do a complete about-face and vote for candidates previously denounced as atheists or Freemasons. Furthermore, it meant engaging in clerical politics without the help of the clergy. Priests might abstain from voting for the government's candidate, but supporting a left-wing candidate, even in the absence of ecclesiastical directives condemning such an action, was too much for

[45] On events in Aachen, see Haas, "Die Wahlen in Regierungs-Bezirk Aachen," pp. 154-55. The political history of the Plaßmann brothers can be traced through Schulte, *Volk und Staat*, p. 706; Hohmann, "Soester Konferenzen," p. 305; STAM RAR I Pr. Nr. 81 Bl. 269; STAM OP Nr. 495 Bl. 118-25; RAR to OPM, Sep. 4, 1858, STAM OP Nr. 500; STAM RAR I Nr. 1419 Bl. 166-69.

them. Only four of the approximately three hundred fifty Catholic priests in the Arnsberg District voted for Progressive electors in 1863.[46]

Attempts at Catholic realignment, embodied in the citizens' associations [Bürgervereine] of Cologne and Münster, were manifest failures. In 1862, the Cologne Catholic notables had taken a militant stand, proclaimed the election a struggle of faith against disbelief, and watched the Progressives win an overwhelming victory. The following year, clerical elements reorganized themselves into a citizens' association and announced that they would support candidates upholding the constitution against the government. Once again, the Progressives were victorious, but, rather than reflecting Catholic interests, they showed in their campaign a growing anti-clericalism. A change in ownership had turned Münster's leading daily, the *Westfälische Merkur*, from a clerical-conservative to a liberal editorial policy. With the journal's support, Catholic businessmen of the city and former 1848 democrats united in a citizens' association to support Progressive candidates espousing a *grossdeutsch* program of national unification. The Bishop of Münster remained firmly committed to the conservative-clerical alliance, and the lower clergy followed his directives. The citizens' association was helpless; sixty percent of Münster's electors voted for the Catholic-conservative candidates, and they were re-elected.[47]

In the less-structured political atmosphere of rural and small town constituencies, liberals and clericals could achieve a certain cooperation. The electors of the constituency Beckum-Lüdinghausen-Warendorf (Münster District) met in a tavern the day before the elections and quizzed the incumbent clerical deputy *Schulze* Hobbeling, a well-respected local farmer. Hobbeling explained to them that he would vote against the ministry's plans for army reorganization, for the parliament's right to determine the budget, and against the reactionary press decree of June 1863. The electors voted him in the next day by a small margin over the Progressive candidate, Viersen, a judge on the Superior Court of Appeals in Hamm, but in the balloting for the second deputy for the constituency several electors switched their votes so that Viersen was elected over the conservative-clerical *Schulze* Geisthövel.[48]

---

[46] STAM RAR I Pr. Nr. 90 Bl. 79-80, 99 ff.

[47] On the citizens' association in Cologne, see Denk, "Die Wahlen in Köln," pp. 149-64; Haas, "Die Wahlen im Regierungs-Bezirk Aachen," p. 151; *Kölnische Zeitung*, Sep. 30, 1863. Its Münster counterpart can be traced through STAM RM Nr. 1175 Bl. 185-90; survey of the press in 1863 in STAM OP Nr. 97; reports on the elections in STAM OP Nr. 501 and STDM Stadtregistratur Fach 9 Nr. 5; *Kölnische Zeitung*, Sep. 9, Oct. 1, 1863 and Mar. 3, 1864.

[48] *Der Patriot* (Lippstadt) Nov. 4, 1863, copy in STAM RAR I Pr. Nr. 90 Bl. 172-

The one constituency in the entire Rhineland and Westphalia where clerical and liberal partisans successfully put up a joint candidate was the *Kreis* Gladbach (Düsseldorf District). Even there, however, more and more liberal electors were chosen in each successive election in the early 1860s and fewer and fewer priests or other sympathizers with the Catholic party. The decline in their strength made the Catholics uneasy, but in spite of considerable tension between them and the liberals there was never a split. This exceptional result was the consequence of the unusual attitude of the *Landrat* of *Kreis* Gladbach, who noted that in his *Kreis*, as elsewhere in the western provinces, there was no one who would support a conservative party; attempting to form one would only "put the administration in a compromising position." Officials elsewhere in the Rhineland and Westphalia frequently made similar observations on the balance of political forces; unlike them, Gladbach's *Landrat* regarded the "existing confessional relationships" as making it "inappropriate to call on the clerical party and in particular the Catholic clergy for help." Since the *Landrat*'s superiors in Düsseldorf did not order him to change his policy and do what the authorities did without trouble everywhere else on the lower Rhine—namely, cooperate with the Catholic party against the liberals—this official abstention saved the Catholic-liberal alliance in this one *Kreis* in all of Prussia's western provinces.[49]

THE STRUCTURE OF POLITICS IN THE EARLY 1860S

The years 1862-1866 were a second and final high point of left-wing influence in the Catholic areas of the Rhineland and Westphalia. Using all the resources open to them in the context of notables' politics, the progressive partisans were able to obtain a majority of the parliamentary seats from the predominantly Catholic constituencies in the Rhineland and Westphalia. Exploiting remnants of *Vormärz* lay-cler-

---

75; LA Kr. Beckum to RM, Oct. 30, 1863, STAM RM Nr. VII-68; RM to LA Kr. Beckum and LA Kr. Warendorf, Nov. 6, 1863, STAM OP Nr. 501. On an apparently similar occurrence in the constituency Borken-Recklinghausen (Münster District), see Pülke, "*Kreis* Recklinghausen," pp. 98-104.

[49] Röttges, *Die politischen Wahlen*, pp. 246, 272-74, 291-92; HSTAD RD Pr. Nr. 565 Bl. 32. There is a twofold explanation for the unique position of the *Landrat* of *Kreis* Gladbach. (1) Close connections between the *Landratsamt* in Mönchengladbach and Protestant industrialists in the *Kreis* (see the documents on the selection of a new *Landrat* in 1871, HSTAD RD Pr. Nr. 1612), which made the *Landrat* reluctant to stir up the largely artisan and proletarian Catholic population against the liberal industrialists and (2) liberal and anti-clerical sympathies among the Düsseldorf district officials, who probably shared the *Landrat*'s position but did not dare express such sentiments in the conflict era; after 1867 and during the *Kulturkampf*, however, their opinions would emerge quite clearly.

ical conflict, they were able to defuse religion as a political issue and convince electors to support their political program centered around opposition to the authoritarian policies of the Berlin ministry, and support for measures to ensure dynamic, capitalist economic growth. These left-wing successes were threatening to the political position of the clergy and the Catholic notables and, for some more apocalyptically minded among them, portents of an imminent collapse of Christian civilization. When the background of the religious revival is kept in mind, the shallowness of the liberal initiative becomes apparent, its success dependent on a unique combination of specific parliamentary conditions and the limitations of notables' politics.

Social and Regional Bases of Clerical and Liberal Support

Protocols of the election of deputies from several rural Westphalian constituencies in 1862 are extant, and an analysis of them shows the social composition of the competing liberal and clerical elites. The *Kreis* Meschede (Arnsberg District) was a liberal-democratic stronghold in the clerical and conservative *Hochsauerland*. A majority of the electors from the *Kreis* had cast their ballots for a Progressive deputy in 1861 and 1862 but had been outvoted in both years by the larger clerical majorities of the neighboring *Kreis* Olpe, with which *Kreis* Meschede formed a parliamentary constituency. Each year the margin was smaller, and in 1863 the Progressive candidate was finally elected. See Table 3.4.

Merchants, industrialists (with their employees), and innkeepers made up forty percent of the liberal electors, while peasants, nobles, and estate owners made up sixty percent of their clerical counterparts. The towns of the *Kreis* and the rural mining and metallurgical districts selected liberal electors, while a majority of the electors chosen elsewhere voted for the Catholic candidate. Yet this opposition—urban-industrial-liberal, rural-agricultural-clerical—seems a little too facile. A majority of the large farmers and the village foremen (usually well-off agriculturalists) serving as electors voted for the liberal candidates, as did about half the peasants. The liberal success was not confined exclusively to the urban-industrial sector of society, as can be seen by considering another constituency without any industrial development whatever.

The electors of the constituency Warburg-Höxter voted in 1862 for the liberal city councillor Lorenz from Beverungen over the clerical judge Hermann Evers, 158 to 122, but then turned around and after two ballots selected Evers as the second deputy from the constituency

TABLE 3.4
Social Composition of the Electors
in *Kreis* Meschede, 1862

Social Group	Clerical No.	Clerical %	Liberal No.	Liberal %	All No.	All %
Noble, owner of noble estate[a]	4	(7.5)	1	(1.6)	5	(4.3)
Non-noble estate owner, estate tenant or large farmer[b]	13	(24.5)	16	(25.8)	29	(25.2)
Peasant[c]	14	(26.4)	11	(17.7)	25	(21.7)
Merchant	2	(3.8)	7	(11.3)	9	(7.8)
Industrialist	1	(1.9)	4			
Other industrial personnel[d]	—	—	7	(17.7)	12	(10.4)
Retailer or innkeeper	2	(3.8)	6	(9.7)	8	(7.0)
Artisan	—	—	2	(3.2)	2	(1.7)
Professional	2	(3.8)	1	(1.6)	3	(2.6)
Official	4	(7.5)	3	(4.8)	7	(6.1)
Village foreman	3	(5.7)	4	(6.5)	7	(6.1)
Clergy	8	(15.1)	—	—	8	(7.0)
Total electors	53	(100.0)	62	(99.9)	115	(99.9)

[a] *Rittergutsbesitzer.*
[b] *Gutsbesitzer, Gutspächter, Oeconom.*
[c] *Ackerer, Ackerswirth, Ackersmann, Landwirth.*
[d] Includes foremen, engineers, and clerks employed by the mine owners and industrialists of the *Kreis.*
SOURCE: Rough draft of the electoral protocols in STAM LA Kr. Meschede Nr. 479.
NOTE: One elector, a peasant, voted for neither the clerical nor the liberal candidate.

over the liberal estate owner Derenthal, 141 to 132. This peculiar turn of events was, as the district governor discreetly noted, "the consequence of accidents and the clumsy . . . operations of certain influential personalities. . . ." What apparently had happened was that the *Landrat* of *Kreis* Höxter, Friedrich Freiherr von Wolff-Metternich, not the most tactful of individuals, had succeeded in some way in offending both the *Landrat* of *Kreis* Warburg and the commander of the Höxter garrison, so that they and several electors under their influence voted on the first ballot against Metternich's candidate. Seeing what results these quarrels led to, the officials patched up their differences in time to defeat the second liberal candidate. In parliament, Lorenz joined the Bockum-Dolffs caucus—the left-liberal allies of the Progressives—and stood for reelection in 1863 as such. In a clear confrontation between liberals and clerical-conservatives he went down to defeat against two different Catholic candidates by votes of 144 to 122 and 144 to 124. Thus, in spite of the personal rivalries present on the first ballot in 1862, the vote on the second ballot gives a good idea of the relative strength of the liberal and clerical elements in the constituency.[50] See Table 3.5.

In *Kreis* Höxter the farmer and peasant electors were split about equally between the liberal and clerical candidates, while in *Kreis* Warburg they voted liberal by a large majority. Urban and commercial electors—merchants, artisans, retailers, and professionals—divided their votes evenly, except for the tavern keepers, who were, not surprisingly, strongly liberal. With a few exceptions in *Kreis* Warburg, the clergy was not at all affected by the personal rivalries among the local leaders of the forces of order and voted solidly for the clerical candidates. The bureaucracy, on the other hand, was divided. Personal rivalries aside (the position of the *Landrat* of *Kreis* Warburg was no doubt the reason for the large number of officials in his *Kreis* splitting their ballots), the decisive element here, as elsewhere in Rhineland-Westphalia, and, indeed, in all of Prussia, was the liberal sympathies of the judiciary and their (at least theoretical) freedom from reprisal for their votes. The converse to the liberal judges and court employees was a group of clerical-conservative schoolteachers, area magistrates, foresters, and gendarmes.[51]

It is possible to approach the question of the social composition of the electorate from another angle. The 1862 electoral protocols also recorded which of the three classes of voters selected each of the electors. Although the connection between voters and electors in an indirect voting system is, admittedly, somewhat tenuous, an interesting pattern emerges. The electors selected by the wealthiest voters in the district were the most likely to vote for the liberal candidate; those selected by the poorest the least likely. In Warburg-Höxter, liberalism

[50] RPMI to OPM, May 17, 1862 and Mar. 2, 1863, STAM OP Nr. 501 and LA Kr. Warburg to RPMI, Oct. 22, 1863, STAD M1 Pr. Nr. 259.

[51] For similar examples of this contrast, see HSTAD RD Pr. Nr. 565 Bl. 45; STAM RAR I Pr. Nr. 90 Bl. 178-83; Anderson, *Conflict in Prussia*, pp. 287-91. The three officers of the Höxter garrison serving as electors cast their votes for both liberal candidates, not returning to the clerical-conservative candidate on the second ballot as did the *Landrat* of *Kreis* Warburg and his subordinates. Was this action simply a mistake, the result of a violent personal antipathy toward *Landrat* Metternich of *Kreis* Höxter, Protestant hostility toward Catholics, or liberal tendencies on the part of the officers of the garrison? The available sources provide no answer.

TABLE 3.5
Social Composition of The Electors in Warburg-Höxter, 1862

Social Group	Clerical		Liberal		Vote Split		Other		All	
	No.	%	No.	%	No.	%	No.	%	No.	%

Kreis Höxter

Social Group	Clerical No.	%	Liberal No.	%	Split No.	%	Other No.	%	All No.	%
Noble, estate-owner	5	(5.4)	3	(4.7)	1	(8.3)	—		9	(4.9)
Large farmer[a]	6	(6.5)	8	(12.5)	4	(33.3)	1	(6.7)	19	(10.4)
Peasant[b]	6	(6.5)	9	(14.1)	2	(16.7)	2	(13.3)	19	(10.4)
Merchant, rentier	4	(4.3)	1	(1.6)	1	(8.3)	2	(13.3)	8	(4.4)
Artisan	3	(3.3)	4	(6.3)	—		2	(13.3)	9	(4.9)
Retailer-innkeeper	1	(1.1)	4	(6.3)	1	(8.3)	1	(6.7)	7	(3.8)
Upper level official	1	(1.1)	11	(17.2)	—		1	(6.7)	13	(7.1)
Middle, lower official	17	(18.5)	3	(4.7)	—		1	(6.7)	21	(11.5)
Local government[c]	13	(14.1)	16	(25.0)	3	(25.0)	1	(6.7)	33	(18.0)
Professional	1	(1.1)	3	(4.7)	—		—		4	(2.2)
Clergy	34	(37.0)	—		—		2	(13.3)	36	(19.7)
Other, unknown	1	(1.1)	2	(3.1)	—		2	(13.3)	5	(2.7)
Total electors	92	(100.0)	64	(100.2)	12	(99.9)	15	(100.0)	183	(100.0)

Kreis Warburg

Social Group	Clerical No.	%	Liberal No.	%	Split No.	%	Other No.	%	All No.	%
Noble, estate-owner	—		2	(3.2)	—		—		2	(1.7)
Large farmer[a]	1	(2.9)	12	(19.4)	1	(4.8)	—		14	(11.8)
Peasant[b]	2	(5.9)	20	(32.3)	8	(38.1)	—		30	(25.2)
Merchant, rentier	1	(2.9)	4	(6.5)	—		—		5	(4.2)
Artisan	—		2	(3.2)	—		—		2	(1.7)
Retailer-innkeeper	2	(5.9)	9	(14.5)	—		—		11	(9.2)
Upper level official	3	(8.8)	2	(3.2)	4	(19.0)	—		9	(7.6)
Middle, lower official	3	(8.8)	1	(1.6)	2	(9.5)	—		6	(5.0)
Local government[c]	2	(5.9)	8	(12.9)	4	(19.0)	— Cut He		14	(11.8)

TABLE 3.5 (cont.)

Social	Clerical		Liberal		Vote Split		Other		All	
Group	No.	%	No.	%	No.	%	No.	%	No.	%
Professional	2	(5.9)	2	(3.2)	—		—		4	(3.4)
Clergy	18	(52.9)	—		2	(9.5)	2	(100.0)	22	(18.5)
Total electors	34	(99.9)	62	(100.0)	21	(99.9)	2	(100.0)	119	(100.1)

[a] Oeconom, Gutspächter.
[b] Ackerer, Ackersmann, Ackerswirth.
[c] Village foremen, mayors and members of city councils.
SOURCE: Election protocols in STAD Ml IL Nr. 71.

TABLE 3.6
Votes of the Electors in Warburg-Höxter, 1862

	Class in Which Elected					
	First		Second		Third	
Vote	N	%	N	%	N	%
	Kreis Höxter					
Clerical	24	(39.3)	32	(52.5)	36	(59.0)
Liberal	27	(44.2)	19	(31.1)	18	(29.5)
Split	4	(6.6)	7	(11.5)	1	(1.6)
Other	6	(9.8)	3	(4.9)	6	(9.8)
Total Electors	61	(99.9)	61	(100.0)	61	(99.9)
	Kreis Warburg					
Clerical	4	(9.8)	10	(27.0)	20	(48.8)
Liberal	28	(68.3)	16	(43.2)	18	(43.9)
Split	8	(19.5)	10	(27.0)	3	(7.3)
Other	1	(2.4)	1	(2.7)	—	—
Total Electors	41	(100.0)	37	(99.9)	41	(100.0)

SOURCE: Election protocols in STAD M1 IL Nr. 71.

appeared as the political expression of the most affluent, non-noble members of rural society. See Table 3.6.

In *Kreis* Meschede, the liberals had the upper hand throughout the first half of the 1860s; in Warburg-Höxter, liberal and clerical elements were about evenly matched; but the deputies from the neighboring constituency Büren-Wiedenbrück-Paderborn remained clerical throughout the conflict era. A study of the social composition of the electorate in this district reveals a third pattern, different from the previous two. See Table 3.7. In this constituency a majority of both the rural and urban electors supported clerical candidates. Even most of the innkeeper electors, elsewhere a bulwark of the left, voted for the Catholic party. Centers of the (admittedly feeble) liberal strength varied. The upper classes of the city of Paderborn—merchants, professionals, judicial officials—led by the 1848 democrat, attorney Kroenig, supported the Progressives, while the artisanate was firmly clerical. The same was true in *Kreis* Wiedenbrück, and the liberals did better there in the towns than in the countryside, but, as in *Kreis* Büren, a definite minority of the rural electors possessed liberal sympathies.[52] Unlike Warburg-Höxter, in these *Kreise* a majority of the electors from all classes supported the candidates of the clerical party. Nevertheless, the liberal minority was strongest among the representatives of the most affluent voters, except in *Kreis* Büren, where, however, the number of liberal electors was very small. See Table 3.8.

Election protocols from large urban constituencies do not seem to have survived, so less definite information about the social composition of the competing parties is available than in the countryside and small towns. Contemporary accounts and modern historians have usually seen the liberals as having their strength among the upper bourgeoisie of entrepreneurs and professional men, and the Catholic party having its primary base of support in the artisanate. These differences would correspond roughly with the confessional structure of many Rhenish and Westphalian cities: the over-representation of Protestants and Jews in the upper classes and Catholics in the lower.[53]

The only quantitative evidence I have been able to find is the membership lists of the Catholic political club in Aachen, the Constantia, and the opposing liberal electoral association from the years 1865-1866. Of all the cities in the Rhineland and Westphalia, Aachen had the largest and most cohesive Catholic bourgeoisie and the membership figures reflect this. Even in Aachen, though, the liberals were noticeably more grand-bourgeois than their clerical rivals. See Table 3.9.

Organized liberalism in Aachen was overwhelmingly capitalist in

---

[52] The towns of Gütersloh and Rheda in *Kreis* Wiedenbrück were predominantly Protestant, and the electors selected there have not been included in this analysis. Unlike almost everywhere else in the west, the Protestant conservatives of *Kreis* Wiedenbrück supported the clerical candidates in 1862.

[53] See, for instance, the report on the elections in Cologne, *Kölnische Zeitung*, Nov. 21, 1861 and in Münster, Nov. 22, 1861; HSTAD RD Pr. Nr. 866 Bl. 46; van Eyll, "Wirtschaftsgeschichte Kölns," 2: 165; Röttges, *Die politischen Wahlen*, pp. 224-27; Kaiser, *Die politischen Strömungen*, pp. 139-50, 191-213.

TABLE 3.7

Social Composition of the Electors in Büren-Wiedenbrück-Paderborn, 1862

	Vote							
	Clerical		Liberal		Other		All	
Social Group	No.	%	No.	%	No.	%	No.	%
Kreis Büren								
Noble, estate-owner	7	(6.3)	1	(4.5)	—		8	(5.8)
Large farmer[a]	4	(3.8)	1	(4.5)	—		5	(3.6)
Peasant[b]	15	(13.4)	12	(54.5)	—		27	(19.6)
Merchant, rentier	4	(3.8)	1	(4.5)	1	(25.0)	6	(4.3)
Retailer, innkeeper	6	(5.4)	1	(4.5)	—		7	(5.1)
Artisan	2	(1.8)	—		—		2	(1.4)
Upper level official	3	(2.7)	1	(4.5)	—		4	(2.9)
Middle, lower official	21	(18.8)	—		1	(25.0)	22	(15.9)
Local government[c]	17	(15.2)	5	(22.7)	2	(50.0)	24	(17.4)
Professional	2	(1.8)	—		—		2	(1.4)
Clergy	30	(26.8)	—		—		30	(21.7)
Other, unknown	1	(0.9)	—		—		1	(0.7)
Total electors	112	(100.7)	22	(99.7)	4	(100.0)	138	(99.8)
Kreis Paderborn								
Noble, estate-owner	4	(3.8)	—		1	(20.0)	5	(3.4)
Large farmer[a]	25	(24.0)	6	(15.4)	3	(60.0)	34	(23.0)
Peasant[b]	10	(9.6)	2	(5.1)	—		12	(8.1)
Merchant, rentier	6	(5.8)	8	(20.5)	—		14	(9.5)
Retailer, innkeeper	5	(4.8)	4	(10.3)	1	(20.0)	10	(6.8)
Artisan	12	(11.5)	3	(7.7)	—		15	(10.1)
Upper level official	6	(5.8)	4	(10.3)	—		10	(6.8)
Middle, lower official	5	(4.8)	2	(5.1)	—		7	(4.7)
Local government[c]	4	(3.8)	5	(12.8)	—		9	(6.1)
Professional	1	(1.0)	5	(12.8)	—		6	(4.1)
Clergy	23	(22.1)	—		—		23	(15.5)

TABLE 3.7 (*cont.*)

Social Group	Vote							
	Clerical		Liberal		Other		All	
	No.	%	No.	%	No.	%	No.	%
Other, unknown	3	(2.9)	—		—		3	(2.0)
Total electors	104	(99.9)	39	(100.0)	5	(100.0)	148	(100.1)
Kreis Wiedenbrück								
Noble, estate-owner	1	(1.2)	—		—		1	(0.8)
Large farmer[a]	41	(50.0)	20	(47.6)	4	(57.1)	65	(49.6)
Peasant[b]	4	(4.9)	1	(2.4)	2	(28.6)	7	(5.3)
Merchant, rentier	4	(4.9)	6	(14.3)	—		10	(7.6)
Retailer, innkeeper	3	(3.7)	5	(11.9)	—		8	(6.1)
Artisan	5	(6.1)	2	(4.8)	—		7	(5.3)
Upper level official	1	(1.2)	1	(2.4)	—		2	(1.5)
Middle, lower official	3	(3.7)	2	(4.8)	—		5	(3.8)
Local government[c]	4	(4.9)	1	(2.4)	1	(14.3)	6	(4.6)
Professional	2	(2.4)	2	(4.8)	—		4	(3.1)
Clergy	13	(15.9)	—		—		13	(9.9)
Other, unknown	1	(1.2)	2	(4.8)	—		3	(2.3)
Total electors	82	(100.1)	42	(100.2)	7	(100.0)	131	(99.9)

[a] *Oeconom, Gutspächter, Colon, Meier, Vollmeier.*
[b] *Ackerer, Ackersmann, Ackerswirth, Halbmeier, Neubauer, Kötter.*
[c] Mayors, village foremen and city council members.
SOURCE: Election protocols in STAD M1 IL Nr. 72.

nature. Fifty-six percent of the members of the liberal electoral association were merchants or industrialists. Their Catholic counterparts were themselves respectably bourgeois, if not so heavily capitalist. Under one-third of the Constantia's membership was composed of the lower middle class of artisans and retailers. Indeed, a majority of the politically organized retailers and a large minority of their artisan counterparts in Aachen were partisans of liberalism.

With the help of another document, the class composition of the two lists can be ascertained more exactly. In an annex to the 1858 industrial census a list was drawn up of all the factories in the city of

TABLE 3.8
Votes of the Electors in Büren-Wiedenbrück-Paderborn, 1862

	Class in Which Elected					
	First		Second		Third	
Vote	No.	%	No.	%	No.	%
Kreis Paderborn						
Clerical	27	(57.4)	36	(66.7)	41	(87.2)
Liberal	19	(40.4)	16	(29.6)	4	(8.5)
Other	1	(2.1)	2	(3.7)	2	(4.3)
All	47	(99.9)	54	(100.0)	47	(100.0)
Kreis Wiedenbrück						
Clerical	22	(55.0)	25	(58.1)	35	(72.9)
Liberal	17	(42.5)	15	(34.9)	10	(20.8)
Other	1	(2.5)	3	(7.0)	3	(6.3)
All	40	(100.0)	43	(100.0)	48	(100.0)
Kreis Büren						
Clerical	33	(80.5)	43	(76.8)	36	(87.8)
Liberal	7	(17.1)	10	(17.9)	5	(12.2)
Other	1	(2.4)	3	(5.4)	—	
All	41	(100.0)	56	(100.1)	41	(100.0)

SOURCE: Election protocols in STAD M1 IL Nr. 72.

Aachen and in *Landkreis* Aachen employing over fifty workers.[54] There were eighty-nine such factories, nine owned by corporations, the remainder in private hands. Of the eighty privately owned factories, it has proved possible to trace the 1865-1866 political affiliations of forty-three of their owners. Thirty-eight belonged to the liberal electoral association and only five to the Constantia.[55] The overwhelming majority of politically active large capitalist entrepreneurs in Aachen were liberals; among the politically active industrialists a much larger proportion of the liberals were big businessmen. The bulk of the clerical industrialists seem to have owned smaller establishments employing under fifty workers, not comparable to a major capitalist enter-

[54] HSTAD RA Nr. 372, annex to the *Gewerbezählung* of 1858.

[55] There were only forty-two factories involved, for Christian and Peter Thywissen of "Thywissen Brothers" textile mill were in the Constantia, but their brother, Eduard Thywissen, was a liberal. Unfortunately, it is not possible to trace the political associations of the corporate executives; most were probably liberals.

TABLE 3.9

Social Composition of the Membership of
Liberal and Clerical Associations in Aachen, 1865-1866

Social Group	Constantia		Liberal Electoral Association	
	No.	%	No.	%
Industrialists	28	(14.0)	82	(23.8)
Merchants	35	(17.4)	107	(31.1)
Rentiers	15	(7.5)	20	(5.8)
Professionals and journalists	19	(9.5)	34	(9.9)
Officials (including local government)	12	(6.0)	—	—
Retailers	19	(9.5)	30	(8.7)
Artisans	37	(18.4)	26	(7.6)
Salaried employees	12	(6.0)	13	(3.8)
Clergy	12	(6.0)	—	—
Other, unknown	12	(6.0)	32	(9.3)
Total members	201	(100.3)	344	(100.0)

SOURCE: HSTAD RA Pr. Nr. 703 Bl. 98-100, 149-58.

prise.[56] Since the membership lists do not record confession, it is impossible to say whether almost all the large entrepreneurs and political liberals in Aachen were Protestants and Jews, or whether their ranks included nominally Catholic big businessmen who had turned their backs on clericalism.

In both rural and urban examples it would seem that the local partisans of liberalism were among the more affluent inhabitants, perhaps also those more oriented toward a capitalist market economy. This did not necessarily mean the urban population of a region; sometimes the larger, affluent farmers were liberals, while the craftsmen and petty merchants of the towns were clerical sympathizers. The observations of the administrative bureaucracy tend to support this contention. The "main leader of the democracy" in *Kreis* Beckum (Münster District) was the estate owner Bernhard von Bruchhausen,

[56] Since there is a seven-year gap between the two lists, it was possible for firms to have gone out of business in the interval, to have changed hands, for new ones to have been founded, for owners to have died or moved away, etc. This clearly happened, but there is no reason to think that it should have affected the clerical industrialists more than the liberal ones.

a man "with great influence over many peasants in the *Kreis*." An area magistrate in *Landkreis* Krefeld, a stronghold of rural liberalism on the lower Rhine, made a similar observation, noting that the peasants there had always supported local notables whom they knew and trusted. In *Kreis* Meschede, the *Landrat* blamed the notables for the Progressive electoral victory in 1863. Leaders of the left included the merchants Schaffer and Eickhoff in Meschede; the affluent farmers Wiese and Meschede, who lived near Velmede; and the "blood-red" mine director Canaris, living in "red Attendorn," a town in the neighboring *Kreis* Olpe. The *Landrat* concluded that "the population of the *Kreis* is basically conservative but is led astray by the more intelligent element who are supporters of the democracy."[57]

The *Landrat*'s observation raises a fundamental question for the historian. Why were the liberal notables so successful in gaining political support in Catholic areas during the 1860s and not at other times? Why were their efforts more successful in some places than others? The usual scholarly answer to these questions is that the decisive element in determining Catholic electoral behavior was not religion as such but hostility to the Protestant Prussian state. When the clerical party was in opposition to the state, in the 1850s and during the *Kulturkampf*, Catholics voted for it, but in the 1860s, when a majority of the clerical politicians supported the Berlin government, Catholic voters abandoned them for the oppositional liberals. Clerical deputies could hope to be elected only if they stressed their opposition to the politics of the reactionary ministry.[58] This thesis, although not without at least a superficial justification, is basically misdirected. It confuses support for the clerical cause with opposition to the government, political orientation in the Berlin parliament with party alignment at the local level, and it makes unproved and probably false assertions about voting behavior.

Where support for the Progressives was strong during the 1860s, putting up anti-governmental Catholic candidates led to nothing, as was shown by the failure of the Cologne citizens' association in 1863

[57] LA Kr. Beckum to RM, Dec. 13, 1862, STAM RM Nr. 260; HSTAD RD Pr. Nr. 566 Bl. 59; STAM RAR I Pr. Nr. 90 Bl. 87-91. The use of the adjective "red" to describe Attendorn is, of course, an exaggeration, but not without all basis in reality. Attendorn had been a democratic stronghold in 1848-1849, a Progressive center in the 1860s, and remained a stronghold of liberalism and religious hetorodoxy well into the *Kulturkampf* era.

[58] This explanation was first propounded by Hermann Wendorf in his 1910 thesis on the Catholic caucus in the Prussian Parliament. Its main proponents have been the students of Max Braubach, whose work has remained largely unpublished. A convenient summary can be found in Müller, "Das Rheinland."

and a similar but equally unsuccessful effort in Bonn that year.[59] In a clerical stronghold, such as the constituency Büren-Wiedenbrück-Paderborn, dissatisfaction with an overly pro-governmental deputy led to the election, not of a Progressive, but of a more anti-governmental Catholic. In 1863, the clerical electors denounced their representative, the prominent and very conservative Catholic politician Hermann von Mallinckrodt, for "taking the position of the extreme right in many instances and not having voted with the [Catholic] caucus on important roll calls." Rather than voting for the Progressive candidate, Striethorst, the majority of the clerical electors nominated the previously unknown estate owner Kleinschmidt, who was elected and duly joined the Catholic caucus in the *Landtag*.[60]

Secondly, all the clerical deputies elected in the northern Rhineland and Westphalia in 1863—in the Minden District, the western half of the Münster District and the northernmost constituencies on the lower Rhine, with a few differences, the same areas in which conservative-clerical candidates were elected in January 1849—stood as official candidates with the help and backing of the state apparatus. Regardless of their positions in the Prussian constitutional conflict, their candidacies in the local arena embodied all the forces of order and opposition to radicalism in the conflict era.

Finally, there is little evidence to support the notion of a crossover of voters from clerical in the 1850s to liberal in the following decade, and a good deal standing against it. In Aachen, there was almost no transfer of membership from the Constantia to the liberal electoral association. Of the 135 members of the Constantia in 1856, only three were organized supporters of the liberals nine years later.[61] For the *Kreise* Warburg, Höxter, Büren, and Paderborn, we can consider the votes of the majority of electors in each precinct (Stimmbezirk) in 1855 and see how the majority from the same precinct voted in 1862. See Tables 3.10 and 3.11.

The clerical precincts of 1855 were by and large the clerical precincts of 1862, while the governmental or mixed precincts of 1855 were the most likely to be liberal in 1862. Protestant enclaves, such as the town of Höxter, strongly governmental during the reaction era, were usually supporters of the left in the 1860s. The continuity is even more striking at the individual level. It is possible to compare the votes of individuals

---

[59] See above, n. 44, and Kaiser, *Die politischen Strömungen*, pp. 191-213.

[60] RPMI to OPM, Nov. 2, 1863, STAM OP Nr. 501.

[61] 1866 Constantia membership list, HSTAD RA Pr. Nr. 780; 1865 membership list of the liberal electoral association, HSTAD RA Pr. Nr. 703 Bl. 149-58. Given the very low turnouts in these elections, the association members were not just the leaders of political life, but the bulk of the participants in it.

TABLE 3.10
Precinct-Level Voting of the Electors in *Kreise*
Warburg and Höxter, 1855 and 1862

Precincts 1855 Majorities	Precincts 1862 Majorities			
	Clerical	Liberal	Neither[a]	Total
Kreis Warburg				
Clerical	3	2	1	6
Governmental	1	3	2	6
Neither[a]	3	5	1	9
Total	7	10	4	21
Kreis Höxter				
Clerical	11	6	—	17
Governmental	1	3	—	4
Neither[a]	4	3	1	8
Total	16	12	1	29

[a] Precincts where a majority of the electors either split their ballots, abstained or where no majority for any particular course of action was present.

NOTE: Because of changes in the precinct boundaries between 1855 and 1862 not all precincts could be compared.

SOURCE: Electoral protocols in STAD M1 IL Nr. 59, 71, 72.

who were electors in both 1855 and 1862. "Oppositional" clerical electors in 1855 were "governmental" clerical electors in 1862. The dominant factor in their voting behavior was not the policy of the Prussian government, but loyalty to the Catholic church and the political party which represented it. See Table 3.12.

The geographical stability of the non-clerical precincts coincided with a sociological transformation of their electors.[62] While in 1855 the authorities could successfully pressure the electors from the non-clerical precincts—village foremen and lesser officials—into voting for the official candidate, or, at least, into splitting their ballots, in 1862 these districts chose as electors affluent farmers, merchants, innkeepers, or judicial officials ready to vote for a liberal deputy. The sociological composition of the clerical electors, on the other hand, remained more or less constant: they were predominantly clergy and lower officials (especially schoolteachers), to a lesser extent artisans and peasants.

[62] It is interesting to note that a much smaller proportion of the liberal, as compared to the clerical, electors had been chosen in 1855. The left had called for electoral abstention in that year.

TABLE 3.11
Precinct-Level Voting of the Electors in *Kreise*
Paderborn and Büren, 1855 and 1862

Precincts 1855 Majorities	Precincts 1862				
	Unanimously Clerical	Majority Clerical	Majority Liberal	Neither[a]	Total
Kreis Paderborn					
Clerical	10	2	—	—	12
Governmental	—	—	—	—	—
Neither[a]	3	4	1	—	8
Total	13	6	1	—	20
Kreis Büren					
Clerical	15	3	3	1	22
Governmental	—	—	—	—	—
Neither[a]	4	—	2	—	6
Total	19	3	5	1	28

[a] Precincts where a majority of the electors either split their ballots, abstained or where no majority for any particular course of action was present.
NOTE: Because of changes in the precinct boundaries between 1855 and 1862 not all precincts could be compared.
SOURCE: Electoral protocols in STAD M1 IL Nr. 59, 71, 72.

The number and proportion of priests selected as electors in these *Kreise* in the early 1860s did not decline, in comparison with 1855. The rural parish priest had not lost anything of his standing and authority; the villagers routinely selected him as their representative. Unlike the reaction era, however, during the 1860s many of the other electors chosen along with the priest did not follow his lead but were convinced or pressured into voting for the liberal candidates. What was the reason for this change?

The same social groups denounced by the clergy for their secular tendencies were also the bearers of liberalism. Innkeepers usually stood noticeably to the left. The Meschede bourgeoisie or the bourgeois Jülich Freemasons, noted as a center of hostility to the missions or as one of secularizing influences in the early 1850s, emerged in the following decade as Progressive supporters. Similarly, the mountain peddlers of the *Hochsauerland* gave their votes to liberal candidates.[63]

[63] STAM RAR I Pr. Nr. 90 Bl. 201-204; Haas, "Die Wahlen im Regierungs-Bezirk Aachen," pp. 142-44; above, p. 62.

TABLE 3.12
Votes of the Electors in 1855 and 1862
in *Kreise* Warburg, Höxter, Paderborn, and Büren

Vote in 1855	Vote in 1862					
	Clerical	Liberal	Split[a]	Abstain	Other	Total
Kreis Warburg						
Clerical	5	3	—	—	—	8
Governmental	2	5	5	—	—	12
Split	—	2	1	—	—	3
Other	—	3	2	—	—	5
Total	7	13	8	—	—	28
Kreis Höxter						
Clerical	15	2	—	—	—	17
Governmental	2	1	—	1	—	4
Split	1	—	1	—	—	2
Total	18	3	1	1	—	23
Kreis Paderborn						
Clerical	16	3	—	—	1	20
Governmental	—	—	—	—	—	—
Split	2	1	—	—	1	4
Total	18	4	—	—	2	24
Kreis Büren						
Clerical	22	1	—	—	—	23
Governmental	—	—	—	—	—	—
Split	3	1	—	—	—	4
Total	25	2	—	—	—	27

[a] Since the *Landrat* split his ballot this might be regarded as the "governmental" vote in *Kreis* Warburg in 1862.

SOURCE: Electoral protocols in STAD M1 IL Nr. 59, 71, 72.

There are two more pieces of evidence which can be presented in support of the connection between religious laxity and political liberalism. Father Hillebrand, director of missions in the Diocese of Paderborn, made it a practice to jot down some observations of the religious and moral conditions in each parish he visited in the course of holding missions. In his yearly reports to the bishop on the missions of 1855 and 1856 he included a copy of his observations. Thirty of the thirty-seven parishes where he preached in those years were in the *Kreise* Meschede, Olpe, Warburg, Höxter, Büren, Paderborn, and Wiedenbrück, for which the 1862 electoral protocols are extant. Although Father Hillebrand's judgments on the piety of a parish were not a perfect guide to the parishioners' political behavior, the most pious parishes were clearly more likely to select clerical electors and less likely to choose liberal ones, while the existence of "bad" elements usually also implied the existence of an influential group of liberals. See Table 3.13.

On a larger scale, we can compare the 1821 judgments of the Rhenish clergy on their parishioners' behavior during pilgrimages and the electoral tendencies forty years later.[64] The zero order coefficient of

TABLE 3.13
Piety and Political Alignment in Thirty
Westphalian Parishes

Votes of Their Electors in 1862	Moral Condition of the Parishes According to Father Hillebrand					
	Unusually Pious		Satisfactory		Immorality, "Bad" Elements or Opposition to the Mission Present	
	No.	%	No.	%	No.	%
Unanimously clerical	5	(36)	—		2	(20)
Clerical majority	3	(21)	2	(33)	2	(20)
Evenly split	2	(14)	2	(33)	—	
Liberal majority	4	(29)	2	(33)	1	(10)
Unanimously liberal	—		—		5	(50)
Total parishes	14	(100)	6	(99)	10	(100)

SOURCES: Father Hillebrand to Bishop of Paderborn, January 2, 1856 and January 1, 1857 AGVP XVI, 13 and electoral protocols in STAD M1 IL Nr. 71-72 and STAM LA Kr. Meschede Nr. 479.

[64] The figures on pilgrimages are from Table 1.3; the figures on elections are from Anderson, *Prussian Election Statistics*, pp. 16-19. The compilers of the election statistics used only two designations: "democratic" and "conservative." In the Catholic areas at this time, however, the clerical party was the only conservative force, and the number of "conservative" votes in the table corresponds roughly to the number of votes cast for the Catholic candidates. Besides the predominantly Protestant *Kreise* of the area, three predominantly Catholic *Kreise* have not been included in the table: Cologne (city) and Krefeld (city), where no Catholic candidate was put up, and Gladbach, where the liberals and the Catholics put up a joint candidate and it is not possible to get any idea of the exact number of specifically Catholic electors.

correlation (Pearson's *r*) between the percentage of the clergy opposing the abolition of pilgrimages and the clerical vote is .65, while the correlation between the percentage supporting such a prohibition and the clerical vote is −.74, both results highly significant. Those areas where, early in the century, the clergy approved of popular religious practices and saw no elements of secularization in them were later strongholds of political Catholicism, even at its weakest moment. Conversely, in the regions where priests deemed these practices suspect, liberal-democratic partisans were present, and in the early 1860s gained the upper hand, as they had previously in 1849. The moral and religious authority of the clergy was directly related to the strength of politicial Catholicism. See Table 3.14.

TABLE 3.14

Lay-Clerical Conflict and Political Alignment
in the Cologne and Düsseldorf Districts

Kreis	Percent Clergy Opposing Prohibition of Overnight Pilgrimages, 1821	Percent Clergy Favoring Prohibition of Overnight Pilgrimages, 1821	Percent Clerical-Conservative Electors, 1862
Cologne District			
Bergheim	70	19	41
Bonn	59	37	27
Cologne (country)	61	26	22
Euskirchen	65	30	36
Mülheim a. Rhein	45	35	36
Rheinbach	31	46	34
Siegkreis	56	33	36
Düsseldorf District			
Düsseldorf	40	44	10
Essen	—	75	26
Geldern	96	—	70
Grevenbroich	56	44	35
Kempen	59	24	50
Kleve	77	10	85
Krefeld (country)	20	60	25
Neuß	52	29	64
Rees	64	29	50

SOURCES: See note 31.

This contention may appear to contradict the assertions of the previous chapter, where it was argued that the influence of the clergy was
on the increase after 1850. A closer look at the electoral statistics will
help to resolve this seeming contradiction. In the Catholic regions of
the Rhineland and Westphalia, the turnout at the elections of the 1860s
was extremely low. While about one-third of all the eligible voters in
the Prussian state turned out to vote in the 1860s, in the western
provinces only about fifteen percent did. In the rural areas of the
Münster District only 7.4 percent of the voters appeared at the polls
on election day in 1863, about one-fourth the average turnout of the
rural voters in the eastern provinces. The contrast between Berlin, with
a fifty-eight percent turnout, and Cologne, the largest city in the west,
where not even half so great a proportion (twenty-six percent) of the
voters went to the polls, is also considerable. Within the western
provinces themselves, turnout was much lower in Catholic than Protestant areas; turnout rates for Catholics were not that much higher
than in the 1850s, while Protestant electoral participation had increased sharply. The overwhelming majority of the Catholic population, even a majority of the most affluent, were politically passive
during the conflict era. As Eugene Anderson has noted, "The Catholics
manifestly found satisfaction for their needs and wishes in some other
way than politics."[65]

In these conditions of political passivity and a very limited electorate,
the importance of religious sentiment was decisive. Areas with a history
of lay-clerical tensions and conflict were likely to have at least a certain
number of notables sympathetic to the left. Led by veterans of 1848-
1849, they broke out of the political passivity and abstention which
had been their lot during the reaction era in 1858-1861, and, engaged
by the constitutional conflict, were able to mobilize enough previously
passive supporters to outvote their clerical counterparts in 1862-1863.
The latter were unsuccessful in bringing the growing religious sentiments of the Catholic masses into play, a consequence of the limited
nature of public participation in the three-class electoral system and
the broader contours of notables' politics, but also a result of the

[65] Anderson, *The Conflict in Prussia*, p. 425; cf. Hamerow, *Social Foundations*, 1:
305-306. 1863 turnout statistics can be found in Anderson, *Prussian Election Statistics*,
pp. 46-63. The turnout in the predominantly Protestant *Kreise* of the Minden District
averaged about fifteen percent during the elections of the 1850s, tripled by 1862,
reaching a high of fifty-one percent of the voters of *Kreis* Bielefeld in that year. In the
Catholic *Kreise* of the district, on the other hand, while turnouts in the 1850s were
similar to those in the Protestant areas, the increase in the 1860s was much smaller,
with turnouts averaging only about twenty-five percent in 1862. (Turnout figures are
from STAM OP Nr. 495 Bl. 79 and STAD M1 IL Nr. 34-38.)

salient political issues of the conflict era, which remained far removed from religion and roused little interest among the bulk of the Catholics one way or the other. Where the authority of the clergy had never been in dispute, what few non-clerical notables were present could find little support, even among the small, politically interested minority, so the Catholic parliamentarians were as easily reelected in the 1860s as they had been in the previous decade. The analysis of social and regional bases of support thus leads to a consideration of publicity and political organization: the means by which progressive and clerical forces were able to rally supporters in the specific political circumstances of the early 1860s.

Organization and Publicity

The development of political organization in the 1860s was still very rudimentary. Standing party organizations did not exist; even permanent local committees were a rarity. Between elections, politics was the concern of a few individuals. In the Arnsberg District, the Progressive Party had a representative (Vertrauensmann) in every city who received material from the parliamentarians in Berlin for use in public meetings or in petitions to be sent to the *Landtag*. Beyond these individuals, there was no formal liberal organization. Partisans met, as in Soest, in a "second-rate tavern" to discuss political questions.[66]

Only at election time did this picture change. Looking back over the previous half decade in 1865, the *Landrat* of *Kreis* Gladbach described the process: "Shortly before the elections, a lively movement of associations appears. Electoral associations are formed—or, rather, a single electoral association is formed, as the great majority of the inhabitants of the *Kreis* belong to the liberal party. After the elections are over, each individual goes right back to work and concerns himself with politics only in that he reads the *Kölnische Zeitung* and in the evenings shoots the breeze [kannengießt] with friends over a glass of wine." Even these associations did not reach beyond the confines of the larger cities. The electors of the small towns and rural communities first became involved in the political process on the eve of the balloting for the deputies. On arriving at the scene of the elections, they were "greeted by the party leaders or their associates and propagandized [bearbeitet] there."[67]

Political organization and popular mass agitation were in no way

[66] STAM RAR I Pr. Nr. 102 Bl. 4-28.
[67] *Landrat* of *Kreis* Gladbach in HSTAD RD Pr. Nr. 866 Bl. 45; Aachen District Governor Friedrich Kühlwetter cited in Haas, "Die Wahlen im Regierungs-Bezirk Aachen," p. 150.

well developed. If anything, the Catholics were better organized than the liberals, even without considering the political uses to which the church organization could be put. The only permanent political associations existing in the Rhineland-Westphalia during the 1860s were clerical ones: the Constantia in Aachen, founded in the 1840s, and its imitations and offshoots in Eupen, Neuß, and several other Rhenish towns.[68]

The Neuß Constantia was particularly effective. Founded in 1861, it held popular agitation meetings both in the town of Neuß and in the rural areas of the *Kreis*. Constantia activists also packed and disrupted liberal election rallies. Enjoying the full support of the clergy and cooperation from a sympathetic *Landrat* and conservative lower officials, the Constantia successfully rallied the generally devout population of the *Kreis* behind the clerical candidates, and throughout the entire 1860s a majority of the electors from *Kreis* Neuß supported the Catholic party but were outvoted by the electors of the more liberal *Kreise* Krefeld (country) and Grevenbroich.[69] Even at the height of the conflict era, a well-organized political Catholicism, supported by an unquestionably devout population, could survive the liberal challenge in spite of the clerical partisans' close association with the Prussian state.

In the absence of mass political organizations, the press played an important role in mobilizing public opinion and rallying support behind the actions of parliamentary groupings. Most historians have asserted the predominance of the liberal press in this period.[70] This has some validity, especially in the Rhine Valley. The liberal *Kölnische Zeitung*, with a circulation of 17,000 in 1865, was one of the leading dailies in Germany. It far outdistanced its Catholic competitor, the Bachem family's *Kölnische Blätter*, which could manage a circulation of only some 5,500. In the predominantly Catholic *Kreise* of the Düsseldorf District—Düsseldorf, Essen, Geldern, Gladbach, Kempen, Kleve, Krefeld, Neuß, and Rees—the liberal and democratic press had a combined circulation of some 15,000, as against 3,500 for clerical papers, 1,500 for the apolitical press, and 5,300 for the conservative journals.[71]

[68] HSTAD RD Pr. Nr. 866 Bl. 84-93 and HSTAD RA Pr. Nr. 712 Bl. 334-36 and Nr. 703 Bl. 74-84.

[69] On the activities of the Neuß Constantia, see Röttges, *Die politischen Wahlen*, pp. 242-44, 269-71, and 292-94.

[70] Cf. Schmolke, *Die schlechte Presse*, pp. 100 ff.; Bachem, *Zentrumspartei*, 3: 151.

[71] At least some of those conservative journals were probably Catholic in orientation, so the actual circulation of the clerical press was somewhat higher. The figures for this and the following paragraph come from the 1865 reports on the Rhenish press in LAK 403 Nr. 7151 Bl. 99-143, and the 1863 reports on the Westphalian press in STAM OP Nr. 97 Bl. 115-49.

The predominance of liberal journalism was far from universal. In many regions the circulation of the Catholic press was equal or superior to that of the liberal journals. The clerical *Echo der Gegenwart* in Aachen was the main newspaper in the district, its press-run of 3,000 more than three times that of its nearest competitor, the liberal *Aachener Zeitung.* There were few newspapers in the Münster District and the Catholic *Kreise* of the Minden District, but by the mid-1860s, following the defection of the *Westfälische Merkur* to the Progressives, such liberal and clerical journals as existed were roughly equal in circulation. In the six predominantly Catholic *Kreise* of the Arnsberg District—Arnsberg, Brilon, Lippstadt, Meschede, Olpe, and Soest— on the other hand, the clerical press enjoyed a crushing predominance: seven Catholic newspapers with a total circulation of 7,700 stood against one liberal and one democratic journal with a combined circulation of 1,680. The newspaper with the largest press run in all of Westphalia (some 3,000) was the twice-weekly *Central-Volksblatt für den Regierungsbezirk Arnsberg*, described by the officials as the "main organ of the ultramontane, *grossdeutsch* party."

Curiously enough, there was no correlation between the strength of the Catholic press and the fortunes of political Catholicism. In the elections of 1862 and 1863, the liberals made major gains in the Arnsberg and Aachen Districts in spite of the predominance of the Catholic press, but could make little headway in the Münster District and the Catholic areas of the Minden District, even though the liberal press was roughly equal in circulation to its clerical competitor. Liberal successes were the result neither of a smoothly functioning electoral machine nor of an influential press. In the small towns and the countryside, formal organization and political propaganda took second place to informal, word-of-mouth contact in ostensibly non-political settings.

In 1863, the *Landrat* of *Kreis* Lippstadt explained how the town and the constituency to which it belonged—Arnsberg-Brilon-Lippstadt—a model of clerical conservatism since 1848, had been captured by the left. His account shows how a small group of notables, working through informal channels, was able to win over a limited group of politically interested countryfolk and townsmen. The process had begun in the late 1850s, when Lippstadt's mayor, Schultz, and the former *Kreis* physician, Dr. Hilbach, succeeded in having a new principal appointed to the town's high school [höhere Bürgerschule]. The principal, a man named Wahlart, was known for his left-wing activities during the revolution. He proceeded to appoint a number of "free-thinking" (freisinnig) teachers who made no secret of their "religious and political" convictions. Having secured a cadre of liberal teachers, he went on to organize the "Progressive clique," which included the "democratic element." Publicity came from the editor and publisher of *Der Patriot*, the town's newspaper, a man named Weinert, who had worn a red cocarde in 1848. A committee, composed of "progressive merchants, industrialists, and judicial officials," provided further (presumably financial) support. With the covert encouragement of the liberal bureaucrats in Arnsberg, "all the wheels were set in motion, to corrupt not just the right-thinking [gut-gesinnt] countryside of *Kreis* Lippstadt, but the entire electoral district." The *Landrat* concluded that, if unchecked, the activities of this group would "bury the good sense of the population and bit by bit drive the Christian faith into the ground."[72]

In 1863, after the electors had been selected but before they met to vote for the deputies, all the electors in the constituency Arnsberg-Brilon-Lippstadt received in the mail a pamphlet attacking the clerical candidates, the Plaßmann brothers, as reactionaries and ultramontanists. The electors of the Allendorf region in *Kreis* Arnsberg met in a tavern, whose owner was a known liberal. There, one of the local Progressives read them the pamphlet and carefully explained how a good Catholic could vote against the clerical candidates. The area magistrate, also a liberal sympathizer, was present and gave his approval.[73]

A variation on this form of electioneering can be seen in the neighboring *Kreis* Beckum (Münster District). The Progressives laid the foundations for their 1863 electoral victory a year earlier at the meeting of the *Kreis* agricultural society when they elected as president the estate-owner Bernhard von Bruchhausen, veteran of 1848-1849, leader of the left in the *Kreis*, and member of the Westphalian provincial committee of the Progressive Party. He used the occasion to canvass for signatures for an address supporting the Parliament against the ministry and invited editor Weinert of *Der Patriot* to make an appeal for subscriptions. The situation was even more favorable for the Rhenish liberals: as early as 1861, the entire provincial agricultural society had endorsed the Progressive candidates.[74]

The characteristic element in all these situations was the opportunity for the liberal notables to discuss politics informally with the upper strata of rural society. In a tavern, or at a meeting of the agricultural society, away from the church and the influence of the clergy, the liberals could defuse the religious issue and emphasize questions of

[72] STAM RAR I Pr. Nr. 90 Bl. 179-83.
[73] STAM RAR I Pr. Nr. 90 Bl. 208-39.
[74] LA Kr. Beckum to RM, Dec. 13, 1862, STAM RM Nr. 260; Kaiser, *Die politischen Strömungen*, p. 142.

political reform and economic improvement: the burdens of taxes, the dangers of militarism and an army outside parliamentary control, the liberation of local self-government from noble privilege and bureaucratic tutelage, the importance of railroad building and trade treaties for the economic development of the region.[75] The liberal position was extremely fragile. Its basis was not an appeal to the mass of the rural and small town population, as the democrats had attempted in 1848-1849, but a cautious and defensive overture to a relatively small group in the countryside. Furthermore, the stability of the social context of this overture was becoming ever more precarious. The religious revival had weakened the position of rivals to the rural clergy—especially the innkeeper—and greatly increased the centrality of both the priest in religious life and religion in rural life. A political strategy based on bypassing or rivaling religion and the clergy was unlikely to enjoy any permanent success. The events of 1866-1867, which brought a return to direct, mass political participation and an increasingly active clerical role, would illuminate the shallowness of liberal support in the countryside.

In the larger cities and industrial areas, the liberal position was more favorable. The *Kölnische Zeitung* and other liberal or democratic journals enjoyed a reasonable circulation among the educated public. The peculiar Prussian suffrage system was favorable to the liberals: its three-class voting gave a grossly disproportionate weight to the often Protestant and usually liberal bourgeoisie, and its public balloting allowed them to oversee their workers at election time. In 1862, the liberal textile manufacturers of Monschau (Aachen District) marched their workers to the polls. Over seventy percent of the eligible voters appeared—an astronomical turnout for the time. Not a single priest or official was selected as an elector, and the Progressives went on to elect both of their candidates (one of whom was an innkeeper) in the constituency Schleiden-Monschau-Malmedy to the *Landtag.*[76]

Even in the cities liberal support was shallow. Liberals may have intimidated the lower classes but they made little attempt to mobilize them. Public election rallies were held on occasion, but without any great frequency. Liberal associations of artisans and liberal workers'

[75] See, for instance, the liberal pamphlet cited above, n. 60; the liberal electoral appeal in the *Olper Kreis Blatt*, Nov. 30, 1861, STAM OP Nr. 500; Haas, "Die Wahlen im Regierungs-Bezirk Aachen," pp. 139-44, to cite just a few examples.

[76] Haas, "Die Wahlen im Regierungs-Bezirk Aachen," pp. 139-47. Industrialists in rural areas could exert a similar influence. See STAM RAR I Pr. Nr. 90 Bl. 187-91, 202-204. The Catholic politicians were well aware of this, and in 1861 the *Kölnische Blätter* called for the introduction of the secret ballot and a more equitable electoral system. Denk, "Die Wahlen in Köln," pp. 135-36.

education societies, very common in southern Germany during the 1860s, were to be found only in a few scattered localities in Rhineland-Westphalia.[77] Beneath a surface of electoral abstention and bourgeois uninterest, "non-political" developments were helping the clerical cause among the Catholic lower classes of the big cities and industrial regions. Rural-urban migration was changing the structure of the lower classes; missionaries were preaching with great effect to workers; sodalities, miners' and journeymen's associations were being formed. As in the countryside, the new political situation after 1866 would reveal the effect of these changes hidden from view by the notables' politics of the 1860s.

THE DILEMMA OF POLITICAL CATHOLICISM IN THE 1860S

Although it is possible for the historian to discern the seeds of future clerical victories in the seemingly difficult political situation of the early 1860s, this consolation was unavailable to the Catholic clergy and politically active laity of the time. What appeared to them was an unbroken string of political defeats at home and a menacing situation abroad—a growing threat to religion and public order by the forces of atheism and revolution. The *Sonntagsblatt für katholische Christen* described the situation after the elections of 1861, when the victories of the Progressives had confirmed the Catholics' worst fears:

> It is unfortunately true that . . . at the elections many Catholics, as a consequence of their religious indifference, have left the field free for Jews and Freemasons. . . . If the program of that [Progressive] party is ever carried out; if the king by grace of God becomes an official of the people, and the sovereign citizen can appeal to the will of the people against this unloved official; if the school is separated from the church and turned into a state institution in which Christians, Jews, and sectarians are taught and religious education excluded . . . if all Christian institutions are robbed of their Christian character and a Jew can be judge and schoolteacher as easily as a Christian, finally, if in foreign policy the right of nations ceases, the ten commandments are no longer applied but are replaced by self-interest—then we will be on the edge of that abyss against which the watchman on the Throne of Peter has warned us time and again. Is it of no importance which conceptions dominate in the law books, Christian

[77] Surveys of the existence (or nonexistence) of these associations can be found in STAM RAR I Nr. 102; HSTAD RD Pr. Nr. 866 Bl. 84-93; HSTAD RA Pr. Nr. 703 Bl. 84-94.

or anti-Christian? Of no importance if usury laws exist or not? Of no importance if commerce and the artisanate are protected in this time . . . of the greatest crisis they have ever experienced? . . . Usurers, certain forms of state loans, distortion of marriage, "liberation" of the artisanate and commerce—all this, little by little, exploits the nation, ruins it morally and physically, and prepares the most dreadful catastrophe resulting from the impoverishment of the masses. This may be called freedom, but it is anti-Christian. There is the feeling in the air not of 1848 but rather of 1793. People take into consideration that . . . the end of Austria and the Papal State is decided . . . Austria shall fall, the Pope shall fall.[78]

The Bishop of Paderborn expressed the same sentiments in a pastoral letter of 1865, which portrayed a universal struggle between the forces of revolution and those of order: "And the secret and open leaders or followers of the worldwide subversive party think only of how they may destroy all authority in the state or church and get rid of the entire Christian order and society. They wish to dethrone all the legitimate princes, so that they themselves may sit on their thrones; they wish to dispose of all existing authority, so they may take its place. All existing divine and human laws shall be trampled, so that they may dictate their own wretched truth to the world as a legal norm."[79]

It is difficult to know how widespread these sentiments were, and if they were shared by the subordinate clergy and the Catholic lower classes. The politically active minority of the Catholic population was probably acquainted with them, since the denunciation of liberals as atheists, Freemasons, and subversives was a common theme of Cath-

[78] *Sonntagsblatt für katholische Christen* 20 (1861): 657-61. Cf. the Lenten pastoral letter of the Bishop of Paderborn on "true and false progress" from the same year, *Amtsblatt für die Diözese Paderborn*, 10 Nr. 2 (Jan. 19, 1861): 10 ff.

[79] *Amtsblatt für die Diözese Paderborn*, 14 Nr. 5-7 (Feb. 1, 1865): 29. For other examples of this sentiment, see *Sonntagsblatt für katholische Christen* 22 (1863): 133 and 23 (1864): 105; 1864 Lenten pastoral letter of the Bishop of Münster on the Freemasons, *Amtsblatt der Diözese Münster*, 7 Nr. 2 (Jan. 26, 1864): 6-7; the 1861 Lenten pastoral letter of the Archbishop of Cologne, printed in *Kölnische Zeitung*, Feb. 3, 1861.

A similar point was made by Karl Bachem in his famous description of the "apocalyptic mood" of German Catholicism in 1866 (*Zentrumspartei*, 2: 192-97). Most authors who quote the comment fail to note that Bachem described the mood not just as a result of the war of 1866, but as the product of a long development, beginning with the revolution of 1848 and building up strongly in the first half of the 1860s. Bachem, himself the product of a later and more secular generation, felt ill at ease with this sort of sentiment, as his comments on it make clear. His contention that the apocalyptic mood vanished during the *Kulturkampf* era is, I would argue, incorrect. Rather, Catholic contemporaries saw the *Kulturkampf* as a high point in the apocalyptic struggle with the forces of atheism and revolution.

olic election rallies and the clerical press. On occasion, such polemics reached a wider audience, as happened in 1861, when the clergy of *Kreis* Jülich preached a cycle of sermons on the subversive history of the Freemasons, from the French Revolution to the "national heroes" of Italy and the editors of the *Kölnische Zeitung*.[80]

For those who accepted this view of the world, the situation seemed desperate. Every fresh report from the political arena was cause for despair. The electoral victories of the Progressives were milestones in the advance of godless revolutionary elements, while the increasingly anti-Austrian tone of Bismarck's foreign policy was an indication that Protestant conservatism and the Prussian state were no longer trustworthy allies.[81]

Two responses were possible. One was a withdrawal from politics into the organizational world of the church. Many Pius Associations, the institutional form of political Catholicism in 1848-1849, concerned themselves in the 1860s with raising money for the Pope or distributing petitions defending the temporal power of the papacy. Prominent Catholic politicians led efforts to found a private, Catholic university in Germany on the Belgian model.[82] Such actions were equivalent to ceding the field of political battle to the Progressives and leaving the struggle for state power up to them. The alternative response was an attempt at the renewal of political Catholicism. The old battle cry, "religion is in danger," seemed increasingly to have lost its attractiveness; a refurbished and expanded political program was called for.

Catholic politicians began to discuss socioeconomic developments, expressing an almost instinctive dislike for laissez-faire and a desire for the preservation or restoration of traditional guild institutions. Spokesmen for the ostensibly more liberal Rhenish Catholics were as likely to raise such demands as their more conservative Westphalian counterparts. In 1861, the *Kölnische Blätter* denounced the abolition of restrictions on industry and commerce in a revealing phrase as a "weapon of red subversion," while the following year, members of the Neuß Constantia took over a liberal election rally and attacked the incumbent deputy, Nücker, for having voted for the abolition of the usury laws. The Westphalians were also active in this direction. Leaders of political Catholicism in *Kreis* Recklinghausen (Münster District), facing in the fall of 1863 imminent defeat in the upcoming elections, published the first electoral program in their history. Any

[80] HSTAD RA Pr. Nr. 681.

[81] The *Sonntagsblatt für katholische Christen* attacked the Prussian recognition of the Kingdom of Italy in such violent terms that the offending issue was confiscated by the state's attorney. *Sonntagsblatt für katholische Christen*, 21 (1862): 481-85 and 507.

[82] Kissling, *Geschichte der Deutschen Katholikentage*, pp. 389, 466-81; HSTAD RD Pr. Nr. 866 Bl. 56-57.

future deputy, they demanded, would have to vote for the preservation
of the guilds and ". . . for the preservation of the usury laws, as their
abolition would deliver the farmer, artisan, and businessman completely into the hands of the usurer. Since every child knows from the
catechism that the usurer is not one whit better than the thief, the
Progressive Party in wanting to free the usurer from the punishment
he so richly deserves, is proceeding in an unfair fashion against the
usurer's twin brother, the thief."[83]

These efforts were, in general, unsuccessful. The clerical politicians
did not strike a responsive chord among the voters in their campaign
for the preservation of the economic old regime, since the guild system
enjoyed little popularity among the Rhenish-Westphalian artisanate
during the 1860s. Tacking on a few corporate paragraphs to a clerical
electoral program was no mechanism for ensuring success at the polls.

The most serious effort at political rethinking came from clerical
partisans in Westphalia. A group of Catholic notables, led by two
noblemen, Hermann von Mallinckrodt and Wilderich von Ketteler,
met several times in the town of Soest.[84] The topics of discussion in
the "Soest Conferences," as these meetings have come to be known,
varied from the political implications of the Syllabus of Errors to the
problems of a *grossdeutsch* plan for German unification. At the center
of the debate stood the declining fortunes of political Catholicism in
Prussia. The participants were inclined to see some variant of the
"social question" as relevant to its revival. They felt the workers were
better off than most people realized, but independent small businessmen and master craftsmen—in contemporary parlance the *Mittelstand*—were in an increasingly difficult position. Unlike many other
Catholic politicians of the time, the conference participants did not
denounce modern industry or call for a restoration of the guilds. Some
way had to be found, they thought, to protect craftsmen without
discriminating against big business.[85] The "unnatural alliance between
the peasantry and modern liberalism" had to be broken, but once
again it was unclear how. Burghard von Schorlemer-Alst discussed the
peasant league he had formed. Although the association was not ex-

[83] Denk, "Die Wahlen in Köln," pp. 135-36; Röttges, *Die politischen Wahlen*, p.
270; Pülke, "Kreis Recklinghausen," p. 161. A similar example from Bonn in 1863 can
be found in Kaiser, *Die politischen Strömungen*, pp. 191-213.

[84] On the following, see the excellent essay of Hohmann, "Soester Konferenzen"; a
few details are added by Müller, "Entscheidung des Jahres, 1866."

[85] This solicitude for the interests of industry is even more surprising when one realizes
that only 9 of the 102 participants in the conference were businessmen—a reflection
of the extent to which politically active Catholics in Westphalia were outside the leading
sectors of the industrial economy.

plicitly political, he claimed that as a result of its work, "political cooperation at the last elections came of itself. . . ." The empire of the future "peasant king" was in the mid-1860s still restricted to the area near Schorlemer's estate, the *Kreis* Steinfurt in the Münster District, a long-time clerical stronghold. With just a few hundred members concentrated in one small area, the league, for all its future potential, was not yet an important political force.

Two years of meetings produced no concrete results. In early 1866, the discussion turned to the upcoming *Landtag* elections, scheduled for the following June. The conference participants could not agree on an electoral program, and a large number of them even felt that the Catholics should not put up candidates at all.

Time had run out on the clerical politics of the early 1860s. While the Soest conferences were proceeding, the struggle between Austria and Prussia for supremacy in Central Europe was reaching its climax. The openly *kleindeutsch* course of Bismarck's foreign policy was repelling even the most conservative and authoritarian of the Catholic politicians. In 1865, a seat became vacant in Heinsberg-Erkelenz-Geilenkirchen (Aachen District), one of the last safe clerical constituencies. The *Landrat* of *Kreis* Heinsberg asked Hermann von Mallinckrodt to stand for the by-election, but the Catholic politician refused. Although strongly opposed to the Progressives, Mallinckrodt could no longer work with the ministry, for he found Bismarck's "particularism"— that is, his adoption of an anti-Austrian, *kleindeutsch* foreign policy— more than he could stomach.[86]

The governmental alliance was dead; the voters no longer seemed to respond to the battle cry of endangered religion; a new sociopolitical program had not been worked out; the likelihood of war with Austria was increasing daily. A sense of hopelessness and futility pervaded the discussions at the final meeting in Soest during the spring of 1866, as the participants realized a war with Austria was imminent. Complementing their despairing sentiments, and perhaps contributing to them, was the feeling of missed opportunity, the sense that somewhere a chance had been passed up to turn the situation around. Schorlemer-Alst wrote to a friend on June 13, 1866: "It seems to me, and no doubt to you as well, that an unusually favorable moment has been missed, in which the Catholic-conservative party could and must have come forth with a manifesto and appropriate candidates. It did not happen. . . ."[87] Two days later, Prussian troops crossed the Austrian border, and the political world of the first half of the 1860s came to an end.

[86] Pfülf, *Mallinckrodt*, pp. 274-75.
[87] Hohmann, "Soester Konferenzen," p. 322.

CHAPTER 4

A POLITICAL TRANSFORMATION: 1867-1871

THE WAR OF 1866

As it became increasingly clear in the course of the spring of 1866 that Bismarck was determined to settle the question of German unification by means of a war with Austria, public opinion throughout Central Europe, never very favorable, turned ever more against him. The denunciation of the planned "war between brothers" was the virtually unanimous theme of the periodical press, public speeches, and political meetings.[1]

Nowhere was the opposition to the war more open and vehement than in the Rhineland and Westphalia. The Catholic population of the region, like their co-religionists elsewhere in Central Europe, despised the prospect of a Prussian war against Catholic Austria in alliance with the anti-Papal Kingdom of Italy. Liberals and progressives saw the war as the latest and most outrageous act of a reactionary ministry. Regardless of religion or political opinion, all the inhabitants of Prussia's western provinces feared a French march to the Rhine, seen as the inevitable consequence of an intra-German war.

In the months preceding the outbreak of the conflict, the Rhinelanders and Westphalians showed no hesitation in letting their feelings be known. Great public meetings were held to express opposition to a declaration of war. Almost every city council of the area, whether controlled by liberal or clerical partisans, as well as the major chambers of commerce, petitioned the government, demanding a peaceful resolution of the diplomatic situation. Virtually the first official act of Paulus Melchers, the new Archbishop of Cologne, whose election by the cathedral chapter and governmental confirmation in May 1866 came after a two-year-long vacancy in the See, was to write a personal letter to the King of Prussia, expressing his diocesans' wish that a war be avoided.[2]

When the war finally came, it was met with unrelieved popular

[1] Höfele, "Königgrätz."
[2] Ibid., pp. 393-416; Röttges, *Die politischen Wahlen*, pp. 299-302; Denk, "Die Wahlen in Köln," pp. 170 ff.; *Kölnische Zeitung*, Apr. 5, 8, 10, 11, 16, 17, 19, May 15-17, 20, 24-27, 29, June 7, 1866.

hostility. The mobilization of the reserves in the western provinces was accompanied by riots, desertions, and near mutinies. Six hundred reservists in Münster refused to be inducted; they were taken to the barracks at gunpoint by regular troops. In Arnsberg, a group of reservists broke away from their column, marched to the district governor's office, and there gave three cheers for the Emperor of Austria.[3] During the two weeks between the outbreak of the war and the battle of Königgrätz, the mood of the population in Catholic areas was unreservedly pro-Austrian. The novelist Heinrich Hardt, then a student at the *Gymnasium* in Münster, recalled the situation in his memoirs:

> The average *Münsteraner* regarded himself almost exclusively as a Catholic. If an inhabitant had a political ideal of any kind (and he was the exception), then he considered himself a partisan of a *Grossdeutschland*. During the campaign of 1866, the population was entirely given over to its antipathy toward Prussia, "the bulwark of Protestantism." If the rumor spread that the Prussians had suffered a defeat, then every house in the city flew a flag in celebration, even on the day when it was reported that the thirteenth regiment, composed almost entirely of local boys, had been virtually annihilated. If news of a Prussian victory came in, then nothing could be felt but doubt, scorn, and bitterness.[4]

While the fighting was still in progress, elections were held for the House of Deputies of the Prussian Parliament. In the eastern provinces, the liberals suffered a major defeat; wartime patriotism led to the election of over one hundred conservative deputies.[5] In the west, the elections took a different course. Still firmly opposed to the war, the inhabitants returned an overwhelming majority of militantly oppositional deputies. The special revulsion toward the war felt by the Catholic population was not reflected in an increase in the number of clerical deputies. Just the opposite occurred: the Catholic parliamentarians had compromised themselves in the eyes of the voters by their support of a government which had engaged in a war against Pope and Emperor. It was, paradoxically, the secular and even anti-clerical left

---

[3] Höfele, "Königgrätz," p. 401.

[4] Cited in Keinemann, *Beiträge zur westfälischen Landesgeschichte*, p. 117, n. 111. See also, ibid., pp. 116-18; Schiffers, *Der Kulturkampf in Aachen*, pp. 26-31; HSTAD RD Pr. Nr. 577 Bl. 6-10; STAM RAR I Nr. 1419 Bl. 51-52; and *Kölnische Zeitung*, May 23, 1866, in which a correspondent from Westphalia, noting the openly pro-Austrian sympathies of the Catholic clergy, asked rhetorically if they could expect better treatment at the hands of "Czechs, Croats, and Panders" than from German Protestants.

[5] Hamerow, *Social Foundations*, 2: 281.

which drew the political profit from the outraged religious feelings of the Catholics.

In the constituency Münster-Coesfeld, the citizens' association succeeded in electing Benedikt Waldeck in 1866 by a narrow margin over the incumbent clerical deputy, Karl von Kleinsorgen. The mayor of Münster described how the liberals were able to conquer a clerical stronghold where their attempt three years earlier had been unsuccessful: "The result of the election is the consequence of the agitation of the democratic party in Münster which succeeded in electing many businessmen as electors. With the help of all the electors chosen in the towns of the *Landkreis* Münster, Telgte and Grevern, they convinced many of the rural electors to vote for their candidate, as the clerical party in general, and the clergy in particular, refused to use their influence in view of their displeasure with the war."[6] The clergy of Aachen and members of the Catholic political club, the Constantia, refrained from voting, ensuring the liberals an easy victory. Priests in several constituencies even openly supported Progressive candidates running under the slogan "Not a penny for the ministry!" In other constituencies, the clerical partisans came to an agreement with their former liberal opponents, united in common opposition to Bismarck's policies. The formation of a "united anti-ministerial party," as contemporaries described it, always worked to the disadvantage of the Catholic parliamentarians. Nowhere was a Progressive incumbent replaced by a clerical deputy in 1866, but Catholic support for liberal oppositionists and clerical-liberal agreements resulted in the election of liberal deputies in such former clerical strongholds as Erkelenz-Geilenkirchen-Heinsberg (Aachen District) and Kempen-Geldern (Düsseldorf District).[7]

There were only eight clerical deputies elected among the forty-five chosen in the predominantly Catholic constituencies of the northern Rhineland and Westphalia; fifteen clerical deputies in all of Prussia. The Catholic caucus in the House of Deputies of the Prussian Parliament dissolved itself. Until the creation of the Center Party in the fall of 1870 there was no supra-regional organization of political Catholicism in Prussia.[8]

[6] Report of the OB Münster on the 1866 elections in STDM Stadtregistratur Fach 9 Nr. 5; further, see the reports on the 1866 elections in STAM OP Nr. 501 and RM to Interior Minister von Eulenberg, Sep. 12, 1868, STAM RM Nr. VII-68.

[7] Haas, "Die Wahlen im Regierungs-Bezirk Aachen," pp. 163-64; Kaiser, *Die politischen Strömungen*, pp. 218-27; Röttges, *Die politischen Wahlen*, pp. 300-309; Weinandy, "Die Wahlen des Regierungsbezirks Köln," p. 233; reports on the 1866 elections in STAM OP Nr. 501.

[8] Bachem, *Zentrumspartei*, 2: 198-204.

While the war of 1866 had brought political Catholicism in Prussia to its nadir, the effect of the war and the postwar political environment was to open up possibilities for a new mass Catholic politics, utilizing the strengthened confessional identity and clerical authority created by the religious revival. In 1867 these new tendencies led to confusion as the Catholic population was politically mobilized but lacked any organization to direct the mobilization. In the following two years, Catholic organizational work was carried out at the local level, so that when the clerical parliamentarians resumed their activity in 1870, they found both mass political support and at least the outlines of a political machine. The political party they created, the Center, was a force to be reckoned with from the moment of its inception.

THE ELECTIONS OF 1867

To institutionalize the result of the war, the victors of 1866 created the North German Confederation, which united the German states north of the Main River in a federal structure under Prussian hegemony. The lower house of the Confederation's legislature, the North German *Reichstag*, was to be elected by universal, secret, equal, and direct manhood suffrage, the first elections of this kind in German history. (Even during the revolution of 1848-1849, the elections had been indirect.) There were two *Reichstag* elections in 1867: the first, in February, was for a constituent North German *Reichstag*; the second, in August, for the first legislative session of the North German Confederation. These elections have been little studied by historians. Complete results were never published, and even in the archives compilations of the returns have only occasionally been preserved. The North German Confederation itself was a short-lived state, replaced by the German Empire in 1871, and many of its political parties were equally ephemeral. Scholars' attention has been focused on the split in the liberals, and the formation of the National Liberal party. Political Catholicism has received relatively little attention.[9]

By switching the focus from parliamentary delegations to events in the constituencies, the elections of 1867 take on a greater interest. Between the introduction of a new form of suffrage and the vast movement of popular opinion occasioned by the war of 1866—the first overtly political event since the revolution of 1848-1849 to have

[9] On political Catholicism in this period, the brief sketch of Lill, "Die deutschen Katholiken," provides a good summary of existing research and notes how many problems remain to be resolved. Windell's study, *The Catholics and German Unity*, is primarily concerned with events in southern Germany, and its discussion of the Rhineland and Westphalia is superficial and often inaccurate.

touched every stratum of society—the possibility existed for the creation of a new kind of mass politics, very different from the notables'
politics of the early 1860s. The pace of events and the swings in public
opinion, however, had rather outrun the awareness of the local leaders
of political life—the provincial and local bureaucrats, the notables,
and the clergy—who frequently continued to think about politics as
they had before 1866, not entirely comprehending the new political
environment. The upshot was a curious situation in which features of
the conflict era, forerunners of the *Kulturkampf*, and unique transi-
tional forms of political life all appeared mixed in together.

As the events of 1866, culminating in the dissolution of the Catholic
caucus in the Prussian Parliament, had left the lay partisans of political
Catholicism disoriented and inactive, political initiative came directly
from the clergy. In January 1867 the Archbishop of Cologne issued a
pastoral letter, calling on Catholics to elect "reliable, insightful, and
pious men . . . upright and forthright adherents of our holy religion.
. . ." His suffragans, the Bishops of Trier, Münster, and Paderborn,
joined his appeal, which acted as a remarkable stimulus to the lower
clergy, everywhere galvanizing them into energetic political agitation.[10]
The energy of the clergy's actions was equalled only by their lack of
direction. There was no Catholic parliamentary caucus, and even at
the local level many clerical notables had since 1862-1863 withdrawn
from politics in disgust. If enough Catholic notables were still politically active, a clerical candidate might be nominated in January 1867;
otherwise, priests and laymen following their lead had to choose between supporting oppositional liberals or nominees of the authorities.

Most of the authorities in the western provinces still saw the 1867
elections in terms of the conflict era, the new circumstances providing
another opportunity to defeat the left opposition. To do this, they
quite naturally turned to the local representatives of the forces of order,
the Catholic clergy and the clerical politicians. As early as 1866, the
Landrat of *Kreis* Meschede (Arnsberg District) had asked the veteran
Catholic parliamentarian Hermann von Mallinckrodt if he would stand
for the Prussian Parliament in the constituency Olpe-Meschede as a
candidate of all the conservative elements, so that the incumbent Progressive deputy might be defeated. Mallinckrodt would not accept
such a proposal since in his eyes Bismarck was no longer a conservative

---

[10] *Kirchlicher Anzeiger für die Erzdiözese Köln*, 16 (1867): 13, also published in the
Kölnische Zeitung, Jan. 31, 1867. Similarly, see *Kirchliches Amtsblatt der Diözese
Paderborn*, 16 Nr. 3 (Jan. 26, 1867): 9. On the effects of the pastoral letter, cf. HSTAD
RA Pr. Nr. 813 Bl. 33-34, 457; STAM LA Kr. Meschede Nr. 235; Denk, "Die Wahlen
in Köln," pp. 161 ff.; Röttges, *Die politischen Wahlen*, pp. 320 ff.; and Weinandy,
"Die Wahlen des Regierungsbezirks Köln," pp. 252-55.

but the man who had realized the radical *Kleindeutsch* program of national unification. Working with Bismarck and his ministry was totally impossible, and he declined the *Landrat*'s offer firmly and immediately.[11]

Nonetheless, the offer was symptomatic of a more general trend. In January and February of 1867, provincial bureaucrats worked to reach an agreement with the Catholics. In the electoral district Hamm-Soest (Arnsberg District), the official candidacy was offered to a Catholic nobleman, the Freiherr von Ledebur; in neighboring *Kreis* Lippstadt, the *Landrat* even suggested putting up a priest as the governmental candidate. The district governor entered into intensive negotiations with the Aachen Catholic political club, the Constantia, and eventually reached agreement on a joint candidate for the Aachen constituency, Chief Justice Jakob Scherer of the Provincial Court.[12]

Even where agreement could not be reached directly, or where there was no organized structure of political Catholicism to deal with, the authorities could put up a Catholic nobleman or official in the hope of obtaining clerical support. Such candidates included Alfred Count von Hompesch in the constituency Erkelenz-Geilenkirchen-Heinsberg (Aachen District), Max Count von Loë in Kleve-Geldern (Düsseldorf District), or Max Bertram Count von Nesselrode in Mülheim-Wipperfürth-Gummersbach (Cologne District). In Brilon-Lippstadt (Arnsberg District), the *Landrat*, Wilhelm Freiherr von Schorlemer of *Kreis* Lippstadt and the Count von Galen both claimed to be the official candidate—the two candidacies being less the result of political differences than of personal rivalries. The elderly Provincial Governor of Westphalia, Theodor von Duesberg, stood as official candidate in two constituencies, Meschede-Olpe-Arnsberg (Arnsberg District) and Borken-Recklinghausen (Münster District), specifically in order to attract the support of the Catholic clergy. In the religiously mixed constituency Bielefeld-Wiedenbrück (Minden District), the government put up General Vogel von Falkenstein, a war hero, for the predominantly Protestant electorate of *Kreis* Bielefeld, but a Catholic war hero for the predominantly Catholic electorate of *Kreis* Wiedenbrück. *Landrat* Friedrich Leopold Devens, official candidate in *Kreis* Essen, although himself a Protestant, counted on obtaining the support of the Catholic clergy in order to defeat his liberal opponents.[13]

---

[11] STAM RAR I Nr. 1419 Bl. 170-72; this interesting episode is not mentioned in Otto Pfülf's standard biography of Mallinckrodt.

[12] STAM RAR I Nr. 1419 Bl. 38-39, 47-48; Lepper, "Regierungsbezirk Aachen," pp. 186-89.

[13] STAM RAR I Nr. 1419 Bl. 51-52, 58-59, 127, 194-201; HSTAD RD Pr. Nr. 575 Bl. 7-9; HSTAD RD Pr. Nr. 577 Bl. 199-200; HSTAD RA Pr. Nr. 813 Bl. 3-6, 32;

While the authorities' attempts to recreate the clerical-conservative alliance of the conflict era succeeded in some constituencies, in others the Catholics refused to cooperate with the men responsible for 1866. Sometimes they put up their own oppositional clerical candidate, but if no such candidate was fielded, the clericals would support militant oppositional Progressives. After all, were these Progressives not opponents of the man who had carried out the revolutionaries' plans to attack Catholic Austria and the Pope, in alliance with the Masonic-dominated Italian government? Some of the leftists were not adverse to accepting support from their former enemies with whom they had already cooperated in the 1866 *Landtag* elections. In the fall of 1867, the *Landrat* of *Kreis* Borken (Münster District) described the new political situation: "About one year ago, the pernicious democratic party threw itself into the arms of the Catholic clergy, which propagandizes [bearbeitet] the peasantry with such success that even previously admired individuals have lost all their influence. . . . In earlier elections, the clergy and the schoolteachers were on my side . . . [but this is no longer the case]. . . . As long as the Catholic clergy, supported by the democrats, propagandizes the masses, no governmental or conservative candidate can be brought through here."[14] During the conflict era the peasantry of *Kreis* Borken had supported the official candidate—he received 80 of 103 votes from rural electors in 1863—but the war had brought about a reversal of alliances: the clergy renounced its connections with an anti-Austrian, anti-Papal ministry and led the peasantry in supporting the only existing opposition. Open clerical support for liberal candidates when there was no specifically Catholic alternative to the government's candidate could also be found in the electoral districts Krefeld and Gladbach on the lower Rhine, Bonn-Euskirchen in the Cologne District, and Düren-Jülich in the Aachen District. In constituencies where Catholics were a minority, both clergy and laity frequently supported the liberal opposition to the government.[15]

By no means all Rhenish-Westphalian liberals held to their pre-1866 opposition. Like their counterparts elsewhere in Germany, they changed their minds about Bismarck, the man who had carried out the *kleindeutsch* program of national unification, and decided to work with

---

Lepper, "Regierungsbezirk Aachen," pp. 193-95; Röttges, *Die politischen Wahlen*, pp. 312 ff.; Weinandy, "Die Wahlen des Regierungsbezirks Köln," pp. 248-50; Moellers, "Reichstagswahlkreis Essen," pp. 58, 68-69.

[14] LA Kr. Borken to RM, Oct. 31, 1867, STAM RM Nr. VII-68.

[15] Anderson, *Prussian Elections*, p. 96; Kaiser, *Die politischen Strömungen*, pp. 231-41; Röttges, *Die politischen Wahlen*, pp. 328-29; Lepper, "Regierungsbezirk Aachen," pp. 192-93; HSTAD RA Pr. Nr. 813 Bl. 47; HSTAD RD Pr. Nr. 575 Bl. 92-93.

rather than against him. For these "nationally" minded liberals, the Catholic opposition to the war of 1866 (which the liberals at the time had shared, albeit for different reasons) was now reinterpreted as treasonous. Mine director Ihre, leader of the militant Progressives in the *Siegkreis* (Cologne District), called on his followers to support the conservative *Landrat* Maurer in the run-off elections in the constituency Sieg-Waldbroel rather than Father Dautzenberg from Siegburg, "a man who wanted the Austrians on the Rhine last summer." The liberal electoral committee in Warstein (*Kreis* Arnsberg) distributed a leaflet asking the voters if they would take the advice of Clemens Count von Westphalen, leader of political Catholicism in the area, "a man whose sons fought against us under Austria's flag." Furious, the Count stormed back that the charge was pure slander, but it was well known that the Progressive candidate, the Cologne attorney Wilhelm Elven, was a member of the Masonic Lodge.[16] The Count's charges are a reminder that the double reversal of alliances at the national level—liberals abandoning their pre-1866 opposition to the ministry and becoming pro-governmental, while the Catholics moved from support of the central authorities into opposition—preserved preexisting clerical-liberal hostilities at the local level. During the *Kulturkampf*, the pair of accusations traded, treason and Freemasonry, were to be the basis of political polemics.

In 1867, only some liberals had moved into a pro-governmental position, and even fewer of the provincial and district authorities were willing to support those who had. The *Landrat* of *Kreis* Kempen noted in January 1867 that previously there had been two "party tendencies, the liberals or Progressive Party and the Catholic clergy. The latter were supported by conservatives of all confessions because this was the only way to defeat the candidates of the former party." As a consequence of the "national achievements," the liberals had become pro-governmental, while the priests made no secret of their sympathies for Austria. The *Landrat*'s request to change course and support the liberals was granted by his superiors in Düsseldorf, whose sympathies probably ran in that direction anyway, but when the subordinates of the Arnsberg District Governor, Heinrich Wilhelm von Holzbrinck, proposed similar moves, he turned them down. Holzbrinck had been appointed to his post in 1862 precisely in order to fight the liberals

---

[16] Weinandy, "Die Wahlen des Regierungsbezirks Köln," p. 246; STAM RAR I Nr. 1419 Bl. 106. Elven was, in fact, a Freemason, or at least had been one, since his name was on the 1850 membership list of the lodge *Rhenania zur Humanität* in Cologne. LAK 403 Nr. 14599 Bl. 39.

in alliance with the Catholic clergy, and he believed the liberals' change of heart to be at best temporary and at worst full of duplicity.[17]

The upshot of these varying attitudes among clergy, clerical notables, liberal notables, and the authorities was an extraordinarily confused electoral situation. Candidates included oppositional liberals who enjoyed clerical support and ones who did not; pro-Bismarckian "national" liberals backed by the authorities and others opposed by the authorities; official candidates with clerical support and other official candidates meeting violent clerical hostility; clerical candidates supported by the authorities and others opposed by them. Three- and four-way races were common. One candidate could be put up in several different constituencies with different groups of supporters in each. Justice Friedrich Bloemer of the Prussian Supreme Court, a nominal Catholic who had sat as an independent in the Prussian Parliament in the first half of the 1860s, belonging to no caucus but sympathetic to the liberals, was nominated three times in three different capacities: in Aachen (country)-Eupen, he was the candidate of the clergy and the officials against the liberals; in Kempen, he was a governmental-National Liberal candidate opposing a clerical one; and in Neuß-Grevenbroich, he was the liberal oppositional candidate against the *Landrat* who had the backing of the clergy and the Neuß Catholic political club, the Constantia.[18]

Whatever the shifting political alliances implied for the nomination of the candidates, the results of the elections showed the enormous political power of the Catholic clergy under universal, equal, and direct suffrage in the post-1866 political environment. In the twenty-seven predominantly Catholic constituencies of the northern Rhineland and Westphalia, sixteen candidates who can be identified as clerical were nominated; thirteen of them were elected. Only in the constituencies Kleve-Geldern, Moers-Rees (both Düsseldorf District) and Paderborn-Büren (Minden District) were the clerical nominees defeated, as a consequence of considerable disunity on the part of the clergy, a large proportion of whom worked for the official candidates, who were either Catholic noblemen or officials. Liberal or conservative candidates backed by the clergy were also victorious.[19]

[17] HSTAD RD Pr. Nr. 574 Bl. 80-82; STAM RAR I Nr. 1419 Bl. 35-48, 142-57. When the *Landräte* of *Kreise* Meschede and Arnsberg supported such a National Liberal candidate, Holzbrinck wrote to the Interior Minister, complaining about their refusal to follow his orders. The Minister replied, ostensibly agreeing with Holzbrinck, but his letter was sent only after the elections were over.

[18] Lepper, "Regierungsbezirk Aachen," pp. 181-86; Röttges, *Die politischen Wahlen*, pp. 321-23, 330-31. A perhaps overly elaborate attempt to tabulate the electoral situations can be found in Sperber, "Rhineland-Westphalia," pp. 238-40.

[19] Election results are in sources cited above, n. 13-17, STAD M1 IL Nr. 74, and *Kölnische Zeitung*, Jan. 24, 30, Feb. 3, 9, 10, 1867.

The priests exerted all the strength of their increasingly influential post-1850 position on behalf of the appropriate candidates. In dozens of instances, sermons were preached, explaining to the faithful whom they should support. Ballots for the clerically supported candidate were passed out by the sexton at the church doors, or by the priest himself after the sermon. In Kempen, all the clergy of the town met on the eve of the elections, and then the chaplains went from door to door, "especially to the houses of the little people," handing out ballots for Father Friedrich Michelis, the clerical candidate—a practice seen in other constituencies as well. Priests stood at the doors to the voting places, handing out ballots. The liberals could in no way match this massive effort, and even the attempts of the officials to employ gendarmes and village foremen to distribute ballots for the official candidate were of little avail—especially as the clergy, when going from house to house, or standing by the polling place, would make sure to tear up the ballots of opposing candidates.[20]

The Catholic schoolteachers were pressed into service, following the orders of the local school inspector, the parish priest. The teachers in Keyen and Schankhuysen (Kreis Moers, Düsseldorf District) had their pupils exercise their penmanship by writing a ballot for the clerical candidate, Dr. Joseph Krebs, and then, for homework, had the children bring the ballots to their fathers. Elsewhere, the church wardens passed out ballots, and the renters of parish lands were asked to vote for the appropriate candidate. In Straelen (Kreis Geldern, Düsseldorf District) the local clergy posted electioneers around the polling place to convince incoming voters to support Peter Reichensperger, the clerical candidate. The electioneers were Vorbeter, laymen who marched at the head of processions, leading the participants in reciting prayers.[21]

Opposing candidates were denounced in specifically religious terms. Chaplain Schmitz in St. Hubert (Kreis Kempen, Düsseldorf District) explained that the governmental-liberal candidate, Bloemer, was a bad Catholic, for he had lived in Berlin too long. In Toenisberg, "a small village, previously loyal [to the government] on every occasion," the rumor was systematically spread on election eve that Bloemer was a lapsed Catholic and Freemason. Count von Westphalen zu Laer, leader of the clerical forces in the constituency Olpe-Meschede-Arnsberg,

[20] While the Reichstag elections were secret, the Australian ballot was not used; rather, the voter wrote a candidate's name on a blank sheet of paper or handed in a pre-written or pre-printed ballot. On clerical agitation, see HSTAD RD Pr. Nr. 574-76; HSTAD RA Pr. Nr. 813 esp. Bl. 47; STAM RAR I Nr. 1419 Bl. 175-87; STAM LA Kr. Meschede Nr. 235; Röttges, Die politischen Wahlen, pp. 320-32; Weinandy, "Die Wahlen des Regierungsbezirks Köln," pp. 242-45.

[21] HSTAD RD Pr. Nr. 574 Bl. 237-38 and Nr. 575 Bl. 3-6. Many similar examples can be found in the sources cited in the previous note.

called upon the voters at a large political meeting in Grevenbrück to support a candidate who believed in the ten commandments, and not a "ministerial official" or a "Progressive Freemason." In this constituency, the government had put up Provincial Governor von Duesberg as its candidate precisely because of his Catholic confession, his close ties to the upper clergy, and his well-deserved reputation as a Prussian bureaucrat favorable to the Catholic church. In spite of this, the parish priest in Hillefeld (*Kreis* Arnsberg) explained to his parishioners that, although Duesberg seemed to be a good Catholic, one could never know whether or not he was a Freemason.[22]

When a clerical candidate opposed a governmental one, the campaign was especially bitter. The war of 1866 dominated the election, Catholics seeing it as a betrayal of their counterrevolutionary alliance with the Prussian state. At a meeting of representatives of political Catholicism from all parts of *Kreis* Kempen on the eve of the February election, the merchant and textile manufacturer Matthias Endepohls from Süchteln referred to the war as the "catastrophe of 1866," and accused the government of having been secretly plotting it for years. A certain Boeker from Bistard explained: "I am no oppositionist and have often been disgusted by the many difficulties which the House of Deputies [of the Prussian Parliament] has made for the ministry, but to say 'yes!' to everything the government wants, that would be even less appropriate."[23] The denial he wished to pronounce was, of course, a denial of the legitimacy of the war against Pope and Emperor. For Boeker, the war was as radical and subversive an action as the opposition of the leftist parliamentarians earlier in the decade.

The area magistrate Plaßmann in Balve, *Kreis* Arnsberg, governmental-clerical *Landtag* candidate in 1863, pillar of the forces of order in the *Hochsauerland*, was selected by the *Landrat* to be one of the government's election agents in the February campaign. To the horror of his superior, Plaßmann proved instead to be one of the leaders of the clerical and anti-governmental forces in the *Kreis*, vehemently opposing the candidacy of the Catholic provincial governor, Theodor von Duesberg. Plaßmann's political associate, Count von Westphalen, explained at a political rally the underlying basis of the clerical position. The commandment, "thou shalt not steal," he said with an unmistakable reference to the war of the previous summer, applied to the relationship between states as well as between individuals.[24]

---

[22] HSTAD RD Pr. Nr. 575 Bl. 10-15; STAM RAR I Nr. 1419 Bl. 178-87; account of the Grevenbrück correspondent of the *Kölnische Zeitung*, Feb. 4, 1867.

[23] HSTAD RD Pr. Nr. 575 Bl. 31-32.

[24] STAM RAR I Nr. 1419 Bl. 58-59, 166-69; *Kölnische Zeitung*, Feb. 4, 1867. On the colorful and eccentric Count von Westphalen, see Keinemann, "Die Affäre Westphalen."

The most spectacular case of this nature involved the *Landrat* of *Kreis* Kleve (Düsseldorf District), Felix Freiherr von Loë. Scion of a prominent Catholic noble family, Loë had been appointed *Landrat* in 1862 after an undistinguished administrative apprenticeship. He was maintained in his position as a symbol of the Catholic-conservative alliance in spite of the low regard in which he was held by his superiors at the Düsseldorf district office, who accused him of gross neglect of his official duties. Loë's predecessor, von Haefter, had been a model of Prussian bureaucratic efficiency, but also of anti-Catholicism, and his religious prejudices had often pushed the conservative clergy of the area into opposition to the government.

On June 26, 1866 Loë chaired a large public meeting in Kleve called to raise funds for wounded soldiers. During the meeting, a report came in of the Austrian victory at Custozza over Prussia's Italian allies, and the *Landrat* exclaimed to the astonished gathering, "God be praised! At last there's some good news." His hostility to a government which had adopted revolutionary policies continued into 1867, when he refused to support the official candidate, his brother, but worked for the clerical opponent. Shortly thereafter, he was dismissed from his post and began a new career as a Catholic politician. During the *Kulturkampf*, he became the leading public speaker for political Catholicism.[25]

Even when there was no clerical candidate running, Catholic circles issued charges of godlessness and Freemasonry. The clergy of the constituency Bonn-Euskirchen supported the Progressive candidate, Karl Freiherr von Proff-Irnich, by denouncing his National-Liberal opponent as a Freemason. Similarly, in Corsenbroich (*Kreis* Gladbach), the word was spread that after the elections "the separation of church and school would be discussed, and if this separation were carried out, it would be the end of religion." The candidate whom the clerical elements were supporting as the defender of religion was Chief Justice Franz Joseph Kratz of the Rhenish Provincial Court of Appeals in Cologne, who sat in the North German *Reichstag* as a left liberal. In the predominantly Protestant *Kreis* Solingen (Düsseldorf District), the Catholic clergy, led by Dean Krey in Opladen, all vigorously supported the Progressive candidate and told their coreligionists that his conservative opponent was guilty of anti-Catholic actions, even though the Progressive was himself a Protestant and Freemason.[26]

In the Catholic areas of Rhineland-Westphalia, the elections of February 1867 were portrayed by the clergy and politically active laity as

[25] See Loë's personnel file, HSTAD RD Pr. Nr. 636 and Röttges, *Die politischen Wahlen*, pp. 310-20.

[26] Kaiser, *Die politischen Strömungen*, pp. 231-41; HSTAD RD Pr. Nr. 575 Bl. 88, 92-93.

a struggle of religion against unbelief—regardless of the actual political affiliation of the candidate whom the Catholic activists were supporting. While the dramatic assertion that religion was in danger had been a staple of political Catholicism since 1848, it had been strikingly ineffective in the elections of the conflict era, so that clerical politicians had frequently abandoned it for other topics. The results of the February 1867 *Reichstag* elections showed that this slogan, far from being obsolete, was more relevant and appealing than ever. Every last Catholic could see that religion really was in danger—what more was needed for proof than the war of 1866? The new electoral system made the vote of every last Catholic count: equal and secret suffrage gave a much greater political weight to the votes of the pious lower classes than had been the case under the three-class electoral system; the introduction of the direct ballot meant it was no longer possible for anti-clerical forces to neutralize the influence of the clergy at the local level by carrying out their electioneering among a small group of electors. Both the impact and the import of these changes were masked by the collapse of political Catholicism in 1866. Beneficiaries of the clerical agitation were often Progressive or sometimes governmental-conservative deputies. The reason they obtained their support from the mass of Catholic voters was not their radical ideas or their loyalty to the victorious King of Prussia, but the endorsement of the clergy as the appropriate defenders of religion in a world where it was menaced by the alliance of atheist subversion and Prussian officialdom.

While the bishops' pastoral letter had touched off this clerical agitation, they were by no means pleased with its results, for both parish priests and lay activists had interpreted their directives in ways divergent from or even directly opposed to what the bishops had in mind. Since there was no Catholic party as such, the lower clergy could and did support candidates repugnant to their superiors. This was most apparent in the Diocese of Münster, where Bishop Johann Georg Müller had attempted, as he had done in the past, to work closely with the authorities and elect governmental conservatives of the Catholic confession. Dean Krins in Kempen had supported the official candidate, Bloemer, while the other priests in the *Kreis* had ignored their superiors' wishes and supported the candidacy of the clerical oppositionist Father Michelis. Chaplain Schmitz in St. Hubert even informed his parishioners that the Dean had been rebuked by the Bishop for supporting Bloemer, thus completely reversing the actual state of affairs. The clergy in *Kreis* Kleve had read Bishop Müller's pastoral letter to their parishioners and explained that it meant, as one official put it, "thou shalt vote for Reichensperger," the clerical candidate even though the official candidate, Count von Loë, was a good Catholic known for his many charitable donations and financial support for the convent in Kevelaer.

Not all the priests of the diocese spurned their bishop's orders. A majority of the clergy in the constituency Moers-Rees supported the official candidate, who was duly elected. Most of the priests in *Kreis* Geldern, unlike their counterparts in *Kreis* Kleve, supported the official candidate, Count von Loë, who then won a narrow victory over Peter Reichensperger in the constituency Kleve-Geldern with the help of the votes of the Protestant minority. The clerical newspaper, *Kölnische Blätter*, denounced the Geldern clergy as cowards and traitors to the Catholic cause for having followed the orders of their bishop and not the advice of the *Kölnische Blätter*.[27]

Even the more independently minded bishops were not pleased with the behavior of the lower clergy in February 1867. The pastoral letter of the Archbishop of Cologne and his suffragans, after stressing the importance of electing good Catholics, had stated: "In any event, one thing is unquestionably both most desirable and essential for the highest and most sacred interests of the state as well as the church: that the people's representatives in the *Reichstag*, who will help decide the future constitution of the North German Confederation, not be atheists, but believing and obedient Christians [nicht Ungläubige sondern gläubige und brave Christen]." As the concluding phrase makes clear, the bishops wished above all to see representatives of the left defeated at the elections. They did not expect parish priests or chaplains to carry out their orders by preaching sermons in favor of Freemasons and militantly oppositional Progressives, disputing with gendarmes, or tearing up the ballots for good Catholic noblemen or officials. Local and district authorities, grown accustomed to regarding the Catholic clergy as reliable electoral allies, were also shocked to find so many priests taking an openly oppositional stance. They protested energetically and demanded that the bishops rebuke this behavior and bring their unruly subordinates back in line.[28]

Following conversations with the provincial governors and correspondence with the Interior Minister in the spring of 1867, the bishops acceded to these demands and ordered the clergy not to take part in the August 1867 elections for the first legislative session of the North German Confederation. Priests were directed not to stand for office, nor to preach on the elections, nor to engage in any other form of

[27] Röttges, *Die politischen Wahlen*, pp. 310-26; HSTAD RD Pr. Nr. 575 Bl. 1-62; Nr. 576 Bl. 46.

[28] STAM RAR I Nr. 1419 Bl. 175-87; HSTAD RD Pr. Nr. 574 Bl. 249; Nr. 575 Bl. 15, 59-62.

political agitation.[29] With scattered exceptions, the clergy obeyed their superiors and remained politically passive. Cut off from their main campaign workers, the lay protagonists of political Catholicism generally did not put up their own candidate but supported another: on occasion, as in Aachen, a governmental conservative, but, more often than not, a radical oppositional Progressive.

The winning candidates in August 1867 were generally the officially supported Conservatives or National Liberals. Oppositional Progressives could pick up only a few scattered constituencies. Unlike February, the support of political Catholicism was not worth much; most of the clerically sponsored candidacies were defeated. Clerical politics without the clergy was a futile affair. This was particularly apparent in Düsseldorf and Essen, where there had been no Catholic candidates in February 1867. Local committees nominated clerical candidates in August, but without the priests on their side they achieved derisory results: under twenty percent of the votes in Essen, barely nine percent in Düsseldorf.[30]

The dominant factor in the August elections was not the victors but the turnout. Participation dropped radically; rates were between one-half and one-third of their February values. The decline in participation was felt throughout the North German Confederation; it reflected the lack of novelty of the August as compared to the February elections; the effects, in the countryside, of the beginning of the harvest season; and, in the predominantly·Catholic areas, the non-participation of the clergy which made the occasion seem not terribly important. The elections to the Prussian Parliament in November 1867 followed a similar course. To all the other causes of a low turnout came the frequently mentioned phenomenon of "electoral fatigue." The Prussian elections were at least the third held in 1867 alone; in many constituencies, because of runoffs in previous elections, they were the fourth or fifth time within ten months that voters were summoned to the polls. Lack of interest and non-participation were virtually universal.[31]

---

[29] STAM RAR I Nr. 1419 Bl. 225-26; HSTAD RD Pr. Nr. 577 Bl. 129; Weinandy, "Die Wahlen des Regierungsbezirks Köln," pp. 251-58; Lepper, "Regierungsbezirk Aachen," p. 200. The Archbishop of Cologne agreed to issue such an order to his clergy only on condition that it not be made public, but the news immediately leaked to the press and was published in the *Kölnische Zeitung*, Aug. 21, 1867.

[30] On the elections of August 1867, see Weinandy, "Die Wahlen des Regierungsbezirks Köln," pp. 251-59; Lepper, "Regierungsbezirk Aachen," pp. 200-221; Moellers, "Reichstagswahlkreis Essen," pp. 80 ff.; Kaiser, *Die politischen Strömungen*, pp. 244-47; HSTAD RD Pr. Nr. 577 Bl. 40-275; STAM RAR I Nr. 1419 Bl. 166-204; STAD M1 IL Nr. 75. For the North German Confederation as a whole, cf. Hamerow, *Social Foundations*, 2: 334-35.

[31] On the elections to the Prussian Parliament in November 1867, see Weinandy,

The February 1867 elections had shown the enormous influence of the Catholic clergy and the political impact of the slogan "religion is in danger," in conditions of universal, direct, and equal suffrage. In these elections, for the first and last time, clerical influence was often applied outside the interests of political Catholicism. Since the Catholic parliamentary caucus had been dissolved, deputies elected with clerical support were spread out over the entire political spectrum, from the Conservatives to the Progressives, from the particularists to the National Liberals. Even in the constituencies it was not always clear who was the "Catholic candidate." The clergy was frequently divided on whom to support; the lay activists could not always count on clerical cooperation. It was not the lack of enthusiasm, or insufficient clerical influence, from which political Catholicism suffered throughout 1867, but a lack of organization. In the following three years, a dense network of Catholic political clubs and associations would be created, programs and manifestoes drawn up, and the cooperation of the clergy successfully solicited in order to channel the inflamed religious sentiments of the mass of the electorate into votes for clerical candidates.

THE REORGANIZATION OF POLITICAL CATHOLICISM, 1867-1871

Catholic Political Clubs

The classic form of nineteenth-century sociability was the club or private association. Members met at regular intervals to hear lectures, read newspapers, or engage in conversation. The association was structured, with dues, bylaws, balloting on the admission of new members, and often a rented or owned regular meeting place. The members typically came from bourgeois circles, although, as the century wore on, these associations became more common among the lower middle classes. Before the existence of centrally directed mass political parties, the club was also the predominant form of local political organization. It could just be a structured version of the informal cooperation of the local notables, or it could be extended downward socially to include the petit-bourgeoisie and, on occasion, the very top strata of the working class.[32]

"Die Wahlen des Regierungsbezirks Köln," p. 265; Lepper, "Regierungsbezirk Aachen," pp. 233-42; Kaiser, Die politischen Strömungen, pp. 249-55; HSTAD RD Pr. Nr. 566 Bl. 17-79; reports of the Landräte in STAM RM Nr. VII-68; electoral results in STAM OP Nr. 501; STAD M1 Pr. Nr. 260. All accounts of this election stress the unusually poor turnout; it is impossible to give exact figures, however, as the Prussian government stopped collecting Landtag electoral statistics in 1866 and resumed the practice only in 1898.

[32] On the clubs as a nineteenth-century form of sociability in Prussia's western prov-

The first example of a politically active Catholic club was the Constantia in Aachen, founded in 1846. During the revolution of 1848-1849, Pius Associations were set up as organs of political Catholicism in all parts of Germany. To a great extent, however, they were just the lengthened arm of the local clergy. The groups proved ephemeral; by the early 1850s most of them had disappeared, a consequence of massive lack of interest in politics. The few that remained generally severed all connection with politics and concerned themselves with religious or charitable matters.[33]

The Progressive electoral victories of the early 1860s provided the first impetus for the formation of clerical political associations in the Rhineland and Westphalia, as Catholics hoped to win back lost parliamentary seats through better organization. Although the electoral efforts were generally unsuccessful, the organizations remained. Between 1867 and 1871 there was a great increase in this organizational activity. Table 4.1 gives an account of all the organizations of political Catholicism existing during the *Kulturkampf* in the northern Rhineland and Westphalia, whose origins can be dated to 1871 or earlier. It is striking how many were founded or reorganized between 1867 and 1871. By 1870-1871, a Catholic political club existed in almost every major city in the northern Rhineland and Westphalia, as well as in a number of smaller towns. Clubs were even to be found in such predominantly Protestant cities as Elberfeld, Ruhrort, Dortmund, Hagen, and Witten. The formation of the Prussian Center Party in the fall of 1870 was preceded by the reorganization of political Catholicism on the local level.

The Westphalian Peasant League

The organizer of the first Catholic peasant league and, indeed, of the first peasant league of any kind in Germany was Burghard Freiherr von Schorlemer, scion of a distinguished family of the Westphalian Catholic nobility. After service in the Prussian army, where he took part in the suppression of the democratic insurrection in Baden in 1849, he purchased the estate Alst in *Kreis* Steinfurt (Münster District)

---

inces, see Henning, *Das westdeutsche Bürgertum*, pp. 58, 173-76, 205-209, 258-59, 312-13, 359-61, 400-403, and 443-49. On the political undercurrents of different social clubs, cf. Ficker, *Kulturkampf in Münster*, pp. 150-51.

[33] See, for instance, STAM OP Nr. 1914 Bl. 19-35, 54-55; HSTAD RD Pr. Nr. 866 Bl. 56-57; HSTAD RA Pr. Nr. 702 Bl. 171 ff.; Aachen Police Commissioner to RA, Dec. 9, 1856 and RA to OPK, Sep. 5, 1853, HSTAD RA Pr. Nr. 780. In Düren (Aachen District), the Pius Association was infiltrated and taken over by the democrats, and in 1850 the embarrassed clergy was forced to dissolve its own creation.

TABLE 4.1
Catholic Political Clubs in the Northern
Rhineland and Westphalia

Place	Name	Founding Date	Remarks
Northern Rhineland			
Aachen District			
Aachen	Constantia	1846	Oldest of its type.
Stolberg	Katholischer Volksverein	1867 (Nov.)	One of the most active of these groups in the 1870s and heavily surveyed by the police.
Eschweiler Burtscheid	Bürgergesellschaft		In existence by January 1871 and helped nominate the Center candidate in the constituency Aachen (country)-Eupen that year.
Düren	Verein	1862	Later renamed Katholischer Volksverein. Founded as a result of the liberal electoral victory in 1862.
Eupen	Constantia	1862	Modeled after the Aachen Constantia.
Cologne District			
Cologne	Neuer Bürger Verein (later Katholischer Volksverein)	1867	Successor to the Bürger Verein founded in 1863 and dissolved c. 1866; according to Karl Bachem, the leading organization in Rhenish political Catholicism.
Bonn	Bürger Verein zur geselligen Erholung	1863	Largely bourgeois membership.
Bonn	Katholischer Verein	1863	Largely petit-bourgeois membership, especially master craftsmen.
Düsseldorf District			
Düsseldorf	Confidentia	1867	Members largely intellectuals and bourgeois.

TABLE 4.1 (*cont.*)

Place	Name	Founding Date	Remarks
Düsseldorf	Constantia	1867 (Jan.)	Members mostly from the well-off lower middle class [gut situierten mittleren Bürgerstand]; the main organization of political Catholicism in Düsseldorf.
Essen and six other towns in *Landkreis* Essen			
	Katholisches Casino (later other names)	Late 1860s	According to the *Landrat*, founded on the urging of the Archbishop of Cologne.
Neuß	Constantia	1861	See above, p. 147
Ruhrort	Unitas	1865	
Mönchen-gladbach	Concordia	Late in 1870	Played an important role in the *Reichstag* elections of 1871.
Viersen	Bürger Verein	1865	Members mostly master craftsmen; founded to influence town council elections in a clerical-conservative sense.
Süchteln	Katholischer Leseverein		Politically active in the February 1867 *Reichstag* elections; probably the most radical of all these groups.
Elberfeld	Parliament		In existence by the late 1860s.

Westphalia
Arnsberg District

Place	Name	Founding Date	Remarks
Dortmund	Katholischer Männerverein	1866	
Dortmund	Geselliger Bürger-verein	1869	Possibly a successor to the above. Ran candidates in the 1869 city council elections.
Witten	Katholischer Männerverein	1863	
Hagen	Katholischer Bürgerverein	1863	Founded to raise money for the local Catholic journeymen's association, but turned to local politics and influenced city council elections.

TABLE 4.1 (cont.)

Place	Name	Founding Date	Remarks
Minden District			
Wieden-brück	Katholischer Verein	1848	Reorganized c. 1870.
Höxter	Katholisches Casino	1868	Founded by "*Bürger* of the ultramontane party" because of "confessional quarrels over the municipal budget."
Münster District			
Münster	Gesellschaft Einstracht	1867	Membership included both the Catholic notables and master craftsmen.

NOTE: This list includes only those organizations whose pre-1871 existence can be proved. Since the 1874 inquiry into Catholic organizations, the main source of information on the existence of Catholic political clubs, rarely includes founding dates of orgnizations, it is probable that this list understates the number of local Catholic political clubs in existence by the end of the 1860s.

SOURCES:

Place	Source
Aachen	See above, pp. 71-72.
Stolberg	HSTAD RA Nr. 4817
Eschweiler and Burtscheid	Lepper, "Regierunsbezirk Aachen," pp. 296-98
Düren	HSTAD RA Pr. Nr. 702
Eupen	HSTAD RA Pr. Nr. 703
Cologne	Denk, "Die Wahlen in Köln," pp. 158, 170 ff.; Bachem, *Zentrumspartei*, 3: 26-27; *Germania* Apr. 21, 1872
Bonn	Kaiser, *Die politischen Strömungen*, pp. 193-94, 250
Düsseldorf	HSTAD RD Nr. 288 Bl. 7-64 and Chaplain Hömmacher to Dean Herten, Oct. 6, 1871 HAEK Gen. XXIII 4 I
Essen	HSTAD RD Pr. Nr. 1233 Bl. 118-21
Elberfeld	Chaplain Hömmacher to Dean Herten, Oct. 6, 1871 HAEK Gen. XXIII 4 I
Neuß	Röttges, *Die politischen Wahlen*, pp. 240 ff., 267 ff.
Ruhrort	HSTAD RD Pr. Nr. 866 Bl. 54-93
Viersen	Same as for Ruhrort
Mönchengladbach	HSTAD RD Pr. Nr. 1233 Bl. 115-16; Müller, *Die christliche Gewerkschaftsbewegung*, pp. 71-72.
Süchteln	HSTAD RD Pr. Nr. 577 Bl. 6-10; Röttges, *Die politischen Wahlen*, pp. 321-28.
Dortmund and Witten	STAM RAR I Nr. 101
Hagen	As with Dortmund and Witten plus Kaufmann Vogelsang (Hagen) to Bishop Martin of Paderborn, Feb. 24, 1864 AGVP XVIII, 1
Wiedenbrück	STAD M1 IP Nr. 363
Höxter	Same
Münster	Ficker, *Kulturkampf in Münster*, pp. 150-53; STAM OP Nr. 1601 IV Bl. 31-41, 50-51, 75-93

from Wilderich Freiherr von Ketteler, brother of the celebrated Bishop of Mainz, Wilhelm Emmanuel von Ketteler. Schorlemer founded the first league, at the time limited to *Kreis* Steinfurt, in 1862.[34]

The ideology of the peasant league was a conservative anti-modernism. Schorlemer denounced the development of industry, the actions of political parties, and the abolition of anti-usury laws. He called for the creation of a Christian and corporate social order and stressed the importance of legally guaranteeing the Westphalian custom of unequal inheritance, so as to preserve economically viable peasant landholdings. He proclaimed drunkenness, immoral behavior, and the lack of piety as major dangers to the existence of a healthy peasantry.

The cloud of traditionalist rhetoric ought not to obscure the actual activities of the organization. It provided cheap fire and veterinary insurance, low interest loans, and free legal advice in drawing up wills. The league sponsored lectures and exhibits on modern agricultural methods; it agitated and lobbied to improve the economic standing of the peasantry—at first for lower property taxes and later for an agricultural protective tariff.

When these activities are considered, the real purpose and addressees of Schorlemer's organization become clear. The Peasant League was not providing emergency assistance for impoverished peasants, about to be overwhelmed by the tidal wave of modernity. Rather, it would help relatively well-off farmers take maximum advantage of the possibilities of a developing capitalist market economy. The heavy dose of traditionalistic religion and morality contained in the league's programmatic statements gave it an entree into the increasingly devout Catholic milieu of rural Westphalia and, in particular, helped gain the enthusiastic support of the clergy for the organization.[35]

These forward-looking activities of the Peasant League formed the basis for the political effectiveness of Schorlemer's creation. It was precisely the more affluent farmers who were the mainstay of rural liberalism. In addressing them, the liberals had worked through the agricultural societies and had stressed the practical benefits of the program of the left: lower taxes, access to expanded markets through railroad building and trade treaties, etc. The Peasant League offered

[34] An outline of Schorlemer's life can be found in the popular biography by Franz Schmidt, *Burghard von Schorlemer-Alst*; the early history of the Peasants' League is best followed from the organization's official history, Kerckerinck zur Borg (ed.), *Geschichte des Westfälischen Bauernstandes*, pp. 378-97. A modern, scholarly biography of Schorlemer and a history of the Peasant League remain a desideratum.

[35] On the support of the clergy, see LA Kr. Recklinghausen to RM, Nov. 8, 1870, STAM RM Nr. VII-68; on the relationship between "traditionalist" ideology and "modernist" practices in peasant organizations, see Lewis, "Lower Austria," passim.

these farmers the practical benefits of liberalism, a patriarchal-conservative ideology useful in dealing with their servants and hired help, and political integration into the dominant religious milieu—an unbeatable combination.

Schorlemer made his ideas available to the reading public in his book *Die Lage des Bauernstandes in Westfalen und was ihm not tut* (The Condition of the Peasantry in Westphalia and What it Must Do), published in 1864. In other *Kreise*, Peasant Leagues began to be formed on the Steinfurt model, the largest and most important of these by the farmer Johannes Breuker of Buer, *Kreis* Recklinghausen, in 1868. The political consequences followed immediately. The League dominated the 1870 *Landtag* elections in the constituency Borken-Recklinghausen, and two clerical candidates were elected for the first time since 1861.[36]

In November 1871 the local organizations united to form the Westphalian Peasant League. The group's 1,820 members, according to a July 1872 membership list, were concentrated in the area of large peasant farming in the Münster District and adjacent regions of the North German plain. There were no members from the mountainous *Hochsauerland*, with its small holdings and impoverished peasantry.[37]

The new association had intimate links to political Catholicism. The League's Chairman (Schorlemer), his deputy (Breuker), and seven of the fifteen members of the executive committee were also members of the Westphalian Provincial Committee of the Center Party. In 1871, Schorlemer was elected president of the Westphalian Provincial Agricultural Society; during the *Kulturkampf* he was able to make political use of his position, as the liberals had done with similar positions in the previous decade.[38] The *Kulturkampf* was fought out with especial vehemence in the rural areas of the Münster District, but, thanks to Schorlemer's actions, the clerical party had already seized the key positions before the struggle began.

Origins of the Christian Social Movement

As with other social groups, the years 1867 to 1871 saw a great mobilization of the Catholic working class. The post-1866 political

---

[36] Pülke, "Kreis Recklinghausen," pp. 121-22, and the material in STAM cited in the previous note.

[37] STAM OP Nr. 1601 I Bl. 4-5, 41.

[38] On the agricultural society during the *Kulturkampf*, see ibid., Bl. 244. The directors of the Westphalian Peasant League are from a list published in Kerckerinck zur Borg (ed.), *Geschichte des Westfälischen Bauernstandes*, pp. 396-97; members of the provincial committee of the Center from an electoral appeal in *Germania*, Dec. 22, 1873.

environment certainly provided a favorable climate for clerical agitation, but the movement began as a reaction to agitation of a very
different kind—that of the social-democrats.

In the early and mid-1860s, the Rhineland had been one of the
centers of the Lassalleans, but their influence was largely confined to
predominantly Protestant areas in the *Wuppertal* and the *Bergisches
Land*. In the Catholic regions, there existed only a few groups in cities
of the Rhine Valley—Düsseldorf (Lassalle's home town), Cologne, and
Mülheim a. Rhein.[39] The 1867 *Reichstag* elections provided a good
forum for social-democratic agitation, and the Lassalleans in the three
towns mentioned above put up candidates in their constituencies—
Düsseldorf, Cologne, and Mülheim-Gummersbach. They obtained only
modest results—7.0, 9.5, and 8.5 percent respectively—but the very
fact of those campaigns showed the red flag as it had not been seen
since 1849. The most spectacular electoral result was achieved in
Essen, where in August 1867 the Social-Democratic candidate finished
third in a five-man field (Conservative, National-Liberal, Progressive,
Catholic, and Social-Democratic), and in a three-way by-election of
March 1868 obtained 49.0 percent of the votes in the run-off against
the Conservative candidate, including a majority in the city of Essen
itself.[40]

The Social-Democrats continued a lively agitation in the closing
years of the 1860s. Meetings were held and local groups founded
among the factory workers and handloom weavers of the lower Rhine
textile districts. The agitation was carried to the mining and metal-
working centers in the predominantly Catholic areas of the *Bergisches
Land* and to the Aachen industrial area. There were twelve hundred
participants at the meeting in Bensburg (*Kreis* Mülheim, Cologne District), a town of some nine thousand inhabitants, in late 1869. In
February 1870, the Düren Police Commissioner claimed there were
five hundred Social-Democrats in the city and inquired about the avail-
ability of troops to suppress strikes and disorders he saw as forth-
coming. The commissioner's fears were certainly exaggerated, but not
entirely without foundation. The Social-Democrats had played a leading role in the 1868-1869 miners' strikes in Eschweiler (*Landkreis*
Aachen) and Essen. The latter, in September 1868, had encompassed
some fifteen hundred workers and was accompanied by street disturbances. Both repressive measures of the authorities and internal
quarrels within socialist ranks—the two rival Lassallean organizations,

[39] Jürgen Reulecke (ed.), *Arbeiterbewegung am Rhein und Ruhr*, pp. 50-80.
[40] STDD II Nr. 28; Denk, "Die Wahlen in Köln," pp. 186-89; Weinandy, "Die Wahlen
des Regierungsbezirks Köln," pp. 248-50; Moellers, "Reichstagswahlkreis Essen," pp.
80 ff. and 127.

led by Johann Baptist von Schweitzer and the Countess Hatzfeld, and, after 1869, representatives of the Eisenachers, were all active in the region—failed to stem the advance of the movement. By the outbreak of the Franco-Prussian War, it appeared to have obtained a definite base of support in the industrial areas of the northern Rhineland.[41]

The Catholic clergy saw in the Social-Democrats the latest form of a godless radicalism they had been battling since 1848, and reacted sharply to socialist efforts. The Vicar Juchem in Steele (*Landkreis Essen*) took direct action when he invaded a Lassallean electoral meeting with some of his parishioners in August 1867, interrupted the speakers and, finally, caused such an uproar that the police intervened and sent everyone home. Elsewhere, the clergy made their opposition known in less dramatic but equally firm fashion.[42]

It quickly became apparent that an exclusively negative approach to the socialist agitation would not suffice to suppress it. From this insight the Christian Social movement was born. In Düsseldorf, at the beginning of 1871, as Chaplain Hömmacher noted, ". . . Schulzeans [i.e., followers of the Progressive advocate of producers' cooperatives Schulze-Delitsch], Lassalleans, and Schweitzerians fought over the terrain, and each of these anti-Christian parties sought to win support among the common people." Consequently, he and several other priests met with "a dozen solid factory workers," wrote out statutes for a Christian-Social Association, got another thirty workers to join, and then held the first public meeting. One hundred fifty new members signed up, and the efforts of the Social-Democrats to disrupt the proceedings were entirely unsuccessful. The new association quickly obtained five hundred members, far outdistancing its socialist competition.[43]

If the political impetus for the Christian Social movement came from the need to counter socialist agitation, the movement's organizational form was an outgrowth of the sodalities, congregations, and related Catholic organizations which had developed in the industrial areas

---

[41] On socialist activities in the Ruhr basin at this time, see Reulecke (ed.), *Arbeiterbewegung am Rhein und Ruhr*, pp. 90-92; Moellers, "Die Essener Arbeiterbewegung," Tenfelde, *Bergarbeiterschaft*, pp. 437-64. For the lower Rhenish weaving areas, see Schmitz, *Arbeiterbewegung im Raum Düsseldorf*, pp. 44-97, 101-106; HSTAD RD Nr. 302 Bl. 233-34, Nr. 303 Bl. 18-122, 184, 200 ff.; HSTAD LA Kr. Kempen Nr. 509. For the *Bergisches Land* and the Aachen industrial area, see Hombach, "Reichs- und Landtagswahlen," pp. 83-87; HSTAD RA Nr. 1633 Bl. 3-20, Nr. 4801 Bl. 16-27.

[42] HSTAD RD Pr. Nr. 577 Bl. 143; cf. Moellers, "Reichstagswahlkreis Essen," pp. 79-80; Hombach, "Reichs- und Landtagswahlen," pp. 86-87.

[43] Chaplain Hömmacher to Dean Herten, Oct. 6, 1871, HAEK Gen. XXIII 4, I. Similarly, see HSTAD RA Nr. 4801 Bl. 38; the report from Düren in HSTAD RA Nr. 4817, and Lepper, "Kaplan Cronenberg," pp. 64-67.

after mid-century. The St. Paul's Workers' Association in Aachen, the largest Christian Social group, counting some five thousand members by the mid-1870s, was founded by Chaplain Cronenberg in 1868 as a congregation for unmarried factory workers, precisely like the other, Jesuit-led congregations of the city, which were intended for members of one specific social class. The Christian Social Associations in *Landkreis* Essen were simply renamed Catholic miners' associations.[44]

The Jesuits hoped to apply to the "social question" the techniques they had used so successfully in the missions. Father H. J. Zurstraessen, superior of the Essen establishment of the Jesuits, hoped to see the creation of a Marian workers' association which would be the basis for a producers' cooperative, as explained in the theories of the "Social Bishop" of Mainz, Wilhelm Emmanuel von Ketteler. The Essen Jesuits led spiritual exercises and preached missionary sermons on the social question. In several towns in *Landkreis* Essen, and in the city of Essen itself, they formed Marianic workers' congregations or transformed existing Marianic congregations into workers' congregations.[45]

The local leaders of the Catholic journeymen's associations, the Kolpingvereine, in their 1870 conference, called for an increased activity of "the oldest Christian Social association" in combatting "the deceptive teachings of a distorted socialism and its egotistical leaders." They wanted to expand the organization's membership by enrolling workers in cities where no Christian Social association existed.[46]

Kolping's associations exerted an important indirect influence on the Christian Social movement. As Chaplain Cronenberg noted, "the blessed Kolping" had provided the solution to the "artisan question"; now the Christian Social associations would provide a solution to the "worker question." Less rhetorically, and more practically, the Düsseldorf Christian Socials modeled their association's statutes on those of the Kolpingvereine, including the latter's celebrated exclusion of "political questions and hateful religious polemics" from the organization.[47]

[44] Lepper, "Kaplan Cronenberg," pp. 64-67; Tenfelde, *Bergarbeiterschaft*, p. 468. On the class-specific Aachen congregations, see above, p. 77.

[45] H. J. Zurstraessen S.J. (Essen) to Archbishop Melchers of Cologne, Dec. 22, 1870 and Feb. 15, 1871; Pf. Hohe (Steele) to Archbishop Melchers, Jan. 14, and Jan. 26, 1871; and Rektor Lenterborn (Dilldorf) to Archbishop Melchers, Jun. 18, 1871, HAEK Gen. XXIII 4, I.

[46] *Generalpräses* Schaeffer (Cologne) to Bishop Martin of Paderborn, Oct. 16, 1869; and a printed memorandum on the meeting of all the *Präsiden* of the Gesellenvereine, dated Cologne, Jun. 24, 1870, in AGVP XVIII, 1. The statutes of such an expanded Gesellenverein, the "Katholischer Junggesellen-Verein," in Hardenberg, founded August 1871, can be found in HSTAD RD Nr. 288 Bl. 68-71.

[47] Lepper, "Kaplan Cronenberg," pp. 64-67; Schmitz, *Arbeiterbewegung im Raum*

The influence of the old forms extended to the point where some priests saw the new groups simply as another version of the old. In 1871, the workers of Gürzenich (*Kreis* Düren), a town in the Aachen industrial area, wished to found a Christian Social association and asked Father Zander, the parish priest, to preside. The clergyman was somewhat skeptical. What is the necessity for such a group, he asked the Archbishop of Cologne in a letter, in his parish there already existed:

> . . . a beautiful death benefit society attached to the Brotherhood of the Heart of Mary, a Marianic League, which sixteen-year-olds join and belong to for several years . . . and, further, a municipal insurance plan with illness and death benefits. I therefore suggested [in place of the Christian Social association] a sewing and knitting school and Sunday school. . . . There are now fifty-eight boys, youths, and men who participate, among them the better part of the workers . . . we practice harmless worldly songs so that the filthy songs may be eventually banished from factories and workshops.[48]

The Vicar Frechen, who was feuding with his superior, went ahead and organized a Christian Social association to spite him. The insubordinate Vicar was eventually transferred, and Father Zander, after "peace and quiet has, thank God, been reestablished in my parish," took over the leadership of the association so that it would not fall into the hands of those "who might endanger the salvation of the workers' souls."

Father Zander's approach to the organization of the Catholic working class—namely, continue the old forms under a new name—may have sufficed in small industrial towns such as Gürzenich, but was clearly not enough in a socially and politically more lively environment. The question posed in Aachen, Essen, or Düsseldorf was how would the forms of the post-1850 religious revival—the clerically-led organization, combining religious, social, and mutual benefit functions—be adapted to political ends? This was an issue hotly debated in political Catholicism. The ideas of Bishop Ketteler of Mainz on the social

---

Düsseldorf, p. 116. Schmitz, although citing the statutes of the Düsseldorf Christian Social Association, seems unaware of the relation of those statutes to the statutes of the Kolpingvereine.

[48] Pf. Zander to Archbishop of Cologne, Dec. 4, 1871 HAEK Gen. XXIII 4, I. For the following paragraphs, see the letters to the Archbishop from Pf. Zander, Aug. 7, 1872 and Feb. 24, 1873; from the *Vorstand* of the Gürzenich Christian Social Association, Nov. 16, 1871, Jun. 6, 1872, and Feb. 11, 1873, and from Pf. Teller (Ladersdorf) Dec. 6, 1871 and Aug. 20, 1872, all in HAEK Gen. XXIII 4, I.

question had obtained a growing audience in the 1860s. The 1868 *Katholikentag*, the meeting of Catholic notables and representatives of Catholic associations from all over Central Europe, had recommended the creation of Christian Social associations, and in the same year the *Christlich-Soziale Blätter*, the theoretical organ of the movement, was founded.[49]

In the late 1860s, all participants in the nascent Christian Social movement were agreed on its relation to the reemerging Catholic political organizations. All three of the laymen among the founders of the Düsseldorf Christian Social Association were also members of the executive committee of the local Catholic political club, the Constantia, and the Catholic bourgeoisie of Essen seems to have played a similar role in helping start the Christian Social Association there. In Stolberg, unlike most of the other industrial towns in *Landkreis* Aachen, a Christian Social Association was never formed; the local Catholic political club, the Volks-Verein, formed a "workers section" (Arbeiter-Abteilung) in its place. The first conference of the Rhenish-Westphalian Christian Social Associations, held in Elberfeld in March 1870, was simultaneously a demonstration of a revived political Catholicism. The meeting was chaired by the Westphalian aristocrat and Catholic politician Burghard von Schorlemer-Alst. Resolutions were passed praising the peasant leagues and calling for the formation of local Catholic political clubs—thus showing that exclusively proletarian questions were by no means the only issues debated.[50]

When the authorities took note of the early Christian Social movement, their opinions of it were generally a reflection of their attitudes toward political Catholicism in general. In Aachen, where governmental and clerical elements continued to maintain good relations into the early 1870s, the authorities put no difficulties in the way of the expansion of Chaplain Cronenberg's St. Paul's Workers' Association, later to become the most radical of all the Christian Social groups and the one the government persecuted with the most vigor. In Essen, on the other hand, where a rapprochement between the *Landrat* and the increasingly "national" liberals had taken place in the late 1860s, the

[49] A good summary of the extensive literature on these developments can be found in Tenfelde, *Bergarbeiterschaft*, pp. 464-66.

[50] See the letter of Chaplain Hömmacher cited in note 47; Tenfelde, *Bergarbeiterschaft*, pp. 466-67; the report of the *Landrat* of *Landkreis* Aachen in HSTAD RA Nr. 4817, and LAK 403 Nr. 7297 Bl. 434-37. Schorlemer, the "peasant king," was also deeply involved in organizing the Catholic miners. In 1867, he sponsored, along with the Catholic publisher Lambert Lensing in Dortmund, the first joint festival of all the Catholic miners' associations in the (predominantly Protestant) eastern Ruhr basin. Tenfelde, "Mining Festivals," pp. 400-401.

authorities were suspicious of the Christian Social Association from the very first, in spite of its repeatedly emphasized anti-socialism and its interconfessional character.[51]

Within the context of loyalty to political Catholicism two definite tendencies emerged in the Christian Social movement. One, centered around the movement's theoretical journal, the *Christlich-Soziale Blätter*, and enjoying the support of prominent Catholic politicians such as Schorlemer-Alst and the Freiherr von Loë, as well as the encouragement of the Archbishop of Cologne, worked to see the Catholic workers' associations closely tied to the local notable leadership of the nascent Center Party. A Christian Social movement organized as a kind of independent, proletarian caucus within political Catholicism—even a caucus under clerical leadership—was most unwelcome to them.

The other tendency, which was working to precisely this end, was centered around a group of young priests in Aachen. Their leader was Franz Cronenberg, Chaplain in St. Adalbert's parish church in Aachen; he was assisted by his friend Chaplain Johannes Laaf, who, like Cronenberg, had been born in Düren, and by Chaplain Hermann Joseph Litzinger, whom Cronenberg had met when they were theology students in Bonn. In 1872, Laaf was transferred to Essen, where he took over the leadership of the Christian Social Association there and found support for his activities among the younger clergy, but reserve and even hostility on the part of the older priests.

Unlike the clerical leaders of the Kolpingvereine, the Jesuits, or even the majority of the clergy active in the Christian Social movement, this group favored a trade-union-like, independent organization of the workers and regarded strikes as socially legitimate, a practice by no means to be abhorred. The difference in attitude between the two wings of the movement can be summed up in the stated purposes of two local Christian Social Associations. In Düsseldorf, where more conservative views prevailed, Chaplain Hömmacher explained the purpose of the organization as leading the workers to "contentedness, thriftiness, Christian sentiment, and work on behalf of the Catholic church, and the Christian religion . . . ," while the Aachen Christian Socials gave a quite different purpose to their group, namely, "the material and spiritual improvement of working people by all legal means."[52]

[51] LAK 403 Nr. 7296 Bl. 595-96; HSTAD RD Pr. Nr. 1233 Bl. 118-21 and HSTAD RD Pr. Nr. 566 Bl. 135-39. According to the *Landrat*, some 450 of the c. 2,300 members of the Essen Christian Social Association in early 1871 were Protestants.

[52] On the two wings of the Christian Social movement, see Lepper, "Kaplan Cronenberg," passim.

Delineating these differences, however, means getting ahead of the narrative. It was only after 1871 that two distinct tendencies emerged within the Christian Social movement.[53] Before that time, a common hostility to liberalism and social democracy and a desire to go beyond purely moralistic and voluntaristic approaches to the "social question" united all those active in the Christian Social movement and played an important role in mobilizing the industrial working class for a revived political Catholicism.

THE TRIUMPH OF POLITICAL CATHOLICISM, 1868-1871

The Petition Movement of 1868-1869

The first campaign of the reorganized or, perhaps more accurately, reorganizing, political Catholicism was the petition movement of 1868 and 1869. Throughout the Rhineland and Westphalia, large public meetings were held and tens of thousands of signatures gathered in defense of confessionally bound public education and in support of the beleaguered position of the Pope.[54] Both of these issues were staples of political Catholicism, but their emphasis in 1868-1869 tended to lead toward a political realignment.

The school petitions meant a break with the liberals. The abolition of separate state school systems and the introduction of a secular system of school inspection in place of the existing clerical one had long been a demand of the left. In 1868-1869, the liberals, especially the oppositional left liberals, pressed the government on this issue, but against the hostility of the orthodox Lutheran Minister of Educational and Religious Affairs, Heinrich von Mühler, they could make no headway.[55]

This liberal demand made apparent the gap between the Progressive deputies from the western provinces and the Catholic voters who had supported them. A striking example was in the constituency Düren-Jülich (Aachen District), where the clergy had successfully supported radical oppositional candidates in both *Reichstag* and the Prussian

---

[53] The beginnings of tension between the two wings in the Essen area can be seen from the letters of Father Zurstraessen (a partisan of the more conservative position), cited above, n. 49, and the report of the *Landrat* in HSTAD RD Pr. Nr. 1233 Bl. 118-21.

[54] On these campaigns, see Kaiser, *Die politischen Strömungen*, p. 257; Lepper, "Regierungsbezirk Aachen," p. 250; Hombach, "Reichs- und Landtagswahlen," pp. 88-89; Moellers, "Reichstagswahlkreis Essen," pp. 161-62; HSTAD RA Nr. 818, *Zeitungsberichte* of the *Landräte* for 1869; *Kölnische Zeitung*, Dec. 21, 1867, Mar. 11, 1868 and esp. Apr. 15, 1869.

[55] Meyer, *Untertanen*, pp. 46-47.

Landtag elections of 1867. When Franz Jakob Freiherr von Hilgers, representing the constituency in both legislatures, supported the liberal call for a more secular educational system, he suddenly found that all his supporters had disappeared.[56]

At the local level as well, the petition movement brought the old clerical-liberal tensions back into strong relief. In *Kreis* Mülheim (Cologne District), the liberals circulated a counter-petition to the Catholics, calling for a secular public educational system. The leader of this movement, city councilman Keller in Mülheim a. Rhein, was, as the *Landrat* noted, "still suffering from the ills he contracted in 1848."[57]

The converse to growing Catholic-liberal tensions was a certain reconciliation of the clerical partisans with the authorities. The retention of a confessionally oriented public school system was an issue on which Catholic politicians and Berlin ministers could agree.[58] A political Catholicism cultivating good relations with the authorities and bad ones with the left was clearly more pleasing to the bishops than the oppositional attitude manifested in 1867. The reorientation of political Catholicism implied in the petition movement was thus the first step in achieving a return of the lower clergy to the political scene, an absolute necessity for the clerical cause.

The petitions in favor of the Pope were important in a similar context. The Catholic campaign in support of the embattled Papacy had begun after the northern Italian war of 1859 and the expedition of Garibaldi in southern Italy the following year. Throughout the first half of the 1860s, petitions were circulated, money collected, special services held, and prayers said for Pius IX. These efforts, however, were not successfully connected to the activities of political Catholicism in Prussia. The movement to rescue the beleaguered Pope flourished, while representatives from the Catholic caucus were defeated in one election after another. Supporting the Pope was an alternative to political action rather than a constituent part of it.[59]

---

[56] Lepper, "Regierungsbezirk Aachen," pp. 278-81.

[57] Hombach, "Reichs- und Landtagswahlen," pp. 98-99.

[58] This is explicitly noted in the 1870 electoral appeal of the Catholic *Essener Volkszeitung*, Nov. 8, 1870, copy in HSTAD RD Pr. Nr. 566 Bl. 137a.

[59] On the movement in support of the Pope during the early 1860s, see *Sonntagsblatt für katholische Christen* 19 (1860): 58-59; 21 (1862): 426-27, 444; *Kirchlicher Anzeiger für die Erzdiözese Köln* 9 (1860): 103 ff.; 10 (1861): 13-19; *Kölnische Zeitung*, Nov. 27, 1859, Jan. 5, 1860. Karl Bucheim, in his well-known book *Ultramontanismus und Demokratie*, asserts that the raison d'être of political Catholicism was rescue of the beleaguered Pope (pp. 1-16 and passim). This view conveniently overlooks the fact that in Prussia, the beginning of pro-Papal movement coincided with the collapse of political Catholicism. It was only after the war of 1866 that the rescue of the Pope became a successful *political* slogan.

The petition movement of 1868-1869 brought the Papacy to the forefront of the ideology of political Catholicism in Prussia. The sufferings of the Pontiff were an effective theme among a mass electorate whose politico-religious sensibilities had been heightened by the war of 1866. Pro-Papal agitation could easily acquire an anti-ministerial tinge—it was, after all, Prussia's Italian allies who were attacking the Pope—and during the *Kulturkampf* this theme would become part of the standard repertoire of speeches by Catholic politicians. In the years 1868-1870, however, another aspect of the Pope's position occupied the foreground. Pius IX became a symbol of the struggle between the forces of atheism and subversion and those of order. At a meeting in Essen in June 1870 in support of the Pope, the merchant Portgens told three thousand listeners: "Behind the attack on the worldly power of the Pope, there lies hidden the hostility to his spiritual power. The hostility is an expression of the struggle against the Pope as Vicar of Christ, as the representative of positive Christianity, and as the bulwark of the social order."[60] This view had been common enough in elite Catholic circles during the 1860s, but the petition campaign of 1868-1870 brought it directly to a mass electorate. By 1870-1871, a vote for political Catholicism was a vote for the Pope.

Local initiatives coincided with national and international developments in this period. The liberals' anti-clerical campaign was by no means restricted to the predominantly Catholic areas of the Prussian monarchy. Stirred up by the liberal press, in August 1869 a Berlin mob attacked and demolished the Franciscans' convent in the working-class suburb of Moabit. Berlin Progressives used this event as a pretext to launch a petition campaign demanding the abolition of the convents, and liberal deputies in the Prussian Parliament proposed measures to restrict and discriminate against the religious orders. The whole campaign came to nothing, as the ministry, looking toward a reconciliation with political Catholicism, refused to support the measures. Rhenish and Westphalian liberals, unlike their Berlin counterparts who had no Catholic voters to worry about, took a disapproving attitude toward the anti-Catholic excesses in the capital. Nonetheless, the "Moabiter Klostersturm," as the event quickly became known, provided a strong impetus toward the recreation of a Catholic political party.

A similar impetus came from the proceedings of the First Vatican Council. The proposed doctrine of Papal Infallibility appeared to the liberals as an outrageous notion and provided all the more ammunition for their anti-clerical campaign. Catholic polemicists responded in kind, and the resulting press feud occupied the entire educated public.

[60] HSTAD RD Pr. Nr. 566 Bl. 137a.

Both lay and clerical leaders of Rhenish-Westphalian Catholicism opposed the doctrine of Papal Infallibility (as was true among leading German-speaking Catholics generally), holding its proclamation at best as inopportune, at worst as foolish or pernicious. The vehemence of the anti-clerical attacks on the Pope, the precariousness of Pius IX's physical position, separated from the hostile Kingdom of Italy by only a French garrison, helped to keep these doubts private and contributed to the use of the Pope as a symbol of Catholic unity.[61]

Events in both narrower and broader arenas thus led toward the recreation of a supra-local political organization with a written program and then the reconstitution of a parliamentary caucus. Between 1868 and 1870 representatives of Catholic political clubs from the industrial areas of the northern Rhineland and Westphalia held yearly meetings. The first systematic initiative, however, came from Westphalian veterans of the Soest conferences, who met in Ahlen in 1869 and in Münster in June 1870 to draw up a program for the *Reichstag* and Prussian *Landtag* elections scheduled for that year. A version of the program was published in the Bachem family's *Kölnische Volkszeitung* (as the *Kölnische Blätter* had been renamed) on June 15, 1870, and endorsed by the Rhenish-Westphalian Catholic political clubs at their meeting in Essen on June 30.

These developments, leading up to a major campaign in the scheduled elections to the North German *Reichstag* in the fall of 1870, were interrupted by the outbreak of the Franco-Prussian War. The elections to the *Reichstag* were canceled, but the Westphalians, meeting once again in Soest in October, issued an abridged version of the program for the Prussian *Landtag* elections, which were held, despite the war, in November 1870. The program was also endorsed at this time by the largest local groups of what would become the following year the Westphalian Peasant League. Finally, after the elections, a group of Catholic parliamentarians gathered in Berlin and accepted the Soest program as the basis for a new political party. After some searching— the names Christian-Conservative Peoples Party and Anti-Liberal Party were considered and rejected—they chose the official title of the former Catholic caucus in the Prussian Parliament and dubbed themselves the Center Party, thus founding a political organization which would exist with unbroken continuity until 1933.[62]

[61] Still the best account of the effect of these events on Catholic politics is Bachem, *Zentrumspartei*, 3: 29-120. See also Lill, "Die deutschen Katholiken," pp. 358-59; Anderson, *Windthorst*, pp. 121-29; Windell, *Catholics and German Unity*, pp. 149-246; *Kölnische Zeitung*, Aug. 18, 1869.

[62] On this and the following paragraphs, see the excellent account in Bachem, *Zentrumspartei*, 3: 99-132.

The political orientation of the nascent party, as was prefigured in
the petition campaign of 1868 and 1869, was noticeably anti-liberal
and, at the very least, not anti-governmental. This was most apparent
in Westphalia, where a number of *Landräte* took part in the drawing
up of a Catholic political program, and the whole project proceeded
with the tacit approval of the provincial and district authorities. Rhenish Catholics may not have identified themselves quite so closely with
the government, but they did not oppose it, either. The mood of 1866-
1867 was not forgotten, but the hostility engendered in that year was
increasingly focused on the liberals and diverted from the government.
The anti-liberal and non-oppositional orientation of political Catholicism helped to dispel the anxieties which the events of 1867 had
created among the episcopate. From 1870 onward, the bishops' attitude toward political Catholicism was one of unreserved support.

The Elections of 1870 and 1871

Elections to the Prussian Parliament were held in November 1870 at
the height of the Franco-Prussian War. Public attention was turned
toward the war, and the electoral turnout was not great. Nonetheless,
these ignored and forgotten elections set the political pattern for the
following decade in the northern Rhineland and Westphalia; they
marked the triumphant return of an organized political Catholicism.[63]
The bishops issued pastoral letters on the elections for the first time
since February 1867, calling on the faithful to vote for good Catholics
and against candidates of the "anti-religious party" (religionsfeindliche
Partei) and encouraging the lower clergy to take an active part in the
elections.[64] Clerical partisans were generally on good terms with the
authorities. The farmer Johannes Breuker, leader of the peasant league
in *Kreis* Recklinghausen, spoke to the *Landrat* after a league meeting
and assured him that the Catholics wished "to go hand in hand with
the government." The two men reached agreement on appropriate
candidates for the constituency Borken-Recklinghausen (Münster District), who were duly elected. In Geilenkirchen-Heinsberg-Erkelenz
(Aachen District) the officials noted with pleasure that sixty-eight priests

[63] On the 1870 elections, see the reports of the *Landräte* in STAM RM Nr. VII-68;
election results in STAM OP Nr. 501; STAM RAR I Pr. Nr. 90 Bl. 385 ff.; STAD M1
Pr. Nr. 260; HSTAD RD Pr. Nr. 566 Bl. 19 ff.; Hombach, "Reichs- und Landtagswahlen," pp. 161-66; Kaiser, *Die politischen Strömungen*, pp. 268-76; Lepper, "Regierungsbezirk Aachen," pp. 263-83; Moellers, "Reichstagswahlkreis Essen," pp. 167
ff.

[64] *Kirchliches Amtsblatt der Diözese Paderborn*, 19 Nr. 21 (Oct. 25, 1870); Kaiser,
Die politischen Strömungen, p. 268; Lepper, "Regierungsbezirk Aachen," pp. 281-83.

had been chosen as electors and "the democratic element has been completely crushed." The reemergence of the clerical party in Neuß-Grevenbroich-Krefeld (country) (Düsseldorf District) gave the authorities a welcome opportunity to defeat the Progressive incumbents who had represented the constituency for eight years.[65]

Just as the events, local, national, and international, of 1868-1869 had recreated a unified political Catholicism, so they brought together various elements of the bourgeois left. The 1866-1867 electoral alliances with the clergy were forgotten; even if anyone had wished to revive them, the growing Catholic organization and increasing saliency of anti-clerical ideas among the liberals would have rendered them impossible. Unlike 1867, Progressives and National Liberals generally did not run opposing candidates in 1870; rather, liberals of all convictions, from the "most extreme Progressive to the most moderate Old Liberal," as the *Landrat* of *Kreis* Essen noted, united to meet the clerical menace.[66] The election results showed that the liberals had had good reason to be apprehensive. Capturing every single seat in the predominantly Catholic constituencies in Westphalia and the bulk of the predominantly Catholic constituencies in the northern Rhineland, the clerical party scored a major victory, a result it had been unable to obtain since the beginning of the conflict era. See Table 4.2.

In spite of the unfavorable suffrage, a reorganized political Catholicism, once more enjoying the active support of the clergy, soundly defeated its liberal opponents in the 1870 elections. The *Reichstag* elections of March 1871 would be the decisive proof of the dominant position of the clerical cause in the Catholic areas of the northern Rhineland and Westphalia. Of the twenty-seven constituencies with a Catholic majority in the northern Rhineland and Westphalia, the Center candidates were elected in twenty-five. In seventeen of them, the Center candidates received more than sixty percent of the votes; in thirteen, over seventy percent; and, in six, over eighty percent.[67]

[65] LA Kr. Recklinghausen to RM, Nov. 8, 1870, STAM RM Nr. VII-68; HSTAD RD Pr. Nr. 566 Bl. 10-20; Lepper, "Regierungsbezirk Aachen," pp. 281-83.

[66] HSTAD RD Pr. Nr. 566 Bl. 135-37. Similarly, the justice Winckelmann, leader of the Progressives in *Kreis* Recklinghausen, told a friend in 1870 that as "a result of the most recent events, he had completely changed his mind," and would vote for a governmental over a clerical candidate. LA Kr. Recklinghausen to RM, Nov. 8, 1870, STAM RM Nr. VII-68.

[67] Election returns in *Statistik des Deutschen Reiches*, old series 14 (1875 part 5): 23-31. The two constituencies where Center candidates were not elected were the proverbial exceptions confirming the rule. In Gladbach (Düsseldorf District), the Chief Justice Kratz was, as in 1867, a joint Catholic-liberal candidate. The clergy actively campaigned for him, and he received sixty-eight percent of the vote while a rival, non-clerical liberal could manage only some twelve percent. On the election, see HSTAD

The electoral campaign combined the clerical-governmental rap-prochement of the previous year with the style of mass clerical agitation developed in 1867. Center candidates in predominantly Catholic con-stituencies usually enjoyed official support, the authorities supporting the Catholics' liberal opponents only in a few scattered instances in the Rhineland.[68] As in 1870, the bishops issued pastoral letters on the election, stressing the dangers to religion, calling on the faithful to vote against anti-Christian candidates and for those who would oppose the introduction of civil marriage or an interconfessional state school system. The lower clergy engaged in an aggressive electoral agitation, as they had done in 1867, this time, however, in greater harmony with their superiors, handing out ballots in church, taking them door to door, or having the schoolteachers distribute them to the children. The priests explained that it was a sin to vote against the Center candidate and denounced the liberals as godless atheists, enemies of the Pope, in one case, as "a Freemason and associate of Garibaldi."[69]

One new element in this election was the energetic action of the Catholic political clubs in the big cities. In Düsseldorf, the Constantia held many public meetings; on election day, "all their people were on their feet the whole day through," getting out the vote. They "deci-sively beat" the National Liberal candidate Anton Bloem and elected a clerical deputy for the first time since 1858.[70]

In 1871, all the elements needed for a clerical electoral victory came together: universal and equal suffrage, the potent electoral slogan of endangered religion, active participation of the clergy in the election campaign, and an effective local, regional, and national political or-

---

RD Pr. Nr. 1233 Bl. 115-16. In Mülheim-Wipperfürth-Gummersbach (Cologne Dis-trict), there were two clerical candidates opposing the National Liberal and former 1848 democrat Heinrich Bürgers. Bürgers ended up in a runoff with the *Landrat* von Niesewand of *Kreis* Wipperfürth. The latter offended Catholic opinion by denouncing ultramontanism on the eve of a runoff and unexpectedly declaring he would sit in the *Reichstag* as a Free Conservative and not join the Center caucus. Many Catholic par-tisans stayed home on election day, and Bürgers, taking ninety-one percent of the vote in heavily Protestant *Kreis* Gummersbach, while managing only some twenty-five per-cent in the predominantly Catholic *Kreise* Mülheim and Wipperfürth, barely squeaked through. See Hombach, "Reichs- und Landtagswahlen," pp. 207-13.

[68] Bachem, *Zentrumspartei*, 3: 119; Lepper, "Regierungsbezirk Aachen," pp. 301-302; Kaiser, *Die politischen Strömungen*, pp. 280-91.

[69] See the pastoral letter of the Bishop of Münster, *Kirchliches Amtsblatt der Diözese Münster* 15 Nr. 14, Jan. 14, 1871, pp. 5-6. On the behavior of the clergy, see the reports in HSTAD RA Pr. Nr. 813 and HSTAD RA Nr. 6279 Bl. 90 ff. as well as Hombach, "Reichs- und Landtagswahlen," pp. 196-201.

[70] Chaplain Hömmacher to Dean Herten, Oct. 6, 1871, HAEK Gen. XXIII 4, I. On similar proceedings in Mönchengladbach, see HSTAD RD Pr. Nr. 1233 Bl. 115-16.

TABLE 4.2
Results of the *Landtag* Elections in Predominantly
Catholic Constituencies, 1862-1870

Year	Liberal or Progressive	Clerical	Free Conservative or Conservative	Unclear
Deputies in Westphalia				
1862	3	12	—	—
1863	5	10	—	—
1866	8	7	—	—
1867	6	9	—	—
1870	—	15	—	—
Deputies in Northern Rhineland				
1862	24[a]	6	—	—
1863	24[b]	6	—	—
1866	26[c]	3	1	—
1867	20[d]	1	6	3
1870	9[e]	12	6[f]	3

[a] One liberal elected with clerical support and two others elected as joint clerical-liberal candidates.
[b] Two liberals elected as joint clerical-liberal candidates.
[c] One liberal elected as a joint clerical-liberal candidate.
[d] Two liberals elected with clerical support.
[e] Three liberals elected with clerical support.
[f] Three conservatives elected with clerical support.
NOTE: I lack information on the 1867 and 1870 elections in the constituency Cologne (country)-Bergheim-Euskirchen.
SOURCES: Election returns in STAM OP Nr. 500-501; STAM RM Nr. VII-68; STAM RAR I Pr. Nr. 90; STAD M1 IL Nr. 73-74; STAD M1 Pr. Nr. 259-60; HSTAD RD Pr. Nr. 565-66 and Anderson, *Prussian Election Statistics*, passim; Denk, "Die Wahlen in Köln," pp. 154-90; Haas, "Die Wahlen des Regierungs-Bezirks Aachen," pp. 139-92; Hombach, "Die Reichs- und Landtagswahlen," pp. 160-66; Kaiser, *Die politischen Strömungen*, pp. 166-276; Lepper, "Regierungsbezirk Aachen," pp. 233-83; Röttges, *Die politischen Wahlen*, pp. 259-309; Weinandy, "Die Wahlen des Regierungsbezirks Köln," pp. 164-265.

ganization. The enormous political potential inherent in the religious revival of the twenty years following mid-century was realized for the first time. In one massive step, political Catholicism emerged as the dominant force in the two western provinces of Prussia. Its sudden emergence ought not to blind us to the decades of pastoral work, social changes, and political organizing which had preceded it.

MESCHEDE AND DÜSSELDORF 1867-1871:
TWO CONSTITUENCIES IN TRANSITION

In this section, the developments in two areas, one in the Westphalian countryside, the other a large urban center in the Rhine Valley, will be examined, using the methods of quantitative electoral analysis. The revealing details brought to light by statistical study will provide a confirmation and a refinement of the general picture of the political tendencies in the region, sketched out above.

Kreis *Meschede*

The *Kreis* Meschede had been a stronghold of rural liberalism in Westphalia during the 1860s. As early as 1861 a majority of the *Kreis* electors supported the Progressive *Landtag* candidate, and this majority was returned again in the elections of 1862, 1863, and 1866. In 1867, *Kreis* Meschede was combined with the neighboring *Kreise* Olpe and Arnsberg to form a *Reichstag* constituency. The election was a three-way race between the conservative-official candidate, Provincial Governor von Duesberg, the clerical politician Hermann von Mallinckrodt, and the Progressive lawyer Wilhelm Elven from Cologne. The campaign was one of the liveliest in the western provinces, but also one of the most bitter, strongly marked by the outcome of the war of 1866. The Catholics did not conceal their pro-Austrian sympathies and responded to liberal charges of treason with counter-accusations of Freemasonry, charges which the clerical partisans directed against the Catholic and conservative provincial governor as well.

Mallinckrodt was elected, with 57.8 percent of the votes in the constituency, although he received only 48.5 percent in *Kreis* Meschede. Precinct level returns for this election have not been preserved; in any event, the results do not give an accurate picture of the strength of the parties, as the liberal candidate Elven announced his withdrawal two days before the balloting, throwing his supporters into confusion.[71]

Mallinckrodt, however, was also elected in another Westphalian constituency, Beckum-Lüdinghausen-Warendorf, and accepted for it, so that new elections were required for Meschede-Olpe-Arnsberg. The political scene for these elections, held in March of 1867, was some-

[71] A summary of the election returns can be found in STAM LA Kr. Meschede Nr. 235. On the campaign, see STAM RAR I Nr. 1419 Bl. 51-52, 90, and 168; the reports of the local authorities in STAM LA Kr. Meschede Nr. 235 and *Kölnische Zeitung*, Feb. 4, 1867.

what different from the one of a month before. Following negotiations, a "fusion" was arranged between "old conservatives and national liberals." The joint conservative-liberal candidate was to be the mine owner Wilhelm Bergenthal of Warstein (*Kreis* Arnsberg), one of the leading industrialists in the area and a local stalwart of the Progressives earlier in the decade. The new clerical candidate was the veteran Catholic parliamentarian Peter Reichensperger. Against the orders of the Arnsberg District Governor von Holzbrinck, the *Landräte* seem to have thrown their support behind the liberal-conservative.[72]

The election in March was as hard fought as the one the previous month. While in February some of the Catholic clergy had supported the Catholic Provincial Governor Theodor von Duesberg over the oppositional clerical Hermann von Mallinckrodt, in March all the politically active priests were for Reichensperger; those not openly in favor of him took no part in the campaign. None had anything good to say about Bergenthal.[73]

Reichensperger was elected, obtaining fifty-four percent of the vote in *Kreis* Meschede. We can divide the precincts of the *Kreis* in two ways. First, they can be divided by their political history, separating those precincts whose electors had voted for the Progressive candidate in 1863 against those whose electors had voted for the Catholic candidate in that year. Secondly, they can be divided by their socioeconomic structure, separating the towns of Meschede and Schmallenberg and the rural areas of the metallurgical and mining industry from the purely rural and agricultural precincts. See Table 4.3.

The old Progressive strongholds were the centers of support for a pro-governmental national-liberalism, while the formerly governmental clerical precincts had gone over to the opposition. Although the liberal and clerical partisans had changed their attitudes toward the Berlin ministry, their hostility toward each other remained the same. Similarly, the bourgeoisie of the towns and the rural industrial areas had been during the early 1860s key supporters of the Progressives; in 1867, areas under their influence stood with the national liberals. The contrast between the two socioeconomically differing groups of precincts is not as sharp as that between the two groups of precincts with differing political histories. In 1867, a number of rural-agricultural areas voted heavily for the conservative-liberal candidate, as had a number of peasant electors in 1862 and 1863.[74]

[72] See above, n. 17.

[73] The reports of the local authorities in STAM LA Kr. Meschede Nr. 235 are quite explicit on this point.

[74] It was suggested in Chapter Three that it was the well-off, larger peasantry which made up the body of supporters for liberalism in the countryside. Statistics on rural

TABLE 4.3
Election Results in *Kreis* Meschede, March 1867

Precinct	Clerical Reichensperger	Conservative-Liberal Bergenthal	Turnout	Total Precincts
Liberal electors 1863	39.3%	60.5%	51.3%	24
Clerical-conservative electors 1863	72.4	27.4	58.1	24
Urban or rural-industrial	44.4	55.2	·60.0	17
Rural and agricultural	61.3	38.5	50.4	31
Kreis Meschede	54.0	45.8	54.3	48

SOURCE: 1867 election returns in STAM LA Kr. Meschede Nr. 235. 1863 electors political affiliation from STAM LA Kr. Meschede Nr. 305. Socioeconomic structure of the precincts from accounts in *Statistische Darstellung des Kreises Meschede, 1861-1873* (Meschede: Selbstverlag des Kreises, 1874), pp. 76-78.

The social and regional bases of liberal and clerical support in *Kreis* Meschede thus remained the same in March 1867 as they had been during the conflict era. Unlike the earlier period however, the new, expanded suffrage gave the Catholic opposition to the liberal notables a powerful weapon in the form of clerical agitation among a mass electorate. Father Nolte, vicar in the village of Eversberg, went, on election day in March 1867, up to the ironworks in nearby Wehrstapel to confront the industrialist Busch, who had posted a placard in his factory, "recommending" to his workers the election of the liberal-conservative Bergenthal. When the vicar arrived, the industrialist was out, but his wife was present. With her help, the priest took from the

---

property-holdings are, regrettably, not reliable or complete enough to test this definitively. It was possible to calculate the coefficient of correlation between the ratio of large pieces of landed property (30-300 *Morgen*) to small pieces of landed property (5-30 *Morgen*) and the conservative-liberal vote. (One *Morgen* equals approximately .7 acres.) The resulting coefficient, for thirty-one rural and agricultural precincts, is .75. This suggests that where large parcels of property predominated over small ones, the liberals did well. Unfortunately, it does not say anything about the relationship of liberal votes to agricultural holdings (a large holding can be made out of many small pieces of property) nor about who owned the property. Finally, the range of values in each category is so wide as to be extremely imprecise.

workers of the factory their ballots, with Bergenthal written on them, and gave them ballots for the clerical candidate, Reichensperger. He then went to the polling place, the local tavern, and announced excitedly, "The workers are trampling Bergenthal's ballots!" The innkeeper, chairman of the precinct election board, and apparently a liberal sympathizer, asked Nolte to cease his electioneering, to leave the polling place, and to "pay more attention to spiritual affairs."[75]

In this case, the priest's efforts to use the new suffrage system in order to break the hold of the liberal notables on political life were not entirely successful, for Bergenthal received fifty-five percent of the votes in Wehrstapel. Nonetheless, the first step had been taken in that direction, and the clerical candidate had obtained a respectable minority in a liberal stronghold which had, to boot, a large Protestant minority (some fifteen percent). Even with the support of the authorities, the liberals could obtain no similar successes in centers of clericalism.

In August 1867 the liberals did not put up a candidate. The election was between the clerical incumbent Reichensperger and Provincial Governor von Duesberg, running once more as a governmental conservative. The campaign was quieter than in the spring and the turnout lower, but the results essentially the same. Reichensperger obtained 52.9 percent of the votes in *Kreis* Meschede to Duesberg's 47.0 percent

TABLE 4.4
Election Results in *Kreis* Meschede, August 1867

Precinct	Clerical Reichensperger	Conservative Duesberg	Turnout	Total Precincts
Liberal electors 1863	34.6%	65.3%	32.5%	24
Clerical-conservative electors 1863	72.5	27.4	37.5	24
Urban or rural-industrial	40.5	59.4	36.8	17
Rural and agricultural	62.1	36.9	33.2	31
Kreis Meschede	52.9	47.0	34.8	48

SOURCE: Election returns in STAM LA Kr. Meschede Nr. 304.

[75] Gendarme Rube (Eversberg) to *Landrat* von Devivere, Apr. 2, 1867, STAM LA Kr. Meschede Nr. 235.

in an election where 34.8 percent of the eligible voters appeared at the polls. See Table 4.4.

The results look suspiciously similar to those of March, a suspicion confirmed by calculation of the coefficient of correlation between the national liberal vote in March 1867 and the conservative vote in August 1867. For all forty-eight precincts of *Kreis* Meschede, r = .67. The Progressive voters of 1861-1863 and the conservative-liberal voters of March 1867 were thus the conservative voters of August 1867. The remarks of the *Landrat* of *Kreis* Arnsberg on the political situation in his *Kreis* seem entirely applicable to the situation in the neighboring *Kreis* Meschede: "The elections to the North German *Reichstag* have shown beyond the shadow of a doubt that in . . . the whole *Kreis* there are only clericals and liberals. In comparison to them, the genuine conservatives [die eigentlichen Konservativen] are just a vanishingly small minority."[76]

In the *Landtag* elections of November 1867, Peter Reichensperger was elected over a liberal-conservative and Progressive opponent by eighty-eight electoral votes to eighty-one, after four rounds of balloting. The electors of *Kreis* Meschede were evenly split between clericals and liberal-conservatives, but the returns are an insufficient measure of the actual political conditions, since one-third of the electors from the *Kreis* failed to appear for the balloting—not for political reasons, but because of an early snowstorm which blocked the mountain passes in an area with very poor roads.[77]

In 1870, the clerical partisans were in command. They elected Peter Reichensperger to the Prussian *Landtag* for the constituency Olpe-Meschede by 179 electoral votes to 36 for the area magistrate Roper from Schmallenberg. In view of this success, the authorities had no doubt that the Center Party would win the first *Reichstag* elections in 1871 with little difficulty.[78] They were right. Peter Reichensperger, who would represent the constituency Olpe-Meschede-Arnsberg in the *Reichstag* until his retirement in 1889, received 83.6 percent of the vote against his National Liberal opponent. In *Kreis* Meschede, the liberals did a little better than in the constituency as a whole, but their performance was still not very impressive. See Table 4.5.

As elsewhere in the Catholic areas of the northern Rhineland and Westphalia, the 1871 *Reichstag* elections were the decisive debacle for the liberals. They could no longer put up any resistance to the agitation of the clergy and the organization of political Catholicism. The liberal

[76] STAM RAR I Pr. Nr. 90 Bl. 366-67.
[77] STAM RAR I Pr. Nr. 90 Bl. 375-76; RAR to OPM Sep. 7, 1868, STAM OP Nr. 495; Bachem, *Zentrumspartei*, 2: 204.
[78] STAM RAR I Pr. Nr. 90 Bl. 385, 407; STAM RAR I Nr. 1419 Bl. 292.

TABLE 4.5
Election Results in *Kreis* Meschede, 1871

Precincts	Center	Liberal	Turnout	Total Precincts
Liberal electors 1863	72.2%	27.8%	43.9%	24
Clerical-conservative electors 1863	91.2	8.8	48.0	24
Urban or rural-industrial	76.0	23.9	53.2	17
Rural and agricultural	85.4	14.5	41.3	31
Kreis Meschede	81.0	19.0	46.1	48

SOURCE: Election returns in STAM LA Kr. Meschede Nr. 128.

vote did not dissolve: for the forty-eight precincts of *Kreis* Meschede, the coefficient of correlation between the liberal-conservative vote in March 1867 and the National-Liberal vote in 1871 is r = .76. The areas which had unusually high liberal percentages in March 1867 still had unusually high liberal percentages in 1871. The liberal vote as a whole, though, had decreased drastically but evenly, declining about equally in all precincts.

The liberal notables of *Kreis* Meschede had retained their attachment to a liberal and anti-clerical politics (although they had, as many liberals throughout Germany, increasingly come to at least a working agreement with Bismarck's ministry), but by 1871 they had lost the battle for the opinions of the mass of the electorate to the clergy and the Catholic nobility. The rest of the 1870s would see them lose what little influence they still retained in 1871.

Düsseldorf

The main candidates in the February 1867 *Reichstag* elections in Düsseldorf were the retired *Landrat* von Frentz as a governmental Conservative and the *Landtag* deputy Alfred Groote, a radical, oppositional Progressive. There were two additional candidates: the lawyer Anton Bloem, a moderate or "national" liberal, and Johann Baptist Schweitzer, Lassalle's successor as leader of the General German Workers' Association, campaigning in Lassalle's home town. Unlike *Kreis* Meschede, which was about ninety-five percent Catholic, there was a substantial Protestant minority—some one-fourth of the population—in the city of Düsseldorf and in the rural areas of *Kreis* Düsseldorf. Nonetheless, a Catholic bloc vote would more than suffice to dominate

TABLE 4.6
Election Results in Düsseldorf, February 1867

Area	Conservative von Frentz	National Liberal Bloem	Progressive Groote	Social Democrat Schweitzer	Turnout
City of					
Düsseldorf	34.0%	3.5%	46.8%	11.5%	44.8%
Landkreis					
Düsseldorf	50.9	11.5	35.4	1.4	46.5
Constituency	42.0	9.4	41.4	6.8	45.6
		Runoff			
City of					
Düsseldorf	38.8	—	61.2	—	55.0
Landkreis					
Düsseldorf	58.2	—	41.2	—	60.2
Constituency	48.4	—	51.6	—	57.4

SOURCE: Election returns in STDD II Nr. 28.

the elections. But how could the Catholics vote in a bloc without a Catholic candidate? See Table 4.6.

Groote won a narrow victory by running up a sufficiently large majority in the city of Düsseldorf to offset the ex-*Landrat*'s edge in the countryside. In our analysis, we will concentrate on the urban precincts. From an 1874 list of voters it has proved possible to reconstruct the confessional composition of the precincts; a sample of occupations from the 1872 address book provides a basis for determining the precincts' social structure as well. This information, necessarily somewhat approximate, nonetheless makes it possible to determine the sources of political support for each party.[79]

[79] The confessional composition of each precinct has been determined from a list in STDD II Nr. 28, dated 1874, which gives the total number of eligible voters of each confession on every street in Düsseldorf. The streets have been combined to form the precincts, according to lists giving precinct boundaries for each *Reichstag* election (also in STDD II Nr. 28), and the assumption has been made that the confessional composition of each street was the same in 1867 and 1871 as in 1874.

The social composition of each precinct has been determined from a random sample of names with professions and addresses drawn from *Adreßbuch der Oberbürgermeisterei Düsseldorf für 1872*, 2 vols. in 1 (Düsseldorf, n.d.) 1: 4-179. (A copy of this book is in the Düsseldorf municipal archives, where I used it.) A random sample of eight persons was drawn from each page, giving approximately 1,400 individuals. (Some

The city of Düsseldorf was divided into twenty-two precincts for the 1867 elections. The twenty-second was made up of the soldiers of the Düsseldorf garrison. They were lined up, marched to the polls, and, in effect, ordered to vote for the government's candidate—which they did, unanimously. The circumstances of the election made a mockery of the secret ballot.[80] The twentieth and twenty-first precincts, Hamm and Flehe-Volmerswerth, although administratively a part of the city of Düsseldorf, were actually villages of truck farmers (a characteristic which they still retain to some extent today), with a drastically different social and confessional structure from the other nineteen civilian precincts. Their inclusion with the others produces serious distortions in the analysis, so they have been considered separately.[81] Finally, the seventeenth and eighteenth precincts (Oberbilk I and II) have been combined, since figures on their confessional composition are available only for both precincts together. There remain eighteen precincts for the analysis.

The population of each precinct has been divided into three social groups: (1) a bourgeoisie of merchants, industrialists, rentiers, professionals, and upper-level officials; (2) a petit-bourgeoisie of craftsmen and shopkeepers; and (3) a proletariat of skilled workers, factory hands, and day laborers.[82] I have calculated the coefficients of cor-

---

addresses were for streets not yet in existence in 1867, so a few names had to be discarded.) The names were arranged by street and the streets combined to form precincts according to the precinct boundary list for each year. As with the religious composition, the assumption has been made that the social structure of each street remained constant throughout the period 1867-1874.

[80] HSTAD RD Pr. Nr. 577 Bl. 235-36.

[81] According to the occupational sample, 52.6 percent of the population of Hamm were truck farmers, as were 42.1 percent of the population of Flehe-Volmerswerth. Only one other civilian precinct had over 20.0 percent of its inhabitants as truck farmers (Bilk, precinct 19); two others had over 10.0 percent truck farmers, six between 1.0 and 10.0 percent, and ten no truck farmers at all. Furthermore, both Bilk and Flehe-Volmerswerth were over 99.0 percent Catholic, while only two other precincts were over 90.0 percent Catholic, and the other seventeen were between 55.0 percent and 85.0 percent Catholic.

[82] Unfortunately, it is not possible to distinguish between master and journeymen artisans, as the address book never distinguished between the two. The book does note that "journeymen and servants" [Gesellen und Dienstboten] were not included, but from the context this does not seem to refer to wage-earners in general, but to those temporarily resident in the city (and probably living with their employers) whose permanent domicile was elsewhere. Wage-earning, head-of-household, permanent resident, journeymen artisans were probably included in the address book. Consequently, the figures used tend to exaggerate somewhat the size of the lower middle class and underestimate that of the proletariat. One to five percent of the inhabitants of each precinct, mostly subordinate salaried employees, did not fit any of these categories and have been excluded.

relation between the turnout and the votes for each of the four candidates and each social group, as well as the correlations between the
electoral data and the proportion of the electorate belonging to the
Catholic confession. Since confession and social structure were deeply
intertwined in Düsseldorf, as in many Rhenish and Westphalian cities
(the bourgeoisie being disproportionately Protestant and the workers
disproportionately Catholic), I have also calculated partial correlation
coefficients to help determine the relative weight of class and confession. See Table 4.7.

The results of the analysis are striking and unexpected. The Catholic
voters tended to reject the Conservative and National Liberal candidates and vote for the left opposition. It is not too surprising that
Catholic voters would reject the National Liberal Bloem, a Protestant
and Freemason, but it is rather more peculiar that they would support
an atheistic socialist and an anti-clerical Progressive over the Catholic
nobleman and ex-*Landrat* who had even been elected to the *Landtag*
from Düsseldorf in 1858 along with Peter Reichensperger.

In 1867, however, class considerations still modified confessional
ones. When social structure is taken into account, Catholic support
for the candidates of the left appears less strong. Precincts with a
disproportionately small Catholic population were also precincts with
a disproportionately large bourgeois population, and these precincts
gave an above-average support to the National Liberals and the Conservatives and a below-average support to the Progressives and Social
Democrats. The relatively low partial correlation coefficients show
that neither the proportion Catholic nor the proportion bourgeois
taken individually played the decisive role in apportioning support to
one of the four parties.

When religion is held constant, the workers showed little particular
inclination to vote for the Social-Democrats, and, oddly enough, a
noticeable tendency to vote for the National Liberals. It thus seems
to have been the heavily Catholic character of the Düsseldorf proletariat which led to its support of the Social-Democratic candidate, and
not the proletariat's class position. It was opposition to the government
and not socialist notions which played the key role in the workers'
votes.[83]

The best way to describe election results in Düsseldorf in February
1867 is to think of the population as being divided into two groups:
one, predominantly Catholic and plebian, composed of non-bourgeois

[83] This strong attraction of the Catholic workers to the oppositional Social Democrats
for distinctly non-socialist reasons was both the cause for the founding of a Christian
Social Association in Düsseldorf and the grounds for its rapid success and the eclipse
of the Social Democrats in the city.

TABLE 4.7
Social Structure, Confessional Identity, and Political
Alignment in the City of Düsseldorf, February 1867

Coefficients of Correlation for the February 1867
Reichstag Elections in the City of Düsseldorf

Between	and	Zero-Order r	Holding Constant	Partial r
Percent Catholic	Progressive vote	+.58	Percent bourgeois	+.15
	Social Democratic vote	+.60	Percent workers	+.36
	National Liberal vote	−.64	Percent bourgeois	−.22
	Conservative vote	−.77	Percent bourgeois	−.35
	Turnout	−.61	Percent bourgeois	−.57
Percent bourgeois	Progressive vote	−.59	Percent Catholic	−.22
	Social Democratic vote	−.57	Percent Catholic	−.12
	National Liberal vote	+.64	Percent Catholic	+.21
	Conservative vote	+.76	Percent Catholic	+.28
	Turnout	+.41	Percent Catholic	−.32
Percent petit bourgeois	Progressive vote	+.21	Percent Catholic	+.09
	Social Democratic vote	+.07	Percent Catholic	−.10
	National Liberal vote	−.46	Percent Catholic	−.41
	Conservative vote	−.07	Percent Catholic	+.19
	Turnout	−.11	Percent Catholic	+.05
Percent workers	Progressive vote	+.40	Percent Catholic	−.07
	Social Democratic vote	+.53	Percent Catholic	+.14
	National Liberal vote	−.18	Percent Catholic	+.61
	Conservative vote	−.61	Percent Catholic	−.06
	Turnout	−.26	Percent Catholic	+.38
Percent bourgeois	Percent Catholic	−.88		

TABLE 4.7 (*cont.*)

Between	and	Zero-Order r	Holding Constant	Partial r
Percent petit bourgeois	Percent Catholic	+.24		
Percent workers	Percent Catholic	+.76		

SOURCES: Calculated from election returns in STDD II Nr. 28 and the occupational sample described in note 82.

social strata; the other, predominantly Protestant, containing mostly representatives of the upper classes. The Progressives and Social-Democrats obtained their most consistent support in the first group; the Conservatives and National Liberals in the second.[84]

In August 1867, the Conservative candidate Micheals was elected in a runoff by a very narrow margin—4,211 to 4,121 over his Progressive opponent, Heinrich Bürgers. Bürgers obtained sixty percent of the votes in the civilian precincts in Düsseldorf, but could not overcome the 300 votes cast for his opponent by the soldiers and the conservative majority in the rural areas of the *Kreis*. A Catholic candidate, Dr. Krebs, managed just nine percent of the vote on the first round of the balloting; the Social-Democrats sank to a dismal 2.6 percent. As elsewhere in the Rhineland and Westphalia, the turnout was light, and interest in the elections was not very great.[85]

In November 1867, the incumbent Progressive *Landtag* deputies were reelected over conservative opposition. The *Landtag* elections of 1870 brought the initial elements of a new political picture. The first deputy elected was a Conservative, defeating the Progressive candidate by 221 to 145 electoral votes. For the second candidate, however, the contest was between a Catholic and a National Liberal. After three

[84] The election results in the truck-farming precincts seem relevant in this context. The Progressives received 83.7 percent of the votes in Hamm and 85.3 percent of the votes in Flehe-Volmerswerth. The truck farmers' vote was thus similar to the plebian urban population, except that they favored the Progressives strongly over the Social Democrats (the latter managing just 2.5 percent in Hamm and 4.4 percent in Flehe-Volmerswerth), but it was not like the rural Catholics of *Landkreis* Düsseldorf who seem to have usually supported the Conservatives.

[85] On these elections, see HSTAD RD Pr. Nr. 577 Bl. 121, 199-200, 226, 230, and 235-36.

rounds of balloting, the liberal was elected by 187 to 155 electoral votes.[86]

Several months later, in the first elections to the German *Reichstag*, the Progressives and the National Liberals agreed on a joint candidate, the attorney Anton Bloem, the unsuccessful National Liberal candidate in 1867. The leaders of the Düsseldorf Social Democrats agreed to support the joint liberal candidate against his Catholic opponent, the *Landesgerichtsassesor* Joseph Bernard.[87] The Center candidate defeated the combined opposition without great difficulty, becoming the first representative of political Catholicism elected from the constituency since 1858. See Table 4.8.

A comparison of the 1867 and 1871 results shows how this turn of events had come about. See Table 4.9. The Progressive and Social Democratic voters of 1867 had moved in the exact opposite direction from their leaders. The Catholic plebians who in 1867 had supported the radical oppositionists now gave their votes to the candidate promising to defend their religion. The leaders of the parties of the left found themselves to be just a small group devoid of any mass support. The only voters in Düsseldorf opposed to the Center were those who in 1867 had supported the National Liberals and, even more, the Conservatives. Once again, this suggests that the Catholics had supported the left-wing opposition in 1867 because it was in opposition to the Prussian state, not because it was left wing. The energetic agitation of the Düsseldorf Catholic political club, the Constantia, and the Düsseldorf Christian Social Association quickly and decisively translated this latent receptiveness for a religiously based politics into votes for the Center Party.

TABLE 4.8
Election Results in Düsseldorf, 1871

Area	Center Bernard	National Liberal Bloem	Turnout
City of Düsseldorf	58.2%	41.5%	53.3%
Landkreis			
Düsseldorf	63.4	35.6	49.2
Constituency	60.7	38.9	51.2

SOURCE: Election returns in STDD II Nr. 28 and *Statistik des Deutschen Reiches*, Old Series 14, 1875 part 1, 23-31.

[86] HSTAD RD Pr. Nr. 566 Bl. 142-43.
[87] Schmitz, *Arbeiterbewegung im Raum Düsseldorf*, p. 117.

TABLE 4.9
Comparison of February 1867 and 1871 *Reichstag*
Elections in the City of Düsseldorf

February 1867 vote	Coefficients of Correlation between:			
	Center Vote 1871		National Liberal Vote 1871	
	All Precincts	without Hamm and Flehe-Volmerswerth	All Precincts	without Hamm and Flehe-Volmerswerth
	r	r	r	r
Progressive	+.77	+.61	−.69	−.54
Conservative	−.89	−.83	+.80	+.74
National Liberal	−.64	−.60	+.52	+.53
Social Democratic	+.24	+.56	−.21	−.48
Total precincts	14	12	14	12

NOTE: Because precinct boundaries changed between 1867 and 1871, it was necessary to combine several precincts in each year in order to obtain compatible units for analysis.
SOURCES: Calculated from election returns in STDD II Nr. 28.

An analysis of the social and religious bases of support for the Center Party in 1871 confirms this analysis. In the *Reichstag* elections of that year the city was divided into twenty-three precincts. The military precinct of 1867 was allowed to disappear, and the soldiers voted in the neighborhoods in which they resided. As in 1867, Hamm and Flehe-Volmerswerth have been considered separately, and the results in the two Oberbilk precincts combined so that twenty precincts remain for the analysis. See Table 4.10.

The Center Party was unquestionably the political representative of Düsseldorf Catholics. Catholics who voted, voted for it, and only Catholics voted for it. Party lines had become definitively fixed by religion. Given the intimate connection between religion and social class in Düsseldorf, the definitive emergence of a confessionally based politics meant the emergence of definite class lines in the voting. The Center Party was the choice of the lower-middle and working classes of the city, while the bourgeoisie spurned it for the National Liberals. In short, the electorate of the Center was very much the heir to the 1867 Progressive and Social Democratic electorates. The main difference between the left electorate of 1867 and the Center electorate of

TABLE 4.10
Social Structure, Confessional Identity, and Political
Alignment in the City of Düsseldorf, 1871

Coefficients of Correlation for the 1871
Reichstag Elections in the City of Düsseldorf

Between	and	Zero-Order r	Holding Constant	Partial r
Percent	Center vote	+.97	Percent bourgeois	+.91
Catholic	Turnout	−.82	Percent bourgeois	−.74
Percent	Center vote	−.91	Percent Catholic	−.73
bourgeois	Turnout	+.59	Percent Catholic	−.30
Percent petit-	Center vote	+.06	Percent Catholic	+.28
bourgeois	Turnout	+.01	Percent Catholic	+.06
Percent	Center vote	+.80	Percent Catholic	+.14
workers	Turnout	−.63	Percent Catholic	+.09
Percent	Center vote	+.88	Percent Catholic	+.58
workers and	Turnout	−.62	Percent Catholic	+.20
petit-bourgeois				

SOURCES: Calculated from the election returns in STDD II Nr. 28 and the occupational
sample described in note 82.

1871 was that Catholic support had grown from predominant to
overwhelming, and bourgeois disinclination from visibly apparent to
extremely strong.[88]

1867-1871: Elements of Continuity and Discontinuity

The candidates and parties of the 1867 Reichstag elections in the two
constituencies just considered were still largely those of the Landtag
elections of the conflict years. In Arnsberg-Meschede-Olpe, the former

[88] Once again, this development can be seen in the truck farmers' precincts, where
Bernard, the Center candidate, received 93.5 percent of the votes in Hamm and 88.6
percent in Flehe-Volmerswerth. The two most Catholic precincts in the city of Düsseldorf
were the two most enthusiastically Progressive precincts in 1867 and also the two
precincts which provided the highest proportion of Center voters of any in the city in
1871. Detailed election returns for Landkreis Düsseldorf are lacking for 1871, but it
would seem that the rural Catholic voters switched from the Conservative candidate
they had supported in 1867 to the Center Party in 1871.

clerical-conservative coalition had split into its separate parts, while in Düsseldorf the democratic-liberal coalition which had been the conflict era Progressive Party also fractured into its component elements, but the lines of continuity, nonetheless, outweighed the elements of novelty.

The continuity of the political parties—and this is the original moment in the 1867 elections—was not entirely matched by a continuity in voting behavior. Although in some cases, the former liberal partisans retained their allegiance, the liberal vote under universal, direct, and equal suffrage was clearly inferior to what it had been under the three-class electoral system. The liberals proved unable to mobilize the new mass electorate; they could only record successes in the Catholic regions with the support of the clergy or as a result of a politicized Catholic religious sensibility; a vote for an enemy of the enemy, for candidates opposing a ministry which had made war on the Pope and the Emperor.

Among the Catholic electorate, the Center Party already existed in 1867; it only remained for the clerical politicians to create it. Once this was accomplished in the following years, the political issues among the Catholic population of the northern Rhineland and Westphalia were settled. Catholics who had given their votes to oppositional liberals or, as on occasion, governmental conservatives in 1867 because there was no clerical candidate to vote for, shifted their allegiance and turned in Center ballots. The supporters of the oppositional clericals in 1867 were also the supporters of the no less clerical if rather less oppositional Center Party of 1871. In either case there was a continuity of religiously-based voting between the two elections.

In some constituencies, the former bases of liberal support disintegrated before the clerical offensive; even where this did not happen, the liberals found themselves more isolated than ever, totally cut off from the great bulk of Catholic voters. Even before the outbreak of the *Kulturkampf*, the Center Party had obtained a dominant position in the Catholic areas of the northern Rhineland and Westphalia; the development of the conflict between church and state after 1871 would merely serve to fortify its position even more strongly.

CHAPTER 5

THE *KULTURKAMPF*

THE PROBLEMATIC OF THE *Kulturkampf*

The political power of the emergent Catholic milieu in the northern Rhineland and Westphalia had been decisively demonstrated in the 1871 *Reichstag* elections. Within a year of those elections, the Catholics found themselves at odds with the Prussian and *Reich* governments. The initial tensions quickly deepened into a bitter conflict, known to posterity as the *Kulturkampf,* which lasted the better part of a decade and dominated political life in the early years of Bismarckian Germany.[1]

The measures of the *Kulturkampf* marked a sharp break with the tendencies of the previous twenty years, which were a time when the Catholic church in Prussia was increasingly freed of any state interference in its internal affairs. During the 1870s, the ministry, with the enthusiastic support of the liberal parliamentary majority, attempted to reassert the predominant influence of the state over the church in several key areas of social and political life, ranging from the control of the educational system to the legal validity of marriage, to the education, appointment and discipline of the Catholic clergy.

Prevalent scholarly opinion offers two explanations for this campaign. One stresses the role of Bismarck, seeing the *Kulturkampf* as

[1] The literature on the *Kulturkampf* is enormous, and just a few indications will be given here. The best of the older studies, and still the most complete history of the conflict, is Kissling, *Geschichte des Kulturkampfes.* Although not having access to ecclesiastical or official archives, the author was able to use private papers since vanished and incorporate the oral tradition of events into his work. Among the more recent studies, Schmidt-Volkmar, *Der Kulturkampf,* has carried out extensive research in the state archives and contains much useful material, but traces of a *völkisch* viewpoint remain (the author is a former SS man), and the work must be approached with a certain skepticism. Much of the literature is concerned with the ostensible intellectual foundations of the struggle. Bornkamm, "Die Staatsidee," is probably the best of this genre, but Franz, *Kulturkampf,* is more metaphysics than history. Margaret Anderson's biography of the Catholic politician Ludwig Windthorst contains an excellent account of the place of the *Kulturkampf* in Catholic political culture; the account in Stürmer, *Regierung und Reichstag,* is also good, but concentrates more narrowly on the parliamentary import of the struggle. Scholle, *Die preußische Staatsjustiz,* is a useful empirical study of the juridical implications of the *Kulturkampf* legislation. The best recent study of the *Kulturkampf* is the work of Weber, *Kirchliche Politik,* which is far more comprehensive than the title indicates.

primarily a ploy on his part (if, perhaps, a ploy that got out of hand) to tie liberal parliamentarians to the ministry and keep them from developing an effective drive toward parliamentary government by offering up the Catholics as a convenient target for liberal hostility. The other interpretation stresses the role of the liberals, seeing their advocacy of an official anti-clerical policy as a conscious move designed to destroy the political power of the clergy (of both confessions) and to push the state apparatus into breaking its ties with clerical and conservative elements, thus ensuring both liberal parliamentary majorities and a ministry which would have to cooperate with them.[2]

The two explanations are less conflicting than complementary since there is no reason to think that the ministry and the liberals could not both have desired the church-state conflict, each hoping to use it to increase its influence over the other. Actions planned in Berlin, however, often led to unexpected consequences in the provinces. While some officials, those especially loyal to the state or with liberal sympathies, were willing to carry out the ministry's anti-clerical measures, they proved to be a minority, especially as many liberal bureaucrats in the provinces with anti-clerical opinions had been purged during the conflict era ten years previously. Large numbers of Catholic officials openly refused to go along with the policy of persecuting the church, and the administrative apparatus in the western provinces began to show signs of collapse. Far from weakening the political power of the clergy, state persecution added the nimbus of martyrdom to a group whose remarkable influence was already apparent in 1870-1871. The strength of Catholic loyalties and the increasingly disruptive effects of attempts to destroy them ultimately led the provincial authorities to loosen their ties to the liberals and to seek an accommodation with the church and political Catholicism.

A study of the course of the *Kulturkampf* in the northern Rhineland and Westphalia is not just useful for showing the distance between plans in the capital and realities in the provinces.[3] Events in the provinces had their own logic, and the response of the politicized Catholic milieu—already in existence by 1870-1871—to the hostile legislative initiatives of the ministry and liberal parliamentary majority provides an excellent example of it. The popular ideology of political Cathol-

---

[2] Schmidt, "Die Nationalliberalen," pp. 208-23.

[3] There are many studies of the *Kulturkampf* in different localities. For the northern Rhineland and Westphalia, the best of them is Schiffers, *Der Kulturkampf in Aachen*. Also useful are the memoirs of Ludwig Ficker, judge and local Catholic politician, *Der Kulturkampf in Münster*. Of less value, but not without interest, are van Gils, "Der 'Kulturkampf,' " which utilizes local chroniclists and oral tradition; Kruse, "Bischof Bernhard Brinkmann"; and Michels, "Kulturkampf in Düsseldorf."

icism in the *Kulturkampf*, the forms—both organized and unorganized—the struggle took on, all testified to the deep influence of a quarter century of religious revival and political conflict. From this perspective, emphasizing the forms of action and varieties of conflict at the local level, the *Kulturkampf* was not the break with the past that it might have seemed from the ministerial offices and parliaments in Berlin, but a continuation and culmination of tendencies existent since midcentury.

THE BEGINNINGS OF THE *Kulturkampf*, 1871-1873

The first legislative initiative of what later acquired the name *Kulturkampf* was the so-called "pulpit paragraph" (Kanzelparagraph), a law passed by the *Reichstag* in the summer of 1871. It prohibited the "misuse of the pulpit for political purposes"—in other words, it was aimed at the election-eve sermons of the Catholic clergy. These sermons were by no means restricted to the Rhineland and Westphalia; the measure had been proposed by the liberal Bavarian Prime Minister Johann Lutz, whose own government was suffering much worse relations with the Catholic church than was the case in Prussia at the time.

Specifically Prussian measures quickly followed. The "Catholic division" of the Prussian Ministry of Education and Religious Affairs was abolished; henceforth one set of bureaucrats would deal with the matters of all confessions. The Catholic division had been established in the 1840s as part of the settlement ending the *Kölner Wirren*; its abolition was taken as a sign of the beginning of an anti-Catholic policy. In 1872, the Prussian parliament approved a government proposal which clearly defined the local school inspectors as state representatives. The parish priest or Protestant pastor was no longer school inspector by virtue of his ecclesiastical position, but only at the discretion of the authorities, who could, if they wished, choose another person for the post. The orthodox Lutheran Minister of Education and Religious Affairs, Heinrich von Mühler, resigned, strongly disapproving this measure. His replacement by the liberal jurist Adalbert Falk showed that the Prussian government had definitely adopted an anti-clerical course.

Further legislative measures followed. In 1872, the *Reichstag* passed a law expelling the Jesuits from German territory. In 1873, the Prussian Parliament approved several governmental initiatives, known from the month of their passage as the "May laws," which formed the legal basis for the coming confrontation between church and state. The most important measure was the "Law on the Education and Appointment of the Clergy," which required priests either to attend a German university or to pass a "cultural examination" devised by state officials. It also required governmental approval of any ecclesiastical appointments; a bishop could no longer appoint a chaplain or parish priest without first obtaining the consent of the provincial governor. Another measure established a "Royal Court for Ecclesiastical Affairs," which claimed final jurisdiction on all matters of internal church discipline. The parliamentary debates on this legislation gave the conflict a name when the Progressive deputy Rudolf Virchow explained that the measures were part of a great "struggle for civilization," a *Kulturkampf*. By this time, the government's religious policy had come to occupy stage center in political affairs, and the entire Catholic population of Prussia was in an uproar over the measures.[4]

In the first half of 1871, Catholic notables and the Rhenish-Westphalian authorities were on good terms, and they had cooperated closely in the March *Reichstag* elections. The passage of the first restrictive laws, the developing debates on others, and the first public confrontations between anti-Infallibilist Old Catholics and their former coreligionists loyal to the Pope began to stir public opinion. As the school inspection law was debated in the Prussian Parliament in the closing months of 1871 and the beginning of 1872, the clergy rapidly spread the word that religion was once more in danger; lay activists from some Catholic political clubs began holding public mass meetings and circulating petitions against the proposal, as they had done in response to the liberal school initiatives in 1868-1869. The actual course of events after the passage of the law helped to assuage the worst fears; rather than the rumored dismissal of all the priests as local school inspectors and their replacement by Jews, the authorities used their new powers simply to confirm the clergy's previous position in the schools. Liberal demands for the expulsion of the Jesuits and the subsequent introduction in the *Reichstag* of such a proposal touched off a large-scale agitation. In December 1872, the Düsseldorf District officials noted: "Hardly a week goes by without a sizeable Catholic meeting being staged [ins Szene gesetzt] somewhere or other. In this way, resistance to the authority of the state is brought to an ever-widening circle of the population."[5]

    [4] Kissling, *Geschichte des Kulturkampfes*, 2: 1-226 and Schmidt-Volkmar, *Der Kulturkampf*, pp. 60-124.
    [5] LAK 403 Nr. 6695 Bl. 189. On the agitation against the school inspection bill and the situation in the first half of 1872, see HSTAD RD Nr. 1257 Bl. 2-9; HSTAD RA Nr. 819 Bl. 40, 135; STAM OP Nr. 1601 I Bl. 19-20, 24-30 and the reports of the *Landräte* of the Arnsberg District in the same volume; STAM RM Nr. 1039 Bl. 20-25; Keinemann, *Beiträge zur westfälischen Landesgeschichte*, pp. 122-23; Pülke, "Kreis

The Mainz Association

This agitation was above all the work of the "Association of German Catholics," commonly known from the location of its headquarters as the "Mainz Association." It was the first mass political organization of German Catholics and had what was probably the largest membership of any political organization in Germany up to that time. The group was founded in July 1872, with the statutory goal of "defending the freedom and rights of the Catholic Church and bringing Christian principles to bear on all aspects of public life." The increasingly anti-clerical policy of Bismarck's ministry and, in particular, the passage of the anti-Jesuit law in the *Reichstag* provided the impetus for the organization's formation.[6]

The location of the association's headquarters in Mainz testified to the patronage of Bishop Ketteler, the leading figure in the German episcopate. There was also a more pragmatic reason for the choice of that city. Had an organization with local branches been formed, the association would have had to deal with the Prussian association laws, which required that the membership list of any political organization be turned over to the police and prohibited organizations from different localities from working together. Instead, all the members of the association, regardless of their actual residence, were enrolled in Mainz, which was in Hessen and thus conveniently out of reach of the Prussian authorities. The practice was a legal fiction: in each locality there was a "business agent" who was actually the chairman of the local group. There were also "district business agents" whose positions were suspiciously similar to those of chairmen of regional organizations.

As its official name indicated, the Mainz Association was to be a nationwide organization, embracing all German Catholics. A separate, independent organization existed in Silesia, however, where the ethnic differences in the Catholic population created a particularly touchy situation. The Mainz Association was also unrepresented in regions where the Catholic population was not ethnically German—Prussian Poland and Alsace-Lorraine. Even in the rest of Germany, there were sharp regional variations in membership.

Although the most prominent families of the Bavarian Catholic nobility were on the executive committee of the Mainz Association— Prince Karl zu Löwenstein, the Freiherr von Franckenstein, Count

---

Recklinghausen," p. 121; reports of correspondents in *Germania*, Dec. 8, 1871, Jan. 7, 11, Feb. 4, Mar. 5-7, 14, 1872.

[6] On the Mainz Association, see Kissling, *Geschichte des Kulturkampfes*, 2:309-25. The founding appeal was published in *Germania*, Jul. 24, 1872.

Ludwig von Arco-Zinnenberg—the ordinary Bavarian Catholics were far too suspicious of the Prussians, no matter what their confession, to join up. The association also had relatively few members in south-western Germany, where the *Kulturkampf* was never as passionate an issue as in Prussia, and where liberal and democratic ideas still influenced a good portion of the Catholic population. The Mainz Association was a Rhenish-Westphalian affair, the two Prussian provinces accounting for over ninety percent of the organization's membership. Within a year of its founding, it counted 59,725 members in the northern Rhineland and Westphalia, with another 8,900 in the southern Rhineland. Membership was most heavily concentrated in the Düsseldorf and Arnsberg Districts, where about twenty percent of all adult Catholic men became members.[7]

The Mainz Association held giant public meetings across the length and breadth of Rhineland-Westphalia. Its president, Felix Freiherr von Loë, who had been dismissed from his post as *Landrat* of *Kreis* Kleve for his Austrian sympathies in 1866, was constantly in motion, traveling from one meeting to another, speaking from Emmerich to Trier, from Aachen to Paderborn. He spoke to enormous crowds. Several attempts by the local authorities to estimate the size of the gatherings suggest that in small towns and the countryside upward of eighty percent of the adult males of the area were present. The proportions were smaller in the large urban centers, but nonetheless impressive. Six thousand people attended a Mainz Association rally in September 1872 in the concert hall in Düsseldorf—perhaps forty percent of the adult Catholic male population of the city and its suburbs. The crowd filled all the seats, spilled over into the halls and side rooms. "Düsseldorf has never seen such a colossal gathering," the correspondent for *Germania*, the Center Party newspaper, reported.[8]

His point was well made. With the possible exception of 1848, and then only in the largest cities and not in the small towns or countryside, such mass political meetings had been previously unknown. The only comparable mass gatherings had not been of an overtly political nature but a religious one—the missions.[9] The Mainz Association meetings

[7] Kissling, *Geschichte des Kulturkampfes*, 2: 314-18; HSTAD RD Nr. 289 Bl. 179.

[8] For crowd estimates, see LA Kr. Ahaus to RM, Oct. 10, 1872; LA Kr. Coesfeld to RM Oct. 25, 1872; *Amtmann* in Telgte to RM Dec. 10, 1872; *Amtmann* in Marl to RM Feb. 18, 1873; LA Kr. Steinfurt to RM Apr. 15, 1873; all in STAM RM Nr. 1039; LA Kr. Büren to RMI Dec. 10, 1872; LA Kr. Wiedenbrück to RMI Oct. 2, 1873, STAD M1 IP Nr. 363. Cf. van Gils, "Der 'Kulturkampf,' " p. 62. On the meeting in Düsseldorf, see HSTAD RD Nr. 1257 Bl. 26 and *Germania*, Sep. 29, 1872.

[9] It should be remembered that missions were held with a renewed intensity after 1866 and continued to be held through early 1872. The Mainz Association meetings began almost exactly as the missions stopped.

were a politicization of the missionary events, a call to the faithful to defend their hard-won religion against the growing ranks of its enemies. Curiously enough, these fervent introductory meetings seemed to have had no follow-up. No organization was set up, no further meetings were held, no trace of the Mainz Association was left at the local level.[10] To grasp the reasons for this is to understand the organization of political Catholicism during the *Kulturkampf*.

Although the Mainz Association had a mass membership, the bulk of its members played no active role in the organization's affairs. The actual work of the association was carried out by the local and district business agents, who were, as exactly as this can be determined, leading figures in the local Catholic political clubs and in the provincial electoral committees of the Center Party.[11] The central office in Mainz acted as a kind of political clearing house, coordinating the work of the clubs, sending out speakers for rallies, distributing surplus funds, and gathering information on local political conditions.

The Mainz Association, in other words, created a mass base for a political organization dominated by the Catholic elites. The ordinary members were expected to pay their dues and cheer the speakers, but not to participate in running the organization. Thus, once an introductory meeting had been held, there was no need for further gatherings. Control over the group and its political work rested in the

[10] See STAM OP Nr. 1601 I Bl. 78 ff.; reports of the *Landräte* of *Kreise* Olpe, Meschede, Brilon, Arnsberg, and Dortmund in 1874 in STAM RAR I Nr. 101; the reports of the *Landräte* from *Kreise* Recklinghausen, Münster (country), Borken, and Tecklenburg in Dec. 1874 in STAM RM Nr. 1039; reports of the *Landräte* of *Kreise* Paderborn, Büren, Höxter, and Warburg in STAD M1 IP Nr. 363; STAM OP Nr. 1601 II Bl. 38-39, 145-47; and the reports of the *Landräte* from *Kreise* Düren and Schleiden in HSTAD RA Nr. 4817 and LA Kr. Jülich to RA Feb. 5, 1873 HSTAD RA Nr. 4816.

[11] This assertion is based on a comparison of the names of local and district business managers of the Mainz Association which can be found scattered through STAM OP Nr. 1601 I-II; STAM RM Nr. 1039-40; STAM RAR I Nr. 101; STAD M1 IP Nr. 363; STAM LA Kr. Borken Nr. 19; HSTAD RA Nr. 4816-17; and HSTAD RD Nr. 287-90; membership lists (or at least lists of leading members) of local Catholic political clubs, which can also be found scattered through these volumes and the names of the members of the Rhenish and Westphalian Provincial Electoral Committees of the Center Party, published in *Germania*, Oct. 3 and Dec. 22, 1873, respectively. The connection between members of the Catholic political clubs and local activists of the Mainz Association was frequently noted by the police. See, for instance, OB Münster to RM, Jul. 29, 1872, STAM RM Nr. 1039; HSTAD RD Nr. 289 Bl. 13-15, 32-33; LA Kr. Schleiden to RA, Jul. 12, 1875, HSTAD RA Nr. 4818.

See the correspondence between the central office and the Warburg business manager, seized in a police raid and preserved in STAD M1 IP Nr. 363. Catholic parliamentarians seem to have had a certain skepticism about the Mainz Association (cf. Anderson, *Windthorst*, pp. 180-81, esp. n. 40) but it would be interesting to know more about the relationship between the Mainz central office and the Center parliamentary caucus.

hands of the Catholic notables and the clergy, who had been the leading elements in political Catholicism before the founding of the Mainz Association and would remain so after the organization's demise.[12]

The Mainz Association was not really a novelty; it was able to grow as rapidly as it did because it built on an already existing network of political clubs. At the same time, the meetings of the Mainz Association in rural areas and small towns contributed to the formation of formal and informal Catholic political clubs in those localities, thus extending the organizational apparatus of the Center Party deep into the countryside.[13]

Within a few months of its formation, the organization came under heavy attack from the state. Officials were prohibited from joining, meetings were closed by the police, raids were carried out on the residences of the local and district business managers. After a lengthy legal battle, the Prussian Supreme Court declared in 1876 that the group was in violation of the association laws and ordered it dissolved.[14] Its disappearance made very little difference to the structure of political Catholicism. The network of political clubs and politically active clergy and notables remained—indeed, it had been considerably expanded in the early 1870s. The Mainz Association had also encouraged the formation of a local press, so that alongside the large Catholic dailies—the *Kölnische Volkszeitung*, the *Essener Volkszeitung*, the *Westfälische Merkur* in Münster or the *Echo der Gegenwart* in Aachen, all of which were in existence before 1871—there appeared a great number of small-town and rural Catholic weeklies, providing a further support for political Catholicism in the countryside.[15]

In the short span of its existence, the Mainz Association, in conjunction with the local Catholic political clubs, organized a massive and unprecedented political propaganda campaign. The speeches held at Catholic meetings before thousands of listeners, the editorials of the newly founded Catholic press: these were the instruments by which Catholic politicians, both laymen and priests, informed the mass of the faithful about the *Kulturkampf* and helped form their view of the

[12] The regional business manager of the Mainz Association for the *Münsterland* was the merchant Joseph Albers in Münster. A small selection of his correspondence from the year 1883 has been preserved in BAM GV IV Nr. A125ᵇ vol. II. The material concerns the organization of a petition drive over a proposed education law and shows quite clearly the survival of the political network of Catholic notables and clergy long after the dissolution of the Mainz Association.

[13] Cf. Bachem, *Zentrumspartei*, 3: 26-27; STAM LA Kr. Ahaus Nr. 92.

[14] Kissling, *Geschichte des Kulturkampfes*, 3: 315.

[15] Cf. the account in HSTAD RD Nr. 290 Bl. 264. The 1881 list of Rhenish newspapers shows that many small-town Catholic journals were started in the early 1870s. LAK 403 Nr. 7155 Bl. 621-714.

political struggle. Memories of the religious and political events of the previous twenty-five years were shaped under the pressure of state hostility into a coherent and lasting *Weltanschauung*.

The Popular Ideology of the Kulturkampf

The primary issue in the *Kulturkampf*, clerical speakers and journalists insisted, was the defense of religion against liberal efforts to destroy it. The accomplishments of the post-1850 religious revival were in danger. As Joseph Racke, national secretary of the Mainz Association, told a meeting in Münster, the liberals hoped to achieve "a state without God, a marriage without God, a school without God."[16]

It was not just the institutional aspects of the religious revival which were under attack, but the spiritual ones as well. At a meeting of the Mainz Association in Wiedenbrück (Minden District) in October 1873, Chaplain Grimmelt from Liesborn, one of the politically most active priests in the area, explained the origins of the *Kulturkampf* with a simple, popularly appealing analogy. When a group of thugs [Spitz-buben], he said, wished to break into a peasant's house, they first took care of the watchdog by putting a muzzle on him so he could not bark. The liberals, he went on, wished to break into the Catholic's house, the church, and steal "our precious treasures stored [there]: faith, hope, love." To do so, they had put a muzzle on the clergy, the watchdogs of the church, through the pulpit paragraph. The attack would continue, he concluded, as long as the liberal "parliamentary heroes" (Kammerhelden) dominated the *Reichstag* and Prussian *Land-tag* and the liberal "gutter press" (Schmutzblätter) slandered the church.[17]

This liberal desire to destroy religion, the speakers insisted, was fundamentally subversive. The contrast between liberal subversion and Catholic defense of order was the main theme, the organizing para-digm, used in explaining the *Kulturkampf*. The liberals were attempt-ing, as Chaplain Horsten from Breyell (*Kreis* Kempen) claimed, to "make a revolution against the Catholic church." These efforts, a certain Boers from Brisbach told two thousand participants at a rally in Rees on the lower Rhine, must be defeated, "obedience to the church must rule, just as the members of a family are obedient to its head."[18]

[16] BM Münster to RM, Aug. 1, 1873, STAM RM Nr. 1039.

[17] STAM OP Nr. 1601 I Bl. 230-34.

[18] HSTAD RD Nr. 1257 Bl. 95-98; among the many other examples of the notion that the *Kulturkampf* represented the effort of a subversive liberalism to destroy religion, cf. HSTAD RD Nr. 1257 Bl. 151-57, 160, 210; HSTAD RD Nr. 287 Bl. 108-109; STAM RM Nr. 1039 Bl. 22-25 and from the same volume (most of which is unpaginated) OB Münster to RM Jul. 29, 1872; BM Bocholt to RM Nov. 11, 1872; LA Kr. Beckum

Even Chaplain Laaf, one of the leaders of the radical wing of the Christian Social movement, employed the language of counterrevolution. He told a meeting in Holstershausen (*Landkreis* Essen) in October 1872: "The enemy of religion is liberalism, whose faith is disbelief and whose mother is the revolution. The word 'liberal' means ˌ freedom, and the slogan 'a free church in a free state' [classic liberal slogan on religion, coined by the Italian Prime Minister Cavour] sounds so attractive, but the true intention of the liberals is to get to the helm of the government and snatch religion away from every single individual."[19]

The *Kulturkampf* was seen in a distinct historical context. Its origins were found in the Enlightenment, and Catholic speakers never tired of reminding their audiences of Voltaire, "écrasez l'infâme," and the godless horrors of the French Revolution.[20] Even more to the point were the events of 1848. Chaplain Büssmann from Essen pointed out, "in the year 1848, the Catholic bishops limited the revolution through their teachings." At the same meeting, textile manufacturer Matthias Wiese from Werden, leading figure in the Center Party of the western Ruhr basin, pointed out the other side of the story: "The liberals talk big today although they still smell of barricade blood." The audience understood him perfectly and roared back "The red Becker!"—referring to Hermann Becker, in 1848 a member of the Communist League, but by 1872 a liberal *Reichstag* deputy and mayor of Dortmund. On another occasion, Wiese pushed the point a little further. "The Catholics stood true to the throne in 1848, and in just the same way they supported the ministry in the conflict era, in 1859 and beyond."[21]

Yet this long loyalty to the forces of order was not recognized by the state. Just the opposite was the case: the authorities protected the liberal subversives as they engaged in their persecution of the church,

---

to RM Oct. 18, 1872; LA Kr. Coesfeld to RM Oct. 24, 1872; BM Ahlen to RM Nov. 17, 1872; *Amtmann* in Telgte to RM Dec. 10, 1872; LA Kr. Recklinghausen to RM Dec. 16, 1872; BM Lüdinghausen to RM Feb. 20, 1873; *Germania*, Sep. 29, 1872 (Düsseldorf), Oct. 3, 1872 (Ahaus), Oct. 6, 1872 (Cologne), Oct. 16, 1872 (Neuß), Nov. 24, 1872 (Aachen), Dec. 29, 1872 (Bonn), Mar. 18, 1873 (Wadersloh), May 9, 1873 (Erwitte).

[19] HSTAD RD Nr. 287 Bl. 108-109; HSTAD RD Nr. 1257 Bl. 151-57.

[20] HSTAD RD Nr. 1257 Bl. 151-57; Police Commissioner Kurtz (Düren) to RA May 31, 1875 HSTAD RA Nr. 4818; LA Kr. Beckum to RM Oct. 28, 1872; LA Kr. Recklinghausen to RM Dec. 16, 1872; *Amtmann* in Beelen to LA Kr. Warendorf Feb. 17, 1873 STAM RM Nr. 1039. Cf. States Attorney Ingahrn (Paderborn) to OPM Jan. 12, 1874 STAM OP Nr. 2159 III.

[21] HSTAD RD Nr. 1257 Bl. 75-89, 139-44; HSTAD RD Nr. 30428 Bl. 124-25. Similarly, see *Amtmann* in Wadersloh to RM Apr. 15, 1873 and the reports of the Cologne correspondent of *Germania*, Mar. 16 and Apr. 5, 1872 and the Düren correspondent Jul. 2, 1875.

or even allowed themselves to be used by the liberals for their nefarious ends.[22] The liberals even wanted to "force their way into the church" and replace the "personal God" with the "ideal state" at the altar. The liberal-revolutionary ideal was the "omnipotent state" which dominated the church and ignored divine and natural law in favor of its own arbitrary creations. This attitude was neatly expressed in a resolution passed at the second national conference of the Mainz Association, in June 1874, which declared that the group saw as its task "the defense of the natural rights of the individual, the rights of the church, and the rights of the German nation against revolutionary and bureaucratic acts of violence."[23]

The clerical politicians vehemently rejected the liberal charges that they were subversive or revolutionary. They were far from glorifying in their role as opposition to the government. Catholics, they insisted, were the true friends of order and opposed only the "modern state" or the "state corrupted by the rule of the political parties."[24] The Catholic opposition to the government's policies was, in the view of the Mainz Association speakers and the clerical press, an attempt to save the state from itself. The notion that religion was the only basis for social and political order ran like a red thread through the discourse of political Catholicism. By opposing religion, liberals were engaging in a "struggle against church and state." In a reiteration of the classic argument of post-French Revolution conservatism, Chaplain Schlunkes insisted: "He who shakes the altar also topples the throne!"[25]

The Catholic polemicists left no doubt that there were indeed altar-shakers and throne-topplers hard at work. Behind the measures of the *Kulturkampf*, behind German and European liberalism, stood the old revolutionary villain, the Masonic Lodge. The lodge, Catholic speakers implied, dominated the Prussian government. When the authorities

[22] The authorities reacted with considerable displeasure to this notion. On at least two occasions, the assertion that the state was carrying out liberal policies led to indictments for slandering the state! STAM OP Nr. 1601 I Bl. 230-34, 248 and a correspondent "from the Sauerland," *Germania*, Feb. 1, 1875. Cf. the marginal comments of *Regierungs-Vizepräsident* Delius to BM Lüdinghausen to RM Feb. 20, 1873 STAM RM Nr. 1039.

[23] *Germania*, Jun. 18, 1874; the sources cited in the previous note and *Amtmann* in Oelde to RM Jan. 6, 1873 STAM OP Nr. 1039; *Germania*, Oct. 6, 1872 (Cologne), Oct. 13, 1872 (Neuß), Nov. 19, 1872 (Cologne), Jan. 9, 1873 (Morsbach).

[24] HSTAD RD Nr. 1257 Bl. 58; *Germania*, Oct. 9, 1872 (Cologne).

[25] HSTAD RD Nr. 1257 Bl. 160, 210. For other examples of the notion that religion was the fundamental basis of social and political order, see LA Kr. Borken to RM Oct. 28, 1872; LA Kr. Coesfeld to RM Oct. 25, 1872; LA Kr. Beckum to RM Sept. 25, 1872; *Amtmann* in Oelde to RM Jan. 6, 1873; LA Kr. Recklinghausen to RM Jun. 30, 1873 STAM RM Nr. 1039; *Germania*, Aug. 21, 1872 (Essen); Oct. 9, 1872 (Cologne); Nov. 18, 1872 (Beckum); Nov. 24, 1872 (Aachen); Nov. 22, 1873 (Cologne).

refused to approve the mayor elected by the clerically controlled city council of Emmerich, Freiherr von Loë told the burghers of the town that they had made a false choice in looking for "men of honor, pious Christians, good Catholics," to serve as their mayor. "But gentlemen!" Loë continued, "you have not gone to the right source. You should have applied to the Masonic Lodge, and they would have procured a mayor for you whom the royal government would have confirmed. . . ."[26]

This was not just the case in Germany. The lodge was perceived as being behind the liberal attacks on the church throughout all of Europe, Chaplain Laaf explained at a meeting in Herten (*Kreis* Recklinghausen). How could these attacks be occurring in every country at once if they were not coordinated by a secret society?[27] The most dramatic account was given by Dr. Engels from Bonn, who told thousands of Catholics at a meeting in Duisburg in 1872 that:

> . . . the mother of liberalism is the lodge, Freemasonry. What the lodge wanted could be clearly read from its periodicals. . . . They all agreed in a twofold goal: namely, everything Christian must go, and all thrones must go. When in France someone is accepted into the Masonic order, he must hold a dagger in one hand and raise the other to swear an oath to devote all his strength to the expulsion of the princes and the annihilation of their thrones; if he does not, then the dagger will bring his death. The true face of the lodge is becoming apparent: men who refuse to recognize any higher being, any God over mankind, but instead wish to deify themselves as half-gods and rule over all.[28]

The accusations seemed only too logical to the vast majority of Catholics accustomed to decades of attacks on Masonry as the epitome of satanic subversion. The riots in Essen which followed the expulsion of the Jesuits in August 1872 climaxed in an attack on the home of a prominent local Freemason. As the police arrived, the crowd was shouting "On to the lodge!"[29]

The tale of revolutionary subversion did not end with the Masons.

[26] HSTAD RD Pr. Nr. 636 Bl. 131.

[27] LA Kr. Recklinghausen to RM Dec. 16, 1872, STAM RM Nr. 1039.

[28] *Duisburger Volkszeitung*, Nov. 5, 1872, copy in HSTAD RD Nr. 1257 Bl. 120. For other examples, see HSTAD RD Nr. 1257 Bl. 95-98, 151-57; LA Kr. Coesfeld to RM Oct. 25, 1872; BM Ahlen to RM Nov. 18, 1872; LA Kr. Recklinghausen to RM Jun. 30, 1873; OB Münster to RM Aug. 1, 1873; STAM RM Nr. 1039; *Germania*, Feb. 27, 1872 (Cologne); May 14, 1872 (Cologne); Oct. 16, 1872 (Neuß); Feb. 14, 1873 (Morsbach).

[29] HSTAD RD Nr. 835 I Bl. 46-53. Cf. Anderson, *Windthorst*, pp. 455-56, n. 25.

The lodge and its liberal associates had, in Catholic eyes, brought forth the most fearsome of all revolutionaries, the Social Democrats. In the growth of the International, Chaplain Hoene, leader of the Catholic political club in Stolberg, informed a Mainz Association meeting in the Aachen suburb of Burtscheid, one could ascertain the "chastizing stick of God" (die Zuchtrute Gottes), as the liberals' own creation had turned against them and would one day annihilate them. Images of the Paris Commune—the burning city, the murdered archbishop— were everywhere proffered and explained as the last, logical consequence of a godless, Masonic liberalism.[30]

Chaplain Schlunkes at a meeting in Hüls, *Landkreis* Krefeld (Düsseldorf District) succeeded in touching on all the main themes of the ideology of political Catholicism in the *Kulturkampf* era in one speech, reported in the clerical *Niederrheinische Volkszeitung* in Krefeld:

> We are not the enemies of the state . . . but the enemies of the church are those who once stood on the barricades and wished to wade up to their ankles through the blood of tyrants. Then he [Chaplain Schlunkes] discussed the lodge, which can tell of many a revolution; the International, an outgrowth of the former, just more inexorable in drawing the consequences [of their common attitudes] finally, "liberalism," also a son of the lodge, which has prepared the way for the International and is even more dangerous to the state because it seems to be its friend. "Liberalism" regards the state as its god and buries religion. But whoever snatches religion from the heart of the people takes away the foundation of the state and brings it to the ground.

The chaplain ended his speech by discussing the Commune and the murder of the Archbishop of Paris. He accused the liberals of working toward the same ends as the Communards and concluded with the statement, "He who shakes the altar also topples the throne!" to the thunderous applause of his listeners.[31]

The speech, and the whole ideology of political Catholicism in the *Kulturkampf* era, testifies to the weight of the political experience of

[30] *Echo der Gegenwart*, Sep. 6, 1872, copy in HSTAD RA Nr. 4816. For the description of the International or the Paris Commune as the final consequence of liberalism, see HSTAD RD Nr. 1257 Bl. 75-89; *Dürener Sonntagsblatt*, Aug. 16, 1874 in HSTAD RA Nr. 4817; LA Kr. Beckum to RM Oct. 28, 1872; LA Kr. Borken to RM Sep. 25, 1872; *Amtmann* in Oelde to RM Jan. 11, 1873, STAM RM Nr. 1039; *Germania*, May 30, 1872 (Cologne); Mar. 22, 1873 (Cologne). Cf. Naujoks, *Die katholische Arbeiterbewegung*, pp. 16-18; Kruse, "Bischof Bernhard Brinkmann," p. 79 and *Germania*, Nov. 23, 1875 (Refrath).

[31] *Niederrheinische Volkszeitung* (Krefeld), Oct. 24, 1872 copy in HSTAD RD Nr. 1257 Bl. 210.

the previous twenty-five years. The church-state conflict was interpreted according to a schema latent in the *Vormärz*, first publicly elaborated in the missions of the 1850s, and brought into political life in the bitter polemics of the 1860s. The challenge to the authority of the church was understood as the result of an international subversive conspiracy of Masons and other revolutionary elements. Their attack on the Catholic religion was the first step in a carefully planned campaign to destroy Christianity and, ultimately, the entire existing social and political order.

The experience of the latter half of the 1860s amplified this interpretation. The portrayal of the Prussian government as the ally of revolutionary and subversive elements was first discussed politically in the 1850s, but the war of 1866 brought the notion from a theoretical proposal about the essentially revolutionary-democratic nature of the bureaucracy to the concrete reality of an armed attack on Pope and Emperor. The biography of Felix Freiherr von Loë is paradigmatic in this respect: he went from the Catholic-conservative *Landrat* in the early 1860s, constantly at odds with his liberal-bureaucratic superiors in Düsseldorf, to the openly pro-Austrian oppositionist of 1866-1867, and, as president of the Mainz Association, he became the leading clerical agitator in Germany, denouncing the Prussian government as under the control of the lodge.

The final element in the clerical picture of the *Kulturkampf*, the growing menace of socialism, heir to godless liberalism, was also a consequence of events in the latter half of the 1860s. At that time, a social-democratic movement had developed out of the bourgeois democracy in the northern Rhineland. Its lively agitation, even if engendering an ultimately successful Catholic counter-agitation, had nonetheless temporarily mounted a challenge to the clerical loyalties of the Catholic workers in the industrial districts of the lower Rhine.

To the contemporary historian, the rhetoric of the struggle may seem extreme, apocalyptic in its portrayal of a decisive conflict between godless subversion and embattled Christianity. The accounts of Mainz Association meetings in police reports and the press leave little doubt that the sentiments expressed in them, both by the speakers and the audience, were genuine and deeply felt. Yet this passionate and extreme interpretation of the course of events did not preclude a shrewd political exploitation of them; rather, passionate conviction and political expediency went hand in hand.

The violent attacks on liberalism made by clerical speakers in the *Kulturkampf* era must be understood in the context of the twenty-five-year-long history of covert tension and open hostility between clerical and liberal-democratic elements which had been the dominant factor of political life in the Catholic areas of Prussia's western provinces. The elections of 1870 and 1871 had been stunning clerical victories; the Catholic parliamentarians used the passions stirred by the religious legislation of the early 1870s to brand their liberal rivals as enemies of religion and human society, thus ensuring they would never again be able to mount a challenge to the clerical position.

No Mainz Association meeting was complete without an exhortation to read Catholic journals and avoid the "wicked" liberal press. Chaplain Laaf told the miners to avoid all the taverns which subscribed to liberal newspapers and to frequent only those which took good Catholic journals, such as the *Essener Volkszeitung* or the Christian-Social *Essener Blätter*. One clerical speaker proclaimed at a Mainz Association meeting that "he who lets a godless newspaper into his house on a daily or weekly basis lets the devil in just as often." The constant reiterations were not without effect: clerical newspapers flourished, and the *Kölnische Zeitung*, against which the clergy and politically active laity had been inveighing for decades, appears to have lost circulation.[32]

We can see this point in a different way by comparing the number of Mainz Association meetings held in the different *Kreise* of the Münster District in the last half of 1872 and the entire year 1873. (Afterward, the authorities succeeded in suppressing such meetings.) Westphalian Provincial Governor Friedrich von Kühlwetter had ordered the authorities to report every single meeting of the Mainz Association; the records of this surveillance in the Münster District have survived in complete form.[33] See Table 5.1.

The two *Kreise* with far and away the most meetings, Recklinghausen and Beckum, were also the two with the longest and most consistent history of left-wing politics. Both *Kreise* had been democratic strongholds in 1848-1849, had chosen a majority of Progressive electors in the 1860s, and had sent Progressives to the *Landtag* or *Reichstag* as late as 1867. The greatest number of Mainz Association meetings were thus held where political opposition to the clerical viewpoint had been strongest.

Between the continuous harassment of the police and repeated indictments for violation of the association laws, the activity of the Mainz Association dropped off to almost nothing by the beginning of 1874. The *Kulturkampf* entered a more militant phase, in which ordered public meetings took second place to mass demonstrations—

[32] HSTAD RD Nr. 1257 Bl. 95-98; *Germania*, Oct. 31, 1873 (Much). Cf. the *Zeitungsbericht* of the LA Kr. Erkelenz for the second quarter of 1874 HSTAD RA Pr. Nr. 821a. On circulation, see the figures in LAK 403 Nr. 7155.

[33] Wegmann, *Verwaltungsbeamten*, pp. 92-94.

TABLE 5.1
Mainz Association Meetings in the Münster
District, 1872-1873

Kreis	Number of Meetings
Recklinghausen	9
Beckum	5
Borken	3
Münster (city)	2
Münster (country)	2
Lüdinghausen	2[a]
Ahaus, Coesfeld, Steinfurt and Warendorf	1 each
Tecklenburg	None

[a] Strictly speaking, these were not meetings of the Mainz Association, but of the "Association for the Furtherance of Catholic Interests in *Kreis* Lüdinghausen," founded in January 1872, and thus predating the Mainz Association. In its structure and function, however, the group was identical to a local branch of the Mainz Association.
SOURCE: Reports of the authorities in STAM RM Nr. 1039.

both organized and spontaneous—and violent clashes between en-raged Catholics and the police. The wave of meetings held in 1872-1873 had contributed to the ideological crystallization of over two decades of political experience. The results would not be forgotten in the phase of more direct action which followed.

THE *Kulturkampf* AT ITS HIGH POINT: 1874-1878

By early 1874 the Berlin ministry found itself confronted with a difficult situation. The attempt to reassert a *Staatskirchentum* had failed. The Prussian bishops, after a brief initial hesitation, refused to obey the May laws and began appointing priests to vacant positions without asking approval of the authorities. The victories of the Center Party in the *Landtag* elections of 1873 and the *Reichstag* elections of 1874 were definitive proof that the mass of the Catholic population stood behind its spiritual leaders.[34]

[34] On the Prussian episcopate, see Kissling, *Geschichte des Kulturkampfes*, 2: 226-

The ministry resolved to go ahead and employ ever more severe measures to break the clerical opposition. Priests acting in violation of the May laws—both the lower clergy and the bishops—were indicted and sent to jail. The government provided financial and legal support for the sectarian, anti-Infallibilist Old Catholics, hoping to win away a portion of the faithful from the Roman Church. New legal measures were proposed and duly ratified by the *Landtag* and *Reichstag*. Civil marriage was introduced in Prussia in 1874 and in the *Reich* in 1876. All the religious orders, with the exception of the nursing sisters, were expelled from Germany. Articles 15, 16, and 18 of the Prussian constitution guaranteeing religious freedom were repealed. The Prussian Ministry of Educational and Religious Affairs denied Catholic priests the right to give religious instruction in the public schools, reserving that task for the schoolteachers under state orders. Many, though not all, of the Catholic clergy were removed from their posts as *Kreis* or local school-inspectors and replaced by laymen. The Ministry drew up plans for the introduction in large cities of *Simultanschulen*—that is, religiously mixed elementary schools with a common curriculum for pupils of both confessions and separate classes only in religious education.

The enforcement of the May laws was tightened by the passage of new legislation. Two laws in 1874 gave the Prussian government the power to confiscate the property of a parish which had no legally (that is, under the May laws) appointed priest and the power to expel from a *Kreis*, a district, or even the country any priest found guilty of violating the May laws if he was indicted a second time. The "breadbasket law" of 1875 cut off all state subsidies to any priest who refused to sign a declaration of support for the government's religious legislation.[35] The state's efforts ultimately proved futile: Catholics vigorously and effectively resisted the government's attempts to enforce these draconian measures in the northern Rhineland and Westphalia.

Demonstrations

Just as the ideology of political Catholicism in the 1870s was formulated out of the experiences of the previous two decades, the organized mass Catholic demonstrations of the *Kulturkampf* era were an adaptation of the new forms of religious festivity which had developed since 1850. The demonstrations took on a political content

---

43 and Gatz, "Bischöfliche Einheitsfront?" For the 1873 and 1874 elections, see the following chapter.

[35] Kissling, *Geschichte des Kulturkampfes*, 2: 349-411, 3: 34-88, 139-49; Schmidt-Volkmar, *Kulturkampf*, pp. 123-46.

less because of conscious efforts to turn them into Center Party election rallies than because of the new political atmosphere created by the experiences of 1866-1867, the campaigns of 1868-1871, and the agitation of the Mainz Association. When the defense of religion became a, or more appropriately the, political issue, then participation in a religious event became a political statement.

PILGRIMAGES AND PROCESSIONS

One example of this form of demonstration was the special pilgrimages organized in the years 1871-1873, especially those to the shrines of the Virgin in Kevelaer. They were first called to ask the intercession of the Virgin in favor of the beleaguered Pope, but by 1873 the position of the Catholic church had become a matter requiring divine intervention, and the pilgrims' prayers were also directed to this end.[36]

Such pilgrimages expressed the post-1850 transformation of Catholic religious life. Neither spontaneous nor traditional, the special pilgrimages were arranged and led by the clergy and Catholic associations. They occurred at novel times, another testament to the development of a post-traditionalist religious sensibility. The pilgrims went to Kevelaer in October of 1871 and 1873, something inconceivable in the religious order of agrarian northern Europe, where October meant field work on the winter wheat crop. Traditional pilgrimages occurred in May-June, or August-September, relatively quiet periods of three-field agriculture before or after the midsummer harvest.

The pilgrimages were not political rallies like the Mainz Association meetings, where elections or public policy were discussed. There was certainly a temptation to use these religious events for overtly political purposes, but the Catholics usually resisted it, as in 1871, when a planned political rally to be held in conjunction with the Kevelaer pilgrimage was called off as incompatible with the religious import of the occasion. (An informal meeting was held afterward in a local tavern to discuss the political situation.) Furthermore, the authorities took great pains to ensure that political questions were not discussed at religious events and threatened to prohibit any such event which showed signs of being explicitly politicized.[37]

[36] On the Kevelaer pilgrimages, see *Germania*, Oct. 9-10, 1871 and Oct. 9-10, 1873; BM Kevelaer to LA Kr. Geldern Sept. 20 and Oct. 6, 1873 HSTAD RD Nr. 29142. Similarly, see "Jahresbericht der Marianischen Congregation für junge Kaufleute zu Köln," 1872 HAEK Gen. XXIII 4 I; *Zeitungsbericht* of the RA for the second quarter, 1873, HSTAD RA Pr. Nr. 821; Police Commissioner in Eupen to OB Eupen Sept. 14, 1874, HSTAD RA Nr. 4818; STAM OP Nr. 1601 I Bl. 62-64.

[37] When the *Echo der Gegenwart* published an antiministerial and rather pro-Austrian

Yet these threats were ultimately pointless. In a situation where the defense of religion had become a major political question, participation in religious events unavoidably took on a political coloration. The Catholic religious revival had always been implicitly "political" in that the practices and beliefs it sponsored had had implications for the structure of the social order. After 1867, and even more so after 1871, the political implications of the new Catholic piety became increasingly explicit. The organizing committee of the 1871 Kevelaer pilgrimage included Catholic politicians such as the Freiherr von Loë, alongside the Archbishop of Cologne and the Bishop of Münster. All twenty thousand pilgrims understood the message in 1873 at Kevelaer when Bishop Ketteler of Mainz—a man who was simultaneously a spiritual and political leader—preached a sermon to the text "Ask and ye shall be answered; knock and it shall be opened unto you."

The decree of 1874 restricting processions and pilgrimages to "traditional" ones—that is, those ostensibly in existence since 1850—brought the practice of special pilgrimages to an end. Through the *Kulturkampf* era, however, the "traditional" religious festivities were exceptionally well attended, and no one had any doubts that the participants in these events by their very participation were showing their opposition to the ministry's policy and their support for the Center Party.[38]

SEDAN DAY AND PIUS DAY

The clash between state and church appeared in festive form, as it were, over the celebration of a national holiday. The quasi-official national holiday (Imperial Germany never had an official national holiday), Sedan Day, September 2, was rejected by Catholics in the 1870s, who contended that the day was exploited by liberals and the authorities to stir up anti-Catholic sentiments. During the *Kulturkampf*, Catholics celebrated instead of Sedan Day June 16, the anniversary of the election of Pius IX as Pope.[39]

---

article on the occasion of the septennial reliquary pilgrimage in Aachen in 1874, the provost of the Aachen cathedral chapter hastened to assure the authorities that there would be "no demonstration but a religious festival in honor of the Lord for the salvation of the faithful," thus heading off the danger of a prohibition. HSTAD RA Nr. 10819 Bl. 198.

[38] Both the authorities and the Catholic press noted the increase in participation in pilgrimages and processions during the *Kulturkampf* and their political implications. See, for instance, HSTAD RD Nr. 1257 Bl. 35; *Zeitungsbericht* of the RA second quarter 1873 HSTAD RA Pr. Nr. 821; HSTAD RA Nr. 10819 Bl. 207-13; *Germania*, Mar. 27, 1872 (Cologne); Jul. 11, 1872 (Münster); Sept. 19, 1872 (Paderborn); Jun. 19, 1874 (Barmen); Jun. 2, 1875 (Dortmund); Ficker, *Kulturkampf in Münster*, pp. 191-96.

[39] Schieder, *Kaiserreich von 1871*, pp. 129-30.

The contrast between the two days was one of the most striking features of the *Kulturkampf* era. In the Catholic areas of the Rhineland and Westphalia, Sedan Day was officially celebrated with military parades, martial music, and patriotic speeches. The large majority of the population, however, went about its everyday business and refused to join the festivities, so the beflagged and illuminated houses of the bureaucrats, Protestants, Jews, and National Liberals stood out, an easy target for stone-throwing in cities and towns full of unadorned buildings. Although the authorities put a great value on the participation of the schoolchildren in the Sedan Day celebrations, the clergy as local school-inspectors would refuse to allow it or even arrange to sabotage the celebration, as happened in Goch (*Kreis* Kleve) in 1874: while the schoolmaster was leading the children in singing patriotic songs, they broke out in cheers of "Long live Pius IX!"—having been prompted beforehand by the chaplain and sexton.[40]

The picture was reversed on June 16. Cities and towns were illuminated, parades were held, the *Schützen*, fully uniformed, marched, firing salvoes in honor of the Pope. In Westphalia between 1875 and 1877, the authorities attempted to prohibit or limit the celebrations, leading to riots and anti-governmental demonstrations. In the little town of Stadtlohn (*Kreis* Ahaus, Münster District), several hundred people poured through the streets on the evening of June 16, 1875, singing to the tune of the Austrian national anthem a song with the words "Pius, our lord and king."[41]

This incident reveals the negative side to the fervent expressions of loyalty to the Pope—hostility to the *Kleindeutsch* national state, whose emergence in 1866 had been a great political defeat for German Catholicism. The distance Catholics felt toward the new *Reich* had been expressed even before the beginning of the *Kulturkampf* on the first Pius Day in June 1871. That year, the twenty-fifth anniversary of Pius IX's accession to the Papacy and the celebration of the victorious conclusion to the Franco-Prussian War had fallen on the same weekend. Whether held simultaneously with the victory celebrations, or

[40] HSTAD RD Nr. 289 Bl. 5-6. For other examples of the celebration of Sedan Day, see RAR to OPM Dec. 7, 1873 (draft) and attached documents, STAM RAR II Nr. 369; STAM LA Kr. Ahaus Nr. 502; STAM OP Nr. 1601 I Bl. 162-67; Ficker, *Kulturkampf in Münster*, pp. 161, 214-15, 234-40; Schiffers, *Kulturkampf in Aachen*, p. 124.

[41] On the Stadtlohn incident, and similar events in the western *Münsterland*, see the documents in STAM LA Kr. Ahaus Nr. 92. On the celebration of Pius Day, see STAM OP Nr. 1601 III Bl. 172 ff., IV Bl. 3-4, 285 ff.; *Zeitungsbericht* for the second quarter of 1877, STAM LA Kr. Meschede Nr 2442; Dean Waeler (Rees) to RD Jul. 9, 1876 HSTAD RD Nr. 30427; HSTAD RD Nr. 120 Bl. 100; Keinemann, *Beiträge zur westfälischen Landesgeschichte*, pp. 124-25; Ficker, *Kulturkampf in Münster*, pp. 232-33.

separate from them, the religious festivities clearly overshadowed the national ones in the Catholic areas of the Rhineland and Westphalia.[42]

Even at the height of the patriotic fervor incumbent on the creation of the new Reich, the Catholic milieu held itself apart. The memories of 1866 were not forgotten. It is no surprise that the response to the government persecution during the *Kulturkampf* was an increasing sense of distance from the national state, a sense of distance which never entirely disappeared down to 1914.

DEMONSTRATIONS IN SUPPORT OF THE CLERGY

The Rhenish-Westphalian bishops replied to the May laws by systematically filling all the vacant positions in their parishes without obtaining the government's consent. The authorities proceeded against the newly appointed priests, accusing them of "illegally exercising a spiritual office." They then tried the bishops for illegally appointing the priests. Fines and jail sentences failed to break the episcopate's will to resist. A second round of indictments was prepared, and, rather than submit to repeated imprisonment, the Bishops of Münster and Paderborn and the Archbishop of Cologne all fled the country. The government then brought suit against them in the "Royal Court for Religious Affairs" and procured a ruling declaring them deposed from office.[43] Thus in the years 1874-1876, it was the Catholic clergy which bore the brunt of the state's persecution. A show of solidarity with them became the main means of demonstrating Catholic unity and resolve.

In 1874, great demonstrations were organized in support of the bishops. In a manner reminiscent of the 1844 pilgrimage to the Holy Shroud of Trier, and the subsequent post-1850 organization of large-scale pilgrimages, each parish or group of parishes was assigned a day to march to the episcopal residence under clerical leadership. Enormous numbers of the faithful appeared. In the course of March and April 1874 some twenty-seven thousand of the Bishop of Münster's diocesans came to Münster to show their loyalty. There were said to have been over ten thousand outsiders in Paderborn on one day in

---

[42] HSTAD RA Pr. Nr. 819 Bl. 346, 350, 371 and HSTAD RD Nr. 120 Bl. 1-6, 22 ff. We do not have to take the bureaucrats' word for it; there was a conscious plan on the part of the clergy and the Catholic notables who led the festivities. In Düsseldorf, "The leaders of the Constantia [the Catholic political club] had the special intention of destroying any opposition that might exist among the people to the doctrine of Papal Infallibility; *for that reason* [my emphasis] they did not wish for the [Papal] jubilee celebration to occur simultaneously with the victory celebration." Chaplain Hömmacher to Dean Herten, Oct. 6, 1871 HAEK Gen. XXIII 4 I.

[43] Scholle, *Preußische Staatsjustiz*, pp. 253 ff. and passim.

1874; by nine o'clock in the morning, the main streets were so packed it was impossible to move in them. The houses of the city were all decked out in Papal flags to greet the demonstrators. Similar crowds thronged through the streets of Cologne.[44]

The bishops, after being convicted of illegally appointing priests under the May laws, refused to pay the fines imposed on them. The authorities resorted to forced sales of the furniture and valuables in the episcopal palaces. No Catholic workmen could be found to carry the objects to the sales; crowds of thousands gathered spontaneously to jeer and throw stones at the Protestants performing the task. Catholic noblemen and merchants then purchased the items at the sale and returned them to the bishops in triumph. When the news spread that the bishops were to be arrested, furious crowds once more gathered at the episcopal palaces to taunt and harass the police. Thousands stood in the cathedral square in Münster, singing "Our baptismal bond shall ever be firm," waiting for Bishop Brinkmann to appear. As he was led out by the police, the entire crowd dropped to its knees to receive his blessing.

Equally large and enthusiastic crowds awaited the bishops upon their release from jail. The streets were covered with flowers, papal flags waved from almost every window, altars were set up at intervals along the way back to the episcopal palace (rather as in the Corpus Christi procession). The carriages of the Catholic nobility and the bourgeois notables were placed at the bishops' disposal; tens of thousands lined the streets, cheering the return of their spiritual leaders. In the evening, torchlight parades and serenades outside the episcopal palace followed—if the authorities did not prohibit them. These scenes were repeated in miniature in scores of parishes after priests returned from serving jail sentences for having violated the May laws or the pulpit paragraph. The same escort of the local dignitaries, cheering crowds, decorated streets, flagged houses, and nocturnal parades or concerts were found in small towns and villages as in the episcopal cities.[45]

As with so many other aspects of the *Kulturkampf*, these demon-

[44] STAM OP Nr. 1601 I Bl. 238-39; LA Kr. Paderborn to RMI Mar. 31, Apr. 18, 1874, STAD M1 IP Nr. 363; *Germania*, Mar. 27-28, 1874 (Cologne); Kruse, "Bischof Bernhard Brinkmann," pp. 71-72.

[45] On the bishops, see: *Germania*, Mar. 20, 1874 (Cologne); Scholle, *Preußische Staatsjustiz*, pp. 97, 102, 127-30, 138-41, 144-45; Ficker, *Kulturkampf in Münster*, pp. 101-104, 128-30; Kissling, *Geschichte des Kulturkampfes*, 2: 405. On the lower clergy, see: STAM OP Nr. 1601 II Bl. 161-162; III Bl. 39 ff.; STAM LA Kr. Ahaus Nr. 501; STAM LA Kr. Brilon Nr. 998 II; *Die Weserbote* (Höxter) Jan. 27, 1875, Circular of the RMI to all *Landräte* Feb. 5, 1875, *Der Patriot* (Lippstadt) Nov. 1, 1875 all in STAD M1 IL Nr. 238; van Gils, "Der 'Kulturkampf,' " p. 61.

strations appeared as events of unparalleled size and intensity. Yet, as again with other aspects of the struggle, they were not unprecedented. The triumphant returns of the bishops and lower clergy from prison had been foreshadowed in similar celebrations during the late 1850s and early 1860s honoring priests who had returned from Rome and a visit with the embattled Pope.[46] Just as the Pope, in Catholic eyes, had been the victim of the alliance between radicalism and the bureaucracy in Italy, the Prussian episcopate was the victim of a similar alliance one decade later. Seen as state policy, the *Kulturkampf* was a reversal of the alliance between two independent powers which had characterized relations between the Prussian state and the Catholic church in the two decades after mid-century and a return to the ideas of a *Staatskirchentum* dominant in the *Vormärz*. The Catholic response, both spontaneous and planned, to the state's persecution testifies more to a continuity than a break: the *Kulturkampf* was seen as the latest battle in a long-planned campaign against religion waged by subversive forces, the Catholic defense another struggle of the *ecclesia militans* as it had come to exist in the religious revival.

Collective Violence during the Kulturkampf

Not all mass gatherings of Catholics ended peacefully. On eleven different occasions between 1872 and 1877 conflicts between the authorities and the Catholic population ended in violent confrontations. There were two distinct varieties of riots occurring in conjunction with the *Kulturkampf*, one taking place in a heavily Catholic environment, usually a small town or rural area, but including a city such as Münster, the other breaking out in a religiously mixed urban area with an appreciable Protestant population—Ruhr basin cities such as Essen or Witten, but also in smaller, religiously mixed towns like Lippstadt (Arnsberg District). A consideration of the causes of these two kinds of riots, the targets of popular anger, and the responses of the authorities provides further clues to understanding the course of the church-state conflict at the local level.[47]

In a predominantly Catholic area, the object of the violence was a representative of the state carrying out some aspect of the *Kulturkampf* legislation or an anti-clerical administrative measure. The mayor of Rheine (*Kreis* Steinfurt), attempting to break up a prohibited nocturnal

---

[46] *Sonntagsblatt für katholische Christen* 21 (1862): 426-27, 444; "Programm zum Empfang des Herrn Kardinal Erzbischofs von Geissel" (printed flyer, dated Jun. 17, 1857) HSTAD PP Aachen Nr. 86 V. I.

[47] For an analysis of these incidents according to the criteria of Richard, Charles, and Louise Tilly, see Sperber, "Rhineland-Westphalia," pp. 401-410.

demonstration on Pius Day in June 1875, was beaten and stabbed by an angry crowd. Area magistrate Schluter, attempting to confiscate the parish records in Balve (*Kreis* Arnsberg), was met by the illegally appointed Chaplain Hoynk, who refused to cooperate by handing over the keys. A threatening crowd of several hundred gathered around Schluter and the two gendarmes and one village policeman who made up his escort. The representatives of authority escaped untouched, but that evening the area magistrate's house was demolished, and he was forced to flee to Arnsberg.[48]

The representative of the state was not always an official. The unfortunate Protestant furniture-maker, whom the government had hired in 1874 to move Bishop Brinkmann's furniture from the episcopal palace to the site of the forced sale when no Catholic workmen would do the job, had his house attacked that evening by a crowd yelling "Judas, come forth!" He was subsequently ostracized—no one would do business with him, his creditors cancelled his mortgage, and he was eventually forced to leave Münster. In Calcar (*Kreis* Kleve), a forced sale of Chaplain Houten's property to pay the fine for his conviction on charges of "illegally exercising a spiritual office" was the occasion for a riot when a crowd attacked the auctioneer. A farmer who rented parish lands which had been confiscated by the government in Brachteln (*Kreis* Geilenkirchen) was similarly attacked.[49]

In the religiously mixed cities, the objects of mass violence were not the representatives of the state but the representatives of what might be called anti-Roman Catholicism. In Essen, after the expulsion of the Jesuits was announced in July 1872, a crowd formed and attacked the home of the merchant Nachtigall, a well-known Freemason. In the other cases, the object of the violence was the sectarian, anti-Infallibilist sect, the Old Catholics. In Lippstadt, an Old Catholic priest, Friedrich Michelis, was attacked when he came to speak; in Witten (*Kreis* Bochum), the Old Catholic congregation was assaulted by an angry crowd after it held its first services in a Catholic Church which the authorities had turned over to it.[50]

A certain social tension was also revealed in these incidents. In every case, the victims of the riots were bourgeois (as will be seen in the next section, the Old Catholics were a heavily bourgeois sect) and the rioters themselves, as best as this can be determined, from the lower-

[48] STAM OP Nr. 1601 III Bl. 5-8 and LA Kr. Arnsberg to RAR Nov. 23, 1875 STAM RAR I Pr. Nr. 91.

[49] Scholle, *Preußische Staatsjustiz*, pp. 127-30, 133-41; HSTAD RD Nr. 252; HSTAD RA Nr. 178 Bl. 26 ff.

[50] HSTAD RD Pr. Nr. 835 I Bl. 46-53; STAM OP Nr. 1601 I Bl. 114-26; STAM OP Nr. 1601 IV Bl. 6-21; STAM RAR II E Nr. 355 Bl. 45.

middle and working classes. The two forms of riot correspond to the two forms of more general political confrontation characteristic of the *Kulturkampf*: (1) the Catholic small-town petit-bourgeoisie or peasantry against the representatives of the Prussian state and (2) the largely Catholic plebians of the large, industrial cities against the non-Roman Catholic (whether Protestant, Jewish, free-thinking, or Old Catholic) upper classes.

The Catholic politicians and the clergy were strongly opposed to the use of violence. "We Catholics need no revolution to uphold our rights" was a constant refrain at Mainz Association meetings, and speakers always emphasized the legal and non-violent means—organization, petition, election of Center Party candidates—for bringing Catholic influence to bear. The clergy strictly warned against violent actions and rebuked anyone who participated in them. Organized and planned Catholic demonstrations were always carried out in the strictest order and discipline; they never turned into riots.[51]

When hostile authorities prohibited these demonstrations in the name of preserving order, they were laying the groundwork for a riot. An unorganized, spontaneous demonstration, involving the mass of the plebian Catholic population without the calming and organizing influence of the clergy and notables would quickly turn violent as soon as the authorities tried to suppress it—as happened on several occasions with Pius Day demonstrations in Westphalia between 1875 and 1877. Official hostility was often accompanied by an arrogant or provocative attitude. The action of the Westphalian Provincial Governor, Friedrich von Kühlwetter, in prohibiting demonstrations on Pius Day in 1875 was provocation enough, but area magistrate Schluter chose that day to carry out the seizure of parish records in Balve (*Kreis* Arnsberg). This action, a direct slap in the face to Catholic sensibilities, triggered a riot.[52]

It was not just hostile bureaucratic attitudes which encouraged violence. Many local authorities of the Catholic confession showed no interest in suppressing a riotous demonstration. When the crowd in Münster attacked the home of the Protestant furniture-maker who

[51] For examples of this clerical attitude, see Ficker, *Kulturkampf in Münster*, pp. 101-103; STAM RAR II C Nr. 11 Bl. 55 and LA *Stadtkreis* Bochum to RAR, Nov. 17, 1876, STAM RAR II E Nr. 354. On the occasion of the demonstrations in support of the Bishop of Paderborn in April 1874, the *Landrat* noted that with ten thousand strangers in the city, trouble could have easily occurred, but the demonstrators all showed "a strong will . . . to avoid any disturbances of order." LA Kr. Paderborn to RMI, Apr. 18, 1874, STAD M1 IP Nr. 363.

[52] STAM OP Nr. 1601 III Bl. 5-8 and LA Kr. Arnsberg to RAR, Nov. 23, 1875, STAM RAR I Pr. Nr. 91.

had carried off the bishop's valuables, the city police refused to intervene, and troops were required to restore order. The Mayor of Rheine, in attempting to suppress the prohibited pro-Papal demonstrations in 1875, had to face the angry crowd alone, since the town policeman somehow lost track of several hundred demonstrators.[53]

In Emsdetten (*Kreis* Steinfurt, Münster District), two men were arrested for having engaged in the forbidden practice of firing salutes on Pius Day in 1876. On the evening of July 24, a crowd of some two hundred gathered in front of the local jail, throwing stones. The following night, their numbers were doubled and, cheering the Pope and the "former Bishop of Münster" (Bishop Brinkmann, living at the time in exile in Holland, had been declared "deposed" by the Royal Court for Ecclesiastical Affairs), they proceeded to demolish the jail and liberate the prisoners. In Emsdetten and throughout the surrounding countryside, people were firing off the forbidden salvoes and making a tremendous racket. Curiously enough, the area magistrate, the gendarme stationed in Emsdetten, and the village policemen all seemed to have overlooked these events and did not attempt to restore order themselves nor to ask for outside help in doing so.[54]

The most spectacular case of this nature occurred in Lippstadt (Arnsberg District), in November 1873, when the Old Catholic priest, Friedrich Michelis, arrived in town to give a speech at the invitation of his fellow sectarians. An angry crowd greeted him at the railroad station and accompanied his carriage to the hotel with threats and jeers and then began bombarding the building with cobblestones. The *Landrat* of *Kreis* Lippstadt, Wilhelm Freiherr von Schorlemer-Overberg, on being informed of the riot, immediately took the next train out of town, claiming that he had family business in Münster.[55]

The attitudes of the authorities in all their different and opposed facets tended to increase the possibility of violence. By arbitrary prohibitions and provocative actions, Protestant and anti-clerical officials turned what might have been peaceful, if angry, demonstrations into riots. On the other hand, once a riot had started, the Catholic authorities often made no move to stop it. These official responses contributed to the paradoxical result that a political movement which stressed its counterrevolutionary sentiments, its respect for law and order, and its subordination to legitimate authority, was responsible for the most widespread outbreak of collective violence in the Rhine-

[53] STAM OP Nr. 1601 III Bl. 24-44; Scholle, *Preußische Staatsjustiz*, pp. 127-30.
[54] STAM LA Kr. Steinfurt Nr. 970.
[55] STAM OP Nr. 1601 I Bl. 114-26. Ironically, Michelis' election to the constituent North German *Reichstag* for the Kempen constituency in 1867 had been a demonstration of a militant Catholicism. Cf. above, pp. 165-66.

land and Westphalia between the revolutions of 1848-1849 and 1918-1919.

It is not by coincidence that 1848-1849 is mentioned in this context. The rural areas where the riots of the *Kulturkampf* era took place—the western *Münsterland*, the *Hochsauerland*, the lower Rhine near the Dutch border—had not experienced disorders in the revolutionary years but had been centers of order, stability, and counterrevolution. Politically, they had been clerical strongholds in 1848-1849 and even at the height of the conflict era when Catholics elsewhere were supporting the Progressives. The rural areas where disturbances had occurred in 1848-1849, where democrats had successfully agitated, and a tradition of left-wing politics had existed through the 1860s—the eastern *Münsterland* and neighboring areas, the Catholic portion of the *Bergisches Land*, and areas on the lower Rhine near Krefeld and Grevenbroich—were peaceful during the *Kulturkampf*. The vast majority of the Catholic inhabitants of those areas had been won over to the Center Party, but the passions of the *Kulturkampf* do not seem to have been quite as strong as they were in the old strongholds of the counterrevolution.

If the disturbances in the rural areas look back toward 1848-1849, those in the cities were indicative of future trends. In the older urban centers of the Rhine Valley and on the left bank of the Rhine—Aachen, Cologne, Düsseldorf, Krefeld, Mönchengladbach—Catholic political action proceeded through a well-organized network of mass associations, predecessors of the institutions of political Catholicism in the Wilhelmine era and the twentieth century. These organizations allowed a clerical and notable leadership to keep an ordering and organizing hand on the Catholic masses, avoiding unorganized and potentially violent demonstrations. In both the smaller cities in Westphalia and in the chaotically growing industrial centers of the Ruhr basin, however, such a network of organizational leadership was, at best, only partially in place. Under the pressure of provocative events, the plebian Catholic population could express its dislike for the enemies of religion in an undisciplined and violent way.

The Old Catholics

Whether shown at meetings, in the streets, or on election day, the Catholic unity expressed during the *Kulturkampf* was firm and impressive. The vast majority of the laity and lower clergy supported the actions of the bishops and refused to bend to the many pressures exerted by the government. Standing at the summit of Catholic loyalty was the Pope, leader and symbol of the church, under attack by the same insidious forces which were regarded as being at work in Germany. No Mainz Association meeting was complete without Papal flags and cheers for the Supreme Pontiff. It was around this key symbol that a small group of Catholics broke solidarity with their coreligionists and founded an independent sect.

The "Old Catholics," as they called themselves, rejected the decision of the 1870 Vatican Council endorsing the doctrine of Papal Infallibility. Theological considerations, however, cannot be regarded as the decisive factor in the emergence of the sect, except perhaps among a small group of intellectuals. Doubts about the doctrine of Papal Infallibility were widespread in leading lay and clerical circles of German Catholics, and the ranks of the skeptics in 1870 included many who would take the most militantly "ultramontanist" standpoint later in the decade.[56]

It seems more fruitful to consider the symbolic rather than the theological significance of Old Catholicism. For a Catholic to support such an anti-Pontifical position in the 1870s was to reject the leading symbol of the church. It meant cutting himself off completely from the Catholic milieu. Only a tiny minority were willing to take that step. Nowhere in the whole northern Rhineland and Westphalia did the Old Catholics make up as much as five percent of the total Catholic population, and in most places they were no more than one percent.[57]

They were a minority despised by their former coreligionists. Old Catholic shopkeepers and craftsmen were boycotted by their former customers. In Cologne, men who had joined the sect were afraid to make their adherence public, keeping it secret even from their wives, fearing their pious wrath. In Witten and Lippstadt, as we have seen, the Roman Catholic anger with those who had betrayed the church in its moment of danger spilled over into violence.

The major inflammatory issue was the use of the sacred precincts by the sectarians. Clergy would not bury them on consecrated ground; if the authorities forced the issue, angry, mocking crowds would ap-

---

[56] Bachem, *Zentrumspartei*, 3: 32-35, 90; Anderson, *Windthorst*, pp. 121-29; cf. Bebel, *Aus meinem Leben*, 2: 257. There is no modern study of the Old Catholics. Becker, *Liberaler Staat und Kirche*, pp. 137-41, 306-309, 331-42, has some interesting comments to make about Old Catholicism in Baden, the main stronghold of the sect. Kehmann, "Die altkatholische Kirche," pp. 217-33, gives the sect's own account of its development in the Rhineland.

[57] Unless otherwise specified, information for this section comes from the following sources, all of which contain information on the number of Old Catholics in various cities: STAM RAR II G Nr. 74; STAM RAR II E Nr. 354-55; STAM RAR II C Nr. 478; STAM LA Kr. Hagen Nr. 512; LAK 403 Nr. 15045, and Buscher, "Krefeld und der Altkatholizismus."

pear, hooting and jeering at the funeral procession.[58] After long controversy, a law passed in 1875 defined the Old Catholics as a separate religious confession, rather than as dissident Roman Catholics. The law stated that if there were a "considerable number" of Old Catholics present in any area, then they had the right to a share in the use of the local Catholic Church. Roman Catholics were horrified at the idea of sharing their churches with the sectarians.

While Rhenish Provincial Governor Heinrich von Bardeleben and his subordinates, most prominently Mayor Hermann Becker of Cologne, usually refused to consider the Old Catholic one percent share in the total Catholic population as a "considerable number," Westphalian Provincial Governor Friedrich von Kühlwetter, with the support of the Minister of Educational and Religious Affairs, overrode his subordinates' doubts and ordered them to grant the Old Catholics an appropriate amount of time each week to use the Catholic Church.[59]

The Roman Catholics responded by first taking from the churches everything which was not nailed down and smashing everything which was. Once the Old Catholics held services in them, the Roman Catholics regarded the churches as having been desecrated and would no longer use them. The first Old Catholic service in a Roman Catholic church in Witten resulted in a riot, when a large crowd attacked the sectarians as they were leaving the church building. A similar riot in Bochum was avoided only by a massive show of force on the part of the authorities. Sixty-two policemen and gendarmes—an enormous number for the time—guarded the Old Catholic worshippers against a threatening crowd of thousands of Roman Catholics. In Dortmund, things went more peacefully, but only because the clergy and the churchwardens spent months beforehand warning against any violent action.

In Krefeld, after some prodding by the central government, the local authorities decided to divide the Catholic Church spatially rather than temporally. Instead of having use of a church at certain times during the week, the Old Catholics were awarded one-half of St. Stephen's Church. The decision was never carried out, because the masons hired

[58] LAK 403 Nr. 15045 Bl. 579 and STAM RAR II E Nr. 354 Bl. 55, 61; the accounts of burials in STAM OP Nr. 2159 V. III and HSTAD RD Nr. 132.

[59] Attitudes of the Rhenish authorities can be followed through LAK 403 Nr. 15045 Bl. 62-78, 623-36, 795-99 and Buscher, "Krefeld und der Altkatholizismus," pp. 160-61. The liberal district officials in Düsseldorf were noticeably more favorable to the Old Catholics than the other Rhenish authorities. LAK 403 Nr. 15045 Bl. 717-27. For the attitude of the Westphalian and the central authorities, see especially Minister of Religious and Educational Affairs to the Roman Catholic church wardens in Bochum, Sep. 12, 1876 STAM RAR II E Nr. 354 and RAR to OPM Nov. 8, 1875 and OPM to RAR Nov. 22, 1875, STAM RAR II E Nr. 355.

to build a wall separating the church in half tore down at night that which they had constructed during the day.[60]

Who were the Old Catholics, and why were they willing to undergo this ostracism and hostility? The Bishop of Paderborn, in an 1874 pastoral letter, referred to Old Catholicism as "a church of statesmen and professors"; less politely, a speaker at a Mainz Association rally in Düsseldorf denounced the sectarians as "men of German scholarship who esteem their academic arrogance more highly than they esteem the Pope and the bishops."[61] The image of arrogant professors and querulous bureaucrats has remained in contemporary scholarship. It is not totally without foundation. All but one member of the Catholic theological faculty at the University of Bonn joined the sectarians; Old Catholic *Regierungsrat* Franz Wulff in Cologne and States Attorney Koppers in Bocholt certainly fit the picture of fanatically anti-Ultramontanist bureaucrats. Ultimately, however, the image is false. But turning from the widely publicized Bonn professoriate toward the obscure congregations in scattered provincial towns we find a different picture of the social composition of Old Catholicism. See Table 5.2.

Although officials did make up between ten and twenty percent of the Old Catholics, they were by no means the dominant element. Far more important were the industrial and professional bourgeoisie and salaried employees who accounted for between one-third and one-half of the sectarians. To a considerable extent, Old Catholicism was a movement of factory owners, merchants, mine directors, lawyers, foremen, and clerks. It was an eminently bourgeois sect.[62]

The bourgeois predominance among Old Catholics is especially clear when one compares the social composition of the Old Catholic and Roman Catholic population of a given area. Relevant records have survived for the town of Witten, which give the profession of every head of household in the Old Catholic and Roman Catholic parishes of the city. The two are not quite identical, as the Old Catholic parish included several individuals living in nearby towns, while the Roman Catholic parish was restricted to the city of Witten itself, but the differences in extent are not very important. See Table 5.3.

Well over three-fourths of the Roman Catholic population of Witten

[60] On the Witten riot, see n. 50; for the other incidents, see LA *Stadtkreis* Bochum to RAR Nov. 17, 1876 STAM RAR II E Nr. 354; STAM RAR II C Nr. 11 Bl. 118 ff.; Buscher, "Krefeld und der Altkatholizismus," pp. 165 ff. Cf. *Germania* Nov. 6, 1872 (Krefeld).

[61] STAM OP Nr. 1601 I Bl. 221-26; HSTAD RD Nr. 1257 Bl. 20. See the choleric comments of Karl Buchheim, *Ultramontanismus und Demokratie*, pp. 201-210, 247, which reproduce the Catholic polemics of the 1870s.

[62] In addition to the examples given in the table, cf. the probably somewhat exaggerated account by the Cologne Old Catholics of the social composition of their congregation, LAK 403 Nr. 15045 Bl. 436.

TABLE 5.2
Heads of Household in Old Catholic Congregations[a]

Social Group	Parish							
	Bochum[b] 1876		Hagen[c] 1876		Lippstadt 1881		Attendorn[d] 1874	
	%	N	%	N	%	N	%	N
Merchant, industrialist rentier	(14.0)	17	(24.2)	16	(27.8)	5	(40.0)	8
Professional	(10.7)	13	(1.5)	1	—	—	(10.0)	2
Salaried employee	(16.5)	20	(13.6)	9	(5.6)	1	—	—
Upper-level state official	(2.5)	3	—	—	—	—	(5.0)	1
Lower, middle-level state official	(13.2)	16	(18.2)	12	(22.2)	4	(10.0)	2
Retailer	(7.4)	9	(4.5)	3	—	—	(15.0)	3
Craftsman or skilled worker	(11.6)	14	(27.3)	18	(44.4)	8	(10.0)	2
Factory worker, miner, laborer	(16.5)	20	(10.6)	7	—	—	—	—
Other, unknown	(7.4)	9	—	—	—	—	(10.0)	2
Total household heads	(99.8)	121	(99.9)	66	(100.0)	18	(100.0)	20

[a] Some Old Catholics were not heads of household—namely, women married to Protestants who found this change of religion a means of relieving a source of domestic discord. Marginal comments on the membership lists suggest that some of the male Old Catholics were married to Protestant women.

[b] Includes members throughout *Kreis* Bochum.

[c] Includes members throughout *Kreis* Hagen.

[d] Technically a "filial" of the Hagen parish, but in practice an independent congregation.

SOURCES: "Verzeichnis der selbstständigen Mitglieder der altkatholischen Parochie Bochum," STAM RAR II E Nr. 354; "Verzeichnis der Mitglieder des altkatholischen Vereins zu Hagen/W.," STAM LA Kr. Hagen Nr. 512; "Verzeichnis der Mitglieder des altkatholischen Vereins zu Lippstadt und ihre Steuer," STAM RAR II G Nr. 350; Altkatholischer Verein Attendorn to RAR, Aug. 18, 1874 and LA Kr. Olpe to RAR, Aug. 14, 1876 STAM RAR II G Nr. 74.

were economically dependent manual laborers or skilled workers, while about half of the Old Catholics were bourgeois or salaried employees. It should be noted that a majority of even the Catholic bourgeoisie remained true to their religion, but a much greater proportion of the bourgeoisie became sectarians than members of any other social group.

TABLE 5.3
Roman Catholic and Old Catholic Heads of Household
in Witten, 1876

Social Group	Roman Catholics		Old Catholics	
	%	n	%	n
Industrialists	(0.1)	2	(2.7)	3
Merchants and rentiers	(1.9)	38	(15.5)	17
Professionals	(0.3)	7	(4.5)	5
Clergy	(0.7)	14	(0.9)	1
Salaried employees	(2.7)	54	(23.6)	26
Upper-level officials	—		—	
Lower, middle-level officials	(1.7)	34	(1.8)	2
Retailers	(1.8)	37	(1.8)	2
Artisans and skilled workers	(38.7)	782	(31.8)	35
Railroad workers	(2.8)	56	—	
Miners	(1.0)	20	(2.7)	3
Factory workers and day laborers	(37.5)	757	(12.7)	14
Servants	(9.4)	190	—	
Other, unknown	(1.4)	29	(1.8)	2
Total	(100.0)	2,020	(99.8)	110

SOURCE: STAM RAR II E Nr. 355 Bl. 62-65, 76-158.

Evidence from elsewhere confirms this picture of the Old Catholics as coming from the most affluent elements of the Catholic population. In Attendorn, twenty Old Catholics, although not even five percent of the adult males of the town, paid twenty percent of the taxes. In Krefeld, the Old Catholic heads of household paid an average of 295 Marks per capita each year in municipal taxes, Roman Catholics about 25 Marks.[63]

Belonging to the bourgeoisie alone did not suffice to make an Old Catholic. There was a large and cohesive Catholic bourgeoisie in the city of Aachen, yet there were only three Old Catholics in the entire Aachen District.[64] Equally important was the presence of Protestants.

[63] Old Catholic Association (Attendorn) to RAR Aug. 18, 1874, STAM RAR II G Nr. 74. Tax figures and Old Catholic population in Krefeld, 1876, from Buscher, "Krefeld und der Altkatholizismus," pp. 164-67. I have estimated the number of Roman Catholic household heads from the 1871 Catholic population. Krefeld's Catholic population certainly grew in the interval, hence the per-capita tax payments of Roman Catholics, as estimated in the text, are, if anything, too high.

[64] Schiffers, *Kulturkampf in Aachen*, p. 137.

Old Catholic congregations in the northern Rhineland and Westphalia existed in cities which were either predominantly Protestant—Witten, Hagen, and Dortmund—or had large, influential Protestant minorities—Bochum, Bonn, Cologne, Düsseldorf, Essen, Krefeld, and Lippstadt. (The only exception to this rule, the town of Attendorn, will be considered below.) Needless to say, the Protestants usually looked with favor on Old Catholics who held their services in Protestant churches for years, unless the government forced the Roman Catholics to surrender one of theirs. Old Catholics adopted a more Protestant-like religion, with a German-language mass and the abolition of clerical celibacy. They condemned "abuses . . . in the granting of indulgences, veneration of the saints, use of scapular medallions. . . ."[65]

This rapprochement with Protestantism was part of a more general one with the *Kleindeutsch* national state, as Old Catholics never tired of reiterating their genuine loyalty to the Emperor and *Reich* as compared with the attitudes of the "ultramontanist" Roman Catholics. In this sense the significance of the Old Catholic repudiation of the Pope becomes apparent. Through this step, a small group of bourgeois symbolically repudiated the whole Catholic milieu which had developed since 1850 and sought to integrate themselves into the world of their Protestant counterparts. They placed their class loyalties, as it were, above their sociocultural ones.

Many Old Catholics had a history of opposition to the Catholic milieu long before the question of Papal Infallibility arose. The lawyers Casper Anton Wrede and Lambert Hagen in Bonn, both local Progressive leaders in the 1860s and National Liberals after 1866, joined the sect. Old Catholicism and National Liberalism were closely linked in Bonn. The lawyer Heinrich Schultz, Old Catholic churchwarden and leading figure in the Old Catholic congregation in Bochum, had been the local representative of the Progressive Party in the 1860s.[66]

The most interesting example of this connection can be found in the little town of Attendorn in *Kreis* Olpe (Arnsberg District). In 1848-1849, Attendorn had been completely dominated by the democrats; unlike any other predominantly Catholic area in Westphalia, no Pius Association had been formed, and the clergy had had no say in political affairs. In the early 1860s, the town had been a Progressive stronghold, its leftist and anti-clerical influence being felt through the entire *Hochsauerland*. Even after 1866, the local liberal predominance remained,

---

[65] Kehmann, "Die altkatholische Kirche," pp. 228-29.
[66] Kaiser, *Die politischen Strömungen*, p. 281; STAM RAR I Nr. 102 Bl. 6 and STAM RAR II E Nr. 354 Bl. 279 and passim.

although the Attendorn liberals (like their counterparts in neighboring *Kreis* Meschede) steered an increasingly "national" course.

Attendorn was the only small town in the northern Rhineland and Westphalia to have an Old Catholic congregation and the most heavily Catholic town (ninety-three percent of its 1,843 inhabitants in 1871 were Catholic) to have one. Two of the Old Catholics, the rentier Müller and the tannery-owner Caspar Frey, had been Progressive electors in 1862; Müller had even been a democratic elector in January 1849.

Led by the Old Catholics, the Attendorn bourgeoisie took a sharply national, liberal, and anti-clerical stance during the *Kulturkampf*. The Vicar Brill led the convinced Roman Catholics of the town on an equally militant course, and for decades afterward "the entire better element of the townspeople" refused to speak to him. The social boycott made no difference. The Center Party obtained a majority in the town council and the *Reichstag* elections. The initial Old Catholics were already middle-aged or elderly. They found no successors in their attitudes among the younger generation, and by 1900 the whole episode was only a memory.[67]

For all the skepticism German Catholics felt about the declaration of Papal Infallibility, the anti-Infallibilist sect never had a chance of success. The decisive issue was not adherence to a theological doctrine but adherence to the Catholic milieu. That milieu had grown so strong between 1850 and 1870 that only a tiny minority with strong ties to Protestants or a long history of anti-clericalism was willing to try disputing it.

Governmental Pressure: Compulsion and Intimidation

The failure of Old Catholicism to attract even a respectable minority of Roman Catholics meant that the ministry could not count on any significant voluntary assistance in carrying out its religious policies. It had no choice but to use compulsory measures in an attempt to break Catholic resistance.

[67] On 1848-1849 in Attendorn, see Brinabend, *Attendorn*, pp. 152-53. On the 1860s, see the list of electors in STAM LA Kr. Meschede Nr. 479 and STAM RAR I Pr. Nr. 90 Bl. 87-91. STAM RAR II G Nr. 74 has information on the development of Old Catholicism in Attendorn. On the events of the *Kulturkampf* there, see STAM OP Nr. 2159 III; STAM OP Nr. 1601 I Bl. 162; Dean Prelatiken (Attendorn) to RAR Nov. 8, 1873, STAM RAR II E Nr. 369; LA Kr. Arnsberg to RAR Aug. 7, 1877 STAM OP Nr. 2150 II; *Germania*, Nov. 11, 1874. A similarly intimate connection between Old Catholicism and liberalism existed in Baden, where local liberal political clubs turned themselves into Old Catholic congregations. Becker, *Liberaler Staat und Kirche*, pp. 137-41, 306-309.

There were two main areas in which this was attempted. The authorities tried to harass and destroy the local institutions of political Catholicism. Meetings were closely surveyed by the police and broken up at the slightest pretext. Catholic political clubs, Christian Social Associations, and the Westphalian Peasant League bore the brunt of a similar mixture of surveillance and harassment. The other victim of the campaign of persecution was the clergy. Wielding the pulpit paragraph, the threat of expulsion, the carrot-and-stick of increased or cut-off state subsidies, the ministry hoped to force the priests to acquiesce in the planned system of *Staatskirchentum* and to renounce their support for political Catholicism.

The policy of compulsion, intimidation, blackmail, and occasional resort to force worked counter to the ministry's intentions. The elections of 1873-1874 were even more impressive triumphs of the Center Party than those of 1870-1871; the vast majority of both the higher and lower clergy defiantly refused to submit to the May laws—and they had the full support and cooperation of the laity in their intransigent stance. Lower-level officials refused to carry out their superiors' orders; even when they did, the means of coercion appeared insufficient; and against a unified Catholic milieu even the most effective weapons in the arsenal of the nineteenth-century state proved to be of no consequence.

THE BUREAUCRACY UNDER FIRE

All the plans formulated in Berlin, the wave of decrees and inquiries which poured out of the Ministries of the Interior and Educational and Religious Affairs in the course of the *Kulturkampf*, were of little value unless they were carried out by the provincial and local authorities. It was at this level that orders of the central government were thwarted, or at least executed in a spirit different from that in which they had been drawn up.

In Neuß (Düsseldorf District), for instance, the policeman assigned to watch over the meetings of the Catholic political club, the Constantia, was himself a member of it. The four area magistrates of *Kreis* Lüdinghausen (Münster District) were among the founding members of the "Association for the Furtherance of Catholic Interests in *Kreis* Lüdinghausen," an organization formed in early 1872, and quickly tagged by Westphalian Provincial Governor Friedrich von Kühlwetter as a hotbed of oppositional Ultramontanism. The mayor of Siegburg (Cologne District) refused to consider the "Catholic Casino" in his town, of which he was an honorary member, a political organization, leading the *Landrat* of the Siegkreis to conclude that his subordinate was either criminally negligent of his duties or attempting to mislead his superiors. A list of such occurrences could be extended almost indefinitely, but the basic point is clear: the close surveillance and harassment of Catholic political associations which the central and provincial authorities wished was virtually impossible to carry out, since many of the local officials who had to do the actual police work were, if not members of the groups, at least sympathizers.[68]

When it came to dealing with Catholic demonstrations and riots, the story was the same. We have already observed how the *Landrat* of *Kreis* Lippstadt and the area magistrate in Emsdetten refused to take measures against pious rioters. The Münster police commissioner resigned his post when ordered to arrest the bishop. In countless communities, the ostensibly forbidden Pius Day ceremonies went on as planned, with the local authorities looking the other way or even taking part. When the Aachen district officials attempted to prohibit parades and festivities in connection with the confirmation journey of the Archbishop of Cologne in 1875, not only did the area magistrates completely ignore their superiors' orders, but several of them even sent their sons to join the forbidden parades as the Archbishop's honor guards.[69]

The most drastic example of bureaucratic disobedience to the government came in the *Landtag* elections of 1873. In spite of official reminders of their duty to oppose the "enemies of the state" and "ultramontanism," no less than 511 officials in the Arnsberg District voted for clerical electors. Hundreds more abstained, including the *Landräte* of *Kreise* Arnsberg and Lippstadt.[70]

The authorities tried to battle the defections in their own ranks. Officials were ordered to resign from the Mainz Association or face dismissal. "Officialdom" was elastically defined to include elected officials—village foremen, mayors, city councilmen, the area magistrates in Westphalia—if their election required governmental confirmation.

---

[68] HSTAD RD Nr. 287 Bl. 66-86; STAM OP Nr. 1601 I Bl. 19-29, 39-48, 61; LA Kr. Siegburg to RK Jun. 18, 1872, HSTAD RK Nr. 7573. For other examples, see LAK 403 Nr. 6695 Bl. 463-65; HSTAD RD Nr. 287 Bl. 76; LA Kr. Schleiden to RA Jul. 12, 1875; STAM OP Nr. 1601 I Bl. 62-64; II Bl. 28; States Attorney Koppers to RM Oct. 17, 1872 and Aug. 14, 1874, STAM RM Nr. 1039. The reports of the *Landräte* of the Münster District on the Mainz Association meetings in STAM RM Nr. 1039 read more like advertisements for the organization than accounts of police surveillance.

[69] STAM OP Nr. 1601 IV Bl. 75-93; BM Lückerberg to RA Aug. 21, 1875, HSTAD RA Nr. 4818.

[70] STAM OP Nr. 1601 III Bl. 183-94 and STAM RAR I Pr. Nr. 90 Bl. 427-42. It is reasonable to assume that among the abstaining officials there were many Catholics who found abstention the easiest compromise between their clerical sympathies and their fears of losing their jobs if they showed these sympathies. Cf. STAM OP Nr. 1601 III Bl. 10-11. Unfortunately, I have not been able to find any account of the number of officials in the Arnsberg District, to say nothing of the number of Catholic officials there, so it is impossible to say what proportion of the officials voted for clerical electors.

A long and at times grotesque inquiry was launched into the political behavior of mailmen who were accused of carrying clerical propaganda along with them on their rounds, the investigation climaxing in the bizarre suggestion of the Minden district governor that all Catholic postmen be transferred to Protestant areas and that Protestants be brought in to move the mail in Catholic regions. He admitted that the suggestion was extreme, but insisted that "the struggle in the religious arena has taken on the dimensions of a virtual state of war."[71]

Mayors elected by clerically controlled city councils were not confirmed in their office by the central government, as happened, to name only the most important cases, in Aachen and Bonn. The provincial governor of Westphalia refused to confirm any of the members of the Dorsten City Council in office, but instead reappointed the liberal incumbents whom the clerical candidates had beaten in several elections during the 1870s. Plans for the introduction of elected area magistrates in the Rhineland were quashed in the well-founded anticipation that local elections in Catholic areas would only bring forth strongly clerical victors.[72]

Large-scale purges were undertaken in the upper levels of the bureaucracy. In 1875, ten of the eighteen Catholic *Landräte* in Westphalia were dismissed for their clerical sympathies; at the same time, Arnsberg District Governor Heinrich Wilhelm von Holzbrinck was pressured into resigning since his superiors were dissatisfied with his lack of energy in combatting "ultramontanism." Similar dismissals, if perhaps on not quite so large a scale, took place in the Rhineland.[73]

The *Kulturkampf* was not the first time the Prussian government had tried to force the bureaucracy into line, obvious precursors being the purge of democratically minded officials after 1849, or the attempt to mobilize the bureaucracy against the Progressives in the early and mid-1860s. Before the 1870s, however, it was left-wing officials who had been the target of administrative measures; membership in Catholic organizations had not been regarded as subversive.[74] Even the tensions raised in 1866 had not led to a mass dismissal of Catholic

[71] STAM OP Nr. 1601 II Bl. 283-85. On these efforts, see STAM OP Nr. 1601 I Bl. 103-105, II Bl. 54-57, 214-16, 229-30, 237-40, 252-59, 261-64, 269-71, 276, 294-97, III Bl. 46-47, 86, 108, 160, 206-30; LAK 403 Nr. 6695 Bl. 157-60, 175-84, 191-92, 211 ff.; HSTAD RD Nr. 290 Bl. 4 ff., Nr. 292 passim.

[72] Klein, *Personalpolitik*, pp. 104-106; Schiffers, *Kulturkampf in Aachen*, pp. 122-24; STAM OP Nr. 1601 IV Bl. 112-37. Cf. Michels, "Kulturkampf in Düsseldorf," pp. 78 ff.

[73] Wegmann, *Verwaltunsbeamten*, pp. 182-83; Schiffers, *Kulturkampf in Aachen*, pp. 121-22; Klein, *Personalpolitik*, pp. 104-105.

[74] See, for instance, STAM RAR B Nr. 18 Bl. 17, where the Arnsberg district officials explicitly excluded the Pius Association from the list of subversive organizations in which membership was forbidden to state servants.

officials—the outspokenness of Freiherr von Loë making him a noticeable exception—and many officials had taken part in the formation
of the Center Party in 1868-1871 with the consent of their superiors.

The victims of the 1870s were the persecutors of the 1860s. *Landrat*
August Heinrich Count Korff von Schmissing-Kerssenbrinck of *Kreis*
Beckum, who had threatened village foremen and area magistrates
with dismissal for having supported Progressive candidates in the elections of 1863, was himself dismissed some twelve years later for his
sympathies with the Center. A similar fate befell the *Landrat* of *Kreis*
Arnsberg, Felix Joseph Freiherr von Lilien, one of the officials who
had spearheaded the ouster of liberal Arnsberg District Governor
Friedrich Wilhelm von Spankeren in 1862.

These examples are part of a more general point which can be made
about the political behavior of the upper level of the provincial bureaucracy. Although there were a few officials—for instance, Westphalian Provincial Governor Friedrich von Kühlwetter, *Landräte* Johannes Freiherr von Deviviere of *Kreis* Meschede or Friedrich Freiherr
von Wolff-Metternich of *Kreis* Höxter—who were able to follow the
ministry in its 180-degree turn and persecute clerical oppositionists in
the 1870s with the same gusto they showed in persecuting liberal
oppositionists in the 1860s, the majority could not carry out whatever
policies their superiors supported without any qualms or hesitations.[75]
Rather, the behavior of the higher officials in the 1870s was usually
a mirror image of their behavior in the previous decade. Heinrich von
Bardeleben, Rhenish Provincial Governor during the *Kulturkampf*,
had enjoyed a close working relation with the clergy and political
Catholicism during his tenure as Minden District Governor between
1858 and 1866. In the 1870s, he acted as a moderating influence,
interpreting the May laws in a relatively lenient fashion, displaying a
skeptical attitude toward the Old Catholics, restraining the intransigent proposals of the liberal Düsseldorf district officials who, in the
1860s, had shown a manifest lack of enthusiasm for the then official
policy of cooperation with clerical elements.[76]

It was among the Arnsberg district officials that a conciliatory attitude during the *Kulturkampf* was most pronounced. Led by District
Governor Heinrich Wilhelm von Holzbrinck, but continuing even after
his forced resignation in 1875, the Arnsberg bureaucrats resisted the

---

[75] All these men were of the Catholic confession, and it is possible that they felt they
had to prove their loyalty as Prussian bureaucrats by acting in a more obnoxious and
persecutory fashion than their Protestant counterparts.

[76] LAK 403 Nr. 6695 Bl. 177-79, 184-86, 189-92; Schiffers, *Kulturkampf in Aachen*,
p. 204; *Germania*, Sep. 11, 1874. Aachen Police Commissioner Hirsch had a similar
attitude to Bardeleben's. Schiffers, *Kulturkampf in Aachen*, p. 205.

vigorous measures against the Mainz Association proposed by Provincial Governor Friedrich von Kühlwetter; they fought for an elastic interpretation of the May laws and displayed little sympathy for the Old Catholics. They regarded the Catholic clergy as the appropriate local school-inspectors and would dismiss a priest from such a position only if he was too open in his support of political Catholicism. The Arnsberg District was the only one in Westphalia where all the Catholic clergy were not deprived of their school-inspector posts. The moderate attitude shaded into open clerical sympathies. In the 1873 *Landtag* elections *Oberregierungsrat* Osterrath and eleven of the clerks and messengers employed at the district office voted for clerical electors. About as many officials, including one *Regierungsrat* and three *Referendare*, abstained from voting—a suspicious act in an election where the lines between government and opposition had been drawn with the utmost clarity.[77]

The position of the Arnsberg bureaucrats was no coincidence, but had arisen as a consequence of the events of the conflict era. There had been a sizeable group of liberal, anti-clerical officials in the Arnsberg District Office then, but they had stood in the way of the ministry's plans for an alliance with the Catholics against the Progressives, so the offending officials were dismissed or transferred. Their replacements, though chosen for their ability to work with the Catholics, were precisely the least appropriate people imaginable for carrying out the policies of the *Kulturkampf*.

The contrast between the 1860s and the 1870s can be extended in another direction. In the conflict era, only a small minority of officials in the Catholic areas, mostly in the upper level of the bureaucracy, supported the efforts of the oppositional Progressives. During the *Kulturkampf*, on the other hand, bureaucratic disloyalty to the government was widespread, reaching deep into the lower ranks of officialdom. Hundreds of gendarmes, schoolteachers, tax-collectors, foresters, area magistrates, mayors, and village foremen—in short, the local symbols of authority—openly controverted official policy.[78] In these circumstances, the claims of Catholic politicians that they were not

[77] On the attitude of the Arnsberg authorities, see STAM OP Nr. 1601 I Bl. 24-30, 37-38, 65, 100 ff., 162-67; IV Bl. 3-4; RAR to OPM Dec. 6, 1886 STAM OP Nr. 1923; circular of the RAR to all *Landräte*, Sep. 5, 1876 STAM LA Kr. Arnsberg Nr. 561; RAR to OPM Oct. 20, 1874, OPM to RAR Nov. 3, 1874, Jan. 14 and Feb. 12, 1875, STAM RAR II C Nr. 4; STAM RAR I Pr. Nr. 91 passim. On the voting in 1873, see n. 70.

[78] The comparison between the accounts of the behavior of the officials of the Arnsberg District in the elections of 1863 (STAM RAR I Pr. Nr. 90 Bl. 79 ff.) and 1873 (see n. 70) is quite instructive in this respect.

really oppositional but represented genuine authority acquired a certain credence.

The pride of the Catholics was the frustration of the liberals. What was to become of the liberal hopes that the state apparatus would implement liberal and anti-clerical policies if that apparatus was shot through with clerical sympathizers? In the best liberal tradition, they turned to self-help. Bonn historian Heinrich von Sybel founded the German Association which claimed some thirteen thousand members in the northern Rhineland. Ostensibly designed as a liberal counterpart to the Mainz Association, its real purpose was to follow the actions of the local authorities and to report any suspiciously pro-clerical behavior to their superiors. The association came to an inglorious end in 1877 when it was revealed that one of its organizers had attempted to use charges of clerical sympathies, not for patriotic purposes, but in order to extort money from the mayor of Münstereifel.[79]

The liberal frustrations were symptomatic of the difficulties of official policy during the *Kulturkampf*. Since 1848 the clerical partisans had been among the leading elements in the forces of order in the Rhineland and Westphalia. It was their order they were upholding, though, which was not necessarily the same as the one conceived of in Berlin. The Catholic officials simply would not accept the post-1866 and post-1871 redefinition of clericalism as "staatsfeindlich," as a danger to the state.

Ultimately, the central officials and their loyal adherents in the provincial governments were faced with the choice of coming to terms with political Catholicism or treating the Catholic areas of the Rhineland and Westphalia like Alsace-Lorraine or Prussian Poland—as conquered provinces to be governed and policed by Protestant outsiders from the provincial governor down to the village policeman. One should certainly not put it past the Berlin authorities to have adopted the second course, but political expediency eventually forced them into the first.

FINANCIAL LIMITS TO COERCION

The attempt to coerce the clergy became an ever more central point of the *Kulturkampf*. The bishops could be imprisoned and eventually forced into exile, the illegally appointed priests arrested and expelled, but these measures left the bulk of the clergy—those priests who already were in their positions at the time of the passage of the May

---

[79] On the German Association, see its letters to the Düsseldorf District Office in HSTAD RD Nr. 120; Kaiser, *Die politischen Strömungen*, pp. 295-300, 375-77; and Moellers, "Das 'Essener *Volksblatt*.' "

laws—untouched. Between 1873 and 1875, the ministry worked out a two-pronged strategy to put pressure on this majority of the lower clergy. First, large sums of money were appropriated to increase clerical incomes; all parish priests were to be given subsidies necessary to bring their income up to 1800 Marks a year. Secondly, the "breadbasket law" of 1875 cut off all state subsidies to priests refusing to sign a declaration promising obedience to the religious legislation. Potent as the combination of these two measures seemed to be, it was actually of little effect.[80]

Unlike the situation in France under the concordatory regime, and unlike the position of Protestant pastors in Prussia, the Catholic clergy in the Rhineland and Westphalia did not derive a large portion of its income from state subsidies. While the properties of the old-regime monasteries or ecclesiastical principalities had been confiscated in the revolutionary era, most of the parish lands had not been (and, where, as on the left bank of the Rhine, they had been confiscated, they were partially replaced under Napoleon by the so-called "dotational" lands). Most priests derived the bulk of their income from parish real-estate, along with fees for saying masses, performing marriages, baptisms, funerals, etc. They received relatively little income that the state could cut off.[81] (See Table 5.4.) The cut-off funds were simply too small to have the desired effect, for they amounted, at most, to about fifteen percent of the average parish priest's income (in the Aachen District) to as little as two or three percent (in the Münster District). When one considers what each Catholic household would have had to have paid to make up for the lost state subsidies, the amount seems even smaller. If every Catholic would skip breakfast once a year, a speaker announced at a meeting of the Catholic political club in Düren in 1875, then the money saved would more than suffice to cover the lost state subsidies.[82]

Of course, averages hid parish-to-parish variations. One priest might have received ninety percent of his income from the state, while his colleague in a neighboring parish received, and needed, no state subsidies at all. To deal with this sort of situation, organizations in each

[80] On the efforts to improve the income of the clergy (ultimately put into effect in 1889), see the material in LAK 403 Nr. 10354-55, 10357; STAM OP Nr. 2112 II-III; STAM RAR II B Nr. 938 and STAM RM Nr. 17301-2. On the use of these efforts to bribe the clergy into supporting the May laws, see Minister of Educational and Religious Affairs to OPM Nov. 12, 1875, STAM OP Nr. 2112 I and OPM to LA Kr. Bochum Oct. 3, 1874 (copy), STAM RAR II C Nr. 4.

[81] The sources cited in the previous note contain a parish-by-parish list of clerical income, broken down by the source of the income.

[82] HSTAD RA Nr. 4806 Bl. 125.

TABLE 5.4
Cut-Off State Subsidies during the *Kulturkampf*
(in Marks)

(Arch) Diocese	Total Funds Cut Off Per Year		Number of Priests[a]	Catholic House- holds	Cut-off Funds Yearly	
	Bishop and Cathedral Chapter	Lower Clergy	Early 1870s	1871	Per Priest[a]	Per Catholic House- hold
Paderborn	114,816	78,686	1,003	111,700	78	1.7
Münster	81,026	91,796	982	131,800	93	1.3
Cologne	55,439[b]	264,132	c.1,880	306,500	140	1.0

[a] Excluding bishop and canons of the cathedral chapter.

[b] These include funds for the cathedral chapter in Aachen [Stiftskapitel] as well as the funds for the Archbishop and cathedral chapter in Cologne.

NOTE on the duration of the cut-off: Subsidies from the state were stopped as of April 1, 1875. In the Diocese of Paderborn, payments were resumed on Apr. 1, 1881; in the Archdiocese of Cologne on April 1, 1882, the cut-off thus having lasted six and seven years respectively. In the Diocese of Münster, state payments were partially resumed on April 1, 1882, resumed for all but a few cases the following year, and were completely resumed on April 1, 1884. In calculating the per-capita figure for the Diocese of Münster, I have used the period between April 1, 1875 and April 1, 1882 as those were the years when the funds were completely cut off.

SOURCES: For the cut-off funds, RMI to OPM Jul. 25, 1882; RAR to OPM Jul. 21, 1882 and RM to OPM Sep. 10, 1883, STAM OP Nr. 2134 III; LAK 403 Nr. 10879 Bl. 363-67.

For the number of priests in the early 1870s: STAM OP Nr. 1923 Bl. 1206; *Schematismus Paderborn*; Schiffers, *Kulturkampf in Aachen*, pp. 112-13 and Reuter, *Bistum Aachen*, pp. 56-58.

For the number of Catholic households: Estimated from figures in *Die Gemeinden und Gutsbezirke*, Vol. VII (Westphalia) and Vol. VIII (Rhineland).

diocese were set up to distribute the offerings of the faithful to the needy clergy.[83]

Of the approximately 1,000 secular clergy in the Diocese of Münster, only 3 were willing to subordinate themselves to the state and have their subsidies continued; in the Diocese of Paderborn, it was 14 of 1,000 priests, and in the Archdiocese of Cologne some 45 of 1,880. The small percentage of clergy who signed the oath to obey the government's religious legislation, and thus continue to receive money from the government, seems to have been impelled primarily by financial motives. The organizations set up to distribute popular contributions did not always work perfectly, and priests living in the

[83] Ficker, *Kulturkampf in Münster*, p. 123; Schiffers, *Kulturkampf in Aachen*, pp. 109-110; RMI to LA Kr. Höxter, Jan. 18, 1874, STAD D 72 Wolff-Metternich Nr. 2.

Catholic diaspora or in impoverished rural areas—the Westphalian mountains, the Eifel districts on the left bank of the Rhine, the Moselle Valley in the southern Rhineland—were vulnerable to government pressure, for their parish lands brought in a meager return, and their parishioners were too poor to make up the lost state subsidies.[84]

Those few who bent to official pressure quickly regretted it. They were ostracized by their colleagues and deserted by their parishioners. Their efforts to preach patriotic sermons were met by jeers and catcalls, as happened in Lindlar (Siegkreis, Cologne District), where the chaplain organized the parishioners to shout down the priest, who spoke to the text "render unto Caesar."[85]

Buttressed by their own resources, supplemented by the gifts of the faithful, the Catholic clergy had little difficulty withstanding the cutting off of state subsidies. The gains from accepting the government's money were so small, the social consequences so unpleasant, that virtually no priests were willing to give in. The policy of coercion failed because the basic element of *Staatskirchentum*, a clergy financially dependent upon the state, was not present.

THE CATHOLIC LAITY AND THE STATE

The final and decisive frustration for the ministry's policy was the attitude of the Catholic laity. With a virtual unanimity, they supported and encouraged the intransigent actions of the clergy; the noncooperation of the laity made the enforcement of the May laws and other *Kulturkampf* legislation impossible.

In 1874, the Bishop of Paderborn issued a pastoral letter condemning the Old Catholics and called on all the clergy of his diocese to read it as part of a sermon. The Westphalian provincial governor was determined to prosecute, on grounds of the pulpit paragraph, every priest who read the letter. In the entire Minden and Arnsberg Districts, the authorities had enormous difficulties finding witnesses who remembered anything about the incriminating sermon. Schoolmaster Wermuth, called to testify on the proceedings in the Market Church in Paderborn, explained that he was at the organ and could not hear; schoolmistress Justus had had a bad headache that day and had paid no attention; other witnesses at the trial suffered sudden memory losses or testified they "knew nothing about it."[86]

The authorities had no more luck enforcing the May laws. No one

---

[84] Minister of Religious and Educational Affairs to OPM Jul. 26, 1875, STAM OP Nr. 2134 I and LAK 403 Nr. 7564 Bl. 206-93.

[85] Schiffers, *Kulturkampf in Aachen*, pp. 115-16; *Germania*, Mar. 27, 1874 (Lindlar); Father Hensbach (Eslohe) to OPM May 6, 1874, STAM OP Nr. 2112 I.

[86] Trial transcript in AGVP II 2 Bischöfe Bl. 434-38. On the whole affair, see STAM OP Nr. 1601 I Bl. 224-41, II Bl. 2-86; Scholle, *Preußische Staatsjustiz*, pp. 81-91.

would testify that priests were saying mass, officiating at marriages, baptisms, and burials without government approval—"engaging," as the legal language had it, "in the illegal exercise of a spiritual office." The frustrated officials began posting police in the church (when they could find reliable policemen) to control the actions of the clergy, leading the clerical *Echo der Gegenwart* in Aachen to comment on one such case: "The positive side of this action is that the police have become diligent in their attendance at St. Jacob's Church recently, and, as we all know, a little prayer never hurt anybody."[87]

Even if convicted, the illegally appointed priests would return to their parishes, and the authorities were often unaware of their return for months at a time. Attempting to arrest all these priests, or even to find them, was often impossible, since all the parishioners—including the local authorities—would warn or hide them at the approach of the police. If, as happened in the later 1870s, all the clergy in a parish had died, a priest from a neighboring parish would come to say mass every other weekend. The action was illegal under the May laws, but nonetheless widespread. The local authorities winked at the violation of the law, and no one could be found to testify that anything had occurred.[88]

After the bishops had been removed from office and forced into exile, the authorities appointed "royal commissioners for the administration of diocesan property." On arrival to take up their duties, they found that all the records had been destroyed, every available piece of property had been sold or leased to front men, and everything imaginable had been done to make their lives utterly miserable. The churchwardens refused to correspond with them about parish property, the lower clergy also refused their cooperation, and the life of the royal commissioners was that of one lawsuit after another.[89]

As Heinrich Schiffers noted in his study of the *Kulturkampf* in the Aachen District, by the latter half of the 1870s the authorities found themselves in a legal morass.[90] Every attempt to determine if a priest was "illegally exercising a spiritual office," every seizure of parish or

[87] Cited in Schiffers, *Kulturkampf in Aachen*, p. 81. See also ibid., pp. 81-87 and STAM OP Nr. 2119-21.

[88] Ibid. See also Anon. (Neuenkiersse) to RMI, May 30, 1875, STAD M1 IP Nr. 961; STAM OP Nr. 2123 I passim; *Amtmann* Hülskötter to LA Kr. Lüdinghausen, Mar. 14, 1876, STAM LA Kr. Lüdinghausen Nr. 1115; STAM LA Kr. Brilon Nr. 998 II Bl. 207, 252. It is impossible to know how many cases were never recorded in the archives because the authorities never found out about them.

[89] Ficker, *Kulturkampf in Münster*, pp. 157-69; STAM RM Nr. 173-82; STAM RAR II C Nr. 56 and II E Nr. 796; Schiffers, *Kulturkampf in Aachen*, pp. 106-107.

[90] Schiffers, *Kulturkampf in Aachen*, p. 203. After plowing through mountains of such documents in the course of my research, I can only agree with him.

diocesan property, was accompanied by an enormous volume of paperwork. Piles of documents, on occasion dating back to the Middle Ages, had to be perused, legal briefs from several different government offices obtained, an extensive inter-office correspondence carried out, civil suits filed, criminal charges made, appeals registered, more appeals to higher courts tended to. Bureaucrats, it may be said, thrive on such paperwork, but every legal victory they won (and the courts did not always see eye to eye with the administrative bureaucracy) brought them no closer to success in their efforts. The clergy remained resistant, the laity no less so.

THE SITUATION BY 1880

By 1878 it was clear that the repressive legislation and the administrative persecution had failed to achieve the results the ministry had hoped for them. Rumors of a settlement were heard, and the first negotiations between Prussian diplomats and the representatives of the Vatican took place. The great transformation in German political life, connected with the passage of protective tariff legislation in 1879, was accomplished only with the support of the Center Party. The liberal era in Imperial Germany came to an end; the resignation of the liberal Minister of Educational and Religious Affairs, Adalbert Falk, more than any other person the symbol of the *Kulturkampf*, was an unmistakable sign of a changing government policy.[91]

Between 1879 and 1882 many of the administrative measures of the *Kulturkampf* were repealed. The Catholic clergy were returned to their posts as local school inspectors (except for those who had never been dismissed in the first place); priests were once more allowed to give religious instruction in the public schools. Plans for religiously mixed elementary schools were relegated to the archives; separate Catholic and Protestant public school systems exist to this day in North Rhine-Westphalia. Priests expelled in the course of the *Kulturkampf* were allowed to return home. They, or neighboring clergy, were allowed to officiate in vacant parishes. The churches given to the Old Catholics were returned to the Roman Catholics. Old Catholicism, deprived of official favor, dwindled into an ever more sectarian existence.[92]

Relations between the authorities and political Catholicism would never be as good as they had been before 1866, but the most blatant

[91] On this change, see Schmidt-Volkmar, *Kulturkampf*, pp. 201-18; Stürmer, *Regierung und Reichstag*, pp. 231-88; Anderson, *Windthorst*, pp. 273-95.

[92] See the district governors' reports from 1883 in STAM OP Nr. 1923; Meyer, *Untertanen*, pp. 153-59; Silbergleit, *Preußens Städte*, pp. 216-17; Buscher, "Krefeld und der Altkatholizismus," pp. 182 ff.; STAM RAR II E Nr. 354.

acts of administrative repression or favoritism—the harassment of clerically dominated local governments or the subsidization of anti-clerical newspapers—came to an end. In heavily Catholic areas, such as the Münster or Aachen Districts, where no National Liberal or Conservative Protestants were to be found who could work with the authorities, the Center Party slowly acquired a certain official approval. In any event, by 1880 the tensions raised by the *Kulturkampf* among the Catholic population had started to dissipate. A slow, never fully completed reconciliation between Roman Catholicism and the *Kleindeutsch* national state had begun.[93]

Things had not quite returned to normal. The return of the bishops from exile, the filling of the vacant parishes, the repeal of much of the *Kulturkampf* legislation was accomplished in the course of the 1880s only after a long and sometimes torturous process of secret diplomatic negotiations accompanied by open political controversy.[94]

The *Kulturkampf* had seriously disrupted the normal life of the Catholic Church. Between 1873 and 1884, no new priests had been appointed in Prussia. Deaths of officiating clergy had left many vacant positions. As late as 1886, one-third of all the parishes in the Arnsberg District had no regularly appointed priest. Even by 1901, the number of secular clergy in the Archdiocese of Cologne had not reached its 1872 level.[95]

Disrupted ecclesiastical administration and vacant parishes were only external signs; they ought not to be confused with the strength of religious loyalties. The successful resistance to the hostile measures of the state was the climax of a quarter-century of religious renewal and revival. By 1880, the Catholic Church in the northern Rhineland and Westphalia was at the height of its popular influence.

[93] Besides the sources cited in the previous note, see STAM OP Nr. 1601 IV Bl. 106 ff.; Schiffers, *Kulturkampf in Aachen*, pp. 200-202; Ficker, *Kulturkampf in Münster*, pp. 370-71, 392, 446-48; Keinemann, *Beiträge zur westfälischen Landesgeschichte*, pp. 130-33; Tenfelde, *Bergarbeiterschaft*, p. 366. In general, on the post-*Kulturkampf* relations of German Catholics to the Empire, Morsey, "Die deutschen Katholiken."

[94] The events are best followed in Weber, *Kirchliche Politik*, passim, and Anderson, *Windthorst*, pp. 201-396. See also Schmidt-Volkmar, *Kulturkampf*, pp. 286-350.

[95] OP von Hagemeister to Ministry of Religious and Educational Affairs, Feb. 1, 1886, STAM RAR II E Nr. 345; Reuter, *Bistum Aachen*, pp. 156-58.

CHAPTER 6

ELECTORAL POLITICS
IN THE *KULTURKAMPF* ERA:
1871-1881

THE DOMINANCE OF THE CENTER PARTY

The fierce loyalty toward the church shown by the Catholic inhabitants of the northern Rhineland and Westphalia in the mass struggles against the *Kulturkampf* legislation was translated on election day into votes for the Center Party, which had established itself by 1871 as the unquestioned representative in the political arena of the Catholic milieu. An elaborate election campaign, as clerical partisans had previously attempted, was unnecessary throughout the 1870s. The rallies of the Mainz Association and the planned and spontaneous resistance to the efforts of the authorities to carry out the state's anti-clerical measures created a condition of permanent political mobilization.[1]

In 1873, forty-two of the forty-five *Landtag* deputies elected in the predominantly Catholic constituencies of the northern Rhineland and Westphalia were representatives of the Center Party. The united National Liberals and Progressives narrowly held onto the two seats from Cologne and the one seat from Krefeld. The equal *Reichstag* franchise was more favorable to the Catholic cause than the plutocratic *Landtag* franchise, and in the 1874 elections every single one of the twenty-seven predominantly Catholic constituencies in the region under study was carried by the Center.[2]

These electoral victories were not just the result of passions temporarily raised by the church-state conflict but had their origins in the restructuring of religious life and growing cohesion of the Catholic milieu which had taken place in the two decades following mid-century. The political consequences of these developments were as en-

---

[1] This is a general observation made in all the dissertations of Max Braubach's students which cover this period. Cf. Lepper, "Regierungsbezirk Aachen," pp. 403-40; Kaiser, *Die politischen Strömungen*, pp. 322-32 or Hombach, "Die Reichs- und Landtagswahlen," pp. 327 ff.

[2] *Reichstag* election returns can be found in *Statistik des Deutschen Reiches* Old Series, 14 (1875) pt. 1: 23-31; *Landtag* returns in LAK 403 Nr. 8440 Bl. 581-97; STAM OP Nr. 501; STAM RAR I Pr. Nr. 90 Bl. 413-20; STAD M1 Pr. Nr. 260; Pülke, "Kreis Recklinghausen," pp. 140-41.

during as the structural changes in popular mentalities and organizational life. In spite of a growing detente between church and state, the Catholics steadily improved their vote totals in the *Landtag* elections, conquering Cologne from the liberals in 1879 and Krefeld in 1885. From that time until the outbreak of the First World War, all the predominantly Catholic *Landtag* constituencies in the northern Rhineland and Westphalia were in the hands of the Center Party.[3]

A similar trend can be observed in the *Reichstag* elections. Although the Center did on rare occasions lose an election in a predominantly Catholic constituency (Essen in 1893, for example), its politically dominant position was threatened only in a few Rhenish constituencies by the Social Democrats on the very eve of the First World War.[4] The vote totals of the Center Party testified to the steadiness of its support. See Table 6.1. Already at a high level in 1871, the Center vote jumped still higher in 1874 and maintained itself at this point through the elections of the subsequent seven years.[5]

TABLE 6.1
Support for the Center Party
in the Northern Rhineland and Westphalia, 1871-1881

	All constituencies of the northern Rhineland and *Westphalia where a Center candidate was put up* *and Catholics were at least forty percent of the electorate*				
Year	*Proportion* *electors* *Catholic* *%*	*Turnout* *%*	*Center Party* *vote as per-* *cent of all* *votes* *%*	*Center Party* *vote as* *percent of* *Catholic* *electorate* *%*	*Constit-* *uencies* *covered*
1871	82.0	50.2	62.5	38.2	29
1874	80.3	67.0	73.7	61.5	30
1877	81.3	62.2	72.9	55.8	29
1878	80.2	68.0	71.6	60.7	30
1881	80.0	56.1	76.4	53.9	30

SOURCES: Election returns in *Statistik des Deutschen Reiches* Old Series, 14 (1875 pt. 5): 23-31; 37 (June 1879): 16-20, 52-57; 52 (March 1882): 14-21.

[3] LAK 403 Nr. 8447 Bl. 224-25, 412-13; Croon, *Die gesellschaftlichen Auswirkungen*, passim.

[4] On the long and painful struggle of the Social Democrats in a predominantly Catholic city in Wilhelmine Germany, see the excellent study of Nolan, *Social Democracy and Society*.

[5] The procedure used here differs from that found in the standard work of Schauff,

Between 1871 and 1874, the proportion of voters supporting the Center Party increased some eighteen percent, while the proportion of eligible Catholic voters supporting the Center jumped sixty-one percent. This very strongly suggests that the variations in the Center Party vote reflected changes in the turnout. The Center did not increase its vote by winning Catholics over from other parties: Catholic voters already supported the Center overwhelmingly in 1871. Rather, the passions raised by the *Kulturkampf* caused previous non-voters to show their support for the beleaguered church by turning up at the polls and casting a Center Party ballot.

By means of regression analysis, it is possible to estimate the proportion of eligible Catholic voters who actually voted. Assuming (and this is hardly unreasonable) that only Catholics voted for the Center Party, it is then possible to use this estimate to determine what percentage of Catholic voters voted for the Center. The regression results are suggestive but they should be understood as plausible estimates rather than mathematically exact figures.[6] See Table 6.2 The *Kulturkampf* solidified the already firm hold of the Center Party on the Catholic electorate. As the struggle drew to a close at the end of the 1870s and the beginning of the 1880s, this hold was stronger than ever.

ANTI-CLERICAL POLITICS IN AN ERA OF TRIUMPHANT CLERICALISM

Bourgeois Liberalism and Political Catholicism

Contemplating the enormous clerical election victories of the 1870s, one cannot help but wonder what had become of the Catholic poli-

---

Das Wahlverhalten der deutschen Katholiken. Schauff claimed that because Catholics had more children than Protestants the proportion of Catholics in the population was larger than their proportion in the electorate, and subjected the official figures to an adjustment factor of his own devising. This procedure is, however, inaccurate. In the 1870s, because of a considerably lower marriage rate, children were, if anything, a smaller proportion of the Catholic than the Protestant population in Rhineland-Westphalia (Knodel, *Decline of Fertility*, pp. 199-202; Reekers, *Westfalens Bevölkerung*, pp. 271-75; Wrigley, *Population Change*, pp. 140-49—a general discussion of this in Sperber, "Rhineland-Westphalia," pp. 120, 124). Unpublished figures for 1874 give the proportion of Catholics among the electorate (cf. STDD II Nr. 28; Regierungsrat von Taske to Landrat von Droste, Jan. 8, 1874, STDM LA Münster A Nr. 6 I; STAM LA Kr. Meschede Nr. 208 or STAM LA Kr. Dortmund Nr. 184), figures virtually identical with the proportion of Catholics in the general population. Schauff's estimate of the proportion of Catholics in the electorate is thus too high, at least for the 1870s in western Germany, and, consequently, his estimate of the proportion of Catholics voting for the Center Party is too low.

[6] For each constituency, the turnout was taken as the dependent variable and the

TABLE 6.2
Proportion Catholic Voters Supporting
the Center Party, 1871-1881

All constituencies of the northern Rhineland and
Westphalia where a Center candidate was put up
and Catholics were at least forty percent of the electorate

Year	Turnout %	Center Party vote as percent of Catholic electorate %	Turnout of Catholic voters (estimated) %	Center Party vote as percent of Catholics voting (estimated) %	Constituencies covered
1871	50	38	44	86	29
1874	67	62	64	97	30
1877	62	56	57	98	29
1878	68	61	62	99	30
1881	56	54	52	99 +	30

SOURCE: Calculated from the sources to Table 6.1.

ticians' former liberal rivals who, a decade earlier, had provided such a stiff opposition to the Catholic cause. There is virtually no evidence to support the notion that the former liberal oppositionists had retained their opposition to the government by going over to the Center. Among the 320 members of the Rhenish and Westphalian provincial electoral committees of the Center Party in 1873-1874, there was not one single individual who could be identified as a former adherent of the left. All the committee members, insofar as their political pasts could be ascertained, were adherents of political Catholicism in the 1860s, when its relations with the Prussian government were very different from the following decade.[7]

Just as the oppositional clericals of the 1850s had become the progovernmental clericals of the conflict era, the oppositional leftists of the 1860s renounced their former hostility to the authorities in the following decade, supporting with what little political strength they retained the state's anti-clerical policies. Justice Adolph Winckelmann, long-term leader of the left in Kreis Recklinghausen (Münster District),

proportion of the electorate Catholics as the independent variable. The turnout of Catholic voters could then be calculated from the regression coefficient created from a regression on all the constituencies (the method is described by Kousser, "Ecological Regression"). The coefficient of variation (r^2) for the 1871 regression equation is .21, for the 1874 regression equation .15, for 1877, .30, for 1878 .43 and for 1881, .14.

[7] Committee memberships according to the signatories of the electoral appeals in Germania, Oct. 3 and Dec. 22, 1873.

retired to Münster in the 1870s and became a liberal activist in that town. A quarrel in Catholic ranks enabled him to stand successfully as a National-Liberal candidate for the city council in 1877. The National-Liberal *Landtag* candidate in the constituency Münster-Coesfeld in 1873 was the merchant August Böhme from Telgte (*Landkreis* Münster), who had been arrested a quarter-century earlier for pasting up democratic placards (probably in connection with the tax-refusal campaign of the fall of 1848) in his home town and who, in 1866, had succeeded with a group of allies in convincing the peasant electors of the constituency to elect the democratic hero Benedikt Waldeck to the *Landtag*.[8] Veteran liberals in the Rhineland acted similarly to their Westphalian counterparts. The liberal *Reichstag* candidate in the constituency Düren-Jülich in 1874 was Freiherr von Hilgers, who had represented the district in the *Landtag* as a Progressive in the early 1860s, and had even stood with clerical support as a radical oppositionist in 1867. Notary Vincenz Jacob von Zuccamaglio in Grevenbroich, a stalwart of the liberal cause since 1848, continued his activities during the 1870s by serving as a speaker for the anti-clerical German Association. Zuccamaglio, a well-respected individual, was able to draw good-sized and attentive crowds, but the political impact of his exhortations, as might be expected, was absolutely nil.[9]

Even in the 1860s, the circle of liberal supporters had been very small. In the *Kreis* Beckum (Münster District), one of the rural strongholds of the left since 1848, there were all of 420 individuals who had voted for Progressive electors in the *Landtag* elections of 1863, representing under five percent of the 9,200 individuals eligible to vote in the *Reichstag* elections of the 1870s. In the whole constituency of Beckum-Lüdinghausen-Warendorf, there were 760 voters who had chosen Progressive electors in the 1863 *Landtag* elections, not so far from the 520 voters who supported the Progressives in the *Reichstag* elections of 1874.[10]

[8] On Winckelmann, see Pülke, "Kreis Recklinghauen," pp. 98, 103, 107-13 and Ficker, *Kulturkampf in Münster*, pp. 285-87; on Böhme, see STDM LA Münster A Nr. 1430 Bl. 21; chapter 4 n. 5; and the 1873 election returns in STDM Stadtregistratur Fach 9 Nr. 5.

[9] On Hilgers, see Haas, "Die Wahlen im Regierungs-Bezirk Aachen," pp. 124-26, 142-44, 156, 189 and Lepper, "Regierungsbezirk Aachen," pp. 192-95, 216-19, 425 (cf. also p. 379). On Zuccamaglio, see Röttges, *Die politischen Wahlen*, pp. 226-27, 331-32; Hombach, "Die Reichs- und Landtagswahlen," p. 83; entry "Vincenz Jacob von Zuccamaglio," *Allgemeine Deutsche Biographie*. The banker Zuccamaglio in Krefeld was a leader of the Old Catholics in the city. Buscher, "Krefeld und der Altkatholizismus," p. 155.

[10] "Uebersicht von den Resultaten der Urwahlen am 20. Oktober 1863 im Regierungs-

While the 760 left voters succeeded in electing about half of the electors and one of the two *Landtag* deputies in 1863 (and the other, clerical, deputy was chosen only after he agreed to support key points in the Progressive program), the 520 left voters in 1874 could provide the Progressive candidate with less than two percent of all the votes cast. The intervening mobilization of the Catholic masses had completely transformed the nature of political life. Even if the former liberal leadership and a majority of the liberal voters remained true to their 1860s loyalties, they were swamped by the great mass of predominantly lower-class Catholics who had previously been politically passive, whose religious sentiments the clergy and lay activists had succeeded in mobilizing for political purposes as a consequence of the events of 1866-1871.[11]

The meager liberal electorate of the 1870s was concentrated in the upper classes of a few cities and towns, "the fat . . . and enlightened bourgeoisie," as one Cologne Catholic described the local supporters of the government in the *Kulturkampf*. In the 1873 *Landtag* elections in Düsseldorf, 165 voters in the first class (the top one-third of the taxpayers) voted for liberal electors, while only 34 voters of the first class supported clerical electors, and 43 abstained or scattered their votes. The liberals also obtained a majority of the votes in the second class, but the Catholic landslide in the third class, where over eighty percent of the electorate was concentrated, gave the Center Party a majority of the electors in the city.[12]

Even in predominantly Catholic areas, a good portion of the Rhenish-Westphalian bourgeoisie were Protestants, and thus unlikely to support the Center Party under any circumstances. Nonetheless, there were particular areas in which Catholic voters unquestionably gave their votes to the liberals. In Cologne, although Catholics were eighty-

---

Bezirk Münster," STAM RM Nr. VII-68; 1874 *Reichstag* election returns as in n. 2; detailed (precinct-level) 1881 *Reichstag* election returns in STAM LA Kr. Lüdinghausen Nr. 492.

[11] This greater participation was not just a reflection of the greater turnout in the *Reichstag* elections with their equal and secret suffrage as compared to the public and plutocratic *Landtag* franchise. Participation rates in the 1870s *Landtag* elections seem to have increased considerably over the 1860s elections. Although the government did not keep regular records of the results of *Landtag* elections between 1867 and 1898, statistical raw material preserved for one *Kreis* shows a large growth in turnout in the 1870s: in *Kreis* Ahaus (Münster District), *Landtag* turnout went from 6.0 percent in 1855 to 13.6 percent in 1862 to 9.2 percent in 1866, but soared to 26.4 percent by 1879. (STAM LA Kr. Ahaus Nr. 374.)

[12] HSTAD RD Pr. Nr. 566 Bl. 226-52; *Germania*, Jul. 1, 1875. For similar examples of the class composition of liberalism, see *Germania*, Nov. 5, 1873 (Cologne), Jan. 12, 1874 (Dortmund); Kaiser, *Die politischen Strömungen*, p. 316; Lepper, "Regierungsbezirk Aachen," pp. 371-400; Moellers, "Reichstagswahlkreis Essen," p. 224.

four percent of the electorate, the Center Party received only fifty-two percent of the vote in the 1874 *Reichstag* elections, where seventy percent of the voters turned out. Even if all the Protestants and Jews in the constituency had appeared to vote and voted for the Progressives or Social Democrats (the other two parties in the election), a sufficient number of votes for these parties remain unaccounted for, so that at least thirty percent of all Catholic voters must have supported them and not the Center. Cologne's adherence to Catholicism had been renowned since the Reformation; Archbishop Paulus Melchers of Cologne had taken a sharp and intransigent stance toward the government's measures in the *Kulturkampf*; and the city was the center of Rhenish political Catholicism. Yet, ironically enough, this arch-Catholic city was also the center of opposition to clericalism, a town with a long liberal and democratic tradition reaching back to 1848 and even earlier.

Cologne was the only constituency in the area under study where parties opposed to the Center must have received a sizeable proportion of Catholic votes in 1874. There were several towns, however, within other constituencies, where this was also the case, including Mülheim a. Rhein, Siegburg, and Bonn in the Rhineland and Meschede, and Attendorn in Westphalia.[13] In all these towns there were powerful pressures exerted on Catholics by liberal businessmen or by the authorities to oppose the Center. Yet this does not seem a sufficient explanation, as there was plenty of political and economic pressure exerted elsewhere without comparable results being achieved. All the above towns were centers of either religious heterodoxy, political leftism, or both. The Catholics there who voted against the Center were the last remnants of a once more numerous and viable opposition to clericalism, an opposition which had been largely eradicated by their religious revival of the years following 1850, and was in its last stages when the heightened Catholic loyalties arising from the persecution of the church dealt it a final blow.

The already hopelessly weak liberal position was further enfeebled by conflicts between free traders and protectionists which emerged after 1873 and cost the liberals the 1876 *Landtag* elections in Düsseldorf. The political dominance of the Center Party was increasingly conceded by their former rivals; even in 1874, many old leftists had given up on the conflict and not come out to vote. The ultra-plutocratic franchise of the city council elections, even more biased in favor of

---

[13] Kaiser, *Die politischen Strömungen*, pp. 323 ff.; Hombach, "Die Reichs- und Landtagswahlen," pp. 327, 330 ff.; 1874 election returns in STAM LA Kr. Meschede Nr. 235.

the rich than the *Landtag* electoral system, made municipal government in some large towns a last refuge of bourgeois liberalism. Industrialists began turning their attention toward the formation of economic interest groups which could influence the state bureaucracy much more efficaciously than political parties had been able to do. Many 1848 democrats retired from political life, having witnessed the total defeat of their political ideals.[14]

Social-Democrats and the Catholic Working Class

Given the close relationship between class and confession, social standing and political affiliation, in the urban and industrial areas of the northern Rhineland and Westphalia, it is not surprising that the conflict between liberalism and clericalism took on aspects of a class struggle. Liberal industrialists threatened with dismissal workers who voted for the Center Party. The German Association, campaigning in the industrial areas, made contact with businessmen and, in effect, attempted to bribe workers into membership by inducing employers to offer time off with pay to proletarians who would attend the association's meetings and rallies. The authorities, especially the liberal Düsseldorf district officials, joined this campaign, denouncing political Catholicism as an ally of the subversive Social-Democrats, in part cynically employing this charge as a weapon in the political struggle but in part seeming really to believe in the identity of two political movements which had little in common except their hostility toward the Bismarckian state.[15]

Rather than being an ally of the clerical cause, workers influenced

[14] LAK 403 Nr. 8447 Bl. 174-55; *Amtmann* in Telgte to LA Kr. Münster, Nov. 28, 1874 STDM LA Kr. Münster A Nr. 6 II; Croon, *Die gesellschaftlichen Auswirkungen*, passim; Ficker, *Kulturkampf in Münster*, p. 392.

[15] On the anti-Catholic policies of industrialists, see Hombach, "Die Reichs- und Landtagswahlen," pp. 389, 444-45; Moellers, "Das 'Essener *Volksblatt*,'" Tenfelde, *Bergarbeiterschaft*, p. 491; *Germania*, Nov. 5, 1873 (Cologne), Nov. 12, 1873 (Krefeld, Düsseldorf, and Essen), Nov. 11, 1874 (Olpe), Jan. 1, 1875 (Sterkrade), Sep. 29, 1875 (Borbeck). On the attitudes of the authorities, most of whom were well aware of the basic disagreements between the clerical and socialist partisans, see STAM OP Nr. 1601 I Bl. 56-58; STAM RAR B Nr. 59 I Bl. 216; HSTAD RD Pr. Nr. 578 Bl. 173-74, 188-93; Moellers, "Reichstagswahlkreis Essen," pp. 334-36; Tenfelde, *Bergarbeiterschaft*, pp. 529-30. One of the more peculiar aspects of the bureaucratic attitude in the *Kulturkampf* was the list of Catholic associations in the Düsseldorf District, which had been closed by the police. This list, drawn up in 1874, had, among the Catholic reading clubs and local branches of the Mainz Association, the "local branch of the Social Democratic Workers' Association," in Süchteln, and the "General German Masons and

by Social-Democratic ideas were virtually the only lower-class Catholics who did not support the Center Party at the peak of the *Kulturkampf*. The identity of those Catholic proletarians who supported the left in those years is somewhat surprising. See Table 6.3. The Social Democrats achieved meager results in Aachen and Krefeld, centers of the mechanized textile industry, and did only somewhat better among the coal mines and steel works of the Ruhr Basin (where Social Democratic supporters may well have been predominantly Protestant) or in the large cities of the Rhine Valley. Rather, it was the artisanal, rural handloom weavers of *Kreis* Kempen who were of all Catholic workers the ones most strongly influenced by the socialists.

The center of Social-Democratic strength in the weaving districts was the little town of Süchteln, an area with an interesting revolutionary past. In 1848, the leader of the democratic forces was the innkeeper Endepohls, who struggled against the conservative parish priest, Father Riegelhaer, attempting to incite the weavers to break down the church doors when the priest refused to have the church bells rung as a signal for insurrection. The post-revolutionary religious revival, sponsored especially by Rieglhaer's successor, who renewed pilgrimages and similar religious practices that his predecessor had scorned, successfully converted some of the democrats. Endepohl's son

TABLE 6.3
Social Democratic Votes in Selected
Urban or Industrial Constituencies, 1874

Constituency	Proportion electors Catholic %	Social Democratic vote as percentage of all votes %
Aachen	96	No candidate
Krefeld	80	1.8
Düsseldorf	76	1.8
Essen	73	6.2
Cologne	84	6.9
Kempen	96	9.6

SOURCES: See Table 6.1.

Stonecutters Association," in Elberfeld. The list circulated widely within the bureaucracy (there are copies of it in LAK 403 Nr. 6695 Bl. 621-29, HSTAD RD Nr. 287 Bl. 12 ff., and STAM OP Nr. 1601 II Bl. 134-37), yet no one seems to have noticed the presence on it of two such distinctly nonclerical, Social-Democratic groups.

Mathias, a merchant and textile manufacturer, even became the leading figure in the Catholic reading club. In 1866, the Catholic partisans were horrified by the news of the Prussian victories, and the following year they organized an energetic election campaign, mobilizing all the priests of the *Kreis* in support of the clerical candidate, Friedrich Michelis, who was successfully elected to the constituent North German *Reichstag*. It seems likely, though, that not all the former leftists had gone over to the clerical cause, for the liberals won a majority of the votes in that election in Süchteln itself.[16]

Shortly thereafter, the Lassalleans began agitating in the area and obtained their greatest successes in Süchteln. Although no tavern keeper would rent the socialists a room for a meeting, a weaver put his house at their disposal, built an extension onto it, and thus formed a gathering place for the "Workers' Casino." Throughout the 1870s, there was a core of some thirty to sixty activists who regularly took part in the work of the association. The group, besides its political work, also sponsored popular festivals, although the authorities on at least one occasion refused to allow a Social-Democratic dance to be held on Ash Wednesday.

Unlike neighboring regions on the lower Rhine, disturbances of public order in Süchteln during the 1870s were not over the government's religious policy. In 1875, angry workers smashed the windows of houses of businessmen (possibly including those of the Catholic leader, Mathias Endepohls) as a reaction to repressive measures taken by the bourgeoisie and the authorities against their organization.[17]

The social Democratic successes in the area were not permanent. A cleverly led Catholic campaign gradually won the leftist minority among the weavers back to the clerical cause by the early 1880s. Technological advances enabled mechanical looms to be constructed which could weave the delicate silk thread which was the specialty of the area. By the mid-1890s, the handloom weavers had disappeared and the region had been largely deindustrialized.[18]

The Süchteln Social-Democrats exemplify the link between an earlier democratic movement and a late-nineteenth-century proletarian rad-

[16] HSTAD RD Pr. Nr. 575 Bl. 10-15, 35-36, HSTAD RD Pr. Nr. 577 Bl. 6-10; Röttges, *Die politischen Wahlen*, pp. 323-24; *Kölnische Zeitung*, Mar. 3, 1867.

[17] HSTAD LA Kr. Kempen Nr. 509; BM Süchteln to LA Kr. Kempen, Apr. 5, 1875, HSTAD RD Nr. 9131.

[18] Tillmann, "Soziale Lage der Handweber." Although Tillmann describes the campaign as a spontaneous movement of naive peasant-artisans, ingenuously putting their trust in a patriarchal monarch, it is clear from his account that political Catholicism was behind the weavers' campaign, especially considering that the weavers' petition, replete with anti-socialist declarations, appeared in the Krefeld clerical newspaper, the *Niederrheinische Volkszeitung*.

icalism. Bourgeois democracy was the school of social democracy, and it was only in those areas where a bourgeois left had been influential that a socialist movement could emerge and maintain itself against clerical hostility.[19] The success of the Catholic religious revival in the decades after 1850 had, to a great extent, cut off the proletariat from the influence of a secularly minded, left-wing bourgeoisie, and thus hampered the emergence of a working-class radicalism.

Splits in the Center Party: Catholic Bourgeoisie and Catholic Workers in Aachen and Essen

The greatest threat to the unity of political Catholicism during the 1870s came from within clerical ranks rather than from outside. For a time, the conflict between bourgeois and working-class wings of the Center Party in Aachen and Essen shook the structure of political Catholicism in those areas. Ultimately, the cohesiveness of the Catholic milieu proved strong enough to deal with internal as well as external challenges.

The conflicts centered around the different tendencies within the Christian Social movement which became ever more apparent in the course of the years 1872 and 1873. The young priests, leaders of the radical faction in the movement, devised a political program calling for genuine parliamentary government, the institution of a secret, equal, and direct franchise in Prussia, legal recognition of the right of workers to organize trade unions and to strike, the passage of worker-protection and social-welfare legislation. It was a strikingly radical program for the time, one of the few examples in political Catholicism of a Christian-Democratic political stance.

These Christian Social clergymen were not content with simply putting forth a program but took steps toward the institutionalization of their movement. A conference of all the adherents of the radical faction was held in Aachen in 1873. In a spectacular incident, which attracted nationwide attention, Chaplain Cronenberg of Aachen, leader of the radicals, gathered funds to support striking textile workers in Eupen.

Attempts by more conservative elements within the church and political Catholicism to combat the movement were unsuccessful. The expulsion of the Jesuits in 1872 removed the leading clerical activists among the moderate Christian Socials. The Archbishop of Cologne attempted to weaken the leadership of the Aachen Christian Social

[19] Following the decline of the Social-Democrats in *Kreis* Kempen, the center of socialist efforts among Catholic workers shifted to Cologne and its suburbs, another old center of the bourgeois left. Ladermacher, "Arbeiterorganisation in der Rhein-provinz," esp. pp. 134-36.

Association, heart of the militant wing of the movement, by transferring to Essen Chaplain Laaf, friend and chief ally of combative Chaplain Cronenberg. The move backfired when Laaf took over the leadership of the Essen Christian Social Association, reviving the position of the more militant faction in the town, which had suffered a blow when its former leader, Chaplain Mosler, had denounced Papal infallibility and become an Old Catholic. After the passage of the May Laws in 1873, any further attempt to limit the movement by transferring the lower clergy was rendered impossible, for such a step would have required the approval of the state—an approval which the ecclesiastical authorities were not willing to request or the Prussian officials to grant.

Demands made on the local Catholic political clubs for the nomination of Christian Social or working-class *Reichstag* or *Landtag* candidates were denied and, consequently, the Christian Social Associations put up their own candidates in Aachen in 1874 and 1877 and in Essen in the latter year. The Christian Socials narrowly lost a run-off election to the Center candidate in Aachen in 1877, but won, by an equally narrow margin, in Essen. The difference between the two constituencies was provided by the behavior of the other political parties: in Aachen, the liberals refused to support either candidate, while in Essen, the liberals, acting to spite their Center Party rivals, and the Social Democrats, out of a sense of proletarian solidarity, supported the Christian Social candidate, metalworker Gerhard Stötzel, who was thus elected.

The movement reached its highpoint in 1877 and then declined with great rapidity. In Aachen, Chaplain Cronenberg was indicted and convicted on what were probably trumped-up fraud charges. The leadership of the Aachen Christian Social Association passed into the hands of a priest chosen by the bourgeois Catholic political club, the Constantia. Membership quickly dwindled, and the organization was dissolved within a few years. Some of the supporters of Chaplain Cronenberg became Social-Democrats, who thus obtained their first foothold in the city, while a majority of former Christian Social adherents returned to the Center Party or lapsed into political apathy.

Chaplain Laaf gradually retired from public life because of a drinking problem (there were several embarrassing incidents of public intoxication). Although not disappearing as completely as in Aachen, the successor organizations to the Christian Social Association which existed in Essen and elsewhere in the Ruhr basin during the 1880s were far from having the numbers and influence of their predecessor.

Gerhard Stötzel joined the Center parliamentary caucus and remained, with an interruption between 1893 and 1898, the *Reichstag* deputy from Essen until his death in 1905. After 1877, however, he stood as a Center Party candidate, and leadership of the local organization of political Catholicism returned to its bourgeois wing, whose most prominent representative was textile manufacturer Mathias Wiese of Werden.[20]

The Christian Social movement in both Aachen and Essen came to an end because of tendencies within it which led beyond political Catholicism and so incurred the considerable opposition of a majority of the clergy and Catholic politicians. The way this process played itself out differed in the two cities because of their differing social and confessional structures. To see this, it is necessary to look at the ideology and activities of the radical Christian Socials a bit more closely.

For all their conflicts with the bulk of the clergy and the Catholic notables, the radical wing of the Christian Social movement saw itself as part of political Catholicism. The Christian Socials vehemently opposed the *Kulturkampf* legislation; in their speeches and literature they followed the counterrevolutionary Catholic ideology, blaming the anti-clerical campaign on the machinations of Freemasons and secret subversives.[21] Yet the Christian Social radicals also called for the "material and moral improvement of the working class by all legal means." This emphasis, when combined with the anti-liberal thrust of political Catholicism, created a socially combative mixture.

The Christian Social priest Father Heggen from Erkrath denounced the liberals for having passed legislation which was "not in the interests of the people but for the money-bags of the liberals . . . for the corporations." Miner Anton Rosenkranz from Essen, a veteran Christian Social lay activist, announced at a Mainz Association meeting in 1872: "Liberalism, whose adherents are mostly rich people, is the natural enemy of the middle class [Bürger] and the workers; it is everyone's duty to struggle against it."[22] The appeal to class solidarity, or at least to a popular solidarity of the lower and middle classes against the bourgeoisie, implicit in these statements was in contradiction to the call of political Catholicism for a solidarity of all Catholics in defense of endangered religion. One of the main and most effective tactics of the bourgeois wing of the Center Party in its fight with the Christian

---

[20] On the course of the Christian Social movement, see Lepper, "Kaplan Cronenberg"; Lepper, "Regierungsbezirk Aachen," pp. 125-46; Tenfelde, *Bergarbeiterschaft*, pp. 464-545.

[21] Cf. above, p. 218, and HSTAD RD Nr. 1257. Bl. 95-98, 120.

[22] HSTAD RD Nr. 1257 Bl. 95-98, 145-46.

Socials was to denounce them for splitting the Catholic cause in the midst of its desperate struggle with the state.[23]

The Catholic industrialists of Aachen saw the very existence of an independent Christian Social movement, with its trade-union-like organization of the workers and support for strikers, as a direct threat to their social position. Although sharply in opposition to the mostly Protestant liberal bourgeoisie and the Prussian authorities, the Catholic bourgeoisie of Aachen shared their hostility to the Christian Social movement and cooperated with their rivals in suppressing it.

The situation in Essen and the western Ruhr basin was somewhat different. The existence of the giant firms in the coal and steel industries, which literally towered over the landscape, and whose activities antagonized a large part of the population, brought forth an opposition from all other social groups adversely affected by their actions—smaller entrepreneurs, peasants, craftsmen, and workers. Since the leaders of the Ruhr heavy industry were almost exclusively Protestant and liberal, and the Catholics were heavily represented in the lower social groups, confessional and class antagonisms tended to coincide. The radical Christian Social program was thus not in and of itself a threat to the Catholic notables of the area, who were ultimately successful in absorbing it.[24]

Unlike Aachen, however, there was in Essen and vicinity a distinct Protestant minority, influenced by socialist ideas, among the workers. The Christian Social call for the improvement of the condition of the working class might well lead to a coalition of proletarians across confessional lines, which would represent a major threat to political Catholicism. In 1877, miner Anton Rosenkranz, as a consequence of his experiences within the Christian Social movement, decided that what the Ruhr coal miners really needed was a non-sectarian trade union, an association which would unite all miners, whether Catholics, Protestants, or freethinkers, clericals, liberals, socialists. Horrified at what their own agitation had wrought, all the Catholic politicians and clergy, including Chaplain Laaf and *Reichstag* deputy Stötzel, vehemently opposed the new organization. The *Rheinisch-Westfälischer Volksfreund,* the newspaper of the Essen Christian Socials, denounced cooperation with the Social-Democrats and called on the workers to choose between "the doubtful hope of an improvement of your earthly

[23] Moellers, "Reichstagswahlkreis Essen," pp. 292-301; Lepper, "Regierungsbezirk Aachen," pp. 420, 495.

[24] The contrast between Aachen and Essen is similar to the account in Naujoks, *Katholische Arbeiterbewegung,* p. 96, which, in spite of its unpleasant polemical tone, seems basically correct. On the antagonisms between the leaders of the giant corporations and the rest of society, cf. Tenfelde, *Bergarbeiterschaft,* pp. 215-18.

conditions and the almost doubtless certainty of your eternal damnation!" Without the support of the Christian Social movement, Rosenkranz's association was captured by the Social-Democrats and disappeared with their prohibition in 1878.[25]

In both Aachen and Essen there were aspects of the radical wing of the Christian Social movement which tended to take it outside the orbit of political Catholicism. A program with a radical set of demands, in which the defense of endangered religion took second place to other issues, an independent (even if clerically led) working-class organization, unafraid of strikes and confrontations with employers, was more than contemporary clerical leaders could tolerate. In the course of the 1870s, the radical thrust of the movement was blunted and the challenge to the leadership of the Catholic notables thrown back. For a minority of the working-class adherents, however, the radical wing of the Christian Social movement was just a way station on the road to the socialists. As was the case with the bourgeois democracy, Christian democracy was, if perhaps to a lesser extent, also a school of Social Democracy. After the end of the Christian Social movement, a distinct suspicion of working-class organization remained among the clergy and Catholic politicians. Even seemingly pious groups might contain within them the seeds of class conflict, irreligiosity, and socialism. The memory of the Christian Social groups was still alive ten or fifteen years later and influenced clerical attitudes toward Catholic working class organizing in the 1890s.[26]

MESCHEDE AND DÜSSELDORF DURING THE 1870s: TWO CONSTITUENCIES IN THE *Kulturkampf* ERA

In this section, the precinct-level analysis begun in Chapter Five will be continued. The more detailed local study will show, as was seen in the general case, the continuation of pre-1871 tendencies during the following decade: the firm loyalties of the Catholic population to the Center Party and the declining strength of any opposition to it.

[25] This follows the excellent account of Tenfelde, *Bergarbeiterschaft*, pp. 514-22.

[26] On this point, see the very interesting letter of the Catholic clergy of Dortmund to the GV Paderborn, Jun. 5, 1890, copy in STAM OP Nr. 2017 II. To discuss the development of the Volksverein and the Christian trade unions, the characteristic Catholic working-class organizations of the Wilhelmine era, would go beyond the scope of this book, but it might be noted that these groups had, from the very beginning, a much greater participation and centralized leadership on the part of the clergy and bourgeois Catholic notables than was the case with the Christian Socials. Cf. Lohn, " 'Arbeiterwohl,' " or BM Altendorf to LA Kr. Essen, Jan. 4, 1894, HSTAD RD Nr. 30427.

TABLE 6.4
Election Results in *Kreis* Meschede, 1874 and 1877

Precincts	Turnout %	Center votes %	Conservative votes %	Number of precincts
		1874		
Liberal electors 1863	62.3	89.5	10.5	24
Clerical-conservative electors 1863	63.9	95.6	4.4	24
Urban or industrial	68.3	87.7	12.3	17
Rural and agricultural	59.7	95.7	4.3	31
Kreis Meschede	63.1	92.3	7.7	48
		1877		
Liberal electors 1863	63.2	95.7	4.3*	23*
Clerical-conservative electors 1863	66.3	98.4	1.6	24
Urban or industrial	71.1	94.7	5.3*	16*
Rural and agricultural	60.4	98.4	1.6	31
Kreis Meschede	64.6	96.9	3.1*	47*

* The number of votes cast for each party are missing in the 1877 election returns for the precinct Ramsbeck—the center of the mining and metallurgical industry and of liberal strength in the countryside. Consequently, the actual nonclerical vote in 1877 is probably slightly higher than in the table.

SOURCES: Election returns in STAM LA Kr. Meschede Nr. 235 and 663.

Kreis *Meschede*

The fall-off in support for the anti-clerical position apparent between 1867 and 1871 continued at an accelerated pace in the following six years, the peak of the *Kulturkampf*. The former centers of liberal strength and of an urban-industrial economy continued to be less clerical than the rest of the *Kreis,* but the adherents of an anticlerical politics had dwindled to a very small number, as the *Landrat* noted in 1874: "The entire population of the *Kreis,* with the exception of a small group in the city of Meschede and scattered individuals in the countryside, is completely devoted to ultramontanism."[27]

The 1870s saw the dissolution in *Kreis* Meschede of the Progressive voting bloc of the previous decade, which had turned increasingly "national" in its politics after the events of 1866. See Table 6.5. The anti-clerical vote of the mid- and late-1870s bore ever less resemblance to its precursors of the previous decade. Even the 1871 National

TABLE 6.5
Comparison of Election Results
in *Kreis* Meschede, 1867-1877

	Zero-Order Coefficient of Correlation between the Liberal-Conservative Vote March 1867 and:				
	Conser-vative vote Aug. 1867	National-Liberal vote 1871	Conser-vative vote 1874	Conser-vative vote 1877	Total pre-cincts
Precincts	*r*	*r*	*r*	*r*	
Liberal electors 1863	.72	.73	.35	.31	24*
Clerical-conser-vative electors 1863	.47	.75	.47	.29	24
Kreis Meschede	.67	.76	.43	.31	48*

	Zero-Order Coefficient of Correlation between the National-Liberal Vote in 1871 and:		
	Conservative vote 1874	Conservative vote 1877	Total precincts
Precincts	*r*	*r*	
Liberal electors 1863	.54	.47	24*
Clerical-conservative electors 1863	.51	.38	24
Kreis Meschede	.54	.44	48*

* Excludes one precinct in 1877. See Table 6.4.
SOURCES: Calculated from election returns given in the sources to Tables 4.3 and 6.4.

[27] *Zeitungsbericht* for the fourth quarter, 1874, STAM LA Kr. Meschede Nr. 2442.

Liberal voters were not entirely compatible with the later anti-clerical vote. What had happened to the one-time liberal voters?

A preliminary answer can be obtained by considering the confessional identity of the voters. Non-Catholics (almost entirely Protestants) made up only 3.9 percent of all voters in the *Kreis* in 1877. Using the figures from that year (and considering the static nature of the *Kreis* population we can assume that the 1877 figures can be applied with accuracy to earlier years) it is possible to analyze the relation between the presence of Protestants and anti-clerical votes. See Table 6.6. Although always positive, the correlation between the presence of Protestants and anti-clerical voters is strong only in 1874. In that year, it would seem, the Protestants of the *Kreis*—mostly executives and engineers of the mining and metallurgical industry or state officials—turned out to meet the "ultramontanist" challenge, while one-time liberal voters of the Catholic confession did not. Both before and after 1874, though, the relation between confession and vote is

TABLE 6.6

Confession and Vote in *Kreis* Meschede, 1867-1877

	Zero-Order Coefficient of Correlation between Proportion Eligible Voters Non-Catholic in 1877 and:					
Precincts	Conservative-liberal votes Mar. 1867 r	Conservative votes Aug. 1867 r	National Liberal votes 1871 r	Conservative votes 1874 r	Conservative votes 1877 r	Total precinct
Liberal electors 1863	.32	.48	.39	.59	.38	24*
Clerical-conservative electors 1863	.26	.22	.21	.63	.27	24
Kreis Meschede	.28	.36	.33	.59	.31	48*

* Excludes one precinct in 1877. See Table 6.4.

SOURCES: Calculated from the election returns given in the sources to Tables 4.3 and 6.4 and from a list giving precinct-level breakdowns of the confession of voters in STAM LA Kr. Meschede Nr. 208.

much less apparent. Another factor must be taken into account—the turnout.

The correlations between liberal vote and turnout rate are negligible for 1871 and not very strong for 1874. In the former liberal precincts in 1877, however, the presence of former anti-clerical voters marks the decisive factor in determining the turnout rate.[28] In that year, the bulk of the former liberal voters gave up as hopeless the struggle against a triumphant clericalism. Even the Protestants, still willing to make an effort in 1874, threw in the towel. The observation of the *Landrat* on the 1877 elections, "the few individuals of another opinion [than the clericals] are hardly of any consequence," may serve as a post-mortem to the efforts to oppose political Catholicism in the area, efforts which had ended in complete defeat. Henceforth only adherents of clericalism would have any voice in the politics of the *Kreis*—a condition which remains essentially unchanged today.[29] See Table 6.7.

Düsseldorf

Complete returns have been preserved only for the 1874 elections in Düsseldorf, but the story they tell is a familiar one. Opposing the clerical incumbent Bernard, the united National Liberals and Progressives put up the democratic veteran of 1848, Heinrich Bürgers. The liberal fusion candidate stood as a Progressive in 1874 and not, as three years previously, as a National Liberal. Also unlike 1871, the Social-Democrats did not support the united liberal effort but fielded their own candidate. See Table 6.8.

In comparison to 1871, the Center Party obtained a slightly higher percentage of the vote, the united liberals a slightly lower one. The chief difference was the turnout which increased from 51.2 percent to 64.6. Political loyalties had changed little since 1871; the political mobilization of the *Kulturkampf* had moved more voters on both sides of the fence to cast their ballots. Statistical calculations bear out this observation: for twenty-one contiguous precincts, the coefficient of

[28] The coefficient of correlation (for the twenty-four precincts which chose liberal electors in 1863) between the turnout rate in 1871 and the turnout rate in 1877 is .67. In other words, in these precincts, the National-Liberal vote in 1871 is better at predicting the 1877 turnout than the 1871 turnout is—a most striking and unusual result for this sort of electoral analysis.

[29] *Zeitungsbericht* for the fourth quarter of 1876, STAM LA Kr. Meschede Nr. 2442. Since the end of the Nazi regime, the *Kreis* Meschede has been a CDU stronghold, and one in which the continuity with the former practices of political Catholicism is still very much apparent. Keinemann, *Beiträge zur westfälischen Landesgeschichte*, pp. 137-45, and Voland, "Ein politisches Lehrstück," *Die Zeit*, Nov. 10, 1977, p. 28.

TABLE 6.7
Former Liberal Voters and Turnout
in *Kreis* Meschede, 1871-1877

*Coefficient of Correlation between Conservative-Liberal
Votes in March 1867 and:*

Precincts	Turnout 1871		Turnout 1874		Turnout 1877		
	Zero-Order *r*	Partial *r**	Zero-Order *r*	Partial *r**	Zero-Order *r*	Partial *r**	Total Pre-cincts
Liberal electors 1863	−.26	−.26	−.23	−.16	−.42	−.43	24
Clerical-conservative electors 1863	+.05	−.08	−.29	−.45	−.24	−.35	24
Kreis Meschede	−.02	−.02	−.22	−.22	−.30	−.31	48

* Holding constant turnout in March 1867.

*Coefficient of Correlation between National-Liberal
Votes in 1871 and:*

Precincts	Turnout 1874		Turnout 1877		
	Zero-Order *r*	Partial *r***	Zero-Order *r*	Partial *r***	Total Precincts
Liberal electors 1863	−.34	−.21	−.68	−.70	24
Clerical-conservative electors 1863	−.09	−.18	−.13	−.20	24
Kreis Meschede	−.21	−.14	−.27	−.22	48

** Holding constant turnout in 1871.
SOURCES: Calculated from the election returns given in the sources to Tables 4.3 and 6.4.

TABLE 6.8
Election Results in Düsseldorf, 1874

Area	Center %	Progressive %	Social-Democratic %	Turnout %
City of Düsseldorf	62.9	33.9	3.0	60.3
Landkreis Düsseldorf	69.0	30.5	0.0	70.8
Constituency	65.2	32.4	1.6	64.6

SOURCE: Election returns in STDD II Nr. 28.

TABLE 6.9
Comparison of February 1867 and 1874
Reichstag Elections in the City of Düsseldorf

Coefficients of Correlation between:

Vote in February 1867	Center Party Vote in 1874 *r*	Progressive Vote in 1874 *r*
Progressive	+.75	−.76
National Liberal	−.52	+.56
Conservative	−.77	+.79
Social Democratic	+.08	−.13
	Social Democratic Vote 1874	
Social Democratic	*r* +.27	
Total precincts	14	14

NOTE: As was the case in Table 4.9, it was necessary to combine a number of precincts to obtain compatible units for analysis.
SOURCE: Calculated from election returns in STDD II Nr. 28.

correlation between the Center vote in 1871 and 1874 is .97, the same as the correlation between the National Liberal vote in the former and the Progressive vote in the latter year.[30] Given this similarity, it is to

[30] Although the city of Düsseldorf was divided into twenty-six precincts for the *Reichstag* elections of 1874, it has been necessary to combine several of them in order to achieve comparable units with 1871.

be expected that the relationship between the February 1867 and 1871 ballots can also be found between those of 1867 and 1874. See Table 6.9.

The Progressive candidate of 1874 was thoroughly rejected by the Progressive voters of 1867 who firmly supported the Center Party,

TABLE 6.10
Social Structure, Confessional Identity,
and Political Alignment in the City of Düsseldorf, 1874

Coefficients of Correlation for the 1874 Reichstag Elections in the City of Düsseldorf				
Between	and	Zero-Order r	Holding Constant	Partial r
Percent Catholic	Center vote	+.96	Percent bourgeois	+.89
Percent Catholic	Turnout	−.43	Percent bourgeois	−.11
Percent bourgeois	Center vote	−.85	Percent Catholic	−.53
Percent bourgeois	Turnout	+.47	Percent Catholic	+.24
Percent workers	Center vote	+.69	Percent Catholic	+.23
Percent workers	Turnout	−.58	Percent Catholic	−.44
Percent workers	Social-Democratic vote	−.26	Percent Catholic	−.22
Percent workers and petit-bourgeois	Center vote	+.89	Percent Catholic	+.60
Percent workers and petit-bourgeois	Turnout	−.44	Percent Catholic	−.17
Total precincts		25		25

NOTE: As was the case in Table 4.7, the two Oberbilk precincts have been combined for purposes of the analysis.

SOURCES: Calculated from election returns in STDD II Nr. 28 and the occupational sample described above, Chapter 5, note 82.

while the former conservatives now made up the mainstay of Progressive support. The 1874 figures thus confirmed the results of the political transformation of the years 1867-1871, when the clerical activists captured the bulk of the former voters for the parties of the left, leaving their bewildered leaders behind. The failure of the Social-Democrats to hold their previous support is also a consequence of these developments.

The confessional and sociological bases of the Center electorate in 1874 were very much like those of three years previously and, in turn, like those of the left electorate in February 1867. See Table 6.10. Once again, the Catholic and lower-class population of the city provided the votes for the Center Party and bourgeois, non-Catholic elements opposed it.[31] The Social Democrats do not seem to have had much support even among Protestant workers in 1874; the energetic agitation of the Düsseldorf Christian Socials (adherents of the more conservative wing of the movement, incidentally) had reduced the socialists to total irrelevance.

In comparison to 1871, the gap between Catholic and Protestant turnout was reduced, the campaigns of the Mainz Association and the passions of the *Kulturkampf* bringing a greater proportion of Catholics out to vote than before. Using the same procedure as was applied in the first section of this chapter, we can produce via regression analysis an estimate of the proportion of eligible Catholics who voted in the 1871 and 1874 elections and thus estimate the proportion of Catholic voters who supported the Center Party. See Table 6.11. The continuity between 1871 and 1874 in Düsseldorf is remarkable, noticeably stronger

TABLE 6.11
Turnout and Support for the Center Party in
the City of Düsseldorf, 1871 and 1874

Year	Turnout %	Center Party vote as percent of Catholic electorate %	Turnout of Catholic voters (estimated) %	Center Party vote as percent of Catholics voting (estimated) %
1871	53	40	46	87
1874	64	49	56	88

SOURCE: Calculated from election returns in STDD II Nr. 28.

[31] Once again, the truck farmers' precincts led all the others in support for the Center: 95.7 and 93.9 percent of the voters in Hamm and Flehe-Volmerswerth respectively casting their ballots for the Catholic party.

than in the average constituency in the northern Rhineland and Westphalia. In a city with a strong liberal and democratic tradition, an
influential and predominantly Protestant bourgeoisie, and a numerous
resident bureaucracy, the pressures on Catholics not to vote for the
Center were considerable and, while the proportion of Catholics voting
increased between 1871 and 1874, the proportion of Catholic voters
supporting the Center Party did not. Although in these respects exceptional, events in Düsseldorf nonetheless exemplify a more general
trend. Building on its overwhelming support among Catholic voters
in 1871, the Center Party solidified its position in the years of the
Kulturkampf and emerged in the new political circumstances of the
following decades in a secure and influential position.

CONCLUSION

Catholic Religion and Social Change, 1830-1870

The development of Catholicism in the northern Rhineland and West-phalia in the years 1830 to 1870 can be roughly divided into two twenty-year periods, breaking in the middle around 1850. Like all periodizations, this one is not precise. Traces of the earlier period can be found in the later one, while forerunners of the events occurring after mid-century can be perceived in the *Vormärz*, especially in its final decade. Nonetheless, each period was characterized by certain predominant tendencies in regard to lay religion, clerical initiatives, the social context of religious practice, and the relationship between ecclesiastical and governmental authority. The interaction of these four factors was different in each period, creating a basically different religious environment. In the *Vormärz*, this environment was one of disruption and disunity, decay of traditional practices, tendencies toward secularization, conflicts within the ranks of the Catholic clergy, between the clergy and the laity, and between the clergy and the secular authorities. The post-1850 atmosphere, on the other hand, was one of renewal and revival: the overcoming of secularizing tendencies through the introduction of new religious practices, the encouragement or benevolent neutrality of the governmental authorities, a growing unification of the clergy, and the consolidation of a Catholic milieu.

During the *Vormärz*, a still largely unreformed old-regime Catholic piety was challenged by two separate developments, each with its own ideology, institutional context, and social basis. One might be described as externally originated secularization, the creation from sources outside Counterreformation Catholic culture—especially the Enlightenment, the French Revolution, and the Prussian state—of organizations embodying Enlightenment ideals and containing a confessionally mixed membership or clientele. Advocates of such new institutions—Masonic Lodges, secular shooting clubs, liberal or left-wing newspapers—understood them as challenges to existing Catholic ones and their Enlightened ideology as a replacement for a self-consciously Catholic view of the world. Devout Catholic circles, hostile to these new developments, nonetheless shared their adherents' interpretation of their significance. These secularizing tendencies were most effective among the Catholic bourgeoisie, especially in the cities of the Rhine Valley, although they were also at work in smaller, more out-of-the-way towns, and in areas of the rural metallurgical industry.

The second kind of development, which could be called inherent laicization, was quite different from the first in virtually all respects. Rather than being external to old-regime Catholicism, it arose from tendencies within it, as the balance between secular festivity and religious devotion, or between lay initiative and clerical control, changed in favor of the former elements. The resulting situation, as it existed in the 1820s, was one of pilgrimages and processions whose high points were the worldly fairs associated with them, of religious brotherhoods whose members spent more time in the taverns than in the church, of relatively high illegitimacy rates and sometimes meager church attendance. Appearing primarily in the lower classes, both in town and country, this development was much more widespread than externally originated secularization, but much less self-conscious. Even while their actions infuriated the clergy and were a cause of frequent conflict with them, the Catholic masses did not regard these actions as anticlerical or non-religious, but continued to perceive them in terms of the old-regime unity of sacred and secular.

Socioeconomic and political developments of the late eighteenth and early nineteenth centuries were favorable to both forms of challenge to the church. The thirty-year-long disruption of normal religious life between 1790 and 1820 had destroyed or severely hampered ecclesiastical administration, clerical recruitment and education, and had driven lay institutions, especially the brotherhoods, into a twilight world of semi-legality and lack of clerical supervision. Among the French revolutionary and Napoleonic administrators, the Prussian bureaucrats and the growing Protestant bourgeoisie resident in previously all Catholic areas, there were many individuals who propagated Enlightened ideas and supported the creation of institutions and associations outside the sphere of the church.

The new authorities' advocacy of laissez-faire also affected religion, since the abolition of previously existing restraints on setting up a household or independent business—the guild system, marriage restrictions—meant a weakening of the religious institutions and practices previously closely associated with them. In a period of rapid population growth and relatively easy access to the means of economic independence and household formation for the lower classes, the morally restrictive aspects of former religious practices appeared less relevant. The socioeconomic environment thus created and lasting well into the *Vormärz* was one which encouraged a maximum of popular festivity and a certain defiance of social authority.

Although conditions in the *Vormärz* were favorable to both inherent laicization and externally originated secularization, the two tendencies existed side by side, never reaching a juncture, as the differences or even opposition between their respective forms and the social and cultural divergences of their bearers were too great. There were a few examples of what might have been the beginnings of an interaction— mutual benefit societies showing Masonic influences, innkeepers preaching atheism to their customers—but they remained isolated influences. The potential danger to religion, inherent in the juncture of these two tendencies, was never actualized.[1]

The historian's hindsight was not available to contemporary participants, and for the Catholic clergy and lay adherents of a "strict" religion the situation appeared difficult enough. Clerical attempts to prohibit overly secularized practices usually led to their continuation without even the former veneer of piety. Yet doing nothing was to allow a bad situation to get worse. The dilemma of the clergy and their lay sympathizers was increased by the actions of the authorities. Positive measures to strengthen Catholic self-consciousness were unwelcome to the Prussian government, for such measures would have increased the differences between the old and the new provinces of the monarchy, or between Catholics and Protestants in the new, western provinces themselves. While having no more love for popular festivities than their ecclesiastical counterparts, the secular authorities judged them by a different measure. Imbued with the spirit of economic liberalism, the bureaucracy was concerned with the relationship of religious festivities to productivity and not to morality. Officials wished to curb the number of non-productive holidays and festivities and not (or only secondarily) to regulate behavior during the celebrations. Though the clergy was aware of these considerations, priests were more interested in improving the existing religious festivities and purging them of secular elements. The two sets of criteria could lead to cooperation between church and state; more frequently, however, they led to conflict and mutual paralysis. Clerical reform initiatives remained scattered or abortive.

After 1850, the negative tendencies of the *Vormärz* were beaten back, and a vigorously pursued religious revival and renewal flourished in a changed social and political environment, transforming the pre-1850 atmosphere into its opposite. At the heart of the religious innovation lay two interrelated processes: the assertion or reassertion of clerical leadership and the transformation of popular festivity. Brotherhoods led by a lay committee gave way to or were transformed into clerically led sodalities and congregations, and the clergy took over from laymen the organization and leadership of pilgrimages and

---

[1] For the analysis of just such a juncture and its politically decisive consequences, see the brilliant work of Agulhon, *La République au Village*.

processions. Following the example of the missions, the sermon acquired a greater importance in church services and the congregation
a greater receptivity for it.

This clerical leadership was the vehicle through which the popular
festivities were transformed. While the new religion was a festive one—
pilgrimages and processions flourished as never before, the missions
provided a remarkable and unique form of religious celebration—the
new festivity was worlds removed from its old-regime or *Vormärz*
predecessors. It took place under priestly supervision in moral and
restrained fashion, practiced in the church and not the tavern or on
the dance floor. Both following a Roman example and innovating on
their own initiative a growing number of Rhenish-Westphalian Catholic priests introduced new, centrally organized, and universally practiced forms of religious devotion—above all the Marian cult, which
grew by leaps and bounds between 1850 and 1870—partially replac-
ing, partially incorporating older, locally oriented forms.

These new practices and organizations replaced their more laic or
secular *Vormärz* predecessors with relatively little opposition. Since
the Catholic masses, even when engaging in practices that the clergy
regarded as morally abhorrent, had always seen their actions in a
religious context, and the self-conscious but bourgeois *Vormärz* secularism never spread widely among the population, there was no mass-
based, effective ideology which might have contested the religious
revival.

The organized and coordinated post-1850 initiatives occurred in a
more favorable socioeconomic environment. The subsistence crisis of
the years 1846 to 1855 had impressed upon the lower classes of the
countryside and non-industrial small towns, the necessity for a more
restricted and sober life-style. Their path to economic survival ran
through delayed marriage, more frequent celibacy, prolonged economic dependence, thriftiness, and denial of pleasure. The glorification
of chastity and renunciation implicit in the new religious practices
helped to justify the adaptation to new and unpleasant economic realities; the new religious institutions provided a social context for the
implementation of these ideas. At the same time, an industrial boom
was drawing hundreds of thousands of migrants from the overpopulated rural areas into the large cities and industrial towns of the
northern Rhineland and Westphalia, creating a Catholic proletariat
unfamiliar with a fully capitalist labor market and an urban-industrial
environment. Clerically led workers' sodalities, Catholic journeymen's
and miners' associations, were islands of stability in a chaotic proletarian sea, an important element in the adaptation of the lower-class
population to urban-industrial life. The process assumed its clearest

form in the cities and mining villages of the Ruhr basin, but it was to be found throughout the entire Rhenish-Westphalian industrial area.

The political circumstances had changed as well, a consequence of the results of 1848-1849, when the Catholic church had proved itself a major force for order in the western provinces, one the Prussian authorities were willing to conciliate. While mutual tensions and suspicions never disappeared and the clashing pretensions of the two autonomous institutions were not dispelled by cooperation, nonetheless the years 1850 to 1870 were a period of good relations between Catholic church and Prussian state, never repeated in the history of the monarchy. After 1850, Catholic efforts at religious renewal could proceed with little bureaucratic interference and frequent official encouragement.

The political implications of the religious revival were not immediately apparent, but in the long run they were decisive in determining the shape of political Catholicism. From the early years of the nineteenth century, even before the formation of political parties, the Rhenish-Westphalian Catholic clergy had, with a few individual exceptions, perceived a connection between revolution and immorality. They saw radical ideas as sinful: democrats were to be placed in the same category as atheists, drunkards, or fornicators. The attitude, one of the many consequences of the French Revolution for European history, was only reinforced by the events of 1848-1849. The post-1850 campaign to improve popular morality was simultaneously designed to counteract "immoral" democratic influences.[2]

The religious revival, as far as the evidence allows judgment, was a success. Its main thrust was directed against inherent laicization and, in dealing with the more self-consciously secular ideologies and the bourgeois social groups where they were most prevalent, the revival was at its least effective. In spite of the attractions of Marianic Congregations of Young Merchants or the post-1849 realization of the pacifying effects of religion on the unruly lower classes, the bourgeoisie remained the least consistent element in the Catholic milieu. This was not because of anti-capitalist or anti-industrial tendencies exhibited in

---

[2] Although in some areas immorality and radicalism could be united in the same group of individuals—as innkeepers whose establishments were gathering places for drunkards and dancers as well as democrats—the sinners and the radicals were usually not from the same social group. The main connection appears to be regional: areas where the politically active, more affluent elements had leftist sympathies were also those areas where the lower classes were given to the immoral practices deplored by the clergy. The two forms of defiance of clerical authority—and this is another aspect of the failed juncture between externally originated secularization and inherent laicization—were never united in the form of a political mass movement.

the religious revival. Outside certain rhetorical flourishes, the thrust of this revival was toward adaptation to an industrial-capitalist economy and society, not opposition to them. Rather, the large proportion of Protestants among the industrial and professional bourgeoisie of the large cities of the Rhineland and Westphalia provided a counter-influence to the efforts of the clergy and its lay partisans. Where, as in Aachen, a Catholic bourgeoisie existed, which was large and coherent enough to form a firm group, then it was precisely these merchants, industrialists, and professional men who were the most intransigently clerical and firmly pious. Even if the religious revival was less successful among the Catholic bourgeoisie than among other social groups—and it was by no means without effect among the bourgeoisie—its very success elsewhere guaranteed that the anti-clerical elements would remain a small, isolated minority. The threat of a massive secularization, present in the *Vormärz*, had been rebuffed by 1870 and replaced with an improved popular morality, a new, widespread set of religious mentalities, practices, and institutions, and a growing Catholic self-consciousness.

RELIGION AND POLITICS, 1848-1880

Political participation varied enormously in the course of the third quarter of the nineteenth century. Broad but inchoate and erratically organized mass movements of the revolutionary years 1848-1849 gave way to an equally vaguely structured but much more restricted period of notables' politics between 1850 and 1866. Starting in 1867 and continuing through the end of this study in 1880 and beyond, mass participation returned to the political stage, but, unlike the previous mass politics of 1848-1849, it took on increasingly organized form, with local and regional political clubs, a far greater number of political newspapers with much larger circulations, and much closer connections between parliamentarians or national organizations and local concerns. Throughout these changing forms of popular participation, political leadership remained in the hands of the notables. In spite of the tendencies toward autonomous popular action apparent in the disturbances of 1848, the strikes of the late 1860s, or the efforts of the early socialist movement, the lower classes in this period did not play an independent political role, self-consciously confronting aristocracy or bourgeoisie, but were involved as they were mobilized by their social superiors. Political life revolved around the opposition or cooperation of different groups of notables and their attempts to mobilize popular support for their positions.

In the Catholic areas of the northern Rhineland and Westphalia, there were two main notables' groups whose politics can be described as liberal-democratic, on the one hand, and clerical-conservative, on the other. A "pure conservative" grouping, as could be found elsewhere in the Prussian state, including the predominantly Protestant areas of the western provinces, did not exist. Even the bureaucracy, if it wished to be effective, especially in electoral politics, had to support one or the other of the two existing groups.[3]

The political orientation of these two groups was not determined by their relations to the policies of the central government. Such relations were flexible and changed frequently, sometimes with disorienting speed, as happened in 1866. Nor were the two groups internally homogeneous. Sub-tendencies existed in each: the left was divided into moderate-liberal and progressive-democratic groups, the latter clearly more radical than the former. Catholic politics is less easily fitted on a left-right scale. The sub-groupings of clerical politicians might be described as authoritarian, on the one hand, and anti-Prussian, on the other. In most elections and in a majority of constituencies at all times, clericals of various stripes worked together, opposing allied moderate and radical leftists, but in a few constituencies in 1849 and again in 1867 Catholic hostility to the Protestant state and democratic hostility to its authoritarian policies might make common cause, opposing the alliance created between moderate clericals and liberals, both desirous of order and willing to work with the authorities.

Regardless of shifting alliances within the two notable groups and between these groups and the government, liberal and clerical notables formed cohesive and mutually impermeable blocs. Movement within them was possible, but movement between them was not. An 1848 radical democrat like Hermann Becker might have softened his militant views by the 1870s and emerged as a National Liberal, or an authoritarian clerical-conservative like Hermann von Mallinckrodt could develop a more strongly oppositional, anti-ministerial stance as a result of the war of 1866, but clerical notables did not become liberal ones or vice versa. Oppositional Catholic electors of the 1850s were pro-governmental electors of the 1860s, not the oppositional Progressives of that decade. Progressive activists in opposition to the government during the Conflict Era did not join the oppositional Center Party of

---

[3] Since Prussia did not have a parliamentary government, it is arguable that the inability to control elections ought not to be seen as proof of bureaucratic weakness. However, the course of the *Kulturkampf* showed that without the consent of the church and political Catholicism many aspects of bureaucratic administration itself could not be carried out. This lesson was not lost on future generations, and even the authorities of the Nazi state—who had much greater pretensions to uninhibited rule than their Prussian forbears and were much more hostile to the Catholic church than they were— were careful to avoid measures which might have provoked a repetition of the *Kulturkampf*.

the *Kulturkampf* but renounced their opposition in favor of their anti-clericalism.

What separated the two notable groups was their respective social milieus. Clerical partisans were less affluent, less closely connected to a capitalist market economy, than their counterparts on the left. These social differences, however, were not articulated in socioeconomic terms. Catholic politics was not a religiously disguised petit-bourgeois anti-capitalism: demands for the restoration of the guilds or attacks on usury were the least effective part of the clerical program. The heart of political Catholicism, its main and most effective slogan and rallying point, was the call to defend an endangered religion. Ultimately, politics in the Catholic areas of the northern Rhineland and Westphalia reduced itself to the distinction between those who accepted this slogan and those who did not.

If defense of religion cannot be reduced to defense of certain social and economic group interests, neither can religion be seen outside a socioeconomic context. The Catholic religious revival was one response to the mid-century socioeconomic crisis. During missions and in sodalities or journeymen's associations, the clergy called on the Catholic lower classes to adopt a restricted and austere life-style, lower their expectations of economic independence and formation of their own households, and respect the shaken authority of pre-capitalist elites—master craftsmen, small-town merchants, peasant paterfamilii, rural noblemen. Defending religion meant defending this way of life, this response to new socioeconomic conditions. The clerical emphasis on confessional issues was implicitly a social program—a far more effective one than the vague formulations used by Catholic politicians in dealing with social questions. Because it was not explicitly tied to petit-bourgeois interest politics, such an implicit social program could be adopted for use in other social contexts: to uphold the authority of the Catholic entrepreneurs of Aachen or to rally the Ruhr basin proletariat to the church.

Support for the left, on the other hand, was closely connected to another implicit social program, an alternative response to the mid-century subsistence crisis: not restriction and retrenchment, but capitalist expansion of the social productive forces. Inherently, this liberal conception of society was as broadly applicable as its Catholic counterpart, but the religious revival's successful suppression of *Vormärz* laicizing tendencies cut off the leftist notables from the Catholic masses and left them no way of disseminating their ideas on a widespread basis.[4]

---

[4] For all the Catholic skepticism about capitalist economic expansion, the implicit social program of the religious revival could be carried out only in the context of the

From the vantage point of the mass politics of 1848-1849, it was by no means clear which group of notables, clerical or left-wing, would ultimately be successful in mobilizing popular support. Toward the end of the subsequent era of notables' politics in the mid-1860s, it even seemed that the left had established itself as the dominant political force in the Catholic areas of the Rhineland and Westphalia. The war of 1866 and the introduction of universal, direct, equal, and secret suffrage in 1867 drastically changed the situation, forcing the competing elites to vie for mass support on an unprecedented scale. Utilizing the leading position it had obtained in the religious revival, the Catholic clergy showed that at the local level it was the master of the new mass politics. Although the disorganization of political Catholicism occasioned by the war meant that clerical influence was not matched by clerical deputies, the new religious-political realities quickly asserted themselves, and a reorganized clerical party triumphed over its liberal rivals in the elections of 1870-1871, demonstrating its dominant position in political life.

A related factor in this new political situation was the ease with which the Catholics defeated the early initiatives of the socialist movement. In Rhineland-Westphalia, as elsewhere in Europe, social democracy grew out of bourgeois democracy. Socialist activists had their first political experiences on the bourgeois left. Liberal and democratic influences in workers' educational and mutual benefit societies gave way to socialist ones. As the religious revival directed the Catholic working class of the region away from *Vormärz* secularizing tendencies and anti-clerical and bourgeois-democratic influence, it cut off the basis for potential socialist support. While in 1848-1849 the Catholic workers of Cologne or Düsseldorf had been no less enthusiastic in their support for radical democracy than their Protestant counterparts in Barmen or Solingen, by the elections of 1871 the socialist movement in the Catholic cities had been reduced to a sectarian existence, a miserable appendage to a feeble bourgeois left; in the Protestant ones, the socialists were already disputing the liberals for the allegiance of the proletariat.

Even before the onset of the *Kulturkampf*, the triumph of political Catholicism and the defeat of its bourgeois and proletarian left-wing rivals in the Catholic areas of the northern Rhineland and Westphalia

post-1850 economic boom. A thriving industrial capitalism provided employment for the "excess" inhabitants of the overpopulated rural and non-industrial areas, thus dampening *Vormärz* social tensions, making austerity a practical possibility (and not a path to starvation), and enabling pre-capitalist elites to reassert their authority. Gradually, Catholic politicians came to realize this and were willing to admit in private—at the Soest conferences, for instance—that capitalism might not be so bad for Catholic interests, after all.

was essentially complete. My research therefore does not support the predominant scholarly opinion which sees the church-state struggle of the 1870s as the origin of the political allegiance of the Catholic masses. While the persecutory actions of the authorities and the bitterness of the struggle certainly helped to mobilize those previously passively favorable and helped to convince waverers and skeptics that religion really was in danger, the conflict was an exacerbating or encouraging rather than an originating factor. Catholic use of organizational forms taken from the religious revival during the *Kulturkampf* or the clerical denunciation of the state's policy as a revolutionary conspiracy show the extent to which the Catholic milieu and the organization of political Catholicism as it existed until 1933 were not spontaneous responses to persecutory actions but products of a complex series of interactions between religious, social, and political developments in the two decades after the middle of the nineteenth century.[5]

More broadly, this whole line of investigation suggests a different, and perhaps more fruitful, way of conceptualizing the relationship between religion (or other forms of popular culture), socioeconomic change, and politics. Most previous research has tended either to see religion as an autonomous entity, existing alongside socioeconomic conditions but independent of them, or to perceive religious issues in modern politics as pretexts for the defense of certain socioeconomic interests—in the case of Catholicism, usually petit-bourgeois or peasant anti-capitalism. The first tendency, exemplified in the work of Max Braubach's students, while pointing to the central importance of religion in the politics of the region takes as unproblematic the question of confessional identity. Religion is just one of many possible forms of group consciousness; why and how did Rhenish-Westphalian Catholics come to identify with their confession so strongly and make it the basis of their politics? Some, at times perhaps most, did not—in 1849 or the early 1860s, for instance. In order to provide a systematic and not an unconvincing ad hoc explanation for this, it is necessary to consider religion as historical, as developing over time in interaction with socioeconomic and political change.[6]

[5] There is an excellent account of the majority scholarly opinion in Anderson, *Windthorst*, pp. 192-200, but her arguments center around potential parliamentary coalitions and simply cannot be applied to developments at the local level. Repgen, in "Klerus und Politik," notes the heterogeneous character of local Catholic politics in 1848 and concludes from it that the *Kulturkampf* created a united political Catholicism, not taking into account the intervening quarter-century. The position I am asserting is very similar to that of Lepsius, "Parteisystem und Sozialstruktur," and the following theoretical suggestions owe a good deal to Lepsius' concept of a "sociomoral milieu."

[6] On the "Braubach school," see above, Chapter 2, n. 14, 15, and 21, and p. 138. Christoph Weber, a student of Braubach's student Konrad Repgen, has provided in his

The second viewpoint, found in the very interesting works of Lothar Gall on the Badenese *Kulturkampf* or David Blackbourn's recent history of political Catholicism in Württemberg, points to this interaction of religion and socioeconomic circumstances, but at times tends to reduce cultural expression to an epiphenomenon of economic interests. If defense of the guild system or support of agricultural protective tariffs were what Catholic politics was really about, why did Catholic politicians stubbornly insist on talking about the defense of religion, and crowds of their listeners cheer them on? Why did Catholic entrepreneurs and proletarians support (and do so disproportionately in comparison to Protestants in the Federal Republic even today) such petit-bourgeois interests?[7]

A preferable way to deal with these interrelationships is to understand religious practices, organizations, and beliefs as being shaped in response to socioeconomic change. They provide ways of interpreting society and suggest, justify, or inspire a certain course of action. Such actions may well fit particular socioeconomic interests best—and since Max Weber, Catholic skepticism of unrestrained capitalist economic expansion seems well established—but are not directly tied to them, and can be used to help reshape them or can be adapted to others. It is this loyalty toward a way of life, a set of beliefs and institutions created in response to given social and political circumstances by a group in which certain socioeconomic interests were most influential—in Rainer Leipsius' words, a "sociomoral milieu"—which can be politically mobilized. Indeed, the political loyalties so created are remarkably tough, durable, and adaptable, more so than ties created by narrower considerations of economic self-interest.

REGIONAL AND CONFESSIONAL PARALLELS
AND CONTRASTS

Rhineland and Westphalia

Although I have treated these two areas as more or less interchangeable, and in comparison to other regions they were very similar, nonetheless there existed distinct differences between the two in their cul-

---

work a very interesting account of the relationship between confessional identity and social environment, from which I have learned much, although I do not agree with it. These remarks about the Braubach school apply, *mutatis mutandis*, to the sociocultural school of American political history as well.

[7] Blackbourn, *Class, Religion and Local Politics*; Gall, "Problematik," *Der Liberalismus als regierende Partei*, esp. pp. 280-302. Cf. the criticism of Gall's argument in Becker, *Liberaler Staat und Kirche*, pp. 147-52.

tural traditions, economic development, and political experience.[8] Such differences were reflected in the religious and political developments considered here. Clerical influence was stronger in Westphalia than in the Rhineland. During the *Vormärz*, lay-clerical conflict, although certainly present in Westphalia, was less pronounced than in the Rhineland; the religious revival began earlier in Westphalia and proceeded more smoothly there. Piety and political influence went hand in hand: Westphalian political Catholicism was more successful than its Rhenish counterpart, more resistant to leftist assaults in 1849 or during the conflict era, and quicker to spring back from war-induced passivity in the late 1860s.

To some extent, the greater clerical power reflected differing regional experiences. The Westphalian custom of unequal inheritance may well have created a greater need for a religiously based family solidarity, involving considerable renunciation on the part of the non-inheriting siblings than the practice of equal division, prevalent in many parts of the Rhineland. Secularizing currents stemming from the French Revolution were certainly greater in the Rhineland, which had been incorporated into the French Republic and Napoleonic Empire for twenty years, while the territories on the right bank of the river spent a briefer time under the administration of the Napoleonic satellite states. In the former areas, the nobility was, with certain exceptions, expropriated, while the Westphalian nobility survived the revolutionary period with its property if not all its privileges intact and provided powerful assistance to the work of reviving the church. Ecclesiastical administration was disrupted during this period on a broader scale to the west than to the east of the Rhine.[9]

Another source of regional differences was the differing combination of similar sub-regions. Many areas with similar socioeconomic structures existed in the Rhineland and Westphalia, and such areas had strikingly similar religious and political developments. The *Kreise* Grevenbroich or Geilenkirchen (Düsseldorf and Aachen Districts, respectively) were regions of relatively prosperous large peasant farming where the presence of lay-clerical conflict in the *Vormärz* enabled non-

---

[8] Drawing distinctions between the two regions is a task complicated by the overlapping of cultural and political boundaries: many areas on the right bank of the Rhine, while belonging to the Prussian Rhine Province, were culturally and socioeconomically more similar to areas in Westphalia than they were to those across the river. Additionally, the changes resulting from urbanization, industrialization, and internal migration tended over time to blur the distinctions between the two regions.

[9] On the relationship between primogeniture and piety among the Westphalian nobility, Reif, *Westfälischer Adel*, pp. 291-99 and passim. A similar study, focusing on the region's peasantry, would be of considerable interest.

clerical notables to mobilize rural support for democracy in 1848-1849 and for the Progressives in the conflict era. *Kreise* Beckum and Recklinghausen (both Münster District) in Westphalia presented exactly the same picture. Merchants and entrepreneurs of the rural metallurgical industry—liberal and disproportionately Protestant—challenged (ultimately unsuccessfully) clerical influence among the otherwise pious rural population of the mountainous Eifel districts in the Rhineland, as they did in the Westphalian *Hochsauerland*. Political Catholicism acquired a proletarian if not exactly class-conscious tinge in both eastern, Westphalian, and western, Rhenish, halves of the Ruhr basin.

There was, however, a basic asymmetry between the two regions. The cities of the Rhine Valley, extending in a belt from Kleve in the north, through the major centers of Düsseldorf and Cologne to Koblenz in the south, were commercial, administrative, to a lesser extent manufacturing centers, with a numerous, influential, liberal, and predominantly Protestant bourgeoisie, an anti-clerical tradition, and an openness to secularizing influences from elsewhere in Europe. In the smaller, less populous, and more isolated Westphalian market and administrative towns—Münster, Paderborn, Soest, or Arnsberg—these elements were present at most to a far smaller degree. The Rhine Valley cities contributed considerably to the creation of a different regional atmosphere.

It is frequently asserted that Rhenish political Catholicism was more liberal than its conservative Westphalian counterpart.[10] I could find little evidence to support such a view. Neither parliamentary deputies nor local clerical activists in the Rhineland were more in favor of laissez-faire or parliamentary government, more inclined to side in parliament with the opposition during the conflict era, more hostile to the Prussian state, than in Westphalia. Indeed, the Westphalian participants in the Soest Conferences of the 1860s showed a more favorable attitude toward occupational freedom and a greater skepticism about demands for restoration of the guilds than their Rhenish contemporaries. While that minority of Rhenish priests and lay activists who supported the democrats in 1849 or allied with the left opposition in 1867 are better known than their Westphalian counterparts, the latter seem to have been no less numerous and active.

Nonetheless, the impression is inescapable that Rhenish Catholics were more liberal than Westphalians. But they were more liberal because they were less clerical—both ideologically and politically. Rather

[10] See, for instance, Reif, *Westfälischer Adel*, p. 425 and p. 670 n. 94. But cf. the comments of Bachem, *Zentrumspartei*, 2: 125-26.

than saying that Rhenish political Catholicism was more liberal than Westphalian political Catholicism, it would be more appropriate to say that Rhenish Catholics were more influenced by political liberalism than Westphalian Catholics.

Catholicism in Central and Northern Europe

Catholics in the northern Rhineland and Westphalia were by no means unique in their nineteenth-century development. Similar tendencies existed throughout northern and Central Europe. If, as I have argued, the disintegrating tendencies in Catholic religious life during the first half of the nineteenth century were largely not the product of industrialization but arose from the anti-clerical policies of an enlightened bureaucracy, on the one hand, and the social tensions of a preindustrial economy, on the other, where existing restraints on marriage and the establishment of economic independence had been broken by rapid population growth, the northern Rhineland and Westphalia would have been areas where the social and political preconditions for a disintegrating piety were present to a lesser extent than in southern and southwestern Germany. There, the post-1815 retention of enlightened governmental policies was more consistent than in Prussia, and the crisis of the preindustrial society more acute than in the north. Declining church attendance, conflicts between clergy and laity, conflicts within the ranks of the clergy, secularized celebration of religious holidays, dancing, frequenting the taverns were common among the Catholics of the southern Rhineland, Baden, and Bavaria before 1850, probably in more widespread and acute form than farther north. In southwestern Germany, the discord reached unprecedented heights when many of the lower clergy joined in and began demanding the abolition of clerical celibacy and reforms in ritual and church organization, including the abolition of individual confession, the introduction of ecclesiastical democracy, and the use of a German language mass.[11]

The religious atmosphere was reflected in the political situation of 1848-1849. South German Catholics were less clerical and more radical than their northern counterparts. Baden, as is well known, was a hotbed of peasant insurrection and militant democracy. The Allgäu, the "Bavarian Switzerland," was also a democratic center where the clergy had little political influence, and no one dared form Pius As-

---

[11] On these developments, see Phayer, *Religion* passim; Weber, *Aufklärung*, pp. 59-65, 74, 102, 108, 185 n. 8, and 207-15; Franzen, "Zölibatsfrage," Hörger, "Mentale Umschichtungen," and Blessing, *Staat und Kirche*, pp. 34-42.

sociations. In the southern Rhineland and the Catholic parts of Bavarian Swabia and Franconia, the democratic left and the clerical partisans were evenly matched with the former, as in the north, gaining the upper hand by late 1848.[12]

As in the north, a Catholic religious revival, tentatively beginning c. 1840, spread rapidly in the south after mid-century. Missions were held; new religious associations founded; the dissident groups among the clergy and the laity, so prominent before 1848, gradually faded away.[13] With this religious revival, political Catholicism gained strength. The "Badenese *Kulturkampf*" of the 1860s, pitting the Catholics against a liberal government, showed the growing influence of clericalism in a one-time democratic stronghold. Clerical partisans in Swabia and Franconia also succeeded, by the early 1870s, in defeating their liberal adversaries, and after a series of events similar to those in the north the Center Party emerged in 1870-1871 as the dominant political influence in the southern Rhineland.[14]

Unlike Rhineland-Westphalia, however, the clerical triumph in the Catholic areas of southern and southwestern Germany was never complete. Eastern Baden, the "Achilles heel of political Catholicism," and the Allgäu in Bavaria continued to send liberal deputies to the *Reichstag* and the respective *Landtage* at least in some elections until the First World War. Both areas were predominantly rural or small town in nature, not very industrialized, and centers of religious heterodoxy. Eastern Baden had been a stronghold of the anti-celibacy movement among the clergy before 1848, and Old Catholicism found many supporters there, as it also did in the Allgäu. Indeed, while the pious workers of Westphalia were physically assaulting any Old Catholic they could get their hands on, the free-thinking peasants of the Allgäu were sending the Old Catholic Joseph Volk, democratic veteran of 1848, to the *Reichstag* as a liberal deputy.[15] In both regions, the

---

[12] Until several very recent studies, which were beginning to appear only after I finished this book, there were no works on 1848-1849 in Baden, and the reader was required to turn to Lautenschlager, *Agrarunruhen*, which appeared in 1915. On the southern Rhineland, see Schmidt, *Wahlen im Regierungsbezirk Koblenz* and Schierbaum, *Wahlen des Regierungsbezirks Trier*, both products of the Braubach school. For Bavaria, see Thränhardt, *Wahlen in Bayern*, pp. 39-47.

[13] Cf. Gatz, *Volksmission*, introduction; Franzen, "Zölibatsfrage," pp. 367 ff. and 378-79; and esp. Blessing, *Staat und Kirche*, pp. 84-97, 132-44.

[14] For Bavaria, see Thränhardt, *Wahlen*, pp. 48 ff. The church-state struggle in Baden can be followed in the accounts of Gall and Becker, cited above, n. 7. On the southern Rhineland, besides the works cited above, n. 9, see Steil, "Die Wahlen in der Stadt Trier."

[15] Thränhardt, *Wahlen*, pp. 71-78; Becker, *Staat und Kirche*, pp. 306-309, 331-42; Zangerl, "Courting the Catholic Vote," pp. 233-34, 238. A glance at the *Reichstag*

resistance of pre-1850 heterodox or secularizing tendencies to the post-1850 efforts at a religious revival seem to have played a major role in the political victories of liberalism over its clerical opponents.

"Old Bavaria," the areas in the kingdom which had also belonged to the old regime Duchy, showed in this respect, as in so many others, an anomalous pattern of development. Although lay-clerical relations there were troubled before 1848, and improved after mid-century perhaps less than elsewhere, the region's rural inhabitants were strongly clerical-conservative during the revolution and continued to be so over the following forty years, a political stance probably influenced as much by Bavarian particularism as by the Catholic church. In the 1890s, however, when such political anti-clericalism as still existed in most rural Catholic areas was clearly on the defensive, it burst out in particularly vehement form in Old Bavaria, and its embodiment, the Bavarian Peasant League, continued, albeit weakened and less influential, until the end of the Weimar Republic and reemerged for a while after the Second World War in that strange political episode, the "Bavarian Party."[16]

This account suggests that the interaction between religious practice, social change, and political development was not unique to the northern Rhineland and Westphalia but could be found in other Catholic regions of Central Europe. If we look farther afield, a similar effort at religious revival can be found in other areas of northern Europe. The first nineteenth-century missions were held in Restoration France, and the practice was copied after 1830 in both Belgium and Switzerland. German Catholics looked at the events of their western neigh-

---

election statistics will show that before the First World War the Social Democrats did much better and the Center Party much worse in the predominantly Catholic cities of southern Germany—Munich, Regensburg, Würzburg, and Mainz—than in Aachen, Cologne, Düsseldorf, Essen, Krefeld, or Mönchengladbach, even though the northern cities were much more heavily industrialized. With regard to German Catholics, the political division into a clerical-conservative south and a secular, left-wing north, so typical of political life in the Federal Republic, is a product of the twentieth century and cannot be read back into the nineteenth.

[16] On Old Bavaria, cf. Hörger, "Mentale Umschichtungen"; Phayer, Religion; the two essays of Farr, "Populism in the Countryside," and "From Anti-Catholicism to Anticlericalism"; Blessing, "Umwelt und Mentalität," and his most recent, detailed study, Staat und Kirche. In that latter work, the author tends to emphasize the religious and political unity of Bavarian Catholicism, downplaying anti-clerical tendencies (as does Möckl, Die Prinzregentenzeit) by contrasting them with developments among Bavarian Protestants. Such a comparison is surely valid, but when Old Bavarian Catholics are compared, not with Bavarian Protestants, but with north German Catholics, it is the lack of unity and the strength of secularizing and laicizing tendencies which stand out. On the Bavarian Party, there is the interesting book of Unger, Die Bayernpartei.

bors during the *Vormärz* with considerable interest; many of the early missionaries in Prussia were German-speaking Swiss or Alsatian priests.[17]

In France, the two decades after 1850 saw a full-blown effort at religious revival—complete with newly created, clerically led pilgrimages and processions, formed or reformed religious associations, and a great expansion of Marian devotion. The results obtained west of the Rhine were not comparable to those east of it; nonetheless, a certain north-south distinction seems apparent as two recent studies testify: in the Diocese of Arras (in the Department of the Pas-de-Calais in northern France), the clerically sponsored innovations were accepted by the laity, and the church was able to consolidate its position in some districts and even regain ground in others; in the Limousin, a poor mountainous region in south-central France, the initiatives of renewal failed, and the area became one of the most violently anticlerical in the whole country.[18]

The model example of a post-mid-century religious revival is to be found in Ireland. Sociologically, it was like a greatly exaggerated version of the Rhenish-Westphalian countryside. The early marriage, rural industry, and enormous parcellization of land characteristic of pre-famine Ireland were accompanied by a disorganized ecclesiastical organization, unable to minister to the religious needs of a swollen rural population, which, in any event, seems to have preferred the tavern to the church. The post-famine scene reveals an even sharper transformation of social and demographic patterns than in northern Germany. Millions emigrated, age of marriage soared, and life-long celibacy became a common rural life-style—all in response to a mid-century subsistence crisis which was the most horrifying of any in Europe. As in the Catholic areas of the Rhineland and Westphalia, this adaptation to a more sober and restricted life-style was accompanied by a whole series of new religious rituals, and clerically led religious associations. Church attendance and popular morality both took a sharp turn for the better. Even before the famine there had been a strong Catholic political

[17] Sevrin, *Les missions religieuses*; Gatz, *Volksmission*, pp. 25 ff. There is a very large if inconclusive body of literature on the influence of Belgian Catholics on the "strict party" in Rhenish Catholicism during the *Vormärz*. See Keinemann, *Kölner Ereignis*, 1: 52-58, and Weber, *Aufklärung*, pp. 82-83, both with further bibliographical references.

[18] Corbin, *Archaisme et modernité*, pp. 678-704; Hilaire, *Une chrétienté au dix-neuvième siècle?*, 1: 373-416 and passim. The political implications of the different outcomes of these religious events paralleled developments in Germany. Politics in the Pas-de-Calais remained, until the rise of the socialists in the mining districts around the turn of the century, dominated by a clerically tinged conservatism (at times monarchist, Bonapartist, or republican), while the Limousin became a stronghold of the extreme left.

movement in Ireland—the name Daniel O'Connell comes immediately to mind—but the further course of nineteenth-century Irish nationalism was closely tied to these new forms of religious life.[19]

The common elements in all these examples point toward the notion of a specifically northern European Catholicism. It was more puritanical and more clerically oriented than its Mediterranean counterpart, less anchored in popular traditions and superstitions (often of pre-Christian origin), and perhaps less superficial as well. More importantly, it was a flexible, adaptable religion, able to transform itself to meet the changing environment of nineteenth-century society.

Catholics and Protestants in Germany

I have not attempted to write a comparative study of Catholics and Protestants, but a few remarks in that direction nonetheless seem in order. Most aspects of the development of Germany's Catholic minority were unique to it, but there were some tendencies which did parallel those among the Protestant majority, and a brief comparison may help to specify further the differing nature of the two groups.

At first sight, it is the differences which are most apparent. The social and economic development of the predominantly Protestant areas in Prussia's western provinces was quite different from that of the Catholic ones. Artisanal protoindustry and mechanized industrial production were more common in Protestant regions than in Catholic ones and appeared at an earlier date. Even in predominantly Catholic areas the Protestants were disproportionately overrepresented in the capitalist class. Both the nature of changes in religious practice and the relationship between social structure and religious practice were different for Protestants than for Catholics. In the *Vormärz*, Protestant opposition to official religion was more likely to be expressed in the form of organized breakaway sectarianism and less likely to take the form of informal secularizing practices than was the case among Catholics, although in both confessions the effects of sectarian and secularizing forms of opposition to the official church tended to blend together. Both tendencies were more common among Protestants living in the industrial areas, including the rural weaving districts, than in the small towns or the agricultural countryside. As the industrial boom of the post-1850 decades got underway, these tendencies were exacerbated: the proportion of the Protestant population less susceptible to official religion increased, and such groups showed less interest in religion. Strict Protestantism tended increasingly to be confined to the

[19] Larkin, "The Devotional Revolution," and Miller, "Irish Catholicism."

peasantry, and the Protestant urban masses grew ever less religious. Although *Vormärz* Protestantism experienced many of the same internal disputes between enlightened and orthodox elements as did *Vormärz* Catholicism, the practical unity achieved by Catholics after 1850 was never obtained by Protestants, further weakening their cohesion. After mid-century the Protestant milieu was in retreat, while the Catholic one was expanding.[20]

The differing religious developments led to different political alignments. Post-1850 Protestant religious disunity was expressed in political terms as well: theological liberals stood politically to the left of theological conservatives. Given the general decline in Protestant piety a politicized Protestant conservatism (or a politicized Protestant liberalism, for that matter) could obtain mass support only in rural areas of traditional and constant piety, like Minden-Ravensberg in eastern Westphalia or the Principality of Lippe. Since the political left had a more clearly secular character than its conservative rivals, both the persistence of religious liberalism and the growing secularism among Protestants after 1850 made them more open to the arguments of the left than Catholics.

In the predominantly Catholic cities of the Rhine Valley or the religiously mixed areas of the Ruhr basin, voting patterns came increasingly to follow confessional lines, pitting Catholic adherents of the Center Party against Protestant partisans of liberalism. The confessional alignments, however, did not derive from the same motive: somewhat exaggeratedly, one could say that the Catholics took the political stance they did because they were religious, while the Protestants took their political position because they were not. The success of the post-1850 Catholic religious revival, the clerically led milieu it created, enabled the notable leaders of the Center Party to rally behind them the Catholic peasantry, the urban proletariat, and the petit-bourgeoisie. Social issues when explicitly expressed were often harmful to the Catholic cause (one need only think of the splits in the Center created by the Christian Social movement), but when subsumed under religious questions had a powerful attractive force. Lacking a com-

---

[20] On tendencies in *Vormärz* Protestantism, see Schulte, *Volk und Staat*, pp. 131 n. 31, 211-17, and Weber, *Aufklärung*, pp. 55-58, 111-12 (an interesting comparison with the situation among Catholics). On Protestant religious life in the Rhenish-Westphalian industrial area, see Tenfelde, *Bergarbeiterschaft*, pp. 369-87; Köllmann, *Stadt Barmen*, pp. 198-211. More generally, the picture of a total decay in Protestant piety painted by Phayer, *Sexual Liberation*, pp. 74-77, who draws perhaps too heavily on Catholic polemicists and impressionistic accounts, should be weighed against the more balanced conclusions reached in the statistical study of Welti, "Abendmahl, Zollpolitik und Sozialistengesetz."

parable religious milieu, the liberal leaders were in the long run unable to mobilize supporters across class lines: by the 1870s, the Protestant working-class was beginning to defect to the socialists; in the longer term, the Protestant petit-bourgeoisie drifted off in a proto-fascist direction.[21]

Even given these differences, there were still certain similarities, certain ways in which the development among Catholics reflected more general trends. In both Protestant and Catholic regions, 1848-1849 marked a high point of nineteenth century social and political radicalism. The success of the Catholic religious revival after mid-century was part of a more general conservative movement in Germany. Since the Catholic religious revival occurred independently of the state's authority, this is one more piece of evidence suggesting that the strength of conservative tendencies in German history is not simply a consequence of the application of state power but a reflection of underlying social processes.[22]

Organizational developments offer another parallel. The replacement of old-regime religious associations, tied to guilds and village government, basically compulsory in nature, with the private and voluntary sodalities, congregations, and other organizations of the religious revival was part of the great nineteenth-century process of the formation of voluntary associations. Those Catholic groups more explicitly political in nature were exemplars of another broad tendency in German history: the creation of conservative mass organizations. A generation before the Agrarian League organized the Protestant peasantry of northeastern Germany under aristocratic leadership, Schorlemer's Westphalian Peasant League had accomplished that task among a group of western Catholics. In a similar way, Kolping's associations represented an organized anti-liberal tendency among the Catholic artisanate some twenty years before a similarly effective

[21] On the relation between Protestantism and liberalism, see Sheehan, *German Liberalism*, pp. 167-69, 242-46. It is frequently asserted in this connection that the Catholics, as a minority, were more likely to be politically cohesive than the majoritarian Protestants. Although the argument is certainly not without justification, it is generally grossly overemployed. At some times, such as the conflict era, the Protestants were politically more united (behind the liberal opposition) than the Catholics, both in Rhineland-Westphalia and Prussia as a whole. In Bavaria, where the Protestants were a minority, they were still politically less unified than the Catholics, and the same is true in the contemporary Federal Republic, where both confessions are about equal in size.

[22] In this general approach, my argument resembles that of Blackbourn and Eley, *Mythen deutscher Geschichtsschreibung*, but is strongly at variance with most of their conclusions, in particular with Eley's downplaying of the consequences of the failure of the 1848-1849 revolution or his disagreement with the idea of an intimate connection between liberalism and a capitalist bourgeoisie.

movement came into existence among Protestants—and that in the 1880s only with extensive state patronage.

For all these similarities and parallels, the predominant impression remains one of distinctly separate developments. The Catholic minority went its own way. The milieu created after 1850 showed an astonishing cohesion, inner unity, and attractive force. It has survived, albeit in weakened form, the social and political storms of the twentieth century and remains apparent even today—a testimony to the great success of the clergy and lay activists in constructing an edifice of religious beliefs and practices in response to a changing world.

SOURCES

1. ARCHIVES

Staatsarchiv Münster
Oberpräsidium der Provinz Westfalen
Regierung Arnsberg
Regierung Münster
Landratsamt Kreis Ahaus
Landratsamt Kreis Brilon
Landratsamt Kreis Coesfeld
Landratsamt Kreis Dortmund
Landratsamt Kreis Hagen
Landratsamt Kreis Lüdinghausen
Landratsamt Kreis Meschede
Landratsamt Kreis Soest
Landratsamt Kreis Steinfurt
Landratsamt Kreis Warendorf
Provinzialschulkollegium

Hauptsaatsarchiv Düsseldorf
Oberpräsidium der Provinz Jülich-Kleve-Berg
Regierung Aachen
Regierung Düsseldorf
Regierung Köln
Polizei-Präsidium Aachen
Landratsamt Kreis Düsseldorf
Landratsamt Kreis Duisburg-Mülheim
Landratsamt Kreis Geldern
Landratsamt Kreis Gladbach
Landratsamt Kreis Kempen
Landratsamt Kreis Solingen

Staatsarchiv Detmold
Regierung Minden
Nachlass Friedrich Freiherr von Wolff-Metternich

Landesarchiv Koblenz
Oberpräsidium der Rheinprovinz

Stadtarchiv Münster
Landratsamt Landkreis Münster
Polizeiregistratur
Stadtregistratur

Stadtarchiv Düsseldorf
Ältere Stadtregistratur

Bistumsarchiv Münster
General-Vikariat

Archivstelle in der Erzdiözese Paderborn
Archiv des General-Vikariats

Historisches Archiv des Erzbistums Köln
Cabinets-Register
General-Vikariat

2. NEWSPAPERS

Kölnische Zeitung (Cologne) December 1859 to December 1869
Germania (Berlin) August 1871 to December 1875

3. PERIODICALS

Kirchlicher Anzeiger für die Erzdiözese Köln vols. 1-19, 1852-1870
Kirchliches Amtsblatt der Diözese Münster vols. 1-15, 1857-1871
Kirchliches Amtsblatt der Diözese Paderborn vols. 1-19, 1852-1870
Sonntagsblatt für katholische Christen (Münster) vols. 9-29, 1850-1870

4. STATISTICS, HANDBOOKS, AND REFERENCE WORKS

Adreß-Buch der Geistlichkeit des Bistums Münster. Münster: Theissingsche
   Buchhandlung, 1851.
Adreßbuch der Oberbürgermeisterei Düsseldorf für 1872. 2 vols. in 1. Düs-
   seldorf, n.d.
Allgemeine Deutsche Biographie
Die Gemeinden und Gutsbezirke des Preußischen Staates im Jahre 1871.
   Berlin, 1875.
Jahrbuch für die amtliche Statistik des Preußischen Staates.
Preußische Statistik
Schematismus der Diözese Münster. Münster, 1907.
Schematismus der Diözese Paderborn. Paderborn: Ferdinand Schöningh, 1872.
Statistische Darstellung des Kreises Meschede 1861-1873. Meschede: Selbst-
   verlag des Kreises, 1874.
Statistische Nachrichten über den Kreis Münster aufgestellt im Jahre 1863.
   Münster: Regensberg, 1864.
Statistische Nachrichten über den Kreis Coesfeld 1862. Münster: Regensberg,
   1864.
Statistische Nachrichten über den Regierungs-Bezirk Münster. Münster, 1860.
Statistik des Deutschen Reiches
*Tabellen und amtliche Nachrichten über den Preußischen Staat für das Jahr
   1849.* Berlin, 1851-1854.

5. OTHER PRIMARY AND SECONDARY SOURCES

Adelmann, Gerhard. "Führende Unternehmer in Rheinland und in Westfalen 1850-1914." *Rheinische Vierteljahrsblätter* 35 (1971): 335-52.

Agulhon, Maurice. *Penitents et franc-maçons de l'ancienne Provence*. Paris: Fayand, 1968.

————. *La République au Village*. Paris: Plon, 1970.

Anderson, Eugene. *The Prussian Election Statistics 1862 and 1863*. Lincoln: The University of Nebraska Press, 1954.

————. *The Social and Political Conflict in Prussia 1858-1864*. 2nd ed. New York: Octagon, 1968.

Anderson, Margaret Lavinia. *Windthorst. A Political Biography*. Oxford: Clarendon, 1981.

Bachem, Karl. *Vorgeschichte, Geschichte und Politik der Zentrumspartei*. 2nd (reprint) ed. 9 vols. Aalen: Scientia, 1967.

————. *Joseph Bachem*. 2 vols. Cologne: J. P. Bachem, 1912.

Bebel, August. *Aus meinem Leben*. 3 vols. Vol. 3 ed. Karl Kautsky. Stuttgart: J.H.W. Dietz Nachf., 1910-1914.

Becker, Josef. *Liberaler Staat und Kirche in der Ära von Reichsgründung und Kulturkampf. Geschichte und Strukturen ihres Verhältnisses in Baden 1860-1878*. Mainz: Matthias Grünewald, 1973.

Blackbourn, David. *Class, Religion, and Local Politics in Wilhelmine Germany: the Centre Party in Württemberg before 1914*. New Haven and London: Yale University Press, 1980.

———— and Eley, Geoff. *Mythen deutscher Geschichtsschreibung. Die gescheiterte bürgerliche Revolution von 1848*. Frankfurt a.M., Berlin, and Vienna: Ullstein, 1980.

Blankenburg, Erhard. *Kirchliche Bindung und Wahlverhalten: die sozialen Faktoren bei der Wahlentscheidung Nordrhein-Westfalens 1961 bis 1966*. Olten and Freiburg i. Br.: Walter, 1967.

Blasius, Dirk. *Bürgerliche Gesellschaft und Kriminalität*. Göttingen: Vandenhoek und Rupprecht, 1976.

Blessing, Werner K. *Staat und Kirche in der Gesellschaft. Institutionelle Autorität und mentaler Wandel in Bayern während des 19. Jahrhunderts*. Göttingen: Vandenhoek und Rupprecht, 1982.

————. "Umwelt und Mentalität im ländlichen Bayern. Eine Skizze zum Alltagswandel im 19. Jahrhundert." *Archiv für Sozialgeschichte* 19 (1979): 1-42.

Bornkamm, Heinrich. "Die Staatsidee im Kulturkampf." *Historische Zeitschrift* 179 (1950): 41-72, 273-306.

Brepohl, Wilhelm. *Der Aufbau des Ruhrvolkes im Zuge der Ost-West Wanderung*. Recklinghausen: Bitter, 1948.

Brinabend, Joseph. *Attendorn, Schnellenberg, Waldenberg und Ewig: ein Beitrag zur Geschichte Westfalens*. Edited and revised by Julius Picht and Karl Boos. 2nd ed. Münster: Aschendorff, 1958.

Buchheim, Karl. *Ultramontanismus und Demokratie. Der Weg der deutschen Katholiken im 19. Jahrhundert*. Munich: Kosal, 1963.

Burger, Annemarie. *Religionszugehörigkeit und soziales Verhalten. Untersuchungen und Statistiken der neueren Zeit in Deutschland.* Göttingen: Vandenhoek und Rupprecht, 1964.

Buscher, Georg. "Krefeld und der Altkatholizismus. Der Kampf der Krefelder Katholiken um die Dionysius und die Stefanskirche 1876-1881." *Annalen des Historischen Vereins für den Niederrhein* 159 (1957): 149-89.

Corbin, Alain. *Archaisme et modernité en Limousin aux XIXᵉ siècle 1845-1880.* Paris: M. Riviere, 1975.

Croon, Helmut. *Die gesellschaftlichen Auswirkungen des Gemeindewahlrechts des Rheinlandes und Westfalens im 19. Jahrhundert.* Cologne and Opladen, 1960.

———. "Die Stadtvertretung in Krefeld und Bochum im 19. Jahrhundert." In *Forschungen zum Staat und Verfassung. Festschrift für Fritz Hartung*, edited by Richard Dietrich and Gerhard Oestrich, pp. 389-403. Berlin: Humboldt, 1958.

Degen, Kurt. "Die Herkunft der Arbeiter in den Industrien Rheinland-Westfalens bis zur Gründerzeit." Ph.D. dissertation, Bonn, 1916.

Denk, Heinz. "Die Wahlen zum Preußischen Abgeordnetenhaus und zum konstituierenden Reichstag des Norddeutschen Bundes in der Stadt Köln in den Jahren 1848-1867." Ph.D. dissertation, Bonn, 1954.

Donner, Hermann. *Die katholische Fraktion in Preußen 1852-1858.* Borna-Leipzig: Robert Noske, 1909.

Dowe, Dieter. *Aktion und Organisation: Arbeiterbewegung, sozialistische und kommunistische Bewegung in der preußischen Rheinprovinz 1820-1852.* Hannover: Verlag für Literatur und Zeitgeschehen, 1970.

Dreyfus, George. *Sociétés et metalités à Mayence dans la seconde moitié du dix-huiteième siècle.* Paris: Armand Colin, 1968.

Eyll, Clara van. "Wirtschaftsgeschichte Kölns vom Beginn der preußischen Zeit bis zur Reichsgründung." In *Zwei Jahrtausende Kölner Wirtschaft*, edited by Hermann Kellebenz 2: 163-266. 2 vols. Cologne: Geis, 1975.

Faber, Karl-Georg. *Die Rheinlande zwischen Restauration und Revolution.* Wiesbaden: Franz Steiner, 1966.

Farr, Ian. "From Anti-Catholicism to Anticlericalism: Catholic Politics and the Peasantry in Bavaria, 1860-1900." *European Studies Review.* 13 (1983): 249-69.

———. "Populism in the Countryside: The Peasant Leagues in Bavaria in the 1890's." In *Society and Politics in Wilhelmine Germany.* Edited by Richard J. Evans, pp. 136-59. London: Croon Helm, 1978.

Ficker, Ludwig. *Der Kulturkampf in Münster.* Edited by Otto Hellinghaus. Münster: Aschendorff, 1928.

Franz, Georg. *Kulturkampf. Staat und Kirche in Mitteleuropa von der Säkularisierung bis zum Abschluß des preußischen Kulturkampfes.* Munich: G.D.W. Callwey, 1954.

Franzen, August. "Die Zölibatsfrage im 19. Jahrhundert. Der 'Badische Zölibatssturm' (1828) und das Problem der Priesterehe im Urteil Johann

Adam Mohlers und Johann Baptist Horschen." *Historisches Jahrbuch* 91 (1971): 345-83.

Gall, Lothar. *Der Liberalismus als regierende Partei. Das Grossherzogtum Baden zwischen Restauration und Reichsgründung*. Wiesbaden: Franz Steiner, 1968.

———. "Die partei- und sozialgeschichtliche Problematik des badischen Kulturkampfes." *Zeitschrift für die Geschichte des Oberrheins* 113 (1965): 151-96.

Gatz, Erwin. "Bischöfliche Einheitsfront im Kulturkampf? Neue Funde zum Kirchenkonflikt im Bistum Hildesheim." *Historisches Jahrbuch* 92 (1972): 391-403.

———. "Kaplan Josef Istas und der Aachener Karitaskreis." *Rheinische Vierteljahrsblätter* 36 (1972): 205-208.

———. "Paul Melchers als Seelsorger." *Annalen des Historischen Vereins für den Niederrhein* 177 (1975): 144-63.

———. *Rheinische Volksmission im 19. Jahrhundert. Dargestellt am Beispiel des Erzbistums Köln*. Düsseldorf: Schwann, 1963.

Gils, J. van. "Der 'Kulturkampf' und seine Auswirkung im Jülicher Land." *Heimat Kalender für den Kreis Jülich* 13 (1963): 59-63.

Gladen, Albin. *Der Kreis Tecklenburg an der Schwelle des Zeitalters der Industrialisierung*. Münster: Regensberg, 1970.

Grenner, Karl. *Wirtschaftsliberalismus und katholisches Denken. Ihre Begegnung und Auseinandersetzung in Deutschland des 19. Jahrhunderts*. Cologne: Bachem, 1967.

Gutman, Herbert. "Work, Culture and Society in Industrializing America, 1815-1919." *American Historical Review* 78 (1973): 531-38.

Haas, Armin. "Die Wahlen zum Preußischen Abgeordnetenhaus im Regierungs-Bezirk Aachen von der Deutschen Revolution von 1848/49 bis zum Deutsch-Französischen Krieg 1870/71." Ph.D. dissertation, Bonn, 1954.

Hahn, Helmut and Zorn, Wolfgang eds. *Historische Wirtschaftskarte der Rheinlande um 1820*. Bonn: Röhrscheid, 1973.

Hamerow, Theodore. *Restoration, Revolution, Reaction: Economics and Politics in Germany 1815-1871*. 2nd ed. Princeton: Princeton University Press, 1966.

———. *The Social Foundations of German Unification*. 2 vols. Vol. 1, *Ideas and Institutions*. Vol. 2, *Struggles and Accomplishments*. Princeton: Princeton University Press, 1969-1972.

Haupts, Leo. "Die liberale Regierung in Preussen in der Zeit der 'Neuen Ära.' " *Historische Zeitschrift* 227 (1978): 44-85.

Heckel, J. "Die Besetzung fiskalischer Patronatsstellen in der Evangelischen Landeskirche und in den katholischen Diözesen Altpreußens." *Zeitschrift der Savigny-Stiftung für Rechtsgeschichte* Kanonische Abteilung 15 (1926): 200-325.

Henning, Hans-Joachim. *Das westdeutsche Bürgertum in der Epoche der Hochindustrialisierung*. Wiesbaden: Franz Steiner, 1972.

Hess, Adalbert. *Das Parlament das Bismarck widerstrebte: zur Politik und sozialen Zusammensetzung des Preußischen Abgeordnetenhauses der Konfliktzeit.* Cologne and Opladen: Westdeutscher Verlag, 1964.

Hilaire, Yves-Marie. *Une chrétienté au XIXᵉ siècle? La vie religeuse des populations du diocese d'Arras (1840-1914).* 2 vols. Lille: Presses Universitaires de Lille, 1977.

Hochstadt, Steve. "Migration and Industrialization in Germany 1815-1977." *Social Science History* 5 (1981): 445-68.

Hohmann, Friedrich. "Domkapitel und Bischofswahlen in Paderborn 1821-1856. *Westfälische Zeitschrift* 121 (1971): 365-450.

———. "Domkapitel und Bischofswahlen in Paderborn von 1857 bis 1892." *Westfälische Zeitschrift* 122 (1972): 191-282.

———. "Die Soester Konferenzen 1864-1866. Zur Vorgeschichte der Zentrumspartei in Westfalen." *Westfälische Zeitschrift* 114 (1967): 293-342.

Hömig, Herbert. *Hömig, Das Preussische Zentrum in der Weimarer Republik.* Mainz: Matthias Grunewald, 1979.

———. *Rheinische Katholiken und Liberale in den Auseinandersetzungen um die preußische Verfassung unter besonder Berücksichtigung der Kölner Presse.* Cologne: Wienand, 1971.

Hörger, Hermann. "Mentale Umschichtungen im Dorf des 19. Jahrhunderts— zum Wandel bäuerlichen Namensgutes und seiner gesellschaftlichen Hintergünde im sudbayerischen Raum." *Zeitschrift für Agrargeschichte und Agrarsoziologie* 19 (1979): 1-42.

Hombach, Heinz-Jürgen. "Reichstags- und Landtagswahlen im Siegkreis sowie in den Kreisen Mülheim/Rhein, Wipperfürth, Gummersbach, und Waldbröl 1870-78." Ph.D. dissertation: Bonn, 1963.

Huber, Ernst. *Deutsche Verfassungsgeschichte seit 1789.* 4 vols. Stuttgart: W. Kohlhammer, 1957-1969.

Hunly, J. "The Working Classes, Religion and Social Democracy in the Düsseldorf Area, 1867-1878." *Societas* 4 (1974): 131-49.

Kaiser, Renate. *Die politischen Strömungen in den Kreisen Bonn und Rheinbach 1848-1878.* Bonn: Röhrscheid, 1963.

Kaufhold, Karl Heinrich. "Handwerk und Industrie 1800-1850." In *Handbuch der deutschen Wirstschafts- und Sozialgeschichte*, edited by Hermann Audin and Wolfgang Zorn, 2: 321-67. 2 vols. Stuttgart: Ernst Klett, 1976.

Kehmann, Karl. "Die altkatholische Kirche." In *Die Rheinprovinz 1815-1915*, edited by Joseph Hansen, 2: 217-33. 2 vols. Bonn: Marcus & Weber, 1917.

Keinemann, Friedrich. "Die Affäre Westphalen. Der Protest des Grafen von Westphalen zu Fürstenburg und Laer gegen die preußische Kirchenpolitik auf den westfälischen Provinziallandtag 1841 und seine Folgen." *Westfälische Zeitschrift* 123 (1973): 189-214.

———. *Ancien Regime, Kulturkampf, Nachkriegszeit: neue Beiträge zur westfälischen Landesgeschichte.* Hamm: Selbstverlag, 1974.

———. *Das Kölner Ereignis: sein Widerhall in der Rheinprovinz und Westfalen.* 2 vols. Münster: Aschendorff, 1974.

―――. "Zu den Auswirkungen der Julirevolution in Westfalen." *Westfälische Zeitschrift* 121 (1971): 351-64.

Kerckerinck zur Borg, Engelbert Freiherr von, editor. *Beiträge zur Geschichte des westfälischen Bauernstandes*. Münster: Aschendorff, 1912.

Kissling, Johannes. *Geschichte der Deutschen Katholikentage*. 2 vols. Münster: Aschendorff, 1920-1923.

―――. *Geschichte des Kulturkampfes im Deutschen Reich*. 3 vols. Freiburg-i-Br.: Herdesche Verlagsbuchhandlung, 1911-1916.

Klein, August. *Die Personalpolitik der Hohenzollernmonarchie bei der Kölner Regierung*. Düsseldorf: Schwann, 1967.

Klein, Ursula. "Die Säkularisation in Düsseldorf." *Annalen des Historischen Vereins für den Niederrhein* 109 (1926): 1-167.

Klersch, Joseph. *Volkstum und Volksleben in Köln*. 3 vols. Cologne: J. P. Bachem, 1965-1968.

Knodel, John. *The Decline of Fertility in Germany 1871-1939*. Princeton: Princeton University Press, 1974.

Köllmann, Wolfgang. *Bevölkerung in der industriellen Revolution*. Göttingen: Vandenhoek und Rupprecht, 1970.

―――. *Sozialgeschichte der Stadt Barmen im 19en Jahrhundert*. Tübingen: Mohr, 1960.

Koselleck, Reinhart. *Preußen zwischen Reform und Revolution*. Stuttgart: Ernst Klett, 1967.

Kousser, J. Morgan. "Ecological Regression and the Analysis of Past Politics." *Journal of Interdisciplinary History* 4 (1973): 237-62.

Kracht, Hans Joachim. "Adolf Kolping und die Gründung der ersten Gesellenvereine in Westfalen." In *Studia Westfalica Beiträge zur Kirchengeschichte und religiösen Volkskunde Westfalens Festschrift Alois Schroeder*, edited by Max Bierbaum, pp. 195-213. Münster: Aschendorff, 1973.

Kruse, Norbert. "Bischof Bernhard Brinkmann von Münster in der Zeit des Kulturkampfes." Staatsexamarbeit: Pädagogische Hochschule Westfalen-Lippe Abteilung Münster, 1974.

Lademacher, Horst. "Wirtschaft, Arbeiterschaft und Arbeiterorganisation in der Rheinprovinz am Vorabend des Sozialistengesetzes 1878." *Archiv für Sozialgeschichte* 15 (1975): 111-43.

Larkin, Emmet. "The Devotional Revolution in Ireland." *American Historical Review* 77 (1972): 625-52.

Lautenschlager, Friedrich. *Die Agrarunruhen in den badischen Standes- und Grundherrschaften im Jahre 1848*. Heidelberg: C. Winter, 1915.

Lepper, Herbert. "Kaplan Franz Eduard Cronenberg und die Christlich-soziale Bewegung in Aachen 1868-1878." *Zeitschrift des Aachener Geschichtsvereins* 79 (1968): 57-148.

―――. "Die politischen Strömungen im Regierungsbezirk Aachen zur Zeit der Reichsgründung und des Kulturkampfes 1867-1887." Ph.D. dissertation, Bonn, 1967.

Lepsius, M. Rainer. "Parteisystem und Sozialstruktur: zum Problem der Demokratisierung der deutschen Gesellschaft." In *Deutsche Parteien vor*

1918 edited by Gerhard A. Ritter, pp. 56-80. Cologne: Kiepenheuer und Witsch, 1973.

Lewis, Gavin. "The Peasantry, Rural Change and Conservative Agrarianism. Lower Austria at the Turn of the Century." *Past and Present* 81 (November 1978): 119-43.

Lill, Rudolf. *Die Beilegung der Kölner Wirren.* Düsseldorf: Schwann, 1962.

———. "Die deutschen Katholiken und Bismarcks Reichsgründung." In *Reichsgründung 1870/71*, edited by Theodor Schieder and Ernst Deuerlein, pp. 345-65. Stuttgart: Seewald, 1970.

Lipgens, Walter. *Ferdinand August Graf Spiegel und das Verhältnis von Kirche und Staat 1789-1835.* 2 vols. Münster: Aschendorff, 1965.

Marrus, Michael R. "Pilger auf dem Weg. Wallfahrten in Frankreich des 19. Jahrhunderts." *Geschichte und Gesellschaft* 3 (1977): 329-51.

Matzerath, Horst. "Industrialisierung, Mobilität und sozialer Wandel am Beispiel der Städte Rheydt und Rheindahlen." In *Probleme der Modernisierung in Deutschland*, edited by Hartmut Kaelble, pp. 13-79. Opladen: Westdeutscher Verlag, 1973.

Meyer, Folkert. *Schule der Untertanen: Lehrer und Politik in Preußen 1848-1900.* Hamburg: Hofmann und Campe, 1976.

Michels, Sigrid. "Die Auswirkungen des Kulturkampfes in Düsseldorf." Schriftliche Hausarbeit zur Ersten Staatsprüfung für das Lehramt an der Volksschule: Pädagogische Hochschule Rheinland Abteilung Neuß, 1967.

Miller, David. "Irish Catholicism and the Great Famine." *Journal of Social History* 9 (1975): 87-98.

Möckl, Karl. *Die Prinzregentenzeit. Gesellschaft und Politik während der Ära des Prinzregenten Luitpold im Bayern.* Munich and Vienna: R. Oldenbourg, 1972.

Möller, Helmut. *Die kleinbürgerliche Familie im 18. Jahrhundert.* Berlin: Walter de Gruyter, 1969.

Moellers, Paul. "Die Essener Arbeiterbewegung in ihren Anfängen." *Rheinische Vierteljahrsblätter* 25 (1961): 42-65.

———. "Das 'Essener *Volksblatt*' als Organ des Deutschen Vereins im Kulturkampf 1875-76." *Beiträge zur Geschichte von Stadt und Stift Essen* 79 (1955): 95-106.

———. "Die politischen Strömungen im Reichstagswahlkreis Essen zur Zeit der Reichsgründung und des Kulturkampfes (1867-1878)." Ph.D. dissertation, Bonn, 1954.

Mönks, A. "Beiträge zur Geschichte des Schützenwesens im Hochstift Paderborn." *Westfälische Zeitschrift* 86 pt. ii (1929): 95-199.

Morsey, Rudolf. *Die Deutsche Zentrumspartei 1917-1923.* Düsseldorf: Droste, 1966.

———. "Die deutschen Katholiken und der Nationalstaat zwischen Kulturkampf und Ersten Weltkrieg." *Historisches Jahrbuch* 90 (1970): 31-64.

Müller, Hans. *Säkularisation und Öffentlichkeit am Beispiel Westfalens.* Münster: Mehren & Hobbeling, 1971.

Müller, Hartmut. "Der politische Katholizismus in der Entscheidung des Jahres 1866." *Blätter für Pfälzische Kirchengeschichte* 33 (1966): 46-75.

Müller, Klaus. "Das Rheinland als Gegenstand der historischen Wahlsoziologie." *Annalen des Historischen Vereins für den Niederrhein* 167 (1965): 124-42.

Müller, Otto. *Die christliche Gewerkschaftsbewegung Deutschlands.* Karlsruhe: G. Braunschen Hofbuchdruckerei, 1905.

Naujoks, Eberhard. *Die katholische Arbeiterbewegung und der Sozialismus in den ersten Jahren des Bismarck'schen Reiches.* Berlin: Junker & Dunnhaupt, 1939.

Nolan, Mary. *Social Democracy and Society. Working Class Radicalism in Düsseldorf 1890-1920.* New York and London: Cambridge University Press, 1981.

Obermann, Karl. "De quelques problèmes et aspects socioeconomiques des migrations allemandes du XIXᵉ siècle." *Annales de demographie historique.* (1971): 120-32.

———. "Die Arbeiteremigration in Deutschland im Prozesse der Industrialisierung und der Entstehung der Arbeiterklasse in der Zeit von der Gründung bis zur Auflösung des Deutschen Bundes (1815 bis 1867)." *Jahrbuch für Wirtschaftsgeschichte* 1972 Teil 1: 135-89.

———. "Die deutsche Auswanderung nach den Vereinigten Staaten von Amerika im 19. Jahrhundert, ihre Ursachen und Auswirkungen (1830 bis 1870)," *Jahrbuch für Wirtschaftsgeschichte* 1975 Teil 2: 33-55.

Pappi, Franz Urban. "Parteisystem und Sozialstruktur in der Bundesrepublik." *Politische Vierteljahrsschrift* 14 (1973): 191-214.

Payne, Howard and Grosshens, Henrig. "The Exiled Revolutionaries and the French Political Police in the 1850s." *Amereican Historical Review* 68 (1965): 954-73.

Pflanze, Otto. *Bismarck and the Development of Germany.* Princeton: Princeton University Press, 1963.

Pfülf, Otto. *Cardinal von Geissel.* 2 vols. Freiburg i. Br.: Herder, 1895-1896.

———. *Hermann von Mallinckrodt.* Freiburg i. Br.: Herdesche Verlagsbuchhandlung, 1892.

Phayer, Michael. "Religion und das gewöhnliche Volk in Bayern 1750-1850." Ph.D. dissertation, Munich, 1970.

———. *Sexual Liberation and Religion in Nineteenth Century Europe.* Totowa, N.J.: Rowman and Littlefield, 1977.

Plum, Gunther. *Gesellschaftsstruktur und politisches Bewußtsein in einer katholischen Region 1928-1933.* Stuttgart: Deutsche Verlags-Anstalt, 1972.

Pülke, Engelbert. "Geschichte der politischen Parteien im Kreise Recklinghausen 1848-1889." *Vestische Zeitschrift* 41 (1934): 3-163.

Reekers, Stephanie. "Beiträge zur statistischen Darstellung der gewerblichen Wirtschaft Westfalens um 1800." *Westfälische Forschungen* 17 (1964): 83-176; 18 (1965): 75-130; 19 (1966): 27-78; 20 (1967): 55-108; 21 (1968): 98-161; 23 (1971): 75-106; 25 (1973): 59-106; 26 (1974): 60-83.

Reekers, Stephanie. *Westfalens Bevölkerung 1818-1955*. Münster: Aschendorff, 1955.

Reif, Heinz. *Westfälischer Adel 1770-1860. Vom Herrschaftsstand zur regionalen Elite*. Göttingen: Vandenhoeck und Rupprecht, 1979.

Repgen, Konrad. "Klerus und Politik 1848. Die Kölner Geistlichen im politischen Leben des Revolutionsjahres—als Beitrag zu einer 'Parteigeschichte von unten.' " In *Aus Geschichte und Landeskunde* edited by Max Braubach, Franz Petri, and Leo Weisgerber, pp. 133-65. Bonn: Röhrscheid, 1960.

———. *Märzbewegung und Maiwahlen des Revolutionsjahres 1848*. Bonn: Röhrscheid, 1955.

Reulecke, Jurgen, editor. *Arbeiterbewegung am Rhein und Ruhr: Beiträge zur Geschichte der Arbeiterbewegung in Rheinland-Westfalen*. Wuppertal: Peter Hammer, 1971.

Reuter, Josef. *Die Wiedereinrichtung des Bistums Aachen*. Mönchengladbach: B. Kuhn, 1976.

Röttges, Otto. *Die politischen Wahlen in den linksrheinischen Kreisen des Regierungsbezirkes Düsseldorf 1848-1867*. Kempen: n.p., 1964.

Rohe, K. "Wahlanalysen im historischen Kontext. Zu Kontinuität und Wandeln von Wahlverhalten." *Historische Zeitschrift* 234 (1982): 337-57.

Ross, Ronald J. *Beleaguered Tower: the Dilemma of Political Catholicism in Wilhelmine Germany*. Notre Dame and London: University of Notre Dame Press, 1976.

Schieder, Theodor. *Das Deutsche Kaiserreich von 1871 als Nationalstaat*. Cologne and Opladen: Westdeutscher Verlag, 1961.

Schieder, Wolfgang. "Kirche und Revolution. Zur Sozialgeschichte der Trierer Wallfahrt von 1844." *Archiv für Sozialgeschichte* 14 (1974): 419-54.

Schierbaum, Hansjürgen. *Die politischen Wahlen in den Eifel- und Moselkreisen des Regierungsbezirks Trier 1849-1867*. Düsseldorf: Droste, 1960.

Schiffers, Heinrich. *Kulturgeschichte der Aachener Heiligtumsfahrt*. Cologne: Gilde, 1930.

———. *Der Kulturkampf in Stadt und Regierungsbezirk Aachen*. Aachen: Kaatzens Erben, 1929.

Schmidt, Franz. *Burghard von Schorlemer-Alst*. Mönchengladbach: Volks-Verein, 1916.

Schmidt, Gustav. "Die Nationalliberalen—eine regierungsfähige Partei? Zur Problematik der inneren Reichsgründung 1870-1878." In *Die Deutschen Parteien vor 1918*, edited by Gerhard A. Ritter, pp. 208-23. Cologne: Kiepenheuer und Witsch, 1973.

Schmidt, Paul. *Die Wahlen im Regierungsbezirk Koblenz 1849 bis 1867-69*. Bonn: Röhrscheid, 1971.

Schmidt-Volkmar, Erich. *Der Kulturkampf in Deutschland 1871-1890*. Göttingen, Berlin, and Frankfurt a.M.: Musterschmidt, 1962.

Schmitz, Heinrich. *Anfänge und Entwicklung der Arbeiterbewegung im Raum Düsseldorf*. Hannover: Verlag für Literatur und Zeitgeschehen, 1968.

Schmolke, Michael. *Adolf Kolping als Publizist*. Münster: Regensberg, 1966.

————. *Die schlechte Presse: Katholiken und Publizistik zwischen 1821-1968*. Münster: Regensberg, 1971.

Schmoller, Gustav. *Zur Geschichte der deutschen Kleingewerbe*. Halle: Buchhandlung des Waisenhauses, 1870.

Schnabel, Franz. *Deutsche Geschichte im 19. Jahrhundert*. 4 vols. Freiburg i. Br.: Herder, 1929-1937.

————. *Der Zusammenschluss des politischen Katholizismus in Deutschland im Jahre 1848*. Heidelberg: C. Winter, 1910.

Schnütgen, Alexander. "Beiträge zur Ära des Kölner Erzbischofs Graf Spiegel. III Die Feiertage in der Kölner Kirchenprovinz auf gesamtkirchlichen und gesamtpreußischen Hintergründe." *Annalen des Historischen Vereins für den Niederrhein* 125 (1934): 38-107.

Scholle, Manfred. *Die Preußische Staatsjustiz im Kulturkampf 1873-1880*. Marburg: N. G. Elwert, 1974.

Schulte, Wilhelm. *Volk und Staat. Westfalen im Vormärz und in der Revolution von 1848/49*. Münster: Regensberg, 1952.

Sevrin, Ernst. *Les missions religieuses en France sous la restauration (1815-1830)*. 2 vols. Saint Mandé: Procure des Prêtres de la Miséricorde, 1948-1959.

Sheehan, James. *German Liberalism in the Nineteenth Century*. Chicago and London: University of Chicago Press, 1978.

Silbergleit, Heinrich, ed. *Preussens Städte*. Berlin: Carl Heymanns, 1908.

Sperber, Jonathan. "Roman Catholic Religious Identity in Rhineland-Westphalia 1800-70: Quantitative Examples and some Political Implications." *Social History* 7 (1982): 305-18.

————. "Social Change, Religious Practice and Political Development in a Catholic Region of Central Europe: Rhineland-Westphalia, 1830-1880." Ph.D. dissertation, University of Chicago, 1980.

————. "The Transformation of Catholic Associations in the Northern Rhineland and Westphalia 1830-1870." *Journal of Social History* 15 (1981): 253-63.

Steil, Hans. "Die politischen Wahlen in der Stadt Trier und in den Eifel- und Moselkreisen des Regierungsbezirks Trier 1867-1887." Ph.D. dissertation, Bonn, 1961.

Stürmer, Michael. *Regierung und Reichstag im Bismarckstaat 1871-1880*. Düsseldorf: Droste, 1974.

Tenfelde, Klaus. "Mining Festivals in the Nineteenth Century." *Journal of Contemporary History* 13 (1978): 378-412.

————. *Sozialgeschichte der Bergarbeiterschaft an der Ruhr im 19. Jahrhundert*. Bonn-Bad Godesberg: Neue Gesellschaft, 1977.

Thränhardt, Dietrich. *Wahlen und politische Strukturen in Bayern*. Düsseldorf: Droste, 1973.

Thun, Alphons. *Die Industrie am Niederrhein und ihre Arbeiter*. 2 vols. Leipzig: Duncker, 1879.

Tilly, Charles, Tilly, Louise, and Tilly, Richard. *The Rebellious Century 1830-1930*. Cambridge, Mass.: Harvard University Press, 1975.

Tilly, Richard. "Zur Entwicklung des Kapitalmarktes im 19. Jahrhundert unter besonderer Berücksichtigung Deutschlands." *Vierteljahrsschrift für Sozial- und Wirtschaftsgeschichte* 60 (1973): 145-61.

Trippen, Norbert. *Domkapitel und Erzbischofswahlen in Köln 1820-1929.* Cologne and Vienna: Bohlau, 1972.

Unger, Ilse. *Die Bayernpartei Geschichte und Struktur 1945-1957.* Stuttgart: Deutsche Verlags-Anstalt, 1979.

Voland, Claus. "Ein politisches Lehrstück." *Die Zeit* Nr. 11 Mar. 10, 1978, p. 28.

Walker, Mack. *Germany and the Emigration.* Cambridge, Mass.: Harvard University Press, 1964.

Weber, Christoph. *Aufklärung und Orthodoxie am Mittelrhein 1820-1850.* Paderborn: Ferdinand Schöningh, 1973.

————. *Kirchliche Politik zwischen Rom, Berlin und Trier 1876-1888. Die Beilegung des preußischen Kulturkampfes.* Mainz: Matthias Grünewald, 1970.

Wegmann, Dietrich. *Die leitenden staatlichen Verwaltungsbeamten der Provinz Westfalen 1815-1918.* Münster: Aschendorff, 1969.

Weinandy, Klaus. "Die politischen Wahlen in den rechtsrheinischen Kreisen des Regierungsbezirks Köln in der Zeit von 1849 bis 1870." Ph.D. dissertation, Bonn, 1956.

Welti, Manfred E. "Abendmahl, Zollpolitik und Sozialistengesetz in der Pfalz. Eine statistisch quantifizierende Untersuchung zur Verbreitung von liberal-aufklärischem Gedankengut im 19. Jahrhundert." *Geschichte und Gesellschaft* 3 (1977): 384-405.

Wendorf, Hermann. *Die Fraktion des Zentrums im Preußischen Abgeordnetenhaus 1859-1867.* Leipzig: Quelle und Meyer, 1910.

Windell, George. *The Catholics and German Unity 1866-1871.* Minneapolis: University of Minnesota Press, 1954.

Wrigley, E. A. *Industrial Growth and Population Change.* Cambridge, England: Cambridge University Press, 1961.

Zangerl, Carl H. E. "Courting the Catholic Vote: the Center Party in Baden 1903-1913." *Central European History* 10 (1977): 220-40.

Zender, Matthias. "Das Kölnische 'Niederland' im Gestalt und Sonderart seines Volkslebens." *Rheinische Vierteljahrsblätter* 36 (1972): 249-80.

INDEX

Library of Congress Cataloging in Publication Data

Sperber, Jonathan, 1952-
    Popular Catholicism in nineteenth-century Germany.

    Bibliography: p.   Includes index.
    1. Catholics—Germany—History—19th century.
2. Catholics—Germany (West)—North Rhine-Westphalia—History—19th century.
3. Germany—Religious life and customs. 4. North Rhine-Westphalia (Germany)—
Religious life and customs. 5. Germany—Politics and government—19th century.
6. North Rhine-Westphalia—Politics and government. I. Title. II. Title: Popular Catholicism in 19th-century Germany.
BX1536.S64 1984   282'.4355   84-42559
ISBN 0-691-05432-0